Translingual Practices in English Language Education in South Asia

LANGUAGE, EDUCATION AND DIVERSITY

Series Editors: **Stephen May**, *University of Auckland, New Zealand*, **Teresa L. McCarty**, *University of California, USA*, **Constant Leung**, *King's College London, UK* and **Serafín M. Coronel-Molina**, *Indiana University Bloomington, USA*

The Language, Education and Diversity series aims to publish work at the intersections of language policy, language teaching and bilingualism/multilingualism, with a particular focus on critical, socially-just alternatives for minoritised students and communities. The series is interdisciplinary, drawing on scholarship from language policy, language education, sociolinguistics, applied linguistics, linguistic anthropology and the sociology of language, including work in raciolinguistics and translingualism. We welcome a variety of methodological approaches, although critical ethnographic accounts are of particular interest.

Topics covered by the series include:

- Bilingual and Multilingual Models of Education
- Indigenous Language Education
- Multicultural Education
- Community-based Education

All books in this series are externally peer-reviewed.

Full details of all the books in this series and of all our other publications can be found on http://www.multilingual-matters.com, or by writing to Multilingual Matters, BLOCK, The Fairfax, Pithay Ct, Bristol, BS1 3BN, UK.

Praise for Translingual Practices in English Language Education

"South Asia boasts a centuries-long history of translingual practices. It is unfortunate that we are forced to rediscover those practices after their suppression and erasure during European colonization. Adopting translingual practices in contemporary educational contexts in the region is a complex exercise that involves creatively applying indigenous communicative practices and language ideologies while critically engaging with changes that have followed the imposition of colonialist institutions and policies. The authors in this book undertake this exercise perceptively, drawing on an intimate knowledge of the educational traditions in diverse communities across South Asia. Scholars in other regions will be motivated to undertake such efforts in their own communities."

Suresh Canagarajah,
The Pennsylvania State University, USA

"Finding a volume that captures the richness of South Asia's linguistic landscapes is rare. Translingual Practices in English Language Education in South Asia: Inclusivity and Equity illustrates how teachers, students, and institutions navigate multilingual realities within colonial and nationalist contexts, along with diverse cultural practices and forms of linguistic activism. Its contributors draw on empirical research, historical and contemporary policy, classroom pedagogy, assessment, and teacher practices throughout the region. They reveal both educators' creativity and the structural barriers that hinder transformative work. The book also emphasizes that translanguaging remains largely unaddressed in national policies and challenges the field to broaden what counts as decolonial language work, advocating for research that considers local classrooms as well as larger power structures.

By synthesizing these insights, the volume demonstrates the potential of multilingual approaches to promote equity, decolonize English language education, and advance linguistic justice across classrooms, institutions, and communities. It is essential reading for anyone seeking to understand and transform language education in South Asia."

Hina Ashraf,
Georgetown University, USA

The policy of Multilingual Matters/Channel View Publications is to use papers that are natural, renewable and recyclable products, made from wood grown in sustainable forests. In the manufacturing process of our books, and to further support our policy, preference is given to printers that have FSC and PEFC Chain of Custody certification. The FSC and/or PEFC logos will appear on those books where full certification has been granted to the printer concerned.

LANGUAGE, EDUCATION AND DIVERSITY: 8

Translingual Practices in English Language Education in South Asia

Inclusivity and Equity

Edited by
Shaila Sultana and Pramod K. Sah

MULTILINGUAL MATTERS
Bristol • Jackson

DOI https://doi.org/10.21832/SULTAN8455
Library of Congress Cataloging in Publication Data
A catalog record for this book is available from the Library of Congress.

Names: Sultana, Shaila editor | Sah, Pramod K. editor
Title: Translingual Practices in English Language Education in South Asia: Inclusivity and Equity/Edited by Shaila Sultana and Pramod K. Sah.
Description: Bristol; Jackson: Multilingual Matters, 2026. | Series: Language, Education and Diversity: 8 | Includes bibliographical references and index. | Summary: "This book presents research from South Asian contexts to explore the feasibility, acceptance and prospects of translingual practices in English language classrooms. It highlights the marginalisation sustained through English language education and persistent monolingual biases and suggests steps to ensure linguistic rights and social justice"— Provided by publisher.
Identifiers: LCCN 2025043347 (print) | LCCN 2025043348 (ebook) | ISBN 9781800418448 paperback | ISBN 9781800418455 hardback | ISBN 9781800418479 epub | ISBN 9781800418462 pdf
Subjects: LCSH: English language--Study and teaching--South Asia | Translanguaging (Linguistics) | Social justice and education--South Asia | LCGFT: Essays
Classification: LCC PE1068.S584 T73 2026 (print) | LCC PE1068.S584 (ebook)
LC record available at https://lccn.loc.gov/2025043347
LC ebook record available at https://lccn.loc.gov/2025043348

British Library Cataloguing in Publication Data
A catalogue entry for this book is available from the British Library.

ISBN-13: 978-1-80041-845-5 (hbk)
ISBN-13: 978-1-80041-844-8 (pbk)
ISBN-13: 978-1-80041-846-2 (pdf)
ISBN-13: 978-1-80041-847-9 (epub)

Open Access

Except where otherwise noted, this work is licensed under the Creative Commons Attribution-NoDerivatives 4.0 International License. To view a copy of this license, visit http://creativecommons.org/licenses/by-nd/4.0/ or send a letter to Creative Commons, PO Box 1866, Mountain View, CA 94042, USA.

Multilingual Matters
UK: BLOCK, The Fairfax, Pithay Ct, Bristol, BS1 3BN, UK.
USA: Ingram, Jackson, TN, USA.
Authorised Representative: Easy Access System Europe - Mustamäe tee 50, 10621 Tallinn, Estonia, gpsr.requests@easproject.com.

Website: https://www.multilingual-matters.com
X: Multi_Ling_Mat
Bluesky: @multi-ling-mat.bsky.social
Facebook: https://www.facebook.com/multilingualmatters
Blog: https://www.channelviewpublications.wordpress.com

Copyright © 2026 Shaila Sultana, Pramod K. Sah and the authors of individual chapters.

All rights reserved. No part of this work may be reproduced in any form or by any means without permission in writing from the publisher. Not to be used for AI training unless licenced.

Typeset by SAN Publishing Services.

Contents

	Contributors	ix
	Foreword *Shaila Sultana and Pramod K. Sah*	xiii
1	English Language Education in South Asia: Possibilities and Prospects for Translingual Practices and Inclusivity and Equity *Shaila Sultana and Pramod K. Sah*	1
2	Translingual Practices in 19th and Early 20th Century Language Education in India: A Case of the State of Odisha *Sunita Mishra and Ramesh C. Malik*	25
3	Examining English Language Education in India through a Translingual Lens *Padmini Bhuyan Boruah*	40
4	Using Translanguaging Pedagogy for Reading Development and Assessment: Considerations for Multilingual Teachers *Lina Mukhopadhyay*	59
5	A Translanguaging Pedagogical Design for Reading Comprehension Development and Implications for Bilingual Classrooms *Abu Saleh Mohammad Rafi*	81
6	Translanguaging as a Decolonial Pedagogy in English Medium Classrooms: Reclaiming Epistemic Identities in an Unequal Language Policy in Nepal *Prem Phyak and Nani Babu Ghimire*	99
7	Equity, Awareness, and Engagement: Translingual Practices in the Linguistic Landscape of Early Childhood Classrooms in the Maldives *Naashia Mohamed*	122
8	Translanguaging in English Language Education in Sri Lanka: Social and Academic Gains *Harsha Dulari Wijesekera*	148

9   Translanguaging and Assessment in English Language
    Learning in Pakistan: Exploring the Affordances
    and Challenges   165
    Tanzeela Anbreen and Pramod K. Sah

10 Translanguaging Pedagogy and Democratizing Higher
    Education in Bangladesh: Possibilities and Challenges   187
    Rowshon Ara and Shaila Sultana

11 Rethinking EMI Through Equity and Inclusiveness
    Lens: Autoethnographic Insights into Anglophonic
    Norms in Pakistan   215
    *Syed Abdul Manan, Muhammad Yasir Khan
    and Liaquat Ali Channa*

    Afterword: Translanguaging for English or Social Justice?   240
    Ajit Kumar Mohanty

    Index   253

Contributors

Editors

Shaila Sultana is the Director and Professor of BRAC Institute of Language (BIL), BRAC University, Bangladesh. She is also a Professor (on leave) and the former Head of the Department of English Language, Institute of Modern Languages, University of Dhaka, Bangladesh. She has been educated at Jahangirnagar University (Bangladesh), Monash University (Australia), King's College London (UK), and the University of Technology Sydney (Australia). Her research interests include critical sociolinguistics, language and nationalism, religionism, and genderism, trans-approaches to language and identity, language in popular culture and social media, and decolonization and deeliticization of English in post-colonial contexts. The first books on sociolinguistics and English language education in Bangladesh, *Language in Society in Bangladesh and Beyond: Voices of the Unheard in the Global South* (Routledge, USA) and *Routledge Handbook of English Language Education in Bangladesh* (Routledge, UK) were edited by Shaila Sultana and her colleagues. Her other recent important publications include a co-authored book, *Popular Culture, Voice and Linguistic Diversity* (Palgrave McMillan, USA), and co-edited books, *Language and Sustainable Development in Bangladesh* (Routledge, UK), *Remote and Online Language Teaching and Learning* (in press, Universiti Sains Malaysia Press, Malaysia) and a Special Issue of *Australian Review of Applied Linguistics* titled 'Translingual Practices Entangled with Semiotised Space and Time'. Shaila Sultana is on the editorial boards of *Language in Society* (Cambridge University Press), *Cambridge Elements in Language and Power* (Cambridge University Press), *Journal of English-Medium Instruction* (John Benjamins), *Ampersand* (Elsevier), *Journal of AsiaTEFL*, *Journal of Education, Language, and Ideology* (JELI), *Crossing, Journal of BELTA* and other journals. With more than 80 articles and chapters in top-tiered peer-reviewed international journals and books, Shaila Sultana has been the most cited author in 'Linguistics and Literature' at the University of Dhaka and Bangladesh since 2021 (according to the AD Scientific Index).

Pramod K. Sah is a South Asian critical applied linguist whose work examines how colonial, liberal and racist language ideologies shape educational and socioemotional inequalities in multilingual societies. He served as an Assistant Professor of English Language Education at the Education University of Hong Kong and holds an Honorary Associate position in the School of Languages and Applied Linguistics at the Open University, UK. He previously held an Honorary Norham Fellowship at the Department of Education, University of Oxford, and worked as a Postdoctoral Associate at the Werklund School of Education, University of Calgary. Recognized among the world's top 2% of most-cited scientists in the field of Language and Linguistics, his scholarship seeks to advance anti-oppressive and asset-based approaches to language education through frameworks such as *critical translanguaging, linguistic citizenship*, and *emotions as entanglement*. His research has been published in leading journals, including *TESOL Quarterly, Applied Linguistics Review, Ethnicities, Journal of Multilingual and Multicultural Development, International Journal of Bilingual Education and Bilingualism,* and *International Multilingual Research Journal*. He is the Founding Editor-in-Chief of the *Journal of Education, Language, and Ideology* and Co-Editor of *Critical Inquiry in Language Studies*.

Authors

Tanzeela Anbreen is a faculty member at the University of Bedfordshire, UK. Her research focuses on EMI, L2 writing, language testing and assessment, social theory and corpus-based approaches in linguistics. As an educator, she is celebrated for making complex linguistic concepts accessible. Her innovative courses on Corpus Linguistics, Language Testing & Assessment and Research Methodologies are highly regarded. She worked across the globe, including Vietnam, Sri Lanka, Pakistan, Nepal, Egypt, Maldives, Oman, Myanmar, Jordan, China, Hong Kong and Trinidad & Tobago.

Rowshon Ara is an Associate Professor and the former chairperson of the Department of English at Eastern University, Bangladesh. Her areas of interest include translanguaging, cultural linguistics, intercultural communication, and language in literature classes. She has published several articles in different peer-reviewed national and international journals. She has recently enrolled as a graduate student in the Department of Educational Studies at the University of British Columbia, Canada.

Padmini Bhuyan Boruah is presently Professor (tenured) and Head of the Department of English Language Teaching, Gauhati University, India. She is a Fulbright-Nehru Academic and Professional Excellence (Teaching and Research) fellow (2019–2020) at the University of San Diego (USD), California. Her recent publications include a Routledge book on English Language

Education and Social Inequality co-authored with colleagues from USD and the University of New Mexico, Albuquerque, and chapters on English language education for Routledge and Springer edited publications.

Liaquat Ali Channa holds a PhD degree in Language and Literacy Education from the University of Georgia, United States of America. He is a Fulbright Alumnus. He is currently a Professor in the Department of English Language and Literature Government College University, Hyderabad, Pakistan. His research interests include English medium instruction, Bilingual and multilingual Education and Educational linguistics.

Dr Nani Babu Ghimire is an applied linguist, studying ideologies, identity and agency of teachers in English medium community schools in Nepal. He is an Assistant Professor at Siddha Jyoti Education Campus, Sindhuli, Nepal. He completed MPhil and MEd in English in Education and Arts from Tribhuvan University. He is interested in teacher professional development, multilingualism, diversity in language education and critical pedagogy.

Muhammad Yasir Khan holds a Master's degree in Applied Linguistics. He is presently doing his PhD at the Graduate School of Education at Nazarbayev University Astana, Kazakhstan.

Ramesh C. Malik teaches at Utkal University. He has a PhD in Translation Studies from the Centre for Applied Linguistics and Translation Studies, University of Hyderabad. He was a UGC-Post-Doctoral Fellow in Linguistics at the Centre for ALTS, University of Hyderabad. He specializes in General Linguistics, Translation Studies and Literary Criticism.

Syed Abdul Manan is an Associate Professor of Multilingual Education at Nazarbayev University Graduate School of Education, Kazakhstan. His research has been published in the top-tier journals that include Language Policy, Language Problems and Language Planning, Journal of Multilingual and Multicultural Development, Multilingua, World Englishes and others. He is co-editor of the books Multilingual Selves and Motivations for Learning Languages other than English in Asian Contexts (Anas & Manan, 2024) and Agency in Multilingual Education Policy and Planning in Asia (Manan & Anas, in press).

Sunita Mishra is a Professor and currently Head of the Centre for English Language Studies at the University of Hyderabad. She researches and supervises in areas like ELT, the History of English education in India, Critical pedagogy and Discourse analysis. She is also interested in Indian media and its changing profile in the last two decades. Presently, she is involved in projects related to the reception of English in Odisha. She is also interested in translating Odia into English.

Naashia Mohamed is a Senior Lecturer at the University of Auckland. Her research and teaching explores how schools and societies can foster equity for racially and linguistically marginalised learners. She highlights the role of home languages and cultures in supporting academic achievement, language development, and positive identity formation. Focused primarily on New Zealand and the Maldives, her work critically examines policies and practices to advocate for asset-based, identity-affirming approaches that value the linguistic and cultural resources of multilingual learners.

Ajit K. Mohanty is an educational psycholinguist working on Multilingual Education (MLE), Language Policy in Education and Education of Indigenous, Tribal, Minority and Minoritized Communities. He was an ICSSR National Fellow after his retirement in 2011 as a Professor of Psychology (and former Chairperson) in the Zakir Husain Centre for Educational Studies, Jawaharlal Nehru University, India. His latest book, *The Multilingual Reality: Living with Languages* (2019), is published by Multilingual Matters, UK/USA. Professor Mohanty drafted the 2014 *Policy for Mother Tongue-based Multilingual Education* of tribal children in Odisha (India). Bhāsā Kathā, Bhāsā Byathā is his recently published book in Odia, dealing with issues of Language and Education.

Lina Mukhopadhyay is a Professor at the Department of Training and Development, School of English Language Education at The English and Foreign Languages University (EFLU), Hyderabad, India. She is also the Director of the Research Acceleration Center (RAC) and All India Language Testing Authority (AIELTA) at EFLU. Her areas of research interest are bi/multilingual education, second language acquisition, second language writing and classroom-based language assessment and evaluation, and she has research publications in each of these areas.

Dr Prem Phyak is an associate professor of language, society and education at Teachers College, Columbia University, USA. He has co-authored a book, *Engaged Language Policy and Practices* (with Kathryn A. Davis), and co-edited a book, *Multilingual Education in South Asia: At the Intersection of Policy and Practice* (with Lina Adinolfi and Usree Bhattacharya). He has published several articles in journals. He is an associate editor of *Diaspora, Indigenous, and Minority Education (DIME)* journal.

Abu Saleh Mohammad Rafi, PhD, is Associate Professor of Linguistics at the University of Liberal Arts Bangladesh and Senior Research Fellow at the University of South Australia. He has published widely on translanguaging pedagogy in top journals and edited volumes. Dr Rafi has delivered keynotes at the University of Witwatersrand and CTGU and convened the 2024 International Conference on The Trans-Phenomenon. His forthcoming edited volume on professional learning will be published by Routledge.

Foreword

Shaila Sultana and Pramod K. Sah

Languages, people, places and ideas of the Global South have not been adequately represented in the Global North scholarship (Pennycook & Makoni, 2019; Sultana, 2022). On the one hand, South Asia, located geographically, politically and economically on the Asian periphery, has received little attention in the international socio- and applied linguistics literature, subsidized mostly by researchers at the 'center'. On the other hand, the domains of applied linguistics research in South Asia have remained largely unexplored by the streams of the recent paradigm shift, which calls for a more fluid understanding of language, gradually shifting from a structured definition to a more nuanced one. This shift reiterates the need for (re)directing our research in applied linguistics towards applications and integrations of novel approaches and perspectives based on a fluid understanding of language in English language education in South Asia.

With the recent transformation in the ways language is reconceptualized in applied linguistics and increased interest in Southern theories, *Translingual Practices in English Language Education in South Asia: Inclusivity and Equity* explores the ethos of translingual practices and applied linguistics issues in relation to translingual practices from a theoretical lens appropriate for the Southern Asian context. To decolonize Southern academia, it is important to study any social phenomenon from locally relevant theoretical constructs. Thus, the book gives a more nascent understanding of applied linguistics at the grassroots level and, most importantly, contributes to the decolonization of the ontology and epistemology of knowledge constructed by the North.

Translingual Practices in English Language Education in South Asia: Inclusivity and Equity fulfils three objectives: (i) it is a comprehensive book on the translingual practices, space and English language education in South Asia and published under a single cover; (ii) the chapters are written by language researchers, practitioners and academics in South Asia, bringing unique perspectives about South Asian languages and societies; and (iii) the editorial responsibility is shouldered by applied linguists and sociolinguists located inside and outside South Asia. Consequently, the book incorporates multiple perspectives about multilingual ecology, ensuring quality on par with the international standard appropriate for a global readership. Thus, the book fills the gap in the field by showcasing the least-represented South Asian countries to the international academia.

1 English Language Education in South Asia: Possibilities and Prospects for Translingual Practices and Inclusivity and Equity

Shaila Sultana and Pramod K. Sah

Introduction

South Asian language ecologies are multilingual, varied and diverse and the communities are multi-ethnic and multilingual in practice, with the presence of 700 spoken languages (Sultana & Bolander, 2021). Among these languages, 454 were found to be actively spoken in India, 124 in Nepal, 77 in Pakistan, 42 in Afghanistan and 40 in Bangladesh. Twenty-two Indigenous languages are used as official languages along with English in India (Bahry, 2020; Davis & LaDousa, 2020). Languages from various language families, such as Indo-Iranian, Dravidian, Austro-Asiatic and Tibeto-Burman, have coexisted and cohabited in the multilingual ecology of South Asia (SA). The communities in these countries are linguistically fluid, with blurry boundaries between many languages and varieties.

The multilingual realities, however, have not been appropriately addressed in certain South Asian countries. For example, no authentic source has been found to determine the number of languages in Bangladesh. The primary reason for this is the lack of mapping of the mother tongues of indigenous and ethnic communities, which comprise the second-largest group in the country after the Bangla-speaking population. There has not been a single comprehensive national survey that examines all ethnic communities and indigenous groups collectively (Mohsin, 2003). Consequently, the existing sources about the number of languages and their speakers are controversial. It is worth noting that there are currently 50 indigenous communities enlisted by the Ministry of Cultural Affairs in the People's Republic of Bangladesh. Unofficially, it is estimated that 54 communities speak at least 36 languages, among which six are non-ethnic minority languages and others are ethnic minority languages (TBS Report, 2022). Besides Bengali, other large groups of people who live in Bangladesh and have their mother tongues are the Chakma (1.1 million), Marma (230,000), Mizo (700,000), Garo (120,000), Rohingya (1.8 million) and Korbok (15,000). Again, within Bangla, there are several varieties, including Chittagonian, Sylheti, Rangpuri, Rarhi, Sundarbani, Manbhumi and Varendi. When the linguistic ecology in Bangladesh and other South Asian countries is multilingual, is multilingualism nurtured in practice in formal and informal domains?

Educational institutions worldwide are becoming increasingly multilingual, driven by the growing international mobility of students. To what extent is multilingualism appreciated in educational institutions in SA or any other countries in the world? In reality, there has been a growing demand for English as a medium of instruction (EMI) in educational institutions in non-English speaking countries, not to mention in SA too (Fang & Dovchin, 2022; Hamid *et al.*, 2015; Hamid & Sultana, 2024; Sah & Kubota, 2022; Sultana, 2014, 2023a, 2024b). Extra English language classes, tuition and out-of-the-classroom coaching sessions for English are getting popular, while mother tongues, minority languages and other foreign languages, such as Chinese, Japanese, Spanish or French, are getting inadequately promoted.

English has become the most desirable commodity in the multi-billion-dollar language industry (Mahboob, 2011). Why do different stakeholders invest so much money, time and energy in learning English? A key justification is that a higher level of English competence or attendance in EMI programs helps individuals earn significantly higher wages and ensures better occupational outcomes in the global economy (Chakraborty & Bakshi, 2016). Consequently, stakeholders, such as employers, teachers, parents and the private education system, continue to prefer English as a foreign language and as a compulsory language for the study of content subjects (Hamid & Nguyen, 2016; Roshid & Sultana, 2023a). In the context of Malaysia, for instance, EMI has been considered advantageous to obtain knowledge for global tertiary education, and English has become 'the universal second language of advanced education' (Rahman & Singh, 2019: 1). In addition, EMI is adopted as a means to make Malaysia the hub of higher education in Asia by attracting international students (Rahman *et al.*, 2021).

Does EMI ensure effective learning, teaching and critical awareness for students and teachers? Mevawalla and Palkhiwala (2022) defined English language learning as a 'Trojan Horse' – 'a "gift" that does more harm than good, perpetuating existing inequalities' (2022: 189). According to Milligan (2022), EMI policy decisions in the Global South are not developed based on educational arguments. English teachers in Asia are on the receiving end of EMI policies that Hamid and Nguyen (2016) identified as 'policy dumping' at the macro level (2016: 26). In addition, the research on EMI seems to be 'descriptive, perceptions-based and lacking in theoretical underpinning' (Milligan, 2022: 1). Consequently, these research studies struggle to come up with effective ways to minimize the hegemonic and neoliberal political roles of English in educational institutions in SA. In addition, it may be questioned whether the English language may be complemented with mother tongues and other linguistic and semiotic resources in the English language education itself.

A more recent term, translingual practices, was introduced to capture the complexity of the language practices and varied semiotic resources in meaning-making processes of the late-modern age (Canagarajah, 2013; Pennycook, 2008). Drawing attention to the preoccupation with the functions of linguistic features of specific languages, translingual practices question the monolingual ideological orientation, such as the one associated with the English language. Translingual practices also problematize the usual fixation with linguistic features associated with specific languages amongst students and teachers, officially claimed as codes and raise concerns that this language attitude ignores the diversity within languages (Bailey, 2012). In a similar vein, Pennycook (2010) questioned terms such as bilingualism and multilingualism, as these terms refer to languages as individual entities with specific linguistic features. According to him, language epistemology, which is preoccupied with the individualistic features of language that divide and separate languages from each other (i.e. English, Bangla or Nepalese), falls short in addressing the contemporary linguistic repertoires made up of mixes of local and global linguistic and cultural resources, as well as the accompanying political baggage associated with different languages and linguistic features.

While Western academia has widely discussed the efficacy of translingual practices (Li & García, 2022), little research has been conducted in the context of SA. English, different national languages, local languages and Indigenous languages in SA have historically, politically, economically and socially occupied hierarchical positions regarding official and national statuses and their acceptance and usage in various formal and informal domains. The hierarchies have also progressively nurtured and sustained a web of linguicism and anglocentrism. The presence of English, the 'mother-tongue' and 'national language' in these contexts is value-laden, relational and paradoxical at the micro level, as these languages are practiced and nurtured by the linguistically minoritized subjects themselves.

Hence, the edited volume explores whether translingual practices have a sustainable chance to survive and even thrive in English language education in SA, where English is given immense importance as a language of the colonizer, a prestigious foreign language, a key medium of instruction, a means to internationalize higher education and most importantly, a ticket to better life chances. The objectives of the book, based on empirical evidence from South Asian countries, are to:

- understand if promoting translingual practices is only a romantic pursuit;
- explore if translingual practices may ensure inclusivity and equity in English language education in the South Asian context.

It is hoped that the empirical research studies in the edited volume will extend and contribute to the ongoing debate about monolingual biases towards English and provide a nuanced understanding of the challenges and opportunities associated with promoting translingual practices in classrooms for inclusivity and equity.

Monolingual Biases in SA

In SA, the linguistic practices in education, in effect, are largely monolingual, and communities are marked by monolingual biases, particularly in favor of powerful languages like English or those designated as the national and official languages (Sultana, 2023b). For nearly 200 years, until 1947, Bangladesh, India, Pakistan and Sri Lanka historically experienced a similar colonial history to India under the British colonizer. Sri Lanka experienced Portuguese and Dutch colonial rule before the British administration started (Low & Pakir, 2022). During the reign of the East India Company for around 100 years, till the early half of the 18th century, Arabic, Bangla, Hindi, Persian, Portuguese, Sanskrit and more were the predominant languages (Clark, 1956). During the latter half of the 18th century, when the British Government took over the management of the Indian subcontinent from the East India Company by passing the 'Government of India Act of 1858', English began to replace Persian, the language of the Muslim ruler, in all domains, including administration, law and the courts. It became the prestige variety of languages and a key to success for the professional middle class, who wanted to be a part of the bureaucracy (T. Rahman, 1997; Sultana & Roshid, 2021). Their incentive grew stronger when Lord Bentinck opened more senior civil service posts to Indians. In summary, 'just like in many other former British colonies, English is seen to be a link language between the British colonial master and the native populace and is viewed as a vehicle to help the Indian, Sri Lankan, and Pakistanis to move up the social ladder as a language of upward social, educational, and occupational mobility' (Low & Pakir, 2022: 5). Till now, English, once the language of the colonizers, is the most coveted in all these countries for its intrinsic and extrinsic value.

A large region of SA, Afghanistan, Bhutan and Nepal did not experience the colonial regime. The Maldives was a protectorate of the British

(Low & Pakir, 2022). Nevertheless, it seems these South Asian countries experienced the British presence through neighboring imperial forces, the military (in Afghanistan's case), an expatriate workforce and the media (Meierkord, 2018; Sah & Li, in press). Afghanistan – a country characterized as 'failed' or 'fragile' in terms of state 'functionality' – seems to struggle with the proper administering of the education system (Pherali & Sahar, 2018: 239). Afghans also seem to have a precarious relationship with the English language. Ahmad & Khan (2019) identified that they were suspicious of the English people and culture, and their religion. According to Coleman (2022), some Afghans considered English as the language of the *kafir*/disbeliever of Allah, while others seemed to accept the need for English for developmental purposes. They also preferred it for its functional and ideological roles, such as its relevance to exam preparation and domestic lingua franca. Afghans also prefer English for studying abroad, escaping abroad, interacting with foreign development personnel and foreign military personnel, and writing graffiti and political statements. However, he predicted that in the long run, English might be 'perceived negatively' (Coleman, 2022: 54). Regardless of these contradictory observations by different authors regarding the role of English in Afghanistan, the monolingual bias towards learning English is visible for its growing need in academic and non-academic domains and for its perceived roles at the national and international levels (Alamyar, 2017). The increased acceptance of English has been more observable since the defeat of the Taliban in 2001 (Alamyar, 2017). Even compared to other foreign languages (such as French, German, or Russian) promoted for peace-keeping, development, political, social and economic opportunities and equality, English seems to be the promising language for the Afghans. Students of public universities in northeastern Afghanistan suggested introducing English as an EMI for the internationalization of universities (Orfan & Seraj, 2022). In Bhutan, the Maldives and Nepal, English has become popular as a foreign language and a medium of instruction compared to other languages.

In Nepal, English was not introduced first by the British colonizers. Instead, the local Nepali elites, the *Rana* oligarchy, Jung Bahadur Rana, the first Rana prime minister, to be precise, first set up the English medium school based on the model of the British education, namely 'Durbar School' (Palace School) for his children, after his return from England in 1850. The initial establishment of English-medium schools across Nepal, later on, was done exclusively for the children of the Ranas, their relatives and associates (Giri, 2015, 2020; Sah, 2021). The objective of the exclusive English was to ensure the monopoly over power and authority with a sociolinguistically and culturally unique 'breed of supporters of the elite regime' (Giri, 2015, 2020: 320).

Following the 1990 Constitution, all languages spoken within the territory of Nepal were recognized as 'national languages', but Nepali – the language of the dominant groups in Nepal – still enjoys the privilege and dominance in education and other domains (e.g. court and business). The Nepali language has always been a threat to the other local and Indigenous languages, as is Bangla for Indigenous languages in Bangladesh (Sah, 2021; Sultana et al., 2021). Regardless of the constitutional provisions, local and Indigenous languages are rarely used in education, while English and Nepali are predominantly used as the language of instruction at almost all levels of education in Nepal (Sah, 2021). All other local and Indigenous languages have been marginalized, initially through oppressive language policies and later under the guise of neoliberal ethos. The role of English in education has been gradually increased in Nepal's language policies: firstly, with the introduction of English as a foreign language and later as the medium of instruction (see Sah, 2021). The desire for English in education has been soaring in Nepal because of the neoliberal ideologies of language influencing the language polices. The undue, unwarranted emphasis on English and other nationally dominant languages has made it important to explore the linguistic ecology of SA with reference to translingual practices, specifically in the context of the formal domain of education, in which official and prestigious languages and monolingual ideologies are usually observed.

The Republic of the Maldives is the abode of an ethnically homogeneous mix of Sinhalese, Tamils and other South Indians, Arabs, Australasians and Africans. English and Dhivehi are both recognized as official languages of instruction in the National Curriculum and the Maldives' constitution. Dhivehi is descended from an ancient form of Sinhalese with origins in Sanskrit and Pali. Dhivehi also borrows from Tamil, Hindi and Arabic, with the linguistic script evolving from Arabic. The government of the Maldives has realized the potential of English for tourism. The large-scale societal and financial transformation based on tourism has made English a vital component of economic activities in the Maldives (Meierkord, 2018). Consequently, English has been adopted as a medium of instruction at the secondary and higher levels of education. However, Mohamed (2020) showed reservations as he empirically found that the modernization and development aided by the English-first policy resulted in inadequate proficiency in Dhivehi in students compared to English.

To challenge the colonizing force of English and Anglocentric obsession with English, there has been a surge of research that examines the efficacy of logocentrism in applied linguistics (Pennycook & Makoni, 2020).

Trans-Turn in Applied Linguistics

The traditional perspective about language does not recognize the features of languages emerging in local practices. The lens used to analyze the interactions was structural, meaning that identifying the linguistic features with reference to different languages in the interaction was the focus. Usually, linguistic features are analyzed with reference to specific phonological, morphological, semantic and syntactical features of a language. This sort of rational and linear understanding of language in applied linguistics has made the discipline disembodied and decontextualized. Hence, Canagarajah (2013) suggested the necessity of a new movement toward a paradigm shift that takes into account an emergent translingual orientation in the ontology and epistemology of applied linguistics.

Underlying the paradigm shift from monolingual bias to translingual orientation had two specific key concepts: first, texts were 'meshed and mediated by diverse codes', with the consequence that communication 'transcend[ed] individual languages', and second, in addition to codes, 'communication involve[d] diverse semiotic resources and ecological affordance' (Canagarajah, 2013: 6–7). Hence, any language-based research is suggested to reconceptualize the traditional definition of language as a combination of discrete, identifiable linguistic features and use research tools that help explore varied linguistic and non-linguistic semiotic resources, trajectories of these resources and time and space of language practices (Canagarajah, 2013; García, 2014).

To support the philosophical underpinnings of the trans-movement in applied linguistics, various research findings may be considered from the past and the present. For example, a spontaneous hybridization of English and Bangla was found in the language practices of the second and third-generation Bangladeshis in the UK. They added the English plural ending suffix -s to a Bangla word 'bondos'/friends (Al-Azami *et al.*, 2010). In an English as an additional language (EAL) class, a group of bilingual learners in a primary school in London translated and transferred cultural knowledge from English to Bangla and vice versa (Kenner *et al.*, 2008). Bilingual teachers in heritage language classes in Birmingham, UK, switched comfortably and spontaneously between English and Bangla with the insertion of common Islamic phrases, such as 'inshallah' (Blackledge & Creese, 2009). The second-generation bilingual Bangladeshis in Manchester, UK, pronounced Bangla phonemes /p, t, k/ with aspiration like English. They added English inflexions, such as -*ing* as a present continuous marker or -*s* for a plural marker, with Bangla root words. They also borrowed Bangla words in English sentences for code-meshing and blended Bangla clauses with English sentences (Al-Azami 2006). Their use of English and Bangla provided insight into the possible ways bilingual Bangladeshi speakers utilized languages and the potential changes they brought to the Bangla language in the process.

Manipulation of languages has been observed in bilingual speakers in other multilingual contexts. A group of English-speaking advanced students of German in a USA institution went beyond the conventions of both languages when they came up with their own language name Engleutschi, that is, English and *Deutsch* or German (Belz & Reinhardt, 2004). They changed the syllabic, phonological, orthographic and syntactic conventions of both languages when they coined new words, such as *Engleutsch* or *Deutlish*, inserted L1 lexical items, or had hybridized syntactic play with English lexicons in German syntaxes. They also deliberately and creatively flouted the conventions of both languages. In a similar kind of research study, an FL learner was found using the Spanish word *pues*, which functioned as a filler word or conjunction in Spanish, in his acts of parody for other playful functions. In the process, its 'semantic and pragmatic parameters' increased and its 'range of potential functions' extended (Pomerantz & Bell, 2007: 569–570). It has also been identified that the borrowing, mixing and blending and flouting of rules were not random or haphazard. Instead, they showed bilingual speakers' keen sense of metalinguistic awareness, 'enriched conceptualization', 'language-related aesthetic sensibilities', greater range of linguistic repertoire, and entertaining style of expressions (Kenner *et al.*, 2008).

Now, what was happening to the 'Bangla language' or the 'English language' as a consequence of all this mixing and blending? The consequences can be seen from the micro level and macro level. At the micro level, the analysis of the data reveals that Bangla/English is not a 'hermeutically sealed property' (García, 2007: xii), 'intrinsically defined object' (Blommaert, 2010), impermeable system, or an artefact that is based on 'decisive indifferences to differences' (Bourdieu, 1991: 287). With diverse elements, Bangla/English becomes messy and chaotic, and it may not be contained within a specific essentialized boundary. The language boundaries are transgressed, and the implicit linguistic ideologies get disrupted and dislocated with the individual and collective language practices. There remains no tangible, structured, prearranged pure language to hold on to or to preserve. At the macro level, mixing and blending refer to the political, historical, social and cultural trajectory of the language. These features reflect the local realities. Hence, Pennycook and Makoni (2020) showed their reservation about the ontology of the traditional science that 'produced a vision of language that had little to do with how people understood language locally' (2020: 79).

In addition, Bilingual speakers are observed to be flexible in their language practices in virtual spaces. Because of the translingual and transcultural flow in the virtual space, they seem to show more creativity in terms of capitalization, punctuation, spelling, word replacement, omission and so on (Maybin & Swann, 2007). For example, bi-lingual Israeli teenagers in Hebrew-language blogs used ASCII characters, like 'k', 'n', 'Y' or '2' that graphically looked like the Hebrew letters for the Fakatsa style of writing. Fakatsa was thus a creative orthographic and typographic marriage of Hebrew scripts with ASCII characters (Vaisman 2011).

Blommaert (2011: 3) defined all these scripts of communication on the mobile space as 'the dialect of the supervernacular':

> The supervernacular is 'English' and the dialects are the actually occurring 'world Englishes': specific local or regional realizations of English, tied to and embedded in local and regional sociolinguistics economies and emerged out of processes that bear all the features of dialects.

Flemish-Belgian, Dutch-speaking young people used the code symbol 'W8' for 'w-acht' in their texting for 'wait' in English and 'wacht' in formal Dutch. They coordinated both the supervernacular English and the core Dutch vocabulary and formed their own dialect. In other words, bilingual speakers' language practices in the virtual space were diverse and complex, and these practices required a multi-layered interpretation. Hence, Dovchin *et al.* (2018) and Sultana and Izadi (2022) identified that transforming the communicative environment and advanced technologies made it vital to move beyond the territorially defined formation of language, culture, and identity. Translingualism is a regular fact of everyday language practices in modern times. In this respect, critiquing the obsession with Standard English, Pennycook (2008) stated, 'To argue for a monolithic version of English is both an empirical and a political absurdity' (2008: 7).

Roles of translingual practices in teaching and learning

The research on translingual practices demonstrates the function of both linguistic and non-linguistic resources in communication and suggests giving importance to these resources in language teaching and learning. Based on research in two universities in Tokyo and Sydney, Otsuji and Pennycook (2018) empirically proved that too much preoccupation with bilingual resources or a narrowly defined cognitive approach to learning might not allow students to take advantage of diverse linguistic and semiotic resources at their disposal. These resources were vital for constructing meaning and engaging with their educational experiences and learning. Canagarajah (2018) observed the communication of international Science, Technology, Engineering and Mathematics (STEM) scholars in a Midwestern American university and identified that these scholars engaged in their communication process as polysemiotic practices. Disregarding what communicative competencies they had, these scholars seemed to practice nonlinguistic, multimodal spatial repertoires, such as PowerPoint and blackboard visuals, gestures, body language and other paralinguistic resources during the interaction that allowed the interaction to become an embodied activity. In other words, linguistic structures do not make translingual practices self-sufficient.

Translingual practices are situated, fluid and expansive. They are embedded in space and time and are given meaning by time and space.

Because of the complexity of the meaning-making processes, translingual practices require a dynamic kind of literacy, which Canagarajah (2015) has defined as 'translingual literacy'. Translingual literacy refers to the competence of students that allows them to use linguistic and semiotic resources and spatial repertoires to engage in meaning-making processes. Canagarajah (2015) pointed out specific benefits of translingual literacy acquisition compared to the older models of literacy acquisition, such as subtractive, additive and recursive:

> The languages are not treated as separate; ... acquisition of language is multi-directional, with influences from languages on each other working in multiple ways; ... competence is integrated, with all languages in one's repertoire making up a synthesized language competence; ... the circulatory nature of acquisition presents proficiency as always evolving. (2015: 4)

It has also been confirmed by the research that translingual practices create better learning opportunities for students, empower them with positive attitudes towards their mother tongues and other languages existing in their linguistic ecology, and allow them to employ appropriate and eclectic linguistic and other semiotic resources to facilitate communication and learning (cf. Fang & Liu, 2020; Kim & Park, 2020; Sultana, 2023a). The research, moreover, suggests introducing the mother tongue as part of the translingual practices to recognize mother tongue-based linguistic performance as maximizing linguistic resources in communication to promote inclusive language use and a de-colonizing pedagogy (Sah & Fang, 2025).

According to translingual literacy, translingual competence, unlike communicative competence (which is language-centric), is always evolving and reconfigured, with individual use and learning of new linguistic and semiotic resources in different times and spaces. In a similar vein, Baker (2011) identified translingual practices as beneficial for classroom practices. Translingual practices legitimize home languages in an official domain like education and thus connect and link school and home languages.

Translingual practices may also become excellent pedagogic resources, allowing the teacher to pair the weaker students with the stronger ones. The pairing helps the teacher to engage students more in classroom activities. Baker (2011) also showed that multilingual competencies were beneficial for translating difficult concepts to students. De Costa *et al.* (2017) suggested the term 'translingual pedagogy' for language classrooms in which students and teachers were allowed to use varied semiotic resources for communicative purposes. All the semiotic repertoires of students are recognized and respected by teachers, and they are allowed to use the repertoires inside the classroom as complementary communicative resources. As a result, students become agentive learners and take advantage of all the possible resources at their disposal for meaningful engagement with content and classroom activities, which eventually ensures optimal learning opportunities for them. Li (2018) identified the multimodal and multisensory nature of interaction. According to him, multilingual language users bring varied resources to their social interaction. Hence, Pacheco *et al.* (2019) concluded that 'instruction must include opportunities for students – and their teachers – to learn languages, learn about languages, and learn content through languages' (2019: 96).

Translingual practices have a compelling impact on individual and collective language and the negotiation of identity. Jones (2020) stated that languaging allows for creative changes to language and helps develop abilities to transform individual and collective selves, self-knowledge and identities. Going beyond the prescribed form of languages, students can indulge in using linguistic resources from different languages creatively. Since there are no hard and fast rules for adhering to any language, students can be agentive in their choices of being creative. Coffey and Leung (2020) identified that creativity in language learning was equally influenced by institutional and sociohistorical ideological factors, but students and teachers exerted their agency against the dominant discourses in translingual practices through their creativity. Lee and Canagarajah (2019) empirically proved the efficacy of transcultural experiences in a multilingual student's translingual writing practices. With linguistic and rhetorical sensitivity and transcultural disposition, students created a flexible space of interaction where their peers and teachers increased their disposition with richer semiotic resources (both linguistic and cultural) and learned to appreciate language diversity and creativity.

Moreover, translingual practices in the classroom create opportunities for critical thinking. Regarding 'translanguaging' and based on a study done on bilingual schools in Wales, Cenoz and Gorter (2017) indicated that different linguistic and non-linguistic resources created opportunities for spontaneous language use with different linguistic repertoires, produced pedagogically convenient pedagogy and the opportunity to use minority languages in classrooms. In a similar vein, De Costa *et al.* (2017) drew attention to the capacity for the transformation of translingual practices. Students were involved in activities where they used semiotic resources from different contexts and questioned the existing unequal hierarchies between languages, language groups and institutions. Hence, Cenoz and Gorter (2017) suggested sustainable translanguaging for regional minority languages.

Most importantly, the translingual approach to language carries the potential for decolonization. Cushman (2016) felt that translingual practices had what he called 'pedagogical possibilities for decolonizing knowledge' (2016: 234). Cushman (2016), citing Walter Mignolo, saw the translingual approach's prospects as 'transforming colonial matrixes of power that maintained hierarchies of knowledge and languages' (2016: 235).

The approach enables students coming from different linguistic and cultural backgrounds to value their own native linguistic and non-linguistic resources in the classroom, have positive self-perception and feel empowered. Allowing students to use their local varieties in the classroom ensures students' right to their language.

Further, Cushman (2016) saw the immense potential in translingual practices to disrupt the traditional ontology of language by focusing on individual and collective imagination and creativity. Translingual approaches to language, learning, teaching and knowledge may allow scholars, teachers and students to problematize the linguistic ideologies, linguicism, approaches to language variations and research methods used in applied linguistics (Cushman, 2016; Sultana & Dovchin, 2019). Scholars, teachers and students may develop critical and metalinguistic awareness that eventually may help them to decolonize their thoughts. The use of multiple scripts, media, languages and English(es) can also be used as a usual and integral part of teaching, learning and the construction of knowledge.

Translingual Practices in the South Asian Contexts of Education

Afghanistan, Bhutan and the Maldives have remained much unexplored in terms of translingual practices in learning and teaching processes. Nevertheless, recent research indicates that translingual practices are a natural phenomenon in multilingual classrooms in SA. Sah and Kubota (2022) identified that translingual practices, even though not a planned pedagogic approach, were traditionally used by students and teachers in South Asian EMI classrooms. When students and teachers did not have adequate communicative competence in English, they fell back on translingual practices as a spontaneous coping strategy.

In the context of Bangladesh, Rafi and Morgan (2022) observed natural translanguaging practices in the classrooms of both public and private universities. Teachers in classrooms with translingual competence played a vital role in transforming the standard or monolingual language ideologies, power relationships and language-based discrimination inside the classroom. According to Rafi and Morgan (2024), students in an anthropology classroom of a Bangladeshi private university benefited when teachers integrated translingual-transcultural approaches to teaching content. Students and teachers used their mother tongue, Bangla, to write in Bangla and use other semiotic resources, such as family photos from American TV shows and real-life family photos of Bangladeshi celebrities, in classroom activities. Teachers used translation as a classroom technique and allowed students to write in both English and Bangla. Thus, the promotion of transcultural-translingual practices ensured holistic learning experiences for students and eradicated proficiency-based discrimination. In other words, students with limited competence in English could participate in classroom activities, and they felt at ease in the classroom environment. The possibilities of discrimination and injustice faced by students due to their backgrounds and English competency were reduced. Rafi and Morgan (2022), thus, recommended translanguaging pedagogies in higher education in Bangladesh to strengthen students' bilingual identities and ensure better language and content learning.

While research about translingual practices predominantly highlights their pedagogic potential, some studies show skepticism on how uncritical adaptation of translanguaging can perpetuate linguistic hierarchies and, thereby, inequalities, including in South Asian contexts (Jaspers, 2018; Mendoza et al., 2024; Sah & Kubota, 2022; Sah & Li, 2022, 2024; Savski, 2024). For example, teachers in private higher education in Bangladesh felt that reimagining a bilingual education is still a romantic pursuit considering the contextual realities, such as students' and teachers' academic literacy in Bangla (the national language in Bangladesh), the poor education system in the primary to higher secondary level of education, and the neoliberal mindset of different stakeholders (Sultana, 2025). Without the appropriate integration of the ethos of translingual practices in curriculum, pedagogy, materials and assessment from the primary level of education to higher education, translingual practices may not be effectively used as pedagogic resources.

Translingual practices may, in their entirety, be the meshing of two dominant languages in the absence of other Indigenous or minority languages. Language ideologies in favor of English and national ideologies in favor of national languages marginalize the existence of local or Indigenous languages in the linguistic ecology and initiate elite bilingualism. Sah and Kubota (2022) showed concerns about the ideology of elite bilingualism that influenced translingual practices with a specific focus on English and dominant national languages (e.g. Nepali in Nepal and Hindi in India). They identified that Indigenous or other local languages and mother tongues were neglected in translingual practices and, instead, teachers selectively used English and the dominant national language (see Sah & Li, 2024). Hence, they argued in favor of a 'critical' stance that might resist neoliberal ideologies of English and nationalist preoccupation with the national language. The historically marginalized language, culture and identity need attention, and translanguaging practices and scholarship should not create additional space for further marginalization (Sah & Kubota, 2022; Sah & Li, 2024)

Sah and Kubota (2022) also suggested that translingual practices should not be valorized since different types of translanguaging practices exist in EMI classrooms. Teachers' pedagogic inadequacies and sociopolitical uncriticality may not allow teachers to do justice to students coming from diversified linguistic backgrounds. They might not be ready to use the different languages of multilingual students. Hence, without appropriate implementation plans, pedagogic translanguaging may not become a liberating or emancipatory tool, but another dominating instructional medium. Therefore, Sah and Kubota (2022) suggested critical translanguaging to oppose nationalist and neoliberal ideologies that unequally treat languages and their users. They believed that critical translanguaging would empower historically marginalized communities, and EMI classrooms could turn into democratic spaces that include mother tongues and thus promote the ethos of 'linguistic human rights'. Hence, a critical lens is required for English language classrooms, which are heavily preoccupied with teaching the standard variety of English across the world, specifically in the context of South Asian countries.

In summary, translingual practices have been observed to be effective for developing students' literacy, knowledge, identity, and sensitivity to different languages and cultures and most importantly, for the decolonization and de-eliticization of English in SA. However, while research studies of translingual practices opt for heterogeneity and consider English as a means to minimize linguistic diversity, the education system in SA, in reality, seems proactive in promoting policies and practices in favor of EMI (Sultana, 2024a). Hence, caution is suggested, so that translingual practices do not become a cause of linguicism, where English and national languages are in a complex relationship with other local, regional, or Indigenous languages. In the meantime, it is important to examine what new affordances translingual practices can offer in English language education within SA, where the presence of multilingual practices is not necessarily a new phenomenon (Sultana, 2023a).

Potentiality of Translingual Practices in English Language Education in SA

The book explores the possible recognition of translingual practices in language policies and practices and English language education in SA, specifically because there is a strong presence of monolingual biases and ideologies. Hegemonic language policies and practices favoring the English language, and negative attitudes towards non-standard varieties of English and other local/Indigenous languages are widely observable in different South Asian countries. It also intends to identify ways to draw the attention of all the possible stakeholders, policymakers and classroom practitioners to initiate a much-needed constructive conversation about the possible positive role of translingual practices in English language education in SA, specifically for ensuring language rights, equality and social justice.

The book includes 10 chapters by established and emerging authors using cutting-edge research approaches and trans-theories in applied linguistics. Applied linguistics research in SA, as mentioned above, has minimal representation in international academia, particularly regarding the recent changes and developments in the approaches to language.

Acknowledging the political, ideological and hegemonic roles of different dominant languages and their demarcated role in the multilingual ecology of SA, this book has challenged the one-dimensional, polarized understanding and domain-specific allocations of languages, which somewhat understate the underlying complexities of language use in the domain of education. Thus, showcasing a collection of empirical research, this book provides a comprehensive view of English education in South Asian countries, sensitizes people about multilingualism, and gives suggestions regarding linguistic rights, linguistic equity and social justice. As a broader term, 'translingual practices' is referred to in the volume, when individual chapters may have used other terms, such as translanguaging.

In Chapter 2, **Mishra** and **Malik** analyze texts written in 19th and early 20th-century Odisha for pedagogic purposes to examine how translingual practice was an ordinary practice in day-to-day communication, art forms and education. Translingual practices were common and accepted in bilingual and multilingual dictionaries, grammar books, thesauruses and literary works like novels, biographies/autobiographies. Mishra and Malik argue that, during the 19th century, it was a planned attempt to use translingual practices in those texts to be used in formal English language education. Similarly, in Chapter 3, **Boruah** examines societal and educational multilingual practices in English language education in India to understand how translingual practices can dismantle hegemonic theoretical models in English language education. In particular, Boruah explores teachers' understanding of, and attitudes towards, the use of children's home language repertoires in learning English at school, which shows that although teachers can be positive towards integrating students' home languages, they lack the pedagogical knowledge to do so. Based on such observation, Boruah presents three key goals of translingual practices in English language teacher education: (a) integrative pedagogy, not assimilatory; (b) situating English in multilingual identity construction; and (c) sharing the responsibility of promoting healthy use of one's languages.

In Chapter 4, **Mukhopadhyay** analogously reviews India's multilingual education policy in the context of English-medium instruction schools, identifying the need for training for language teachers. Based on a series of interventions in multilingual education, Mukhopadhyay provides a translanguaging model of providing language inputs through learners' home language(s) and English. In her translanguaging model, the emphasis is placed on scaffolding multilingual students' reading comprehension skills in emergent languages, and it also underlines multilingual assessment strategies for teachers. **Rafi**, in Chapter 5, presents a pedagogical translanguaging design for reading comprehension development in the English language at two Bangladeshi public and private universities. His study demonstrates the potential of translanguaging instructional design to help students utilize their complete linguistic repertoires and maximize their participation in class discussions. In particular, Rafi showed that the strategic selection of Bangla and English texts supported reading development and comprehension in both these languages and even enhanced students' agency and confidence.

Likewise, in Chapter 6, **Phyak** and **Ghimire** examine how teachers in English-medium instruction programs utilize translanguaging to claim their own and students' epistemic identities in the context of Nepal. Drawing on their analysis of classroom language practices, they argue that translanguaging serves as a 'decolonial pedagogy' as it not only creates a flexible and inclusive interactional space for multilingual teachers and students but also claims their epistemic identities. Their study also shows teachers question, resist and transform the hegemonic domination of monolingual English pedagogy through their translanguaging pedagogies. Their claim of translanguaging as a decolonial pedagogy is based on two key grounds: (a) teachers' translanguaging pedagogy did not focus on named standard languages but rather engaged students' full linguistic repertoire and teachers' agency; and (b) it involved deliberate efforts to bring change.

In Chapter 7, **Mohamed** investigates the linguistic landscape (e.g. artefacts displayed in the classroom) of early childhood classrooms in the Maldives to understand how teachers and students translanguage and engage in interaction with that visual landscape, in addition to exploring the social justice implications. Mohamed's study shows that both teachers and students utilized their integrated semiotic communicative repertoire, in which they used multiple languages and responded through gesture, gaze and engagement with artefacts. However, Mohamed argues that those translingual practices had a decolonial limit because the classroom discourse privileged literary over vernacular language, and textual over oral and multimodal literacy. In those translingual practices, the instrumentalist approach to instruction positioned English as more privileged than national and indigenous languages. Mohamed argues that teachers' and students' engagement in translingual practices by privileging English and lacking awareness of key concepts in Dhivehi indicates the hegemonic language ideology within the classroom practices. Sah and Li (2022) call such practice 'unequal languaging', which cautions against the uncritical and liberal promotion of translanguaging.

In Chapter 8, **Wijesekera** examined the context of English-medium instruction within the bilingual education approach in Sri Lanka. Reporting on two studies (the first was an ethnography in a multi-ethnic bilingual education school and the second one was action research in a monoethnic ESL classroom), the chapter shows that translanguaging can facilitate second language learning and give voice to low-proficient students and, in the meantime, students can navigate their flexible linguistic and ethnic identities.

Anbreen and **Sah**, in Chapter 9, examined the intersection of translanguaging and assessment in English language education in higher education in Pakistan. Their analysis of classroom interactions, interviews and written exam scripts shows that while translanguaging can aid comprehension of the content knowledge, the monolingual assessment practices not only create challenges for students in their written exams, but also limit their flexible translingual practices. Therefore, Anbreen and Sah argue that such a discrepancy between the classroom linguistic ecology and assessment practices necessitates ideological clarity and policy reforms to embrace multilingual realities and, thereby, enhance academic success and equity and inclusivity in English language education.

In Chapter 10, **Ara** and **Sultana** also demonstrate a case of 'unequal languaging'. They examined teachers' translanguaging strategies and techniques in English in four different programs at private universities in Bangladesh. Their analysis of classroom observations, interviews and focus group discussions reveals that teachers used translanguaging as a pedagogic resource but in limited ways. For example, while English and Bangla (a national dominant language) were flexibly used in those classrooms, Indigenous or ethnic minority languages never existed as a point of reference. Guided by the ideology of elite bilingualism, teachers and students did not even see the importance of using Indigenous and other minority languages. Ara and Sultana argue that linguicism and nationalist language ideology are often reinforced in the form of English-medium instruction in Bangladesh, and if translanguaging is romanticized without considering its ideological complexities, such inequalities will be reproduced even through translingual practices.

Finally, in Chapter 11, **Manan, Khan** and **Channa** present a collaborative autoethnography on their experiences of teaching in an EMI university in Pakistan to analyze how de jure institutional policies promote Anglophone norms in teaching and learning practices and how, in response, these three teachers negotiated the policy in favor of linguistically disadvantaged students. In particular, they demonstrated their agentic response to the monolingual and Anglo-centric policies to create meaningful spaces for linguistic inclusivity, students' empowerment and equitable employment of translingual practices within the classrooms.

Based on the empirical research studies presented, the book has:

(1) identified diverse language uses in sociolinguistically unexplored formal domains of education in SA and explored their role in English language learning and teaching;
(2) provided suggestions regarding translingual pedagogies to address contextual realities;
(3) created opportunities for sensitizing people about multilingualism in SA and raised awareness about marginalization and injustice sustained through the English language in SA;

(4) suggested steps to ensure linguistic rights, linguistic equity and social justice in classrooms;
(5) drawn the attention of intelligentsia, language educators and practitioners and policymakers, both local and international, to the socially and spatially situated nature of translingual practices; and
(6) supported readers from Western academia to understand the sociolinguistic profile and English language education in contemporary SA (generally accepted and perceived as monolingual, monocultural and peripheral) with contemporary theories and empirical evidence.

Conclusion: Translingual Practices for Decolonization of English Language Education

The chapters above highlight how classroom practitioners across different South Asian contexts are increasingly aware of the role that local and Indigenous languages, including mother tongues and other semiotic resources, can play in creating more inclusive classrooms. These linguistic practices not only foster a more cooperative and respectful learning environment but also enrich teaching and learning. They consistently show that when teachers draw on a range of semiotic resources in their pedagogy, it positively impacts their teaching. Through translingual classroom practices, teachers are engaging in what can be called 'epistemic decolonization' – a shift in how they understand language and language education, one that challenges the dominance of English and powerful national languages in knowledge production. These chapters suggest that teachers, when empowered to act agentively, can make informed, purposeful decisions about using multiple languages to support student learning in multilingual classrooms (Phyak *et al.*, 2022). In doing so, many embark on new paths as 'language-activist-scholars'. Their openness to collaboration, solidarity and respect for all languages – and the necessity of multilingual resources for effective teaching – has led to meaningful changes in classroom practices.

At the same time, these chapters reveal a persistent gap: language policy and planning across SA are yet to meaningfully recognize or support the ethos of translingual practices. Without any support from language policies and practices, classrooms remain isolated pockets where teachers adopt translingual pedagogy on their own initiative, often without broader institutional backing. This raises a critical question: How much impact can translingual practices truly have if they remain confined to individual classrooms, disconnected from systemic support? If language policies and educational institutions continue to uphold monolingual norms and linguistic ideologies from the colonial era, teachers alone may struggle to bring about broader societal change through language education. To truly support transformative teaching, educational programs must create opportunities to engage policymakers and institutional leaders. By doing so, they can raise awareness of the potential impact of these classroom innovations – not only on students and schools, but also on communities at large.

There should be a longitudinal study about the efficacy of trans-movement in applied linguistics and English language teaching in resource-deficient contexts, specifically with the engagement of students, teachers, teacher educators and other stakeholders, such as heads and principals. A more constructive discussion among stakeholders may be held about the assessment system, doing justice to the ethos of translingual practices. If we decolonize the classroom pedagogies but remain chained to the old assessment system, we may not keep the decolonization process alive. Hence, Takaki (2020) suggested to 'transform the official exam and assessment in decolonial ways' (2020: 51). Charamba (2021) suggested an ambitious objective that may take a while to execute, but there should be further research to identify the possible ways of execution.

To decolonize the minds of policy-makers and other stakeholders, such as education ministers or directors of government bodies involved in education and language education, there is a necessity for 'knowledge activism', so that they realize the necessity of translingual literacy and pedagogy. Knowledge activism discourages the meaningless movement of knowledge from one platform to another. Instead, it encourages knowledge as a way of 'thinking otherwise and knowledge to be treated to become politically significant' (Gillies, 2014: 282). For example, the Sindhi Language Authority (SLA) in Pakistan arranges national and international conferences and publishes books on the Sindhi language, culture, history, and politics to preserve the Sindhi language from the encroachment of Urdu, the national language of Pakistan and English, the foreign language. In addition, SLA arranges cultural events to involve the community members and produces songs and dramas for various platforms. Engaging social media, SLA ensures the participation of the young Sindhi and other language-speaking communities in language revitalization and makes the voices of the Sindhi speakers audible to the communities beyond the Sindh province. The entanglement of language, nature and life is displayed with compelling issues, such as the encroachment of the river and land in the Sindh province. For example, Sanam Marvi's 'Sindhu Wahando Rahando' written by Dr Ishaque Samejo has become an anthem for Sindhis protesting against the canal project in the Sindh province. Saman Marvi is a popular Pakistani singer, and Dr Ishaque Samejo (a professor of Sindhi language and literature at the University of Sindh) is the lyricist, a poet and the Chairman of SLS (Lakho, 2025). This sort of knowledge activism may have stronger possibilities of drawing the attention of policymakers and stakeholders in promoting the ethos of trans-movement in the formal domains of education in SA and beyond.

References

Abrar-ul-Hassan, S. (2021) Linguistic capital in the university and the hegemony of English: Medieval origins and future directions. *SAGE Open* 11 (2). https://doi.org/10.1177/21582440211021842

Ahmad, A. and Khan, A. (2019) Pashto and English in Afghanistan. *Pashto* 48 (658), 11–19.

Alamyar, M.N. (2017) Emerging roles of English in Afghanistan. *INTESOL Journal* 14 (1), 1–12.

Al-Azami, S. (2006) Linguistic manipulation in the Bengali language by Bangladeshis in Manchester. *South Asian Cultural Studies* 1 (1), 53–59.

Al-Azami, S., Kenner, C., Ruby, M. and Gregory, E. (2010) Transliteration as a bridge to learning for bilingual children. *International Journal of Applied Linguistics* 13 (6), 683–700.

Bahry, S. (2020) Towards 'mapping' a complex language ecology: The case of Central Asia. In S. Brunn and R. Kehrein (eds) *The Changing World Language Map* (pp. 3–41). Springer.

Bailey, B. (2012) Heteroglossia. In M. Martin-Jones, A. Blackledge and A. Creese (eds) *The Handbook of Multilingualism* (pp. 499–507). Routledge.

Baker, C. (2011) *Foundations of Bilingual Education and Bilingualism* (5th edn). Multilingual Matters.

Belz, A.J. and Reinhardt, J. (2004) Aspects of advanced foreign language proficiency: Internet-mediated German language play. *International Journal of Applied Linguistics* 14 (3), 324–362.

Blackledge, A. and Creese, A. (2009) 'Because tumi Bangali'. *Ethnicities* 9 (4), 451–476.

Blommaert, J. (2010) *The Sociolinguistics of Globalization*. Cambridge University Press.

Blommaert, J. (2011) Supervernaculars and their dialects. *Working Papers in Urban Language and Literacies* 81, 1–13.

Bourdieu, P. (1991) *Language and Symbolic Power*. Polity Press.

Canagarajah, S. (2013) *Translingual Practice: Global Englishes and Cosmopolitan Relations*. Routledge.

Canagarajah, S. (2015) Clarifying the relationship between translingual practice and L2 writing: Addressing learner identities. *Applied Linguistics Review* 6 (4), 415–440.

Canagarajah, S. (2018) Translingual practice as spatial repertoires: Expanding the paradigm beyond structuralist orientations. *Applied Linguistics* 39 (1), 31–54.

Cenoz, J. and Gorter, D. (2017) Minority languages and sustainable translanguaging: Threat or opportunity? *Journal of Multilingual and Multicultural Development* 38 (10), 901–912. https://doi.org/10.1080/01434632.2017.1284855

Chakraborty, T. and Bakshi, S.K. (2016) English language premium: Evidence from a policy experiment in India. *Economics of Education Review* 50, 1–16. https://doi.org/10.1016/j.econedurev.2015.10.004

Charamba, E. (2021) From colonisation to self-colonisation: Efficacy of translanguaging as a socially just decolonising pedagogy. In F. Maringe (ed.) *Higher Education in the Melting Pot: Emerging Discourses of the Fourth Industrial Revolution and Decolonization* (pp. 111–124). https://www.researchgate.net/profile/Erasmos-Charamba/publication/358662455_From_Colonisation_to_Self-Colonisation_Efficacy_of_Translanguaging_as_a_Socially_Just_ Decolonising_Pedagogy/links/620e2a6908bee946f3875051/From-Colonisation-to-Self-Colonisation-Efficacy-of-Translanguaging-as-a-Socially-Just-Decolonising-Pedagogy.pdf

Clark, T.W. (1956) The languages of Calcutta, 1760–1840. *Bulletin of the School of Oriental and African Studies, University of London* 18 (3), 453–474.

Coffey, S. and Leung, C. (2020) Understanding agency and constraints in the conception of creativity in the language classroom. *Applied Linguistics Review* 11 (4), 607–623.

Coleman, H. (2022) The roles of English in Afghanistan. *World Englishes* 41 (1), 54–71.
Cushman, E. (2016) Translingual and decolonial approaches to meaning making. *College English* 78 (3), 234–242.
Davis, C.P. and LaDousa, C. (2020) Introduction: Sign and script in South Asia. *Signs and Society* 8 (1), 1–7.
De Costa, P.I., Singh, J.G., Milu, E., Wang, X., Fraiberg, S. and Canagarajah, S. (2017) Pedagogizing translingual practice: Prospects and possibilities. *Research in the Teaching of English* 51 (4), 464–472.
Dovchin, S., Pennycook, A. and Sultana, S. (2018) *A Popular Culture, Voice and Linguistic Diversity: Young Adults On- and Offline*. Palgrave Macmillan.
Fang, F. and Liu, Y. (2020) 'Using all English is not always meaningful': Stakeholders' perspectives on the use of and attitudes towards translanguaging at a Chinese university. *Lingua* 247, 102959.
Fang, F. and Dovchin, S. (2024) Reflection and reform of applied linguistics from the Global South: Power and inequality in English users from the Global South. *Applied Linguistics Review* 15 (4), 1223-1230.
García, O. (2007) 'Foreword'. In S. Makoni and A. Pennycook (eds) *Disinventing and Reconstituting Languages* (pp. xi–xv). Multilingual Matters.
García, O. (2014) Countering the dual: Transglossia, dynamic bilingualism, and translanguaging in education. In R. Rubdy and L. Alsagoff (eds) *The Global-Local Interface and Hybridity: Exploring Language and Identity* (pp. 100–118). Multilingual Matters.
Gillies, D. (2014) Knowledge activism: Bridging the research/policy divide. *Critical Studies in Education* 55 (3), 272–288.
Giri, R.A. (2015) The many faces of English in Nepal. *Asian Englishes* 17 (2), 94–115.
Giri, R.A. (2020) Nepali English. In K. Bolton, W. Botha and A. Kirkpatrick (eds) *The Handbook of Asian Englishes* (pp. 317–336). Wiley Blackwell.
Hamid, M.O., Nguyen, H.T.M. and Baldauf Jr, R.B. (2013) Medium of instruction in Asia: Context, processes and outcomes. *Current Issues in Language Planning* 14 (1), 1–15.
Hamid, O. and Sultana, S. (2024) English as a medium of instruction in Bangladesh. In K. Bolton, W. Both and B. Li (eds) *Handbook of English-medium Instruction in Higher Education* (pp. 352–364). Routledge.
Jaspers, J. (2018) The transformative limits of translanguaging. *Language and Communication* 58, 1–10. https://doi.org/10.1016/j.langcom.2017.12.001
Jones, R.H. (2020) Creativity in language learning and teaching: Translingual practices and transcultural identities. *Applied Linguistics Review* 11 (4), 535–550.
Kenner, C., Gregory, E., Ruby, M. and Al-Azami, S. (2008) Bilingual learning for second and third generation children. *Language, Culture, and Curriculum* 21 (2), 120–137.
Kim, K.M. and Park, G. (2020) 'It is more expressive for me': A translingual approach to meaningful literacy instruction through Sijo poetry. *TESOL Quarterly* 54 (2), 281–309.
Lakho, A. (2025) Sanam Marvi's 'Sindhu Wahando Rahando' has become an anthem for Sindhis protesting against the canal project. *Images*, 15 May. https://images.dawn.com/news/1193558/sanam-marvis-sindhu-wahando-rahando-has-become-an-anthem-for-sindhis-protesting-against-the-canal-project
Lee, E. and Canagarajah, S. (2019) The connection between transcultural dispositions and translingual practices in academic writing. *Journal of Multicultural Discourses* 14 (1), 14–28.
Lewis, M.P., Simons, G.F. and Fennig, C.D. (eds) (2013) *Ethnologue: Languages of the World* (17th edn). SIL International. http://www.ethnologue.com/ethno_docs/distribution.asp?by=country#7
Li, W. (2018) Translanguaging as a practical theory of language. *Applied linguistics* 39 (1), 9–30.
Li, W. and García, O. (2022) Not a first language but one repertoire: Translanguaging as a decolonizing project. *RELC Journal*, 00336882221092841.

Low, E.L. and Pakir, A. (2022) English in East and South Asia: Context and issues. In E. Ling Low and A. Pakir (eds) *English in East and South Asia: Policy, Features and Language in Use* (pp. 1–16). Routledge.

Mahboob, A. (2011) English: The industry. *Journal of Postcolonial Cultures and Societies* 2 (4), 46–61.

Maybin, J. and Swann, J. (2007) Everyday creativity in language: Textuality, contextuality, and critique. *Applied linguistics* 28 (4), 497–517.

Meierkord, C. (2018) English in paradise: The Maldives: English is rapidly establishing itself as a second language in a society transforming from fishing to tourism and trade. *English Today* 34 (1), 2–11.

Mendoza, A., Hamman-Ortiz, L., Tian, Z., Rajendram, S., Tai, K.W.H., Ho, W.Y.J. and Sah, P.K. (2024) Sustaining critical approaches to translanguaging in education: A contextual framework. *TESOL Quarterly* 58 (2), 664–692. https://doi.org/10.1002/tesq.3240

Mevawalla, Z. and Palkhiwala, S. (2022) English language learning as a Trojan horse? Examining early childhood teachers' views of teaching young children in an English-medium NGO in India. In D. Hill and F.K. Ameka (eds) *Languages, Linguistics and Development Practices* (pp. 189–220). Palgrave Macmillan, Cham.

Milligan, L.O. (2022) Towards a social and epistemic justice approach for exploring the injustices of English as a medium of instruction in basic education. *Educational Review* 74. https://do.org/10.1080/00131911.2020.1819204

Mohamed, N. (2020) First language loss and negative attitudes towards Dhivehi among young Maldivians: Is the English-first educational policy to blame? *TESOL Quarterly* 54 (3), 743–772.

Mohsin, A. (2003) *The Chittagong Hill Tracts, Bangladesh: On the Difficult Road to Peace*. Lynne Rienner Publishers.

Orfan, S.N. and Seraj, M.Y. (2022) English medium instruction in Higher Education of Afghanistan: Students' perspective. *Language Learning in Higher Education* 12 (1), 291–308.

Otsuji, E. and Pennycook, A. (2018) The translingual advantage: Metrolingual student repertoires. In J. Choi and S. Ollerhead (eds) *Plurilingualism in Teaching and Learning* (pp. 70–88). Routledge.

Pacheco, M.B., Daniel, S.M., Pray, L.C. and Jiménez, R.T. (2019) Translingual practice, strategic participation, and meaning-making. *Journal of Literacy Research* 51 (1), 75–99.

Pandey, S.B. (2020) English in Nepal. *World Englishes* 39 (3), 500–513.

Pherali, T. and Sahar, A. (2018) Learning in the chaos: A political economy analysis of education in Afghanistan. *Research in Comparative and International Education* 13 (2), 239–258.

Phyak, P., Sah, P.K., Ghimire, N.B. and Lama, A. (2022) Teacher agency in creating a translingual space in Nepal's multilingual schools. *RELC Journal* 53 (2), 431–451. https://doi.org/10.1177/00336882221113950

Pennycook, A. (2008) Translingual English. *Australian Review of Applied Linguistics* 31 (3), 301–309.

Pennycook, A. (2010) *Language as a Local Practice*. Routledge.

Pennycook, A. and Makoni, S. (2020) *Innovations and Challenges in Applied Linguistics from the Global South*. Routledge.

Pomerantz, A. and Bell, N.D. (2007) Learning to play, playing to learn: FL learners as multicompetent language users. *Applied Linguistics* 28 (4), 556–578.

Rafi, A.S.M. and Morgan, A.M. (2022) Linguistic ecology of Bangladeshi higher education: A translanguaging perspective. *Teaching in Higher Education* 27 (4), 512–529.

Rafi, A.S.M. and Morgan, A.M. (2024) A pedagogical perspective on the connection between translingual practices and transcultural dispositions in an Anthropology classroom in Bangladesh. *International Journal of Multilingualism* 21 (1), 236–257.

Rahman, T. (1997) The medium of instruction controversy in Pakistan. *Journal of Multilingual and Multicultural Development* 18 (2), 145–154.

Rahman, M.M. and Singh, M.K.M. (2019) Language ideology of English-medium instruction in higher education: A case study from Bangladesh. *English Today* 36 (4), 40–46. https://doi.org/10.1017/S0266078419000294

Rahman, M.M., Islam, M.S., Hasan, M.K. and Singh, M.K.M. (2021) English medium instruction: Beliefs and attitudes of university lecturers in Bangladesh and Malaysia. *Issues in Educational Research* 31 (4), 1213–1230.

Roshid, M.M. and Sultana, S. (2023) Desire and marketizing English version of education as a commodity in the linguistic market in Bangladesh. *The Qualitative Report* 28 (3), 906–928.

Sah, P.K. (2021) Reproduction of nationalist and neoliberal ideologies in Nepal's language and literacy policies. *Asia Pacific Journal of Education* 41 (2), 238–252. https://doi.org/10.1080/02188791.2020.1751063.

Sah, P.K. and Kubota, R. (2022) Towards critical translanguaging: A review of literature on English as a medium of instruction in South Asia's school education. *Asian Englishes* 24 (2), 132–146. https://doi.org/10.1080/13488678.2022.2056796.

Sah, P.K. and Li, G. (in press) Multilingual English language education in South Asia: A historical and future perspective. In Chi-Kin John Lee (ed.) *Handbook of Asian Educational Innovation Towards the Futures of Education*. Springer Nature.

Sah, P.K. and Li, G. (2022) Translanguaging or unequal languaging? Unfolding the plurilingual discourse of English medium instruction policy in Nepal's public schools. *International Journal of Bilingual Education and Bilingualism* 25 (6), 2075–2094.

Sah, P.K. and Li, G. (2024) Toward linguistic justice and inclusion for multilingual learners: Implications of selective translanguaging in English-medium instruction classrooms. *Learning and Instruction* 92, Article No. 101904. https://doi.org/10.1016/j.learninstruc.2024.101904

Sah, P.K. and Fang, F. (2025) Decolonizing English-medium instruction in the global south. *Tesol Quarterly* 59 (1), 565–579.

Savski, K. (2024) (Trans)languaging, power, and resistance: Bordering as discursive agency. *Language in Society* 53 (3), 371–393. https://doi.org/10.1017/S004740452300012X

Sultana, S. (2014) English as a medium of instruction in Bangladesh's higher education: Empowering or disadvantaging students? *Asian EFL Journal* 16 (1), 11–52.

Sultana, S. (2023a) English as a medium of instruction in the multilingual ecology of South Asia: Historical development, shifting paradigms, and transformative practices. In R.A. Giri, A. Padwad and M.M.N. Kabir (eds) *English as a Medium of Instruction in South Asia: Issues in Equity and Social Justice* (pp. 31–56). Routledge.

Sultana, S. (2023b) Indigenous ethnic languages in Bangladesh: Paradoxes of the multilingual ecology. *Ethnicities* 23 (5), 680–705.

Sultana, S. (2024a) English as a medium of instruction and translingual practices: Reality vs. dream for the South Asian education system? In H. Kayi-Aydar and L. Mahalingappa (eds) *Contemporary Perspectives on English as a Medium of Instruction* (pp. 77–96). Information Age Publishing.

Sultana, S. (2024b) EMI in the neoliberal private higher education of Bangladesh: Fragmented learning opportunities. In G.F. Fang and P. Sah (eds) *English-Medium Instruction in Multilingual Universities: Politics, Policies, and Pedagogies in Asia* (pp. 83–103). Routledge.

Sultana, S. (2025) Reimagining bilingualism in English-medium private higher education in Bangladesh: Reality vs. dream. In R.A. Giri, A. Padwad and M.M.N. Kabir (eds) *Equity, Social Justice and English Medium Instruction: Case Studies from Asia* (pp. 185–206). Springer.

Sultana, S., Ahmed, T.N., Bhuiyan, F.N. and Huda, S. (2022) Linguistic governmentality, neoliberalism, and communicative language teaching: Invisibility of indigenous ethnic languages in the multilingual schools in Bangladesh. In S. Makoni and A. Bassey (eds) *Southernizing Sociolinguistics: Colonialism, Racism, and Patriarchy in Language in the Global South* (pp. 251–269). Routledge.

Sultana, S. and Dovchin, S. (2019) Relocalization in digital language practices of university students in Asian peripheries: Critical awareness in a language classroom (special issue). *Linguistics and Education*, 62. https://doi.org/10.1016/j.linged.2019.100752

Sultana, S. and Bolander, B. (2021) English in a multilingual ecology: 'structures of feeling' in South and Central Asia. *Multilingua* 41 (4). https://doi.org/10.1515/multi-2020-0141

Sultana, S. and Fan, F. (2024) English as a medium of instruction and mother-tongue-based translanguaging: Challenges and prospects for tertiary education in Bangladesh and China. *International Journal of Educational Development*. https://www.sciencedirect.com/journal/international-journal-of-educationaldevelopment

Sultana, S. and Roshid, M.M. (2021) English language and English language education in the multilingual ecology of Bangladesh: Past, present and future. In S. Sultana, M. Roshid, Z. Haider, N. Kabir and H.M. Khan (eds) *The Routledge Handbook of English Education in Bangladesh* (pp. 1–14). Routledge.

Sultana, S. and Izadi, D. (2022) Translingual practices entangled with semiotized space and time. *Australian Review of Applied Linguistics* 45 (2), 127–134.

TBS Report (2022) Languages of Bangladesh. *The Business Standard*, 21 February. https://www.tbsnews.net/supplement/languages-bangladesh-373636

Takaki, N.H. (2020) Exercising southern and decolonial (self) critique in translanguaging: For a juntos stance. *Revista X* 15 (1), 32–54.

Vaisman, C. (2011) Performing girlhood through typographic play in Hebrew blogs. In C. Thurlow and K. Mroczek I (eds) *Digital Discourse: Language in the New Media* (pp. 177–198). Oxford University Press.

2 Translingual Practices in 19th and Early 20th Century Language Education in India: A Case of the State of Odisha

Sunita Mishra and Ramesh C. Malik

Introduction

Translanguaging and bilingual education have always been notable features in the Indian subcontinent. The widely prevalent multilingualism necessitated translingual communication in everyday life and literary and folk-art forms. In the contemporary sense of the term, however, it has roots in the beginning of 'modern' and 'Western' education in the early 19th century. Interestingly, education in modern Indian languages began along with English education in the 19th century. Before that, teaching and learning of languages used to take place in the Madrasas, the Tolls and the Pathshalas. These systems flourished in mutually exclusive environments, although there was no dearth of linguistic exchanges in folk art forms that used more than one language. The Moghul Tamsa, for example, is a kind of Jatra (popular drama performed in the open air) prevalent in Odisha, on the Eastern coast of India. This was performed in the Mughal courts by the Odia artists and often became the platform to voice the complaints of small-time traders and businesspeople. The language used here moved freely between Odia and Hindi/Urdu, making possible some rudimentary communication between the common Odia-speaking population and the Urdu-speaking representatives of the Moghul Emperor. A similar phenomenon was the tradition of Manipravalam, which used a language that freely traversed between Sanskrit and the Dravidian languages, especially Tamil. This hybrid language variety was prevalent in the 14th century and has been used in several manuscripts in the South of India. With the introduction of the 'modern' English education system that was increasingly getting centralised under a unified

British administration, the existing multilingualism got transferred to the teaching-learning processes, resulting in the use of multiple languages in dictionaries, grammar books, and other teaching/learning materials.

This chapter presents an analysis of a few such dictionaries and grammar books from early 20th century Odisha. Apart from analysing the textbooks, the chapter also looks at the multilingual, sociocultural and political contexts that necessitated the use of translanguaging.

The Concept of Translanguaging

Since the beginning of the use of the word translanguaging or *trawsieithu* in 1994, it has been used to suggest a pedagogical practice where bilingual/multilingual students are encouraged to alternate between languages to achieve better comprehension or production. Williams (2002) emphasises the value of translanguaging as a pedagogic tool that could have important educational outcomes. He sees it as a cognitive strategy to use one language to strengthen the learner's ability to use another. According to Williams, 'translanguaging entails using one language to reinforce the other to increase understanding and to augment the pupil's ability in both languages' (as cited in Lewis *et al.*, 2012: 4). Baker (2011), on the other hand, focuses on the sociocultural implications of the practice, stressing the need to implement it in a planned strategic manner to maximise learning. He says, 'The teacher can allow a student to use both languages, but in a planned, developmental and strategic manner, to maximize a student's linguistic and cognitive capability, and to reflect that language is sociocultural both in content and process' (Baker, 2011: 290). The perspectives of Creese and Blackledge (2010) and Lewis *et al.* (2012) are very similar. They stress the pedagogic utility of translanguaging and discuss the intentional and planned two-language usage of bi/multilingualism. Creese and Blackledge (2010) primarily focus on 'spontaneous translanguaging' where pupils utilise both their languages to maximise understanding' (2010: 655). García (2009) not only acknowledges the pedagogic value of translanguaging as a tool but also pushes it further as a shaping experience in the bi/multilingual world. For her, 'translanguaging is indeed a powerful mechanism to construct understandings, to include others, and to mediate understandings across language groups' (as cited in Lewis *et al.*, 2012: 7). Popularly known as 'dynamic bilingualism', this refers to 'the multiple language interactions and other linguistic interrelationships that take place on different scales and spaces among multilingual speakers' (García & Li, 2015: 223–224).

García and Li (2015) propose that the possibility of translanguaging in the bilingual/multilingual pedagogic context enables students to engage their entire language repertoire to create a meaningful language experience for themselves. According to them, it allows them to 'acquire not only new ways of speaking and acting, of languaging, but also of being, of knowing, and of doing' (García & Li, 2015: 229). For teachers, they suggest, this could even involve moving between languages to give instructions and illustrations in what has been called language for academic purposes. Findings by Phyak *et al.* (2022) demonstrate that translanguaging is already used effectively as a tool in multilingual classrooms in Nepal to teach content subjects as well as English. They see the 'translanguaging space' as a dialogic space for teachers to operate effectively, while creating a safe environment for students. In another study, Sah and Kubota (2022) show that translanguaging has always been an accepted norm in schools in South Asia, but it is not necessarily a planned pedagogic approach. Lightfoot *et al.* (2022), in a similar study conducted in Delhi and Hyderabad, report the overwhelmingly multilingual nature of teaching English language and mathematics classes in schools. Sah and Li (2020) look at it as 'a transformative pedagogic approach to teaching both academic content and language for minoritized children as it allows equal space and opportunity for ALL learners in the classroom' (2020: 3). Often, in these studies, translanguaging is a part of spontaneous pedagogic practice used during classroom interaction. Suresh Canagarajah's technique of 'code-meshing' extends this to teaching writing. He uses translanguaging as a pre-planned systematic strategy to improve the academic writing skills of students (Canagarajah, 2011).

Significantly, all these studies look at translanguaging as a recent development, an effort to empower students and make classrooms inclusive. Contrary to these assumptions, the present chapter shows how translanguaging was operationalised in the multilingual context of late 19th and early 20th-century India as a well-planned pedagogic strategy, built into language teaching materials and probably used within classrooms too. Specifically, it focuses on how translanguaging, or the seamless use of multiple languages, was instrumental in establishing and furthering 'modern' English education in the Indian subcontinent. For this purpose, this chapter looks at 'translanguaging' as a broad approach that includes features like bilingualism, altering between languages, using mixed codes, etc., for teaching or any other kind of communication.

Multilingual Practices in the Indian Subcontinent

The Indian subcontinent, as mentioned earlier, has always been a place of multiple language use – as a sociocultural practice and in literary and performative art forms. When the British colonisers assumed control over the country in the 18th century, apart from *Pathasalas* for education in the vernaculars, there were already many well-established language education systems in place for Sanskrit, Persian and Arabic. With the increasing British hold over the administrative, financial and legal systems, there was growing pressure to introduce English language education and train a sizable number of English-educated Indians for administrative and other positions. There was also constant pressure from the missionaries and the Indians themselves who asked for English because it gave them access to economic as well as cultural capital. All this galvanised a movement towards modern education, a big part of which was English education. It is necessary to point out that after the armed rebellions that erupted in several parts of the country against the East India Company rule in the last part of the 18th and 19th centuries, the British were apprehensive about introducing exclusive English education. Hence, their policies stressed on the continuation of vernacular education along with the introduction of English.[1]

There was the establishment of Anglo-vernacular schools around the 1820s. These schools focused on teaching several subjects in the modern Indian languages with English as a subject from the secondary level onwards. This, in a major way, has promoted English education among the Indian population. The inclusion of Indians into the Indian civil services and the establishment of the Supreme Court in Calcutta, where English was becoming an increasingly important language was another reason to learn English along with other modern languages. By the 1860s, Indian civil services were open to Indians. There was a need for translators in the High Courts and the Supreme Court. The bureaucracy needed English-educated Indians to help with the administration at all levels and there was a growing need for English-educated people to teach in schools, colleges and universities. The first colleges were established in the first quarter of the 19th century. The first universities were established in 1857 (Calcutta, Bombay and Madras). All these developments point to growing exposure to English literacy and the need in the system to create an English-educated population.

Simultaneously, there was a growing need for education in the modern Indian and classical languages. The English bureaucrats posted in India had to have a reasonable command over the Indian languages. The missionaries also needed to learn the local languages to reach out to the Indian public for proselytisation. In addition, the Orientalists/linguists wanted to learn the Indian languages for reasons of academic interest. All this created a situation where there was a need to evolve pedagogy for multilingual learning. Hence, there began the prolific production of multilingual dictionaries and grammar books, many of which were used as textbooks in schools and colleges. Added to all these factors was the money allocated in the 1813 Charter Act[2] for 'the revival and improvement of literature and encouragement of the learned natives of India and for the introduction and promotion of knowledge of the sciences among the inhabitants of the British territories in India' (Krishnaswamy, 2006: 17). This resulted in the establishment of the Centers of Oriental Learning and Translation. As the Orientalist-Anglicist controversy[3] gathered steam and culminated in Macaulay's Minute in 1835,[4] there were influential voices like Campbell and Brian Hodgson, who argued for liberal funding and furthering of vernacular education. They saw it as a way out of the Orientalist-Anglicist controversy.

The complex dynamics of all these pressure systems eventually resulted in the formalisation of 'modern education' which included English at the higher levels and the vernaculars or the modern Indian languages at the primary and secondary levels. The growing nationalist movement and the rise of sub-nationalisms (region-based nationalism/identity formation like Odia or Tamil nationalism) also furthered the cause of teaching/learning the vernaculars. The outcome of all this was the growth of different types of colonial/vernacular modernities of which multilingualism was a vital part.

In the Indian subcontinent, colonial modernism took many forms and different contours. Enmeshed with the struggle for hierarchy and power, it contoured modern education, administration and law. As Chatterjee (1997) points out, colonial modernity defined itself as 'objective', 'modern', 'progressive', 'secular' and 'scientific', but above all, 'national'. It was constructed in the public consciousness as the '*nabya*' (the new) against the old. Therefore, the site of modern education, especially language education, became a space for nurturing sub-nationalisms like Odia, Bengali, Telugu or Tamil nationalism with a strong need for linguistic identity based on ethnicity. Interestingly, the increase in the need for exclusive language-based identities accompanied by the struggle for power did not become a hindrance in teaching/learning multiple languages or the need for translanguaging in the bi/multilingual platforms. This was possible probably because, construction of national/subnational identities based on a single language was largely a creation of 19th century colonial modernity. But for centuries, it was the norm in the Indian subcontinent for a single community to have multiple languages and practice active translanguaging for communication. The *Mani Prabalam* and the *Moghul Tamsa* are examples of this in literary and popular performative art forms. After the institution of a centralised modern education system, this kind of active/dynamic multilingualism necessitated the use of all the available linguistic repertoire to ensure comprehension. This eventually led to the need to develop bi/multilingual teaching materials, grammar books and dictionaries. Here, unlike the earlier instances of translanguaging between Indian languages, English became a major point of reference. From this point onwards, in the field of modern education at least, there was frequent translanguaging between one or more than one Indian language and English.

Multilingual Education in the State of Odisha

In the subsequent parts of the chapter, we will illustrate translingual practices in the State of Odisha, drawing on written texts (grammar books, dictionaries and thesaurus) that were used for pedagogical purposes. The texts have been collected from archives, old book shops and an old Odia textbook collection repository – '*Srujanika*'.

The Odisha province was established on the 1st of April, 1936, under the British Raj. This was possible after relentless efforts to unite the Odia-speaking areas from Bengal, Madras and Bombay Presidencies (administrative units created by the British administration). Interestingly, however, both before the formation of the independent province and after, Odisha retained its multilingual character and Odia, Bengali, Hindi, Persian and Telugu were used in different parts of the province for cultural and pedagogical purposes.

The first primary English schools in Odisha were established in the 1820s by British missionaries. In 1835, the British Government established the first English school in Puri. Thereafter, Zillah (District level) schools were set up in Cuttack, Sambalpur and Balasore (Samantarai, 1964: 52–59). However, the growth was slow and schools had to be closed down at times owing to the lack of students. One of the important factors that spurred the growth of education in the second half of the 19th century was a terrible famine – the *na anka durbhiksha* – in 1866, which killed almost a million people in the state. The Commissions set up to enquire into the cause of this disaster stressed the immediate need to strengthen the economy, improve means of transport, strengthen systems of administration and modernise education. As part of this, English and Anglo-vernacular schools were set up in different parts of the state and the administration made considerable effort to encourage education. According to the statistics presented in *Growth of Modern Education in Odisha* (2018), North Odisha had 12 High schools and 82 Middle English (ME) schools by the end of the 19th century. Meanwhile, South Odisha had four high schools and 26 ME schools. These were Anglo-vernacular schools that the East India Company (EIC) set up. The medium of education in these schools was the respective local language of the region and English was taught as one of the languages. Apart from these, there were also English schools set up by missionaries in different parts of the state and private schools established by Rajas and groups of socially aware/progressive people. Since exposure to English was limited and there was a growing need for a sizable English-educated population, bilingualism became popular in school education. Hence, we have a plethora of bilingual/multilingual dictionaries prepared for both local and English speakers in this period.

Discussed below are some of the dictionaries/textbooks used widely to teach in educational institutions and to learn languages independently.

Translingual Practices in Dictionaries and Textbooks

One of the first bilingual dictionaries in Odia was Amos Sutton's *An English and Odiya Dictionary* (1841). In the 'Preface' of this volume, the author briefly talks about the use of this book and describes the Odia language as distinct from Bengali and very similar to Sanskrit. He even dwells on phonetic differences between these closely related languages. As is evident in the sample below, the book was primarily meant for the readers who were fluent in English but could read and understand Odia. It was meant for learners who would like to understand Odia grammar and structure. The following two images (Figures 2.1 and 2.2) are from the book: the first talks about the kinds of verb classes and the second about the structure of the Odia sentence.

Sutton was part of the Baptist missionary service and knowing/understanding the local language was important for him and his colleagues. Considering the teaching/learning context, explaining the Odia language by freely moving between English and Odia was probably the most appropriate pedagogy. As the extracts presented here illustrate, the grammatical explanations are in English and the features being talked about are retained in Odia. In Figure 2.1, reproduced above, we have the explanation of four verb classes, categorised according to their phonetic behaviour. Here, except for the verb forms and the sounds that change, the explanations are in English. Figure 2.2 explains the structure of the Odia sentence. Again, the grammatical terms for the 'subject' and the 'predicate' are provided in Odia. But the constitution of these categories is explained in English. Further, the examples used to describe the subject and the predicate are first given in Odia and then translated into English (2nd and 3rd para. of Figure 2.2).

The presentation style indicates that the book's target reader was expected to be proficient in English and have knowledge of Odia orthography. The objective was to provide an understanding of the morphological and syntactic structure of Odia. It is possible that this was a pan-Indian tradition because we find grammar books written in a similar style in Bengali, too. One such book is the first grammar book written in the Bengali language in 1778. The book was titled *A Grammar of Bengali*

Verbs may be separated into four classes. 1. Those formed like କରିବା ପଢ଼ିବା, &c. These reject the final ଇବା, or ବା, to form the root, leaving କର, ପଢ଼.

2. Those formed as ଯାଇବା, ଖାଇବା, &c. These reject the final ଇବା to form the root, leaving ଯା, ଖା, &c.

Those formed like ବଳିବା, ଚେଡ଼ିବା, &c. These reject the final ବା only, to form the root, leaving ବଳି, ଚେଡ଼ି, &c.

4. Those which are irregular. This class is very small: the most important verb of this kind is ହେଉଛି, *being*, which will be fully explained in its proper place.

The Oriyas often prefer the gerund viz. କରିବା ଯାଇବା ଚେଡ଼ିବା &c. to the verbal noun from which to conjugate the verb, in which case the Gerund termination ବା has to be rejected.

Figure 2.1 Verb classes (Sutton, 1841: 14).

According to native grammar, sentences may be divided into two parts; the বিশেষ্য, or words to be described, and বিশেষণ, or words which describe, if the বিশেষ্য be a noun or pronoun, the বিশেষণ is its adjective; if a verb, its adverb.

The বিশেষণ usually precedes the thing to be described. Exam. ଲକ୍ଷ୍ମୀବର ବିଘ୍ନନ ଘନ ମୂଷିକବାହନ ଗଜବନ୍ଦ ମହାକାୟ୍ ଏମନ୍ତ ଏଯ ଗଣେଶ ଚାହ୍ୟାକୁ ନମସ୍ୟାର କର. The long-bellied, the destroyer of misfortune, the rat-borne, the elephant-toothed, the large-bodied, viz. Gunésha, him I salute.

Compound sentences are of course made up of subordinate বিশেষণ and বিশেষ্য. Exam. ଅଭିଷେକାର୍ଥ ସିଂହାସନ ସମୀପସ୍ଥି ଭ ଶ୍ରୀ ଶ୍ଲୋକ ଗଳାକୁ ଦେବୀ ଅଙ୍ଗବନୀ ଥିଲ୍ଲୀ କହ୍ଥି ଲା. The fifteenth image, seeing the illustrious raja Bhoja, (who) had approached the throne, for the purpose of installation, said.

Figure 2.2 Structure of the Odia Sentence (Sutton, 1841: 34)

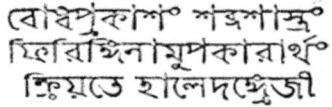

Figure 2.3 Cover Page (Halhed 1778, Cover page)

Language and was written by Nathaniel Brassey Halhed, an Orientalist and philologist. Illustrated above is part of the book's title page (Figure 2.3), which indicates the kind of translanguaging we find in the entire text.

The book was commissioned by the East India Company when there was an increasing demand for Company employees with knowledge of Bengali. A similar book in Telugu is *The Grammar of the Telugu Language,* which was written by C.P. Brown in 1857. The book was printed in Madras at the Christian Knowledge Society's Press. The books mentioned here are bilingual in parts. But often, there is the simultaneous use of two languages – Odia, Bengali or Telugu, as the case might be – without translation, for ease and exactness of comprehension.

The other book of significance is *Child's Easy First Grammar,* written after almost 80 years in the 1920s, when colonial modernity was very much a part of the curricular framework and knowing English was a means of gaining access to better opportunities. The early 20th century was a period of the growth of nationalisms and sub-nationalisms. This was also the time when there were serious attempts in Odisha to draw the marginalised sections of society into the mainstream education system. Foremost among these endeavours was the *Satyabadi* school set up in the vicinity of Puri in 1906. The school was set up by Pandit Gopabandhu Das, a nationalist and social worker, who was also instrumental in establishing Odia nationalism and carving out an independent state for the Odia-speaking population. Some of the most educated (i.e. English-educated) young men of the times joined him in establishing and teaching at the school. The philosophy of the school was to train children from all classes and sections (especially the marginalised) to be part of a modern growing India, yet be loyal to their Odia identity. The education here was highly experimental and aimed at producing 'ideal' citizens of the times.

Acharya Harihara Das, the author of *Child's Easy First Grammar*, was one of the teachers in the *Satyabadi* school. He was also an eminent Gandhian, a committed social worker, and a Nationalist. *Child's Easy First Grammar* is a book of English Grammar with explanations and instructions in Odia, probably used to teach English at *Satyabadi*. The book presents the grammar of English by using both English and Odia translingually. And if the presentation style is anything to go by, the teaching in the classes was probably translingual. Quoted below are parts of the book that show how the two languages – Odia and English – were used translingually for purposes of better comprehension. Significantly, the book does not have a publication date. It was probably printed informally for wider circulation and is still used widely in Odisha for English learning in vernacular medium schools. The latest reprint available is from 2014.

The author, in the text, designs exercises to identify kinds of Nouns and Verbs in the following way:

ନିମ୍ନ ଲିଖିତ word ଗୁଡ଼ିକ କି କି noun ଚିନହେଇଦିୟ-
Love, iron, care, baby, leisure, crowd, India, God, rice, wisdom, cotton, shop, ...etc.
Noun ର number (ବଚନ), gender (ଲିଙ୍ଗ), person (ପୁରୁଷ), ଏବଂ case କାରକ ଅଛି.

Verb ଦୁଇ ପ୍ରକାରର -- transitive (ସକର୍ମକ) ଏବଂ intransitive (ଆକର୍ମକ)
ଯେଉଁ verb ର ଗୋଟିଏ object (କର୍ମ) ଥାଏ, ତାହାକୁ transitive verb କହନ୍ତି, ଯଥା, he loves his brother (ସେ ତାହାଙ୍କ ଭାଇଙ୍କୁ ସୁଖ ପାଆନ୍ତି). ପ୍ରଶ୍ନ - ସେ କାହାକୁ ସୁଖ ପାଆନ୍ତି? ଉତ୍ତର ଭାଇଙ୍କୁ (brother). ଅତଏବ ଏଠାରେ loves ଏହି verb ର object ହେଲା ବରତହେର.
Adapted from Vennela & Mishra, 2023: 16

The first part of this extract is an exercise on Noun types. The author frequently moves between Odia and English, providing instructions in

Odia interspersed with grammatical terms in English. The first line of the extract, for example, is the instruction for the exercise followed by nouns (provided in English only) which the students are expected to categorise. Additionally, information about nominal criteria like number, gender, person and case has been provided with Odia equivalents in the next line. The second half of the extract deals with Verb types. The explanation here is in Odia and the grammatical terms are in English with Odia equivalents wherever possible. Unlike the previous books, this book was probably aimed at Odia speakers learning English grammar. Translanguaging, or the movement between languages, was a method to make learning easy and ensure better understanding of form and function through the semantic integration of the two languages.

The third book of interest is titled *Odia Self-Taught*. It was written by Chakradhara Mahapatra and published in 1955. As stated by the author, the purpose of this book was 'to enable foreign tourists, travelers, and research scholars to understand Odia… the dialect and the script of the land' (Mahapatra, 1955: *Preface*). The author specifies the objective of the book stating, 'Another objective, which is of equal importance, is to enable public officers of Odisha hailing from beyond the State to pick up the language and the script through the medium of this book' (Mahapatra, 1955: *Preface*). Primarily, the book describes vowels, consonants, the different parts of speech and the sentence types. The writing has been done primarily in English, with Odia brought in as examples. Given below is an example of how he explains pronouns. In a Note on pronoun types he says,

1. In other cases they are declined as in 'ଏହା', viz., ଯାହାଦ୍ୱାରା by that, ଯାହାଙ୍କ ଠାରୁ from whom, ଯାହାଠାରେ with whom, ଯେଉଁ ମାନଙ୍କ ଠାରୁ from whom.............etc.
2. Reflexive pronoun is expressed by using the word ନିଜେ, viz., ମୁଁ ନିଜେ I myself, ସେ ନିଜେ he himself, ସେମାନେ ନିଜେ they themselves, ତୁମେ ନିଜେ You yourself, …etc.

(Mahapatra, 1955: 50)

We find here that the text assumes fluency in English and attempts to teach Odia structure to learners who can read and understand basic Odia. In the sample provided in Note 1, the kind of pronoun being talked about is stated in English, followed by examples of the same in Odia with the English equivalents following immediately. The next sample (Note 2) explains the behaviour of pronouns in English, followed by Odia examples and their English equivalents. Presumably, an English proficient reader with minimum familiarity with the Odia orthography would be able to understand the Odia structure as well as the meaning of it in the given context.

The second example from the book is an explanation of Passive Verbs. In a section titled *Passive voice of Verbs* (କ୍ରିୟା ର କର୍ମ ବାଚ୍ୟ) the author gives the following examples to show the change of voice:

Examples of Active voice
କରିବା — do
କରିଅଛି — has done
କରିଥିଲା — did
କରିବ — will do

Examples of Passive voice
କରାଯିବା, କାରହବା — be done
କରାଯାଇଛି, କରାହେଇଛି — has been done
କରାଯାଇଥିଲା, କରାହେଇଥିଲା — was ଦନେ
ପଢ଼ାଯାଇଅଛି, ପଢ଼ାହେଇଅଛି — has been read
(Adapted from Mahapatra, 1955: 76)

Unlike the first example where the reader would need only basic familiarity with Odia, the explanation here puts more emphasis on knowledge of Odia. While explaining the Passive voice, for example, more than one Odia sentence with minimal style or usage variation has been translated into a single English sentence. Structures like 'has been done', 'was done' and 'will be done', have been provided with more than one Odia equivalent, showing the usage-based difference. In the latter example (Examples of Passive voice), though the format is that of translation, one would need a fair amount of knowledge in both languages to see the parallels and the differences. In a way, this would necessitate the reader or teacher to move between the formal structure and the semantic system of both languages to get a grasp of each.

Translanguaging in Other Domains

Apart from education, we find translanguagism in other sources too – in documents like public debates and autobiographical accounts of leading intellectuals of the times. One such important document is the *Atmacharita (The Autobiography)* of Phakhirmohan Senapati (1843–1918), who is also known as the usherer of modernity in Odia literature. Phakirmohan was the first Odia novelist, translator and administrator. The *Atmacharita* was written in the last two years of his life, around 1916. It was serialised in *Utkal Sahitya*[5] in his lifetime but was published in book form in 1927, nine years after his death. In the book, he often refers to the wide prevalence of multilingualism in the public and private spheres. Apart from Odia and English, he refers to the wide use and acceptance of Persian as the language of court and administration, which was eventually changed to English and then Odia. The book has been translated into English more than once. Here is an excerpt from the translation done by Paul St Preire in 2010.

> At the time English or Persian-educated Babus considered it an insult or a sin to pick up an Oriya book or to speak Oriya correctly. The clerks spoke in half-Persian and half-Oriya, and their writings read like a strange dialogue between the two languages. They even recorded their household expenditures in Persian. (St Preire, 2010: 22)

Phakirmohan was one of the important supporters of Odia in the war of languages[6] that rocked Odisha in the later half of the 19th century. He was also largely responsible for establishing Odia as an independent language in the face of onslaught by intellectuals from Bengal claiming that Odia was a dialect of Bengali. Hence, his disappointment at the attitude of some Odia speakers towards their mother tongue. The reference to 'Half Persian and Half Odia' in speech and writing, however, is definitely an instance of translanguaging in both formal and informal circumstances.

Discussion

Samples of texts discussed in the chapter show the wide prevalence of translanguaging in the Indian subcontinent during the 19th and early 20th centuries. The presence of a large number of dictionaries, thesaurus, grammar books and other documents indicates that the use of multiple languages and translanguaging between these languages was always acceptable in the field of education. More importantly, these were attempts to formally make translanguaging a part of language education and use it as an acceptable strategy to enhance language learning. The 'forewords' and 'prefaces' of many of these texts mention that they were sometimes commissioned by the administrators or funding agencies who placed prior orders for these books to be used in educational institutions. Thus, one can safely assume that they were part of the 'formally approved' teaching/learning strategy of the times. It can be argued further that translanguaging in the 19th-century Indian subcontinent was not just an informal classroom strategy to promote language learning or create a safe learning environment as has been reported by most studies on translingual practices in the present times (some of them have been discussed in the literature review of this chapter). It was a formally accepted pedagogy, approved and widely used as a tool for its highly functional and practical utility. Probably, this was because the Indian subcontinent has always been multilingual, with a variety of languages used on formal and informal occasions. Further, there was a robust language learning tradition that easily accepted and accommodated more than one language, ideologically and functionally. Interestingly, many of these texts are still in circulation and used as supporting texts for English language learning in rural and semi-urban contexts. Unfortunately, however, they no longer feature as prescribed texts in any curriculum for language learning.

Conclusion

In India, on the one hand, English is still a language that holds the key to upward social mobility and global opportunities and learning English is still a challenge for the majority of the population who do not have access to privileged schooling. On the other hand, increased networking of employment opportunities within the country and internationally has created the need to be proficient in, or at least develop familiarity with multiple languages in the corporate sector. Given such requirements, it would be worthwhile to revisit the existing translingual traditions in India and look at how they can be revived to suit the present needs. Given the resurgence in the recognition of translanguaging as an accepted pedagogic strategy, it is possible to revive the texts discussed and maybe contemporise them for learning English and other languages. To achieve this, it might be necessary to recognise that translanguaging was a formally accepted teaching/learning pedagogy with strong roots in India's traditional language learning systems and see it as a means to sustain the rich linguistic ecosystem that is historically part of its sociocultural fabric. The texts discussed in this chapter are from Odisha. But a few texts cited here are from other regions, too. Overall, the number of texts found in the translingual format across India is a definite pointer to the success of this pedagogic strategy in the past and the possibility of its success in the present times.

Interestingly, translanguaging is an important feature in the new Indian media and is increasingly becoming acceptable in formal contexts like online discussions and debates. This points at the formation of new and contemporary Indian identities, especially among the youth. Along with acknowledging and accepting translanguaging as a successfully tried and tested language learning strategy, expanding the educational pedagogy to recognise the changing features in new media and accommodating them formally could be an important step for the current education system in India.

Notes

(1) Important among the policies that stressed vernacular education is the Woods Despatch (1854). But even Macaulay, known as the foremost votary of English education, talked about vernacular education.
(2) The officials and influential members of the Board of East India Company who were not in favour of missionary education pressurised the Board to include the following section in the Charter Act of 1813: 'It shall be lawful for the Governor General in council to direct that out of any surplus, which may remain …. a sum of not less than 1,00,000 of rupees in each year shall be set apart and applied to the revival and

improvement of literature and encouragement of the learned natives of India and for the introduction and promotion of knowledge of the sciences among the inhabitants of the British territories in India.' (In Krishnaswamy, 2006: 17).
(3) The Orientalist-Anglicist controversy was primarily about the nature of education that the Company should impart in the conquered territory. The Orientalists favoured encouragement to Sanskrit, Arabic and Persian while the Anglicists wanted English and missionary education.
(4) Macaulay's Minute forms an important chapter in the history of English in India. He says: 'But I would strike at the root of the bad system which has hitherto been fostered by us. I would at once stop the printing of Arabic and Sanscrit books, I would abolish the Madrassa and the Sanscrit College at Calcutta'. (In Krishnaswamy, 2006: 37)
(5) Utkala Sahitya was one of the most important Odia periodicals that began in 1897. Edited by Viswanath Kar, it became one of the major platforms for the debate on Odia language. It was also the platform where vernacular modernity was formulated and concretised in Odisha.
(6) The reference here is to the language debate in Odisha that was active between 1868 and 1870 in Odisha. A detailed analysis of this movement can be found in the essay 'British Language Policy in the 19th Century and the Oriya Language movement' by Panchanan Mohanty (2022). *Utkal Dipika (1868–1873)*, edited by Gaurisankara Rai, was a magazine that served as a major platform to voice perspectives on the language movement in Odisha.

References

Baker, C. (2011) *Foundations of Bilingual Education and Bilingualism* (5th edn). Multilingual Matters.
Brown, C.P. (1857) *The Grammar of the Telugu Language*. Christian Knowledge Societies Press.
Canagarajah, S. (2011) Codemeshing in academic writing: Identifying teachable strategies of translanguaging. *The Modern Language Journal* 95 (3), 401–417. https://doi.org/10.1111/j.1540-4781.2011.01207.x
Chatterjee, P. (1997) *Our Modernity*. The CEPHIS and CODESRIA.
Creese, A. and Blackledge, A. (2010) Translanguaging in the bilingual Classroom: A pedagogy for learning and teaching. *Modern Language Journal* 94 (1), 103–115.
Das, A.H. (n.d) *Childs Easy First Grammar*. Available print, 2014. Cuttack Trading Company.
García, O. (2009) *Bilingual Education in the 21st Century: A Global Perspective*. Wiley-Blackwell.
García, O. and Li, W. (2015) Translanguaging, bilingualism, and bilingual education. In W.E. Wright, S. Boun and O. García (eds) *Handbook of Bilingual and Multilingual Education* (pp. 204–223). Wiley Blackwell.
Growth of Modern Education in Odisha (2018) History of Odisha. See https://historyofodisha.in/growth-of-modern-education-in-odisha/ (accessed on 21 May 2023).
Halhed, N.B. (1778) *A Grammar of the Bengal Language*. Endorse Press.
Krishnaswamy, N. (2006) *The Story of English*. Cambridge University Press.
Lewis, G., Bryn, J. and Colin, B. (2012) Translanguaging: Origins and development from school to street and beyond. *Educational Research and Evaluation. An International Journal on Theory and Practice* 18 (7), 655–670. http://doi.org/10.1080/13803611.2012.718490
Lightfoot, A., Balasubramanian, A., Tsimpli, I., Mukhopadhyay, L. and Treffers-Daller, J. (2022) Measuring the multilingual reality: Lessons from classrooms in Delhi and Hyderabad. *International Journal of Bilingual Education and Bilingualism* 25 (6), 2208–2228. https://doi.org/10.1080/13670050.2021.1899123

Mahapatra, C. (1955) *Oria: Self Taught*. The New Students Stores Ltd.

Mohanty, P. (2002) British language policy in the nineteenth century and the Oriya language movement. *Language Policy* 1, 53–73.

Phyak, P., Sah, P.K., Ghimire, N.B. and Lama, A. (2022) Teacher agency in creating a translingual space in Nepal's multilingual English-medium schools. *RELC Journal* 53 (2). https://doi.org/10.1177/00336882221113950

Sah, P.K. and Li, G. (2020) Translanguaging or unequal languaging? Unfolding the plurilingual discourse of English medium instruction policy in Nepal's public schools. *International Journal of Bilingual Education and Bilingualism* 25 (6), 2075–2094. https://doi.org/10.1080/13670050.2020.1849011

Sah, P. K. and Kubota, R. (2022) Towards critical translanguaging: A review of literature on English as a medium of instruction in South Asia's school education. *Asian Englishes* 24 (1), 132–146. https://doi.org/10.1080/13488678.2022.2056796

Samantarai, N. (1964) *Odia Sahityara Itihasa: 1803–1920 (The History of Odia Literature)*. Kalinga Mudrani.

Senapati, F. (2019) *Atmacharita*. First published in 1927. Friends Publishers.

St. Preirie, P. (2010) Translation and multilingualism in nineteenth century India: A view from Odisha. *Translation Today* 7 (1), 9–35.

Sutton, A. (1841) *An Oriya Dictionary in Three Volumes. Vol I. An Introductory Grammar, An English and Oriya Dictionary*. Orissa Mission Press.

Vennela, R. and Mishra, S. (2023) Alternative forms of bilingual education in colonial India: Prologue to the methods era. *Language and History* 66 (3), 1811–1920. https://doi.org/10.1080/17597536.2022.2147686

Williams, C. (2002) Ennill iaith: Astudiaeth o sefyllfa drochi yn 11–16 oed [A language gained: A study of language immersion at 11–16 years of age]. http://www.bangor.ac.uk/addysg/publications/Ennill_Iaith.pdf

3 Examining English Language Education in India through a Translingual Lens

Padmini Bhuyan Boruah

Introduction

India is currently poised at a historically significant moment in terms of education policy and practice, having begun to implement the curricular and administrative guidelines of the National Education Policy (NEP) (2020). Amid neoliberal pressures for English medium instruction (EMI), this NEP calls for nurturing India's rich multilingual and cultural heritage through education in the mother tongue from the Foundational stage of education (NEP 2020: 4.12). The NEP aims to achieve this by 'promoting multilingualism and the power of language in teaching and learning' (2020: 5). In terms of implementing a multilingual approach to education, the NEP (2020) promises to 'invest in large numbers of language teachers in all regional languages around the country, and, in particular, for all languages mentioned in the Eighth Schedule of the Constitution of India' (2020: 13). Pedagogical preparation for this would include efforts where '[t]eachers will be encouraged to use a bilingual approach, including bilingual teaching-learning materials, with those students whose home language may be different from the medium of instruction' (2020: 13).

The NEP (2020), however, departs considerably from previous policies with its silence on English as one of the languages in education. While previous policies tried to accommodate the Indian public's aspirations to learn English for social uplift, economic success and global mobility, the NEP (2020), while not being overtly hostile, has chosen not to discuss the undercurrents arising out of the desire to learn/teach English for upward mobility. In other words, India is at a crossroads: on the one hand, it needs to find effective ways of resisting the global neoliberal trends that have redefined both the objectives and pathways of English education in the 21st century, and on the other, it has to respond adequately to the call to adopt translingual pedagogical practices that value and promote traditions of rich Indian multilinguality while accommodating English in education (Boruah & Mohanty, 2022). Although national education policies (NPE, 1968, 1986; NEP 2020), the National Curriculum Framework (NCF, 2005), the NCF for School Education (NCFSE, 2023) and the NCF for Teacher Education (NCFTE, 2009) have all adopted celebratory rhetoric on India's multilingual heritage, this has not translated into a corresponding reframing of language education curricula in both school/university education and teacher education. The country needs a robust multilingual pedagogy framework for English, informed by research emerging out of multilingual South Asian contexts, to respond critically to the neoliberal trends, identity concerns, linguistic rights movements and language pedagogy theorizations that have remained sites of dominance, subjugation and inequity in the country.

In this chapter, we first look in more detail at how multilingualism itself is framed in Indian society, education policy, language education and teacher education practices. While doing so, we look at multilinguality through a teacher lens to examine teachers' understanding of, and attitudes to, the use of children's home language repertoires in learning English at school. Situating translingual pedagogies as ideology and as praxis, we then look at ways in which language teacher education curricula and pedagogy might promote translingual practices for teaching English alongside other languages. This, in turn, would help dismantle hegemonic linguistic ontologies (Boruah & Mohanty, 2022; Cushman, 2016; Fang *et al.*, 2022; Phyak, 2021) and prevent linguistic epistemicide (Santos, 2014).

Societal Multilingualism in India

MacSwan (2017) provides a detailed overview of the popular terminology employed by scholars[1] to describe multilingual speakers' systematic and conscious use of multiple languages in the same or different domains of use. Some of the most widely used terms include *translanguaging*, *heteroglossia*, *polylanguaging*, *polylingual languaging*, *metrolingualism*, *codemeshing*, *translingual practice* and *multilanguaging*, and India is a robust illustration of these various kinds of languaging practices. Most Indians, for example, routinely communicate with one another with varying degrees of proficiency in two or three 'discrete' or 'named' languages, including English, in the same or different contexts (in a kind of *sequential multilingualism*). Most people also use features (morphemes, words, phrases, metaphors, etc.) from several cognates (such as Assamese-Bengali) or non-cognate (such as Tamil-English) languages effortlessly in the same syntactic construction (a kind of *simultaneous multilingualism*). In addition, they can move across varieties of the same language in diglossic contexts or while conversing with people from other varieties or languages (a kind of *dialectal multilingualism*). These phenomena are historically prevalent practices, much like the first language acquisition practices well attested in language acquisition research (Mohanty, 2019; Taylor & Mohanty, 2021), and are born of visual, verbal and semiotic mechanisms and artifacts that multilingual children in Indian societies are exposed to from infancy; they are also an illustration of what is now popularly termed 'translanguaging'.

The Interpretation of Multilingualism in Indian Education Policy

Indian education policies recognize this complex societal multilinguality and conceptualize multilingualism in two related, but different ways. Firstly, multilingualism is discussed in terms of the promotion, maintenance and revitalization of indigenous languages and dialects to preserve India's cultural heritage and safeguard every child's linguistic human rights. The NCF for School Education (2023), for example, conceptualizes 'the word "language" [to] denote all variants of the language, without affixing any particular variant as "the language" and the rest as "dialects"' (2023: 136).

The second interpretation of multilingualism in education policy is as a matter of choice of languages in education by schools, learners and teachers. This is in recognition of the complex societal language practices, the language hierarchies that have lodged themselves firmly in education and the continuing demands from smaller language communities for inclusion of their languages in education. The Kothari Commission on education (1964–1966) devised a Three Language Formula (TFL) in school education as the most efficacious way to allow Indian multilingualism to thrive while promoting national unity within linguistic and cultural diversity. The TLF stipulated the compulsory introduction of three languages at the primary level (Kindergarten through Grade 8; ages 4 to 13) in a graded sequence. The child's home language (L1) was to be introduced first, preferably as the medium of instruction and the language of early literacy, followed by a regional language (L2/L3) and a language for national unity and/or global presence (L2/L3).

The TLF was designed to ensure that all Indian children received an education in three languages that could best serve their individual, community and national needs. Children would begin literacy in their home language to make sense of their immediate society and environment and develop pride in their linguistic and cultural heritage. They would then learn the language of the larger community for regional integration, and/or Hindi for national unity, and English compulsorily,[2] to prepare for higher education and professional success. The iteration of the Three Language Formula (TLF) in the latest national education policy formulations as the study of 'at least three languages [by students] in their school years' (NCF for School Education, 2023: 138) reflects the two related positions described above. The NEP (2020) has mandated 'early implementation of the three-language formula to promote multilingualism; teaching in the home/local language wherever possible' (2020: 54). It has also taken cognizance of the marginalization, in mainstream language education, of children from minority language groups, declaring that '[a]ll efforts will be made early on to ensure that any gaps that exist between the language spoken by the child and the medium of teaching are bridged' (NEP, 2020: 11).

However, the well-meaning but misrepresented aim of multilingual education, as the teaching of three or more languages (in succession) and the compartmentalized pedagogical training of teachers for separate languages, is problematic in terms of the aims of Indian education, and it also raises concerns of a possible backfiring of the social justice agenda. As Phyak (2021) warns, '[t]he logic of "choice" of languages in a multilingual context misrecognizes the complexities of multilingual experiences and supports the "we-vs-them" discourse'. Phyak argues that choice of language, especially in the context of learning English, becomes a politically charged discursive tool 'to reproduce sociopolitical, economic, and cultural capitals, wrought by the neoliberal market...and to validate the legitimacy of monolingual ideologies in education' (2021: 226). In other words, language choices in Indian education continue to be guided by people's aspirations to learn English for economic success, and this demand for English makes it difficult to dislodge pedagogies borrowed from western monolingual theorizations. These pedagogies propagate deficit ideologies that devalue and erase traditional epistemologies of language learning practiced by diverse multilingual communities, as these are not attested by Western scholarship. For example, smaller languages that do not yet have written grammars are not included as languages in education, because of a residual colonial mindset that still regards grammar teaching as an integral part of language teaching.

A related and alarming consequence of this kind of ideology is the homogenising of language pedagogies 'into a global, neoliberal monoculture' (Meighan, 2022: 3), where language pedagogy training is offered to teachers through 'universal' principles of language acquisition without submitting these to contextual realities. In India, for example, curricular frameworks for the teaching of English subscribe to pedagogies designed for English as a second language (ESL) contexts, even where English is hardly present in the learners' environment (see Kalyanpur *et al.*, 2022). This has failed to develop the English proficiency of many learner groups, especially those from disadvantaged backgrounds. Scholars have warned of such '*colonialingual* ideologies and pedagogies' (Meighan, 2022) arising out of Eurocentric orientations towards English language teaching, even in multilingual societies. Bonnin and Unamuno (2021), Jasper (2018), Kubota (2020) and Meighan (2022) refer to such privileging practices as 'epistemological racisms', which may prevent multilingual classrooms from achieving the agenda of social change and transformative education through translingual pedagogies. Bonnin and Unamuno (2021) warn that if such Eurocentric epistemologies are so deeply entrenched in education, 'minority speakers' sociopolitical struggles' (2021: 247) may not be acknowledged even in translanguaging pedagogies. People's proclivity towards English medium instruction at the cost of literacy in home languages (Boruah & Mohanty, 2022; Chacko, 2020; Jayadeva, 2019; Mathew & Lukose, 2020; Tooley & Dixon, 2006; Xiong & Yuan, 2018, and others) has also added to the already tenuous relationship between the linguistically privileged and the marginalized in multilingual contexts.

Multilingualism in English Teacher Education

As the previous section argues, multilingualism is a central focus in policy formulations for both school education and teacher education, and yet it has not led to a corresponding incorporation of translingual pedagogies in language teacher education. As multilingualism has been interpreted in education policy as the teaching of several individual languages, either as medium of instruction or as language 'subjects', pedagogical training of language teachers is conceptualized in terms of separate 'Methods' or 'Teaching' courses for each language (e.g. Teaching English/ Gujarati/Assamese) in BEd Programs. Furthermore, in most pre-service language teacher education programs, even when included, any discussion of multilingualism is just a tokenism; it does not translate into multi- or translingual pedagogical suggestions. A representative survey of the 'English methods/Pedagogy of English' course syllabi of Bachelor of Education (B.Ed) programs of six universities from the north, south, central, east and north-east regions of India[3] was conducted to understand in what ways multilingual education practices were conceptualized for English pedagogy courses. The term 'multilingualism' was found to occur mostly in the syllabi of a generic course named 'Language-across-the-Curriculum' (LAC). The term 'translanguaging' was mentioned in the BEd Syllabi of only two universities (Uttarakhand Open University, 2017 and Mizoram University); the first as an example of good practice and the second as a topic on a list of contents, both within the LAC courses. No critical discussion on the inadequacy of reliance on Western pedagogical theorizations or ways to adopt translanguaging pedagogies in teaching English was found in any of the syllabi. Such programs and courses thus fail to operationalize language teaching from a multilingual education or translingual pedagogy lens, contradicting the aim of language education to provide all children with equitable access to education and adequate support to develop their multilingual identity.

The NCFFS (2022) does make an observation on multilingual repertoires in passing, advising that '[l]anguages need not be taught and learned in watertight compartments at separate times. There can be a mixing of languages, and children should get an opportunity to learn new concepts and languages using the foundation of their L1 as scaffolding' (2022: 77). Findings from recent research on multilingual classroom practices and student learning in India (Alobaid, 2023; Tsimpli *et al.*, 2020) have also strongly recommended the adoption of multilingual strategies in lesson delivery for the development of learners' conceptual knowledge. However, pedagogical guidelines on how to incorporate L1 scaffolding in learning other languages or subjects and how to help students transition fluidly from their familiar languages to English, remain absent in English language teacher preparation, even though in India, English teachers' classroom practices have historically been framed through the use of several languages. Legitimate instances of authentic language practice (Heugh, 2018), such as explaining, translating, paraphrasing lesson content and giving instructions in the learners' languages are commonplace, and yet these have hitherto gone undocumented in Indian language education and language teaching. Legitimizing such acts of translanguaging in language teacher education, by acknowledging teachers' efforts at transcending the strict compartmentalization of lexis, grammar, pronunciation and idiom as properties of individual languages, could serve to decolonize and challenge monolingual ideologies of language teaching.

Translingual practices as a pedagogical stance in English teacher education

In this chapter, the term 'translingual' as a theoretical stance is based on three pedagogical principles offered by De Costa *et al.* (2017) – 'a broadened understanding of semiotic resources, student repertoire expansion, and critical awareness development' (2017: 465). In their definition, the prefix 'trans', which was earlier 'used to refer to practices beyond individual languages (treating them as mobile verbal resources), … is beginning to be applied to ways of looking at communication beyond language itself, to accommodate diverse other modalities and semiotic resources' (2017: 470). The authors add that '[i]n this sense, translingual points to the way words align with the body, objects, space, and environmental ecology, among other symbol systems, for making meaning' (2017: 470). They also point to the political use of 'trans', where the term can refer to a transformative process emerging from 'the contact and synergy between languages' and capable of 'transforming existing hierarchies and unequal statuses between language groups and institutions' (2017: 470).

Translingual practices for English language education, through translanguaging pedagogy, offers decolonizing support in two ways: by helping teachers explore learners' cognitive resources as 'a holistic multi-competence' (Li, 2018: 27) and by offering resistance to the colonial mentality inherent in '*colonilingual* ELE' (Meighan, 2022: 4). Translanguaging pedagogy is a response to deficit ideologies that justify the underperformance of children from marginalized linguistic communities as an outcome of pre-existing intellectual, socioeconomic and other deficiencies. To counter such deficit ideologies, English language education and teacher education in India would need to centre teachers' multimodal pedagogies for *all* children. This is also crucial to avoid existing roadblocks in English teacher education, such as the focus on teacher accountability rather than teacher support, and to establish a robust culture of equitable translingual language education. It is important to ensure that teachers do not have to 'set aside their own social and cultural beliefs and assumptions about knowledge, the process of learning and their views of learners, once they enter the hallowed portals of teacher education institutions' (Batra, 2005: 4351).

It is equally important to investigate teachers' own attitudes towards the methodology they follow while teaching (English) to students in multilingual classes, since teachers in India have historically been indoctrinated, either consciously or involuntarily, in the philosophy that knowledge comes from 'outside experts'. This message forces them to use their instincts, common sense, experience and intuition in surreptitious ways (Boruah, 2017) or to devalue them. Dislodging teachers or policymakers from such rigid structures of educational theorization is, of course, not easy. Pedagogical practices that have gained traction by having originated in contexts where the currency of scholarship is 'objectivity'/'scientific'/ 'rational'/'positivist' are unlikely to be critiqued or altered without resistance. Acceptance of new practices rooted in translanguaging theory would depend on how closely these are aligned to teachers' existing beliefs and perceptions of multilingual education, and their conviction that invoking learners' home languages in teaching a new language or teaching content is actually an educational gain. Several studies mentioned here have tried to document teachers' attitudes and beliefs towards their own translingual pedagogical repertoires and their multilingual contexts. This allows the classroom to become 'a space for interrogating language relationships, expanding participants' repertoires, and developing metalinguistic awareness, among other valuable educational outcomes' (DeCosta *et al.*, 2017: 470). In the section below, we look at some of how teachers conceive of their multilinguality in terms of delivering language lessons. Following that, we discuss ways in which education policy dispensations and stakeholders' beliefs, attitudes and translingual practices can converge to build appropriate pedagogies for language teacher education.

Teachers' perceptions of multilingual teaching

Recent research on teachers' attitudes to translanguaging pedagogies reveals at least three trends: A favorable attitude towards multiple language use (e.g. Alobaid, 2023; Dewaele, 2018; Ellis & Shintani, 2014; Tsimpli *et al.*, 2020); a negative view of code switching, language mixing or using children's first language to teach a new language (e.g. Doiz & Lasagabaster, 2018; Hall & Cook, 2012); or a positive position that is not reflected in their teaching practices (Edstrom, 2006) either from a sense of guilt or from not being convinced of the cognitive or linguistic benefits of students' home languages as a resource for learning new languages (Singleton & Flynn, 2022). These studies also report that while many teachers have affirmed the benefits of teaching a new language (say, English) through learners' (kn)own languages, they contradict their own stance by restricting the use of learners' home languages only to matters relating to classroom management.

Boruah (2022) and Lasker and Boruah's (2023) research on teachers' perceptions about using students' home languages to teach English and their attitudes towards teaching Maths and Science in English[4] show a similar trend: Teachers in these studies reported that they were 'forced' to use students' home languages as the students did not understand English, even though they 'know' that English needs to be taught through maximum exposure to the language. The first study (Boruah, 2022) revealed a mixture of attitudes. While the teachers responded with 'strongly disagree' to statements suggesting that it is better to teach one language at a time, they marked 'strongly agree' on statements that asked if using multiple languages in the class to teach a new language can cause confusion. One teacher (T5) marked 'strongly agree' on the statement 'Learners learn and enjoy learning when you use different languages or use their home languages in the classroom'. Yet, in a different question, they stated that '[l]earners must be taught in English only without use of any other language (sic) from the beginning'. In the second study (Lasker & Boruah, 2023) conducted with more than 500 secondary school teachers teaching multilingual populations, 57.9% reported that their students do not have English in their environment and hence they favored learning subjects such as Maths and Science in their home languages: 'English is just a language. Knowledge can be gather (sic) through mother language too'. However, a majority of the respondents (91.2%) reported that their students would benefit from learning Maths and Science in English:

> Having English knowledge and words [in] maths and science subjects will greatly help the students when they pursue higher education, as almost all terms and words used in higher courses are in English. (T6)

Yet another confusion is evident in teachers' responses to teaching English to multilingual students. A research study being conducted in the northeast Indian state of Nagaland (Walling, 2023) has revealed that deeply entrenched language hierarchies continue to be accepted uncritically by teachers. Nagaland is a multilingual, multi-ethnic tribal state where the government has adopted English as the medium of education in the absence of a majority ethnic Naga language. In a pilot survey on 10 primary government school English teachers working in one of Nagaland's districts, the first author (Walling) elicited data on teachers' use of multiple languages in the English class. All teachers listed Naga tribal languages such as Ao, Chang, Konyak, Khiamniungan, Sangtam, Phom, Yimchungru and Lotha – and non-Naga languages such as Nepali, Bihari and Assamese – as the different mother tongues of their students on the survey questionnaire, and reported in another question that they used students' mother tongues while teaching English. It was only through interviews that the researcher realized that the teachers interpreted 'mother tongue' not as the home languages of all students but as Ao, the language of the dominant ethnic Naga tribe of that particular district.

Findings from another study (Alobaid, 2023) – conducted by Macmillan Education India to explore teachers' attitudes towards multilingualism – have also shown that teachers perceived English and/in multilingualism in different ways. At least 57.2% of the teachers understood multilingualism as the use of multiple languages in the classroom, while 27.4% interpreted it as the teaching of regional languages along with English. Around 10% of teachers understood it to mean using home languages while teaching English. However, all the participating teachers welcomed the use of multiple languages in their classrooms. One of the reasons cited for this was the belief that this would help 'build an equitable, accessible and inclusive educational system' (2023: 9). Other reasons provided by the teachers to justify their use of several languages in the English classroom included improving understanding of concepts in the absence of equivalent terms, developing or retaining identity, for sociocultural expression, to accommodate the listeners' or speakers' proficiency in one of the languages used, or to explain something quickly. Teachers in this study also saw societal benefits of using multiple languages in lesson delivery, mentioning benefits such as sociocultural knowledge development and respect and acceptance of peers from diverse (smaller) language groups to counter their feeling of exclusion or inferiority. These studies show that most teachers of English have a positive attitude towards learners' home languages, relating it to the development of linguistic competence as well as mutual respect. However, in the absence of a robust pedagogical framework for incorporating learners' languages in the teaching of English, or an orientation on ways of supporting learners' linguistic identity development, teachers continue to disregard, downplay or reject their intuitive beliefs and translingual practices as unsound pedagogy.

Bridging the gap between societal multilingualism and translanguaging pedagogy for teacher education

Given such varied understanding of teachers on the value of tapping into multilingual children's existing language learning strategies and resources, translingual practices will have to be incorporated in Indian English language teacher education with both sensitivity and caution.

Prescribing translanguaging pedagogies as an obligatory mandate or ignoring teachers' existing classroom languaging practices is not likely to promote a healthy translingual stance in teacher education. Responses from teacher participants in the studies discussed above indicate that most teachers of English are already familiar with the practice of using learners' languages to teach English. In the Macmillan Education study (Alobaid, 2023) discussed above, teachers provided many strategies that they either used in the classroom or supported:

- encouraging learners to ask questions or share opinions in their own languages;
- using culture-specific phrases/sentences in drama-based activities;
- making learners greet one another in their home languages;
- encouraging learners to engage in conversations in their mutually intelligible languages;
- asking learners to search for and share names of regional items specific to their languages;
- explaining topics first in home languages, followed by explanations in English;
- using videos from learners' languages for teaching.

However, it is important to note that many of these strategies may still be used through the majority of speakers' home language. Teachers may still face linguistic barriers that prevent them from accessing or helping learners from minority language communities activate their translingual repertoires. Teachers' (positive or tolerant) attitudes towards the use of several languages in the English classroom can be considered the foundation of their translanguaging proficiency, and pedagogy training can be designed around this. Even when the teacher is multilingual but does not know the learners' languages, translingual pedagogy training can help them activate learners' linguistic resources. Teachers can be encouraged to use a two-pronged approach to accelerate students' learning of English: the first, by engaging learners in pedagogical activities that encourage them to use cognitive strategies from all their known languages, and the second, allowing learners to express themselves in their most familiar language. As Anderson (2023) notes, '[c]rosslinguistic mediation involves using our stronger languages to help others to understand something encoded in a weaker language (English in our classrooms)' (2023: 49). These are asset-based conceptualizations of translanguaging that can inform language teacher pedagogy for English and also serve as the bedrock for culturally sustaining pre-service English teacher education syllabi.

Contextually appropriate translingual pedagogies in English language teacher education

The discussion above suggests that any pre-service English language teacher education (ELTE) program that seeks to serve the language needs of multilingual learners, especially those from disadvantaged and marginalized speech communities – needs to be formulated through an asset-based approach to translanguaging pedagogy and translingual practices. In this section, I discuss three important goals that would need to underlie translingual approaches to English teacher education. These goals are essential for the training of teachers in equitable pedagogy and transaction of syllabi from a social justice lens, as well as a means of countering the hegemonic hierarchies of English education.

Goal 1: Integration, not assimilation

Pedagogical theorizations for English in education in post-colonial India have traditionally been driven by ESL and second language acquisition (SLA) research emanating from European and American contexts, and teacher education programs have not yet seriously considered the societal implications of such pedagogies. In English-speaking countries, the ESL/TESOL field of study became the default pedagogical framework to teach English to children of immigrants who needed English to *assimilate* into an English-speaking society. These pedagogical practices complemented the need for learners to practice English in 'real-life contexts', as learners encountered English the moment they stepped out of their homes for social, professional and academic purposes.

Indian English Language Teaching (ELT) adopted such ESL/TESOL pedagogies without submitting these to the Indian learners' contexts, which are varied, complex, heterogeneous socioeconomic spaces, and where exposure to English in the environment can range from near-full exposure to complete absence of English. In other words, English has never been uniformly a second (or foreign) language in India. For complex and layered multilingual contexts like India, the goal of English for education has to be moored in a philosophy of *integration*, where English is taught within a holistic framing of language education that responds adequately to the societal, educational and socioeconomic needs of different groups of Indians. A philosophy of integration dissolves the boundaries between Us and Others ('English for native speakers' vs 'English for speakers of other languages') and reduces the hierarchical distance that a philosophy of assimilation internalizes. Integrative translingual pedagogies have the potential to reduce the psychological distance between English as a desirable goal and home languages as hindrances to accessing English.

Goal 2: Situating English in multilingual identity construction

In India, a deeply painful colonial past has created a divide between champions of 'Indian languages' and those who see English as a strategic tool for development. The National Education Policy (2020) in its draft form (2019: 81–83) used a very hostile rhetoric to describe the role of

English, comparing it unfavourably with Indian languages. Against this construction of English as an intruder that has strategically tried to displace the wisdom and logic of Indian languages, there are arguments declaring English as 'the great equalizer against linguistic oppression' (Chidambaram, Member of Parliament, 2020: paragraph 3), a 'precious thing' and 'an Indian language' (Infosys founder Narayan Murthy, 2021: paragraph 7) and 'a lingua franca for the people of multilingual nations like India' (Nandi, 2019: 143). Contesting attitudes and claims over English, such as these impact on the development of linguistic identities of multilingual Indians. This is especially pertinent since India's NEP 2020 has acknowledged the impact of language and culture orientation on identity creation and citizenship building (2020: 53).

A multilingual identity is 'relational, mediated and as highly situated' as well as 'dynamic, multiple and shifting' (Block, 2006: 34), and is influenced by 'factors such as language use habits, open-mindedness, future multilingual self and beliefs about multilingualism' (Forbes & Rutgers, 2021: 400–1). In South Asian multilingual societies such as India, we need to be sensitive to the impact of English on the development of a child's multilingual identity. We need to study the *reciprocity value* of English in identity formation, that is, the interplay of factors around the learning of English that contribute to multilingual identity formation vis-a-vis the prestige value of English and its impact on society, culture and multilingualism. When developing a translingual approach to English language pedagogy, we need to take into account learners' investment in English language learning and their emotional attachment to the languages in their environment. A conscious and reflexive process of 'negotiation' (Fielding, 2021) between themselves and their languages will help learners position English equitably in the development of their multilingual identities.

English teachers' reflexive reading of their own identity is also an important part of translingual pedagogy training for multilingual learners. Teachers' reflections on the role of English in the development of their multilingual identity are likely to help them take a more empathetic stance and build appropriate pedagogies to bridge their learners' known languages and English. This 'identity education', or 'the purposeful involvement of educators with students' identity-related processes or contents' (Schachter & Rich, 2011, in Forbes, 2022: 222) is crucial from a social justice perspective, as it helps both teachers and learners confront language hierarchies and dismantle artificial barriers in multilingual identity development arising out of undue attention to dominant and powerful languages such as English. Meredith (2011), discussing Stein (2008) points out that 'valuing diversity is not about denying access to dominant discourses of power, but rather is about valuing and building on students' complete array of representational resources… and positioning children as active transformers of culture as they assert their identities' (2008: 558). Although Indians rejoice in their multilinguality, in existing practices, an individual's social worth is still valued in proportion to their level of proficiency in English. If the teaching of English can be framed within the familiar linguistic contexts in which children live and grow, the development of their linguistic identities and sense of self will no longer be impacted by or measured in terms of their proficiency or access to English (or the lack of it).

Goal 3: Sharing the responsibility of promoting healthy use of one's languages

When English sits comfortably in translingual practices in Indian classrooms, teachers would have achieved the 'pedagogical breakthrough' (Agnihotri, 2007: 197) required in colonized South Asian contexts like India to counter the hegemonic, Western-centric language pedagogical norms traditionally accepted as best practices. The successful dismantling of hierarchies is more likely to happen if English teacher education engages in a healthy critique of the current local sociopolitical contexts of language learning. In other words, transformative translingual education is dependent on the extent to which both consumers of educational reform (i.e. trainee teachers and in turn, their students) and producers of new curricular practices (e.g. teacher educators and in turn, their trainees) take equal responsibility to create and maintain a safe space for all languages to thrive. A 'heterogeneous, inclusive educational space' (Tian, 2020: 217) can arise when teacher trainees' and learners' known language practices are incorporated 'strategically' in pedagogy. Creating a space in the English classroom and teacher education for sharing of experiences and apprehensions around English in the environment, in life and society is the first step towards a social justice orientation in language education. This is especially important, as for too long English language education has been conceptualized around sanitized pedagogies that focus on developing language skills through inherited methods and methodology, without a consideration of users' past, present and future relationship with English.

Here is an example from my personal language education experience. Our English-medium classrooms in the 1980s exposed us to a variety of words, structures, concepts and an English idiom. We developed conceptual knowledge of the world around us in English, and we developed the language to define, explain, discuss, narrate, compare and argue about academic concepts. However, we were never taught to be self-reflexive; there was no space in our classes to talk about our own languages and our own relationship with English. Outside the classroom, we spoke in a mixture of languages, but these were the languages (English, Assamese, Hindi and Bengali) already visible at school, in administration and media. We were discouraged from using any language other than English at school, and it did not occur to us that this would lead to an erosion of our multilingual abilities. We denied visibility to our linguistic selves, thought of lesser-used languages or varieties as quaint. The lesson for current English language and teacher education pedagogy is that until the English classroom foregrounds learners' beliefs and attitudes towards their known languages and their translanguaging practices, language pedagogy will remain unresponsive to societal multilingual needs and language functions. The English learned by children within the limited confines of textbook lessons and grammar tests will remain an inadequate resource, unable to provide students with the tools for effective meaning-making in their multilingual contexts.

Implications and Recommendations

In this concluding section, we consider once again how English language teacher education in India – both pre-service and in-service – can prepare teachers for transformative translingual education. The task of implementing language education curriculum and pedagogy to provide Indian children with equitable and globally relevant language education has been entrusted to teachers, many of whom have not been adequately trained for the purpose. English language teachers have also been caught between the ideological agenda of language education in India, neoliberal market expediencies, the language practices and aspirations of learners and inadequate translingual pedagogical orientation in teacher education curricula. Much of this disconnect stems from an inability to map societal language practices onto language pedagogy, which, in turn, is a result of the absence of a provision in language teacher education to center teachers' own and their students' natural multilingual practices. There is an urgent need for English language teacher education and language teaching praxis to consider multilingual identity development as part of translingual pedagogies. The field also needs to carefully consider the goals of English language teaching, which currently have not been built on the everyday classroom practices of teachers who teach multilingual learners.

In short, a bottom-up, constructivist and contextually relevant formulation of translanguaging theory and practice needs to be adopted for English language education and teacher education. There are many advantages of adopting contextually appropriate translingual pedagogies in the Indian context, one of which is arresting the poor performance of learners in English at school. The Annual State of Education (ASER) (2023) report shows that out of almost 700,000 children assessed, only about 17.5% of children could read simple English sentences in Grade 5. State governments have taken these statistics seriously, threatening the closure of schools with poor-performing students. For many of these schools, situated mostly in rural contexts, adopting contextually relevant translanguaging strategies for the teaching of English could be one way of bringing about positive change in exam performance. Adoption of equitable translingual pedagogies would also enable pre-service language teachers to adequately prepare for the sociopolitical realities of culturally and linguistically diverse classrooms and communities and counter the 'neoliberal precarity' (Sharma & Phyak, 2023: 3) that forces teachers to valorize certain forms and practices in English language education (such as developing a 'neutral accent') that are disconnected from the realities of teachers' and learners' multilingual contexts.

When structural inequities stemming from language hierarchies are ignored, minority languages begin to be overlooked and 'treated as mere resources, important only for their exchange value rather than cultural significance' (Pennycook & Makoni, 2020: 98). In such scenarios, minority language speakers may be pushed to adopt 'identities of resignation' (Nakagawa & Kouritzin, 2021: 304), which lead to a constant and unrewarding struggle to adapt their own practices to fit better into dominant language cultures. Such deficit forms of translanguaging may even lead to language loss (Singleton & Flynn, 2022). English language teacher education pedagogy will thus need to look at translanguaging practices from at least two perspectives: (a) as a tool for minority language maintenance and/or (b) to teach a new language (English in this case) using learners' existing funds of knowledge (Gonzalez *et al.*, 2005) across their available languages. Teachers' attitudes towards learning about and using translanguaging pedagogies will be affected by these two positions, which suggests that a critical discourse around inclusive translanguaging strategies needs to become a focal area in English language teacher education curricula. It is important to remember that although 'using more than one language is natural for multilingual teachers and learners, multilingual lesson delivery requires organization, lesson planning and scaffolding so that language use will be associated with specific activities and teacher–learner or peer interaction' (Tsimpli *et al.*, 2020: 23). A tiered pedagogical process which introduces translanguaging practices through successive stages of self-reflexive inquiry, familiarization, modelling and implementation might help situate such practices in inclusive multilingual teacher education.

Notes

(1) Such as Baker (2011), Canagarajah (2011, 2012), García (2009), Mohanty (2019), Nguyen (2012), Otsuji and Pennycook (2011), Williams (1994) and others.
(2) The NEP (2020) and the National Curriculum Framework for school Education (2023) have now made English an optional rather than a compulsory subject in the TLF. However, it is unlikely that English will be removed from school syllabi given its high demand in society.
(3) Links to the syllabi of the B.Ed. syllabi of the six universities (Delhi, Gauhati, Gujarat, Mumbai, Tamil Nadu and Uttarakhand Universities) are provided in the references.
(4) The first data set is from a study on English teachers' multilingual practices conducted in India and Malaysia as part of a 2021 study consortium of colleagues from one Malaysian and two Indian universities. The second set is from a 2023 government funded training mandate for primary teachers to prepare them to teach and train colleagues to use English while teaching mathematics and Science.

References

Agnihotri, R. (2007) Towards a pedagogical paradigm rooted in multilinguality. *International Multilingual Research Journal* 1 (2), 79–88. https://doi.org/10.1080/19313150701489689

Alobaid, A. (2023) *Understanding Multilingualism in India's Classrooms*. Macmillan Education India Pvt. Ltd. https://macmillaneducation.in/wp-content/uploads/2023/02/MLE-Report-1.pdf

Anderson, J. (2023) Translanguaging in the ELT classroom. *Modern English Teacher* 32 (2), 46–50.

Annual Status of Education Report (2023) https://img.asercentre.org/docs/ASER%202022%20report%20pdfs/allindiaaser202217_01_2023final.pdf

Baker, C. (2011) *Foundations of Bilingual Education and Bilingualism (Vol. 79)*. Multilingual Matters.

Batra, P. (2005) Voice and agency of teachers: A missing link in the national curriculum framework. *Economic and Political Weekly* Vol. 40 (October 1–7), 4347–4356.

Block, D. (2006) *Multilingual Identities in a Global City: London Stories*. Palgrave Macmillan. http://books.google.com/books/about/Multilingual_Identities_in_a_Global_City.html?id=O10TKgAACAAJ.

Bonnin, J.E. and Unamuno, V. (2021) Debating translanguaging: A contribution from the perspective of minority language speakers. *Language, Culture and Society* 3 (2), 231–254. https://doi.org/10.1075/lcs.20016.bon

Boruah, P. (2017) Learning English in a low-cost semi-urban English-medium school in India: Challenges, interaction patterns and domains of use. In H. Coleman (ed.) *Multilingualisms and Development* (pp. 289–306). British Council.

Boruah, P. (2022) Examining English teachers' multilingual pedagogy choices: A study of teacher perceptions about using home languages in teaching English. *Unpublished manuscript*.

Boruah, P. and Mohanty, A.K. (2022) English medium education in India: The neoliberal legacy and challenges to multilingual language policy implementation. In J. Daghigh, J.M. Jan and S. Kaur (eds) *Neoliberalization of English Language Policy in the Global South, Language Policy 29* (pp. 51–72). Springer. https://doi.org/10.1007/978-3-030-92353-2_4

Canagarajah, S. (2011) Codemeshing in academic writing: Identifying teachable strategies of translanguaging. *The Modern Language Journal* 95, 401–417.

Canagarajah, S. (2012) Teacher development in a global profession: An autoethnobiography. *TESOL Quarterly* 46 (2), 258–279. https://doi.org/10.1002/tesq.18.

Chacko, M.A. (2020) English-educated as 'ready-made' leaders: Re-inscribing distinction through the student police cadet project in Kerala, India. *South Asia Journal of South Asian Studies* 43 (4), 1–18. https://doi.org/10.1080/00856401.2020.1775356

Chidambaram, K.P. (2020, August 31) It's time we get over this erroneous assumption that English is a "foreign" language. English is now native to India. @ShashiTharoor @chetan_bhagat @cdivakaruni @RealVikramSeth @devduttmyth. [Tweet]. Twitter. https://twitter.com/KartiPC/status/1300320376791003137?s=08

Cushman, E. (2016) Translingual and decolonial approaches to meaning making. *College English* 78, 234–242.

De Costa, P.I., Wang, X., Singh, J.G., Fraiberg, S., Milu, E. and Canagarajah, S. (2017) Pedagogizing translingual practice: Prospects and possibilities. *Research in the Teaching of English* 51 (4), 464–472. https://doi.org/ 10.58680/rte201729121

Delhi University. Two Year B.Ed syllabus. https://cie.du.ac.in/userfiles/downloads/Academic/Syllabus/BED/Bed_syllabus.pdf

Dewaele, J.M. (2018) Online questionnaires. In A. Phakiti, P. De Costa, L. Plonsky and S. Starfield (eds) *The Palgrave Handbook of Applied Linguistics Research Methodology* (pp. 269–286). Palgrave Macmillan.

Doiz, A. and Lasagabaster, D. (2018) Teachers' and students' second language motivational self-system in English-medium instruction: A qualitative approach. *TESOL Quarterly* 52 (3), 657–679. https://doi.org/10.1002/tesq.452

Edstrom, A. (2006) L1 use in the L2 classroom: One teacher's self-evaluation. *Canadian Modern Language Review* 63 (2), 275–292. http://doi.org/10.1353/cml.2007.0002

Ellis, R. and Shintani, N. (2014) *Exploring Language Pedagogy Through Second Language Acquisition Research*. Routledge.

Fang, F., Zhang, L. and Sah, P.K. (2022) Translanguaging in language teaching and learning: Current practices and future directions. *RELC Journal* 53 (2), 305–312.

Fielding, R. (2021) A multilingual identity approach to intercultural stance in language learning. *The Language Learning Journal* 49 (4), 466–482. https://doi.org/10.1080/09571736.2021.1912154

Forbes, K. (2022) We are multilingual: Identity education to promote engagement and achievement in schools. *Languages, Society and Policy*. https://www.lspjournal.com/post/we-are-multilingual-identity-education-to-promote-engagement-and-achievement-in-schools

Forbes, K. and Rutgers, D. (2021) Multilingual identity in education. *The Language Learning Journal* 49 (4), 399–403. https://doi.org/10.1080/09571736.2021.1918850

García, O. (2009) *Bilingual Education in the 21st Century: A Global Perspective*. Wiley Blackwell.

Gauhati University (n.d.) *Two year B.Ed. syllabus*. https://collegeofeducationmorigaon.org/B.Ed.NEW%20SYLLABUS%202%20Year.pdf

Gonzalez, N., Moll, L.C. and Amanti, C. (eds) (2005) *Funds of Knowledge: Theorizing Practices in Households, Communities, and Classrooms*. Lawrence Erlbaum Associates Publishers.

Ministry of Education, Government of India (1966) Report of the Education Commission 1964–66 (Kothari Commission). http://www.academics-india.com/Kothari%20Commission%20Report.pdf

Ministry of Home Affairs, Government of India (2017) Constitutional Provisions Relating to Eighth Schedule. www.mha.gov.in/sites/default/files/EighthSchedule_19052017.pdf.

Government of India (1968) National Policy on Education. https://mhrd.gov.in/sites/upload_files/mhrd/files/document-reports/NPE-1968.pdf

Government of India (1986) National Policy on Education. https://www.education.gov.in/sites/upload_files/mhrd/files/upload_document/npe.pdf

Government of India (2005) National Curriculum Framework. www.ncert.nic.in/rightside/links/pdf/framework/english/nf2005.pdf

Government of India (2017) The Eighth Schedule of the Constitution. https://www.mha.gov.in/sites/default/files/EighthSchedule_19052017.pdf

Government of India (2019) Draft National Education Policy. https://mhrd.gov.in/sites/upload_files/mhrd/files/Draft_NEP_2019_EN_Revised.pdf

Government of India (2020) National Education Policy. https://static.pib.gov.in/WriteReadData/userfiles/NEP_Final_English_0.pdf

Government of India (2022) National Curriculum Framework for Foundational Stage. https://ncert.nic.in/flipbook/NCF/National_Curriculum_Framework_for_Foundational_Stage_2022/mobile/index.html

Government of India (2023) National Curriculum Framework for School Education. https://ncert.nic.in/pdf/ncfse2023.pdf

Gujarat University (2017) *Two Year B.Ed. Syllabus*. https://www1.gujaratuniversity.ac.in/data/pdfs/syllabus/110_B.Ed.%20Syllabus_In%20Force%20From_June_2017_final.output.pdf

Hall, G. and Cook, G. (2012) Own-language use in language teaching and learning. *Language Teaching* 45 (3), 271–308.

Heugh, K. (2018) Multilingualism, diversity and equitable learning: Towards crossing the 'abyss'. In P. Van Avermaet, S. Slembrouck, K. Van Gorp, S. Sierens and K. Marijns (eds) *The Multilingual Edge of Education* (pp. 341–367). Palgrave.

Jasper, J. (2018) The transformative limits of translanguaging. *Language & Communication* 58, 1–10. https://doi.org/10.1016/j.langcom.2017.12.001

Jayadeva, S. (2019) English-medium: Schooling, social mobility, and inequality in Bangalore, India. *Anthropology & Education Quarterly* 50, 151–169. https://doi.org/10.1111/aeq.12287

Kalyanpur, M., Boruah, P.B., Molina, S. and Shenoy, S. (2022) *The Politics of English Language Education and Social Inequality: Global Pressures, National Priorities and Schooling in India*. Routledge.

Kubota, R. (2020) Confronting epistemological racism, decolonizing scholarly knowledge: Race and gender in applied linguistics. *Applied Linguistics* 41 (5), 712–732. https://doi.org/10.1093/applin/amz033

Lasker, S.N. and Boruah, P. (2023) Teaching mathematics and science in English in Assam government schools: What are government teachers' perceptions of its utility? Manuscript in preparation.

Li, W. (2018) Translanguaging as a practical theory of language. *Applied Linguistics* 39 (1), 9–30.

MacSwan, J. (2017) A multilingual perspective on translanguaging. *American Educational Research Journal* 54 (1), 167–201. https://doi.org/10.3102/0002831216683935.

Mathew, L. and Lukose, R. (2020) Pedagogies of aspiration: Anthropological perspectives on education in liberalising India. *South Asia: Journal of South Asian Studies* 43 (4), 691–704. https://doi.org/10.1080/00856401.2020.1768466

Meighan, P.J. (2022) Colonialingualism: Colonial legacies, imperial mindsets, and inequitable practices in English language education. *Diaspora, Indigenous, and Minority Education*. Open Access. https://doi.org/ 10.1080/15595692.2022.2082406

Meredith, K. (2011) Identity and language learning: Multiple critical perspectives. *Language Teaching* 44 (4), 551–561. https://doi.org/10.1017/S0261444811000279

Mizoram University (2019) Two Year B.Ed. Syllabus. https://iasemz.edu.in/storage/source/Syllabi/BED%20Syllabus%20Revised%202019.pdf

Mohanty, A.K. (2019) *The Multilingual Reality: Living with Languages*. Multilingual Matters.

Murthy, N. (2021) It is time we accepted English as an Indian language and encourage it as any other Indian language. *Money control,* 27 July. www.google.com/amp/s/www.moneycontrol.com/news/business/it-is-time-we-accepted-english-as-an-indian-language-and-encourage-it-as-any-other-indian-language-infosys-founder-narayana-murthy-7227061.html/amp

Nakagawa, S. and Kouritzin, S. (2021) Identities of resignation: Threats to indigenous languages from neoliberal linguistic and educational practices. *Journal of Language, Identity & Education* 20 (5), 296–310. https://doi.org/ 10.1080/15348458.2021.1957679

Nandi, P.S. (2019) United by a "foreign" language: The evolution of English in multilingual India. In B. Mahanta and R. Sharma (eds) *English Studies in India* (pp. 143–154). Springer.

National Council for Teacher Education (2009) *National Curriculum Framework for Teacher Education: Towards a Humane and Professional Teacher*. NCFTE. https://ncte.gov.in/website/PDF/NCFTE_2009.pdf.

Nguyen, H.H. (2012) The multilanguaging of a Vietnamese American in South Philadelphia. *Working Papers in Educational Linguistics* 27 (1), 65–85.

Otsuji, E. and Pennycook, A. (2011) Social inclusion and metrolingual practices. *International Journal of Bilingual Education and Bilingualism* 14 (4), 413–426. https://doi.org/10.1080/13670050.2011.573065

Pennycook, A. and Makoni, S. (2020) *Innovations and Challenges in Applied Linguistics from the Global South*. Routledge.

Phyak, P. (2021) Epistemicide, deficit language ideology, and (de)coloniality in language education policy. *International Journal of the Sociology of Language* 2021 (267–268), 219–233. https://doi.org/10.1515/ijsl-2020-0104

Santos, B. de Sousa (2014) *Epistemologies of the South: Justice Against Epistemicide*. Routledge.

Schachter, E.P. and Rich, Y. (2011) Identity education: A conceptual framework for educational researchers and practitioners. *Educational Psychologist* 46 (4), 222–238. https://doi.org/10.1080/00461520.2011.614509

Sharma, B.K. and Phyak, P. (2023) Neoliberalism in multilingual education. In C.A. Chapelle (ed.) *Encyclopedia of Applied Linguistics* (pp. 1–6). Wiley.

Singleton, D. and Flynn, C.J. (2022) Translanguaging: A pedagogical concept that went wandering. *International Multilingual Research Journal* 16 (2), 1–12. https://doi.org/10.1080/19313152.2021.1985692

Stein, P. (2008) *Multimodal Pedagogies in Diverse Classrooms: Representation, Rights and Resources*. Routledge.

Tamil Nadu Teachers Education University (2021) *Two Year B.Ed. Syllabus*. TNTEU. https://www.tnteu.ac.in/admin/file_storage/cms/B.Ed.%20Regulations%20&%20Syllabus%20%20%20Semester%20Pattern%202021-2022%20-182%20pages.pdf.pdf

Taylor, S.K. and Mohanty, A.K. (2021) Challenges to implementing best practices in complex plurilingual environments: The case of South Asia. In E. Piccardo, A. Germain-Rutherford and G. Lawrence (eds) *Routledge Handbook of Plurilingual Language Education* (pp. 385–393). Routledge. https://doi.org/10.4324/9781351002783

Tian, Z. (2020) Faculty first: Promoting translanguaging in TESOL teacher education. In S.M.C. Lau and S. Van Viegen (eds) *Plurilingual Pedagogies: Critical and Creative Endeavors for Equitable Language in Education* (pp. 215–236). Springer International Publishing. https://doi.org/10.1007/978-3-030-36983-5_10 215-236

Tooley, J. and Dixon, P. (2006) 'De Facto' privatization of education and the poor: Implications of a study from sub-Saharan Africa and India. *Compare: A Journal of Comparative & International Education* 36 (4), 443–462.

Tsimpli, I.M., Balasubramanian, A., Marinis, T., Panda, M., Mukhopadhyay, L., Alladi, S. and Treffers-Daller, J. (2020) *Research Report of a Four-Year Study of Multilingualism, Literacy, Numeracy and Cognition in Delhi, Hyderabad and Patna*. University of Cambridge.

University of Mumbai (2019) *Two Year B.Ed. Syllabus*. MU. http://mu.ac.in/wp-content/uploads/2019/02/Education-Two-Year-B.Ed_.-Revised-Syllabus-2015-16.pdf

Uttarakhand Open University (2017) *Two Year B.Ed. Syllabus*. UOU. https://uou.ac.in/sites/default/files/slm/CPS-5.pdf

Walling, S. (2023) Role and pedagogical challenges of nagamese as the language of mediation in teaching english to multilingual learners in government schools of Mokokchung District of Nagaland. Unpublished manuscript.

Williams, C. (1994) *Arfarniad o ddulliau dysgu ac addysgu yng nghyd-destun addysg uwchradd ddwyieithog* [An evaluation of teaching and learning methods in the context of bilingual secondary education]. Unpublished doctoral dissertation, University of Wales, Bangor.

Xiong, T. and Yuan, Z. (2018) "It was because I could speak English that I got the job": Neoliberal discourse in a Chinese English textbook series. *Journal of Language, Identity & Education* 17 (2), 103–117. https://doi.org/10.1080/15348458.2017.1407655

4 Using Translanguaging Pedagogy for Reading Development and Assessment: Considerations for Multilingual Teachers

Lina Mukhopadhyay

Introduction

Multilingual education (MLE) is based on the premise that children who do not share the language of instruction, often the majority language of a nation-state or a region (Ortega, 2020), as their home language, can get an opportunity to study through their mother tongue or a home language. A vast majority of children worldwide are bi/multilinguals due to factors like bi/multilingual parents, history of migration and/or the pursuit of higher education. Therefore, to cater to the needs of such children, MLE is conceptualized as an inclusive and equitable model of education. It can warrant every child the right to education.

A large body of studies in multilingual contexts provides positive evidence that MLE helps children become more successful, especially when they attend education in their mother tongue (or home languages) (May, 2017). This strengthens the claim of using home language(s) as cognitive and affective resources in learning English as a second (or a foreign) language. It guarantees an ethically just teaching-learning environment (Mohanty, 2019; UNESCO GMR, 2016). Integral to the success of MLE is the use of multilingual assessments that uphold the development of multi-competence of learners. However, in India, teacher training on using multilingual resources to harness reading skills and using multilingual assessments to scaffold learning are both under-researched. I aim to explore these two areas in this chapter.

The chapter is organized in the following manner: I begin with a review of the learning advantages and unique abilities of multilingual learners, their learning needs and why they can benefit from the mother tongue-based MLE model. Thereafter, I discuss the MLE context in India, focusing on the need for Indian teachers to know (i) how to employ learners' multilingual resources for instructional benefits and (ii) how to use multilingual assessments to suit the needs of young learners. The learners in question are the ones who come from low socioeconomic status families and experience a mismatch between their home language(s) and the language of instruction. Furthermore, they do not get any additional academic support at home. Consequently, they are at a severe learning disadvantage (UNESCO GMR, 2016). In the second part of the chapter, I review translanguaging pedagogy in Indian classrooms. Thereafter, I present a translanguaging model to deliver systematic ML instruction using the home language resources of the learners. The model can be adapted in primary reading classrooms. Finally, I conclude with some multilingual strategies that teachers can adopt to assess the reading comprehension of young learners.

Learning Advantages of Bi/Multilingual Learners and their Unique Abilities

First language acquisition and by extension, simultaneous bilingual acquisition, is easy. This is because complex neural mechanisms and rich linguistic environments support the incredible task to be accomplished within the first five to six years of age (Sanchez-Alonso & Aslin, 2022). However, to assume that the ease of first/bilingual language acquisition in the naturalistic environment can be pedagogically replicated in the second/foreign language (SL/FL) classroom is impractical. This is because the quality and quantity of L2 input are much diminished. At the same time, the communicative intent and fluency of the SL users have a lot of individual variation (Lightbown & Spada, 2020). Furthermore, success in SL learning, a complex dynamic process, is mediated by the age of exposure (DeKeyser, 2020), individual multilingual, psychological and social skills, the interactional quality of the linguistic environment and so on (Singleton & Leśniewska, 2021).

Language learning becomes more intricate when the SL classroom is located in a multilingual setting (Mohanty, 2019). Input variability heightens, impacting the individual's capacity to learn languages other than one's home language(s). Though bi/multilingual learners have access to two or more languages, either at home and/or outside, developing academic proficiency in the language of instruction in school plays a key role in their academic success and, subsequently, in furthering their job prospects.

Research on bilingualism and cognition has shown that the cognitive benefits of bilinguals are more flexible and open to abstraction due to the routine practice of managing two (or more) jointly activated but conflicting language inputs (Bialystok, 2017). However, the bilingual cognitive advantage claim has also met with some controversy in that the impact is small, variable and not proven true of all bilinguals. Rather, it is restricted to a smaller learner group under specific circumstances (Lowe *et al.*, 2021). Aside from the controversy, two recent reformulations of the cognitive advantage are as follows: One, linguistic environment and experiences give rise to different degrees of bilingualism in individuals. This, in turn, pervasively and directly modulates their executive functioning and integrative cognitive processing, such as the theory of mind, creativity and critical thinking. Secondly, there is a dynamic interplay between bilingual abilities and cognitive functioning (Chung-Fat-Yim & Bialystok, 2022).

Defining Bi/Multilingual Abilities

In addition to research on cognitive functioning in bi/multilinguals, defining their abilities has been tricky. The operationalization of the construct has not yet met with any consensus. However, for the practical purposes of teachers' understanding and application in pedagogy and assessment, we need to consider which features in bi/multilinguals should warrant our careful attention. It can help in operationalizing the construct for educational purposes. This is a key concern of the current chapter.

From a multitude of definitions, I extract the following features to understand bi/multilingual abilities that would (a) aid in language education planning and (b) lead to training teachers working in ML contexts to adopt inclusive classroom practices. Firstly, bi/multilingual abilities need to be considered within an ambit of dominance (or balance) based on the relative ease/fluency in using the languages, with the possibility of significant individual variations. Secondly, it can range from a wide compass of general proficiency across languages to more localized pragmatic competencies and language identities, owing to individuals' varied life experiences in picking up multiple languages from their surroundings (Treffers-Daller, 2019). Thirdly, it refers to Cummins' (2017) recent modified construct of the interdependence of cognitive-linguistic skills (also termed CALP), which can support the processing of lexical, syntactic features along with text or discourse competence, knowledge integration through speech (De Houwer, 2007) and writing (Reyes, 2022). Lastly, as a result of the simultaneous processing of two or more languages, unique communication behaviors such as translation (Malkoff, 1992) and code-switching (Treffers-Daller, 2022) need to be considered. Translation is a higher-order metalinguistic skill. An average bilingual child, as early as 3rd grade, can practice this mode of communication without getting confused between the two linguistic systems (Malkoff, 1992). Code-switching, a highly skilled behavior (Poplack, 1980) and distinct from cross-linguistic influence, happens with remarkable ease at both intra- and inter-sentential levels (Jisa, 2000). The behavior surfaces owing to typological differences, processing constraints and societal factors (Muysken, 2013). It gives us insights into a unified lexical storage of the bi/multilingual brain. In the instructional context, both code-switching and translation can be used to give rise to a third dimension of multilingual classroom communication called 'translanguaging'. It constitutes 'an alternation between two or more languages' and their fluid use to plan lessons and communicate in class (García & Li, 2014). The construct will be further reviewed and its application in the development of reading comprehension skills and its assessment will be presented later in this chapter.

Bi/multilingual learners' classroom needs

Alongside defining bi/multilingual abilities, the use of multiple languages (i.e. learners' home languages) as a classroom resource needs to be considered. In this context, it is imperative to recall that the use of other languages in English classrooms has had a chequered history, where L1 use was frowned upon a few decades ago. More recently, the natural co-occurrence of languages has gradually been accepted in multilingual Asian (Anderson & Lightfoot, 2018; Kalyanpur *et al.*, 2022) and African societies (Charamba, 2020). However, there is a need to move beyond using ML resources (especially translation) merely as a coping strategy in classroom instruction to using them in a more planned and resourceful manner (Sah & Kubota, 2022). As ML practices in class are further constrained by language ideologies and language policies at the national and micro levels (e.g. teachers' language ideologies and school-level language policy), their systematic use and positive impact on learners can better inform language policymakers. However, these practices have to guard against perpetuating the dominant state or national languages and employ languages of minority speakers and learners from migrant families (Sah & Kubota, 2022).

In the following section, I build on theoretical and ideological insights for teachers about why the use of learners' multilingual resources in the form of translanguaging is natural and important (García & Li, 2014). It would provide an opportunity to enhance children's cognitive-linguistic and socioaffective skills in their home languages (and not just the dominant state/regional language) and transfer such skills in the language of instruction. Such a model can promote inclusivity by affording optimal conditions to creatively explore and exploit an entire gamut of children's linguistic, affective and cultural resources.

Mother Tongue-based MLE and its Use in EMI Schools

Societies have a deep impact on the education system because their speech communities influence the choice of language(s) of communication among their speakers. It also drives the selection of the language of instruction. For instance, dominant monolingual societies may have multilingual groups, but they covertly support the use of only the dominant language in educational setups with assumptions of knowledge development in only the dominant language (Skutnabb-Kangas & Dunbar, 2010). In contrast, in culturally multilingual and multicultural societies like those in Asia and Africa, people use multiple languages often with fluid boundaries, as their key concern is to engage in meaningful communication using their multilingual repertoire (Mohanty & Skutnabb-Kangas, 2022). The language of instruction has a key role to play in any society as it paves the path for cognitive and linguistic development in the young population. Over time, proficiency in the language of instruction becomes the foundation of knowledge across different domains and learners' all-around development (Sah, 2022). So, we need a critical lens to consider the role of language of instruction in culturally multilingual societies. This is because it would be counter-intuitive to use the monolingual instructional mode in rich sociolinguistic settings of multilingual countries.

Globally, 40% of children who come from ethnolinguistic minority groups and low SES status families are often forced to study in a language that is not their home language (UNESCO GMR, 2016). This is an outright violation of their linguistic human rights (Mohanty, 2019; Skutnabb-Kangas & Dunbar, 2010). It perpetuates a suppression of not using the home languages of minority speakers in class; school policies mandate them to learn school languages through which their academic growth is recorded (Sah & Kubota, 2022). Consequently, a majority of children from low SES families and minority languages suffer dire consequences from early dropouts from schools, low attainment of cognitive and academic skills and loss of mother tongue, identity and self-esteem (Skutnabb-Kangas & Dunbar, 2010). Hence, language teachers need to be sensitized about the significance of using the home languages of learners who come from minority and marginalized backgrounds. In its absence, there can be a language divide and eventual language loss, as is commonly experienced in several South Asian countries (Mohanty, 2019).

We need to be especially critical of the poor learning outcomes of children from low-SES families attending English-medium instruction (EMI) schools in multilingual countries. In such schools, all or most subjects are assumed to be taught through English (Mohanty, 2019; Sah, 2022). The low outcomes arise from the sharp mismatch between learners' home language(s) and the language of instruction (Boruah, 2017). To counter the negative impact of such subversive education policies, one needs to turn to MLE research that gives robust evidence of positive impact on the lives of multilingual children as they enjoy cognitive, linguistic and socio-affective benefits when they are taught in their mother tongue (May, 2017) or using home languages to scaffold EMI (Phyak et al., 2022). Unfortunately, in the present times, frequent violations of linguistic rights and opportunities in education often get neglected in both monolingual and multilingual societies owing to reasons of power, politics and coercion (Mohanty, 2019).

One challenge to counter is the equity logic that access to EMI schools means that children would have larger global access to life with English as the linguistic capital (Bourdieu, 1993; Sah & Li, 2018). This argument has propelled many countries, especially those with a colonial past, to introduce EMI at primary grades even before a threshold level of proficiency is attained in a child's home language(s). Hence, what seems to be equitable in effect denies the right to be educated through home language(s). It perpetuates inequality and injustice by ignoring the local realities of the children growing up in multilingual and multicultural societies (Sah, 2022). These children have little or no exposure to English outside class (Boruah, 2017). It rather establishes the coercive colonial power structures and racial/ethnic inequalities that could eventually lead to language loss (Kalyanpur et al., 2023). Thus, advocating for a mother tongue-based (or home language-based) MLE model becomes a crucial step in planning for inclusive, equitable and sustainable language education for children during their formative years of growth. Developing cognitive skills in their home language(s) can support the development of other school languages subsequently (Mohanty, 2019; Mohanty & Skutnabb-Kangas, 2022; Sah, 2022).

Using Translanguaging in Multilingual EMI Contexts to Support Learning

In multilingual societies like India, we need to take cognizance of the fact that children move from simpler home language(s) context to a wider societal context where negotiations have to be made with a higher level of the multilingual network (Mohanty & Skutnabb-Kangas, 2022). Through such negotiations, children learn to process in multiple languages and effectively communicate outside the home.

A natural extension of this fluid languaging is to be found in the classroom space as translanguaging, where the language of instruction is often officially 'English' (like in a host of Indian states). Children are expected to develop a high level of proficiency in the language of instruction and any other language included in the curriculum (e.g. the dominant state language and its standard variety, a foreign language and so on). However, in reality, children would spontaneously use fluid language boundaries or code-switch during classroom communication and to express comprehension (Anderson & Lightfoot, 2018; Kalyanpur et al., 2023). The frequency and quality of code-switching can be constrained by children's degree of bilingualism and the amount of multilingualism the language environment in and out of class promotes (Chung-Fat-Yim & Bialystok, 2022). In essence, translanguaging overlaps with code-switching (refer to

Treffers-Daller, 2024, for a critical review) whereby meaningful associations are forged between learners' home languages and the target language of instruction (here English). This is what situates translanguaging in class, mostly to negotiate for meaning and express understanding using language alternation for pedagogic purposes (García & Li, 2014; García & Lin, 2018).

There are various ways in which translanguaging is practiced in classrooms. In this paper, I propose the use of translanguaging one in which a teacher makes a conscious effort to utilize different home language resources for input and output, which has been conceptualized as planned or 'pedagogical translanguaging' by Cenoz and Gorter (2022). In keeping with multilingual speakers' fluid use of languages for communication, the researchers have gathered evidence from a wide set of classroom examples on planned translanguaging. Based on the results, they have operationalized it as a pedagogy that can be practiced in two or more languages and class levels, with a wide range of activities to promote comprehension, knowledge integration, communication (through social coordination) with peers and develop metalinguistic awareness. By participating in such tasks, learners experience heightened cognitive stimulation. However, the researchers concur that despite the interest and motivation in using this pedagogy, there could be sceptics who would believe in the language separation ideology or the two-solitude notion (for a critique, refer to Cummins, 2008). It would stem from their assumption that bilingual children need to reach L1 like ultimate attainment in each language. Additionally, I would refer to the Cummins' notion of cross-linguistic translanguaging theory (2019, 2021) in which he considers the transfer of conceptual and linguistic academic skills across languages. This theorization further builds on the construct of pedagogical translanguaging as it proposes teaching using multiple registers to help multilingual learners connect the resources of their home languages for educational purposes.

One way to support the use of translanguaging pedagogy would be to support teachers' multilingual agency in aiding children to use their home languages in learning concepts, developing critical thinking skills and transforming learning experiences (Phyak *et al.*, 2022; Lightfoot *et al.*, 2022). To further understand the benefits of pedagogical translanguaging, in the remaining part of this chapter, I present a brief overview of what research has shown us about its use specifically in reading classes (for a full review, refer to Mukhopadhyay *et al.*, 2022a, 2022b). Thereafter, keeping in mind the needs of the vast majority of primary school teachers in India who struggle with the overarching EMI system, I will describe how such a pedagogy can be employed to support the development of reading for meaning (assuming that decoding skills have developed) and inference generation skills, followed by assessment of multilingual ability with a specific focus on vocabulary, syntactic awareness and reading comprehension.

Translanguaging in EMI Classrooms in India

English language education in a multilingual society like India has progressed greatly from the colonial mindset of using monolingual and heavily structural teaching methods to bi/multilingual methods. Now, we recognize and acknowledge the benefits of using translanguaging pedagogy to scaffold learning in English classrooms (Anderson, 2022; Mukhopadhyay, 2020; Mukhopadhyay et al., 2023).

Recent research in low-cost EMI government and private schools in India reveals that while translanguaging pedagogy is practiced (Anderson & Lightfoot, 2018), much of it is only a coping strategy (Sah & Kubota, 2022). It is unplanned and spontaneous, where teachers largely use it for lexical access and meaning comprehension in English as a subject (Anderson & Lightfoot, 2018; Kalyanpur et al., 2023; Mukhopadhyay et al., 2023, 2025) and content classes (Lightfoot et al., 2022).

A key idea pursued in this chapter is that reading comprehension, a linguistic-cognitive skill, can be activated in multiple languages and/or through the route of a known (home) language in which literacy is already developed into an emergent language (Cummins, 2017), here English. This kind of pedagogical model, where multiple linguistic resources can be alternated upon, will open up discussions among language and subject teachers on how to use the rich linguistic-cognitive resources of multilingual learners, who come from low SES families with negligible exposure and/or use of English as a language for social communication. However, due to their varied and challenging life experiences, these children acquire cognitive skills quite early on, especially inference generation skills, as evident from their oral comprehension in home languages (Mukhopadhyay et al., 2020), mental math skills and metalinguistic awareness (Mohanty & Panda, 2017). The model will build upon what children *know* from their everyday experiences and oral fluency in their home language(s) to use such resources to learn the target language(s). The attempt will be to use multilingual resources without coercing them to learn English or to develop content knowledge only through the dominant language of instruction.

Using Multilingual Pedagogy to Develop Reading Comprehension

Reading is a complex psycho-linguistic process dependent on a set of attendant sub-skills such as word decoding, oral comprehension, vocabulary knowledge and syntactic and metalinguistic awareness. Working memory span helps to comprehend a text. Comprehension levels vary from literal to inferential levels, along with knowledge integration with background knowledge (or schemata). Lastly, successful comprehension results in creating a whole-text representation or story structure in the reader's mind (Cain & Oakhill, 2007).

Research bears evidence that reading is not a monolingual process, as multilingual learners access their home language resources through the process of mental translation to understand the meaning of L2 texts they find difficult (Malkoff, 1992). They actively use cognitive processes from home language(s) to confirm comprehension, predict text and content structure, monitor text characteristics and reading strategies in L2 (Upton & Thompson, 2001). All of this is possible as learners mediate their thinking through home language(s) to build on L2 reading.

In the current times, the role of home language(s) on L2 reading has been further explored through translanguaging. Classroom-based research has shed light on multiple purposes for which translanguaging pedagogy can be systematically used to develop reading comprehension and its attendant skills as vocabulary knowledge and syntactic awareness (see Mukhopadhyay *et al.*, 2022a). The following purposes of pedagogic translanguaging for reading have emerged: In one set of studies, teachers have consciously considered using translanguaging to help learners identify word-meaning correlates across L1-L2 in typologically distant (Vaish & Subhan, 2015) as well as cognate languages (Cenoz & Santos, 2020). These strategies have helped learners understand concepts, develop vocabulary knowledge and look for cross-linguistic comparisons. In executing all these tasks, learners have engaged in deeper cognitive processing across languages. In a second set of studies, researchers have exploited translanguaging pedagogy in the reading classroom in a planned manner through a series of tasks to (i) develop learners' inferential skills by integrating background knowledge with text meaning and answer questions of an English text in their L1s (Desmond & Makalela, 2013), (ii) read texts in two or more languages to gather more information, analyse text structure and report their understanding through writing tasks in more than one language (Cenoz & Santos, 2020) and (iii) express text comprehension by paraphrasing main ideas from sub-parts of a text and convey meaning across languages (Hungwe, 2019).

All these studies provide evidence that when learners engage in reading tasks utilizing the translanguaging mode, their meaning making gets enhanced. It is because they get a chance to express their understanding by using their multilingual repertoire. This, in turn, positively impacts their general proficiency in all the languages employed.

Translanguaging and reading in Indian classrooms

In Indian primary-level classroom observations from low-cost government schools done in a recent four-year longitudinal project (from 2016 to 2020) called MultiLiLa (Tsimpli *et al.*, 2020), the researchers have shown that teachers spontaneously resort to using a combination of the state language (Hindi or Telugu) along with children's home language(s) to teach English and other subjects, as is practiced in EMI settings. The observations revealed that teachers made a range of language choices based on learner needs and their own proficiency in the language of instruction (Lightfoot *et al.*, 2022). The EMI model was brought in hastily in several Indian states (e.g. in Telangana) roughly around the time when the MultiLiLa project was conducted. However, the teachers were not ready to use English in their classroom transactions and, therefore, they used spontaneous translanguaging in their lessons. Unplanned use of translanguaging certainly exploited learners' known language resources for meaning-making and drawing similarities in lexico-morphemic features across English and learners' home languages (Mukhopadhyay, 2020). Taking into account how much the learners benefitted from the translanguaging moves, Lightfoot *et al.* (2022) recommended that teachers benefit from more focused training in using pedagogic translanguaging.

A seminal finding in terms of learning outcomes from the MultiLiLa project was that when children are made to learn in a language not spoken at home, it affects their learning negatively (Tsimpli *et al.*, 2020). It does not allow them to think critically in a language that they are not proficient in. Consequently, they fail to show an adequate understanding of academic content. Therefore, teachers must be trained to systematically use learners' home language resources to develop comprehension skills in L2 and other subjects in a systematic manner. This would serve the twin purposes of developing language proficiency and supporting content understanding. It would also help learners feel more confident and boost their motivation, which are socioaffective factors to aid comprehension, as found in current research on reading (Savage, 2022). To this end, I will now present an example of multilingual pedagogy by proposing a translanguaging-based reading model (TLP). I will explain its design and how teachers can use this model in class.

Teaching Reading Comprehension using Translanguaging Pedagogy: A Model

The translanguaging pedagogy (TLP) reading model is based on the simple view of reading that comprehension is based on decoding and linguistic comprehension (Gough & Tunmer, 1986). Alongside this, reading for comprehension is dependent on oral language skills, domain and background knowledge, motivation and engagement with reading (Savage, 2022).

The model proposed here uses multilingual lexical support to help children establish links between key ideas and learn to comprehend the whole text (see Mukhopadhyay *et al.*, 2022b, for a full discussion). Their expression of comprehension is planned in the bi/multilingual mode as a breakaway from the typical monolingual ways of expressing comprehension only through the target language. The reading model builds on teachers' multilingual agency (Phyak *et al.*, 2022). Therefore, they are likely to find this useful, as it does not assume teacher proficiency in only the dominant language of instruction.

The TLP reading model is diagrammatically presented in Figure 4.1 (from Mukhopadhyay *et al.*, 2022b: 268).

The reading model presented above is based on the cognitive framework of the simple view of reading (Gough & Tunmer, 1986) that linguistic skills need to be developed to aid comprehension, as included in Steps 1 to 4 in Figure 4.1. The model is further linked with more recent directions on how to teach reading (Savage, 2022). Here, reading is operationalized with its sub-skills – vocabulary and different levels of comprehension from factual to inferential, local and global and whole-text representation (Cain & Oakhill, 2007). The development of these skills is presented through Steps 5 and 6. In addition to the cognitive basis of reading, the model considers reading not as a monolingual process but as a translanguaging process.

Unknown words pose a maximum challenge for early readers (Laufer, 2020). Hence, children can benefit from focused instruction in vocabulary while reading texts. Children from low-SES families do not have access to rich oral input in the target language because the school language (state language and/or English) is not available at home. However, oral fluency in the target language is necessary for developing reading comprehension in that language (Cain & Oakhill, 2007). In such a context, teachers need to use pedagogical translanguaging to plan the reading instruction in such

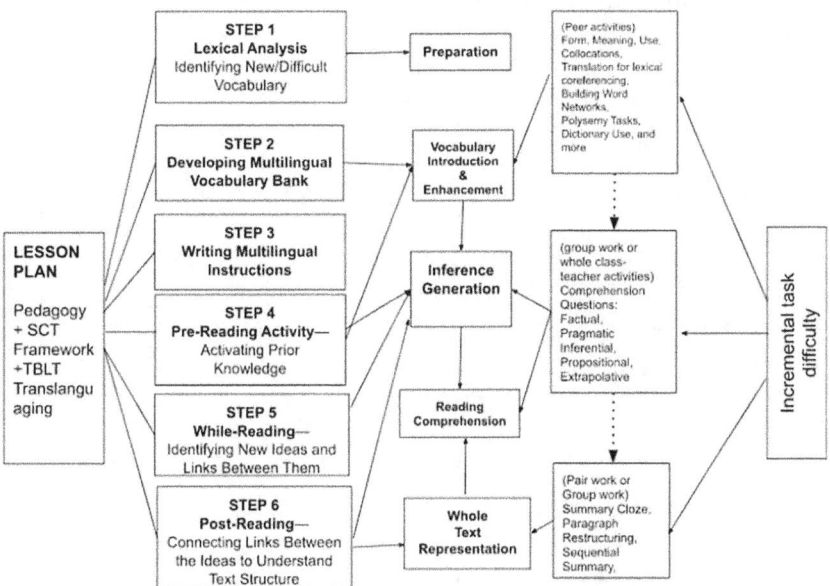

Figure 4.1 Translanguaging pedagogy-based reading comprehension model

a manner that children can experience vocabulary enhancement through multilingual inputs in class. In other words, they can get additional vocabulary support by comparing multilingual lexical resources (e.g. creating bi/multilingual word and phrase banks). This can help children experience the use of home language(s) in class to become more engaged and motivated to learn the school language(s). This would lay a strong foundation for their language comprehension development.

Furthermore, this model is based on the socioconstructivist framework in which it is believed that reading development happens through a social process of scaffolding from the teacher(s) and peers, along with individual attempts at mental translation (Shepherd-Carey, 2020). Across all six steps in Figure 4.1, peer activities can be incorporated. Reading as a social activity can result in knowledge integration and the acquisition of comprehension skills. These can, in turn, positively impact production skills (speech and writing).

Steps in using the model

Teachers can use the reading model with the elaboration of translanguaging inputs and outputs as shown in Figure 4.2 (for details, refer to Mukhopadhyay *et al.*, 2022b). Steps 1 to 5 from Figure 4.1 are elaborated through example tasks in Figure 4.2 to help teachers develop translanguaging-based lesson plans to teach reading.

The model taps learners' background knowledge through translanguaging moves. It supports vocabulary development to aid content understanding. It also attends to text structure, which can help to develop inference generation skills.

Step 1: Attempt lexical analysis of text using lexical tutor(https://www.lextutor.ca/) (Cobb, 2004)

Step 2: Plan and insert bi /multilingual instructions

Step 3: Create pre-reading tasks (to activate schemata)
Step 3a: Pre-reading Task type 1: Picture-based discussion, interpretation
Step 3b: Pre-reading Task type 2: Enhancing lexical coverage [tasks to explain difficult words identified through lextutor analysis, create semantic networks, bi/multilingual glosses, word/phrase banks]

Step 4: Create while-reading tasks (to aid text-based comprehension)
Step 4a: While-Reading Task type 1: Enhancing lexical depth: word polysemy and association (synonymy, hyponymy, binomials)
Step 4b: While-reading Task type 2: Comprehension questions [factual, propositional, pragmatic, evaluative]
Step 4c: While-reading Task type 3: Enhancing lexical depth [tasks on lexical co-referencing through pronominal usage, lexical substitution, and linkers]

Step 5: Create post-reading task (to generate whole-text representation)
Step 5a: Bilingual sequential summary
Step 5b: Unit-based reading assessment (MCQs & short answers with bi/multilingual inputs and outputs as part of formative assessment)

Figure 4.2 Steps to follow the TLP Reading: Inputs and outputs

Method of teaching: Based on current research findings and a review of instructional steps from Savage (2022), here are a few pedagogical steps to practice in the reading class. Since teachers have to be able to support all the learners in their journey of comprehension development, the model is to be used at the whole-class level for maximum benefits. Teachers can focus on building oral language fluency in the language of instruction, taking the help of home languages as required. With this translanguaging interaction, they can help learners respond in class and support the use of reasoning skills. Teachers can also develop domain and background knowledge by elaborating on content or themes. They can offer focused instruction on narrative structure and other text structures (e.g. those of exposition and argumentation).

In teaching comprehension, teachers will also have to deal with individual learner differences and needs. They may have to try out whole-class instruction followed by specific small group interventions where peers can discuss and get teacher support based on what they need. The needs can differ from oral language development support to specific linguistic support in vocabulary development or sub-skills of reading comprehension (refer to Figures 4.1 and 4.2). Lastly, teachers can provide emotional and motivational support to the learners through dialogic engagement and additional reading exposure, as these have been found to positively impact children's reading goals and outcomes (Shepherd-Carey, 2020).

To add to the discussion on using the model in class, a recent teacher training project in Telangana in India that used the multilingual reading model has borne evidence that teachers in low-cost multilingual classrooms have been able to use the model successfully (refer to Mukhopadhyay *et al.*, 2025, for the full report). The usefulness of the model has been to create inclusive multilingual spaces by scaffolding reading subskills and it has increased learner engagement and autonomy (Mukhopadhyay *et al.*, 2023).

Assessing bi/multilingual reading abilities

In this last section, I briefly discuss critical issues in assessing bi/multilingual children in primary to secondary grades, firstly to monitor progress and secondly for summative purposes.

Alongside developing general proficiency skills and reading skills in particular, teachers need to know how to assess their learners in the target language, which may not overlap with learners' home language(s). So, teachers need to be informed about the multilingual assessment framework. A review of the assessment of bilingual speakers points to a fallacy in that their abilities are overwhelmingly compared with monolinguals in the target language (like English). Using the same test instruments meant for monolinguals has proven to be harmful in the interpretation of results from bilingual learners' performances. Conclusions have been drawn that bilinguals are deficient or lacking in age-appropriate proficiency levels (as summarized in Treffers-Daller, 2019).

Interestingly, in the last four decades, there has been a positive turn to defend the abilities of multilingual learners in their rights. Several researchers have strongly countered the dominant monolingual and deficit view by demonstrating that – one, not much difference exists in test-taking abilities shown through performance on grammar cloze (Alderson, 1980), writing and reading between L1 and L2 users of English (Hamilton *et al.*, 1993) and two, the term native speakers need not be reserved for only monolinguals (Treffers-Daller, 2019).

Methods to assess reading comprehension through the multilingual mode

A realistic goal for a teacher would be to consider how a multilingual learner employs a multiple set of mental abilities to comprehend texts. The teacher also needs to consider how the learner can express thoughts using strategies such as mental translation and code-switching, which are part of translanguaging behavior. Since success in reading comprehension of young learners would be incumbent on the micro features of linguistic knowledge, such as vocabulary knowledge (at least at the K2 level) and syntactic awareness, teachers can consider including multilingual assessment of these features to predict reading success (or conversely diagnose difficulties).

Assessing bi/multilingual vocabulary

In the first language reading context, children's oral proficiency and vocabulary knowledge aid reading comprehension (Ouellette & Beers, 2010). However, this is not true of ESL/EFL learners, as the quality and quantity of exposure to the target language are variable. Furthermore, research on bilinguals shows that their verbal proficiency is lower than L1 age-matched children (Chung-Fat-Yim & Bialystok, 2022). Hence, bilingual learners' vocabulary knowledge becomes an important area to assess as it can predict comprehension success and improve cognitive performance. Teachers can use varied formative ways of collecting information about children's vocabulary through narrative accounts. They can also make classroom notes on learners' preferred uses of multilingual vocabulary learning strategies.

One novel way of assessing bi/multilingual learners' vocabulary would be to use the Multilingual Assessment in Narratives (MAIN) tool, which includes picture-based storytelling and retelling tasks across languages. The instrument can be used to draw lexical estimates of bilingual/multilingual learners in a contextualized manner. It is a useful instrument that has gained a lot of attention recently. Developed by Natalia Gagarina and her team in 2012 and subsequently revised and made available in 92 languages (Gagarina *et al.*, 2019), MAIN serves as an integrative and non-intrusive tool for bilingual ability assessment across reading and/or listening and speaking and/or writing abilities. It can also be used to gather estimates of children's emergent vocabulary and syntax knowledge.

Assessing multilingual syntactic awareness

Syntactic awareness as a grammatical correction task can influence reading ability indirectly, further mediated by variance in vocabulary knowledge and memory in children with English as L1 (Cain & Oakhill, 2007). In an L2 context, morpho-syntactic skills are influenced cross-linguistically, owing to the transfer phenomena; this, in turn, positively impacts L1 and L2 reading skills (Tong *et al.*, 2022). Therefore, taking a cue from such empirical evidence, teachers can prepare grammar error correction tasks based on the structures ESL learners encounter in their textbooks and commonalities across home language(s) and L2. Performance on such tasks will help build learners' syntactic awareness and notice commonalities across home language(s) and language of instruction. Such meta-linguistic knowledge would help them comprehend texts better. Further, teachers can measure growth in syntactic ability in a formative manner through measures of mean length of T units (Lanauze & Snow, 1989) in written performance. They can build meta-linguistic awareness by giving contingent feedback in home language(s) about L2 structures (Cenoz & Gorter, 2022).

Assessing multilingual comprehension

Using the MAIN tool, children's comprehension knowledge can also be assessed through the modalities of listening and/or reading. It can be done by presenting the text of picture-based stories and asking children to answer comprehension questions included in the tool. For instance, the story-retelling task is quite useful as a classroom-based assessment tool involving Indian primary-grade learners from low SES families. This task served as dual assessment task: one, of oral vocabulary knowledge, a precursor to reading comprehension (Cain & Oakhill, 2007), both as lexical breadth (through ratio of new words over total number of words used) and lexical depth (through counting morphologically derived words from the root) (Treffers-Daller *et al.*, 2022); and two of oral inference generation ability, based on listening to the story and retelling it (Mukhopadhyay *et al.*, 2020). Additionally, the retelling can also serve as an assessment tool for multilingual children's discourse and pragmatic abilities (Huang & Bailey, 2022).

Assessing reading comprehension (and, by extension, assessment of content knowledge) calls for estimating learners' cognitive skills as well as background knowledge. These can be assessed through local and global inferences respectively (Cain & Oakhill, 2007). The usual measures of reading comprehension are: (i) multiple choice question (MCQ) items, where learners have to access their cognitive processing skills and heavily rely on working memory (Rupp & Choi, 2006); (ii) answering open-ended short answers, where they have to employ their background knowledge, text integration and paraphrasing skills (Ozuru et al., 2013). While designing MCQ items is challenging and requires training, building estimates through sample answers in short answer items is subject to inter-rater reliability issues (Cushing & Tywoniw, 2020).

Just as L2 reading is not a monolingual act and the bi/multilingual learners have recourse to their L1 (home language(s)) comprehension skills (Upton & Thompson, 2001), L2 reading assessment need not be monolingual at primary stages. It can gradually move from being multilingual to more of expressing understanding through L2. Planned in this manner, learners would be able to use their comprehension strategies and home language literacy skills to improve performance on L2 reading assessments. Implicit in this suggestion is that learner proficiency may not match the proficiency of the L2 text and/or question difficulty (Cox et al., 2019); therefore, until readers reach higher levels of L2 proficiency, assessment should take place in home language(s) or mediated through the latter. This would be the translanguaging model of reading assessment (Huang & Bailey, 2022).

Translanguaging assessment of reading

I now look at some ways of using translanguaging reading assessment for teachers to consider. ESL/EFL teachers can assess bilingual reading comprehension skills either separately in two languages or in a translanguaging manner (alternate input and output bilingually), using both the item types: MCQs and short answer questions. In the translanguaging model, the question language for MCQ items can be alternated between home language and L2 based on the difficulty of the text and the complexity of the questions asked (Cox et al., 2019). For instance, factual questions can be easy to comprehend in L2, though inferential questions would need home language(s) support (e.g. read text in L2 and design MCQs in home language(s) and at later stages in L2).

Short answers as the second type of reading assessment can be used as they entail advanced comprehension skills such as inference generation, identifying inter-textual relationships and base-level writing ability. What teachers need to keep in mind is that such tasks can be reliably used provided there is a holistic rubric for measuring learner responses. Cushing and Tywoniw (2020) have proposed such a rubric by linking content and language performance across all the responses of a text to arrive at a holistic grade. As assessing the open-responses is time-taking, therefore Cushing and Tywoniw advise that for classroom assessments where the stakes are low, individual item scoring can be replaced by a holistic score. The holistic score (or grade) can be used to measure reading comprehension. I go a step further to suggest that teachers can use home language as the question language initially and eventually in L2. They can also develop the rubric in home language(s) and if required translate it to L2, for ease of understanding, comparing and marking responses. The responses can also be accepted as home language-mediated L2 answers (Lanauze & Snow, 1989). This is because learners are seen to perform better when they can use home language resources to compose texts in L2. This will be a good practice for literacy maintenance in home language(s). It would also provide a strong cognitive base to develop L2 writing skills (Hsin & Snow, 2017).

In sum, although the assessment of multilingual learners is a promising and necessary area of exploration, the fact that learners can be heterogeneous on account of varying age of exposure, quality and quantity of input, assessing their academic proficiency in a target language like English (globally dominant as a language of access to opportunities and power) is rather challenging. It would impact the design validity for education and accountability purposes (Huang & Bailey, 2022). A way to address the heterogeneity of the learners, as well as utilize their variations of language and cultural knowledge, teachers can be trained to use dynamic translanguaging assessments (mediated through translanguaging feedback) (for details, refer to Kadam & Mukhopadhyay, 2023).

Conclusion

In this chapter, I have reviewed the basic tenets of multilingual education, unique language and cognitive behavior of bi/multilinguals, followed by how teachers can employ bi/multilingual abilities for classroom purposes. I have demonstrated the use of translanguaging pedagogy to develop and assess reading comprehension skills of young multilingual children studying in challenging contexts, as they are from low SES families. It is hoped that the operationalization of the translanguaging-based reading model and multilingual assessment strategies would help teachers working in global multilingual contexts use and/or adapt the model and find its impact on learners.

The reading model is presented as a tool of social and linguistic justice to the majority of Indian learners (and other learners in similar socially disadvantaged contexts) with evidence from recent projects in India about the usefulness of the model in creating equity and inclusivity in language education as well as supporting learner agency in exploiting home language resources to build on reading comprehension skills (Mukhopadhyay et al., 2023, 2025). This is because the compulsion to become literate and acquire high proficiency in English is high across all SES groups, owing to the equity logic and the opportunities proficient users of English get in life. So, learners would be able to develop comprehension skills through multiple language resources and learn to value their home language resources and cultural knowledge for educational purposes. This can lead to better learning, as their other home languages would scaffold inferential and critical thinking skills in English.

However, to gain wider validation of the translanguaging reading approach and extend it to other skills and in content classrooms, further research is currently underway in India. The implication of the reading model and suggestions for multilingual assessments would be to inform pre- and in-service teacher education practices in India as well as similar Global South contexts. It would also be for educational policymakers to understand the role of using multilingual and multicultural resources in class and promote home language-mediated English teaching and assessment modes.

Acknowledgement

The multilingual reading model referred to in this chapter has been used in a teacher training project in Telangana, India, that was funded by the British Council, English Language Teaching Research Partnership Awards, UK (ELTRA, Lead Ref: G106298) with Professor Ianthi Maria Tsimpli as the Principal Investigator from the University of Cambridge in collaboration with The English and Foreign Languages University, India.

References

Alderson, J.C. (1980) Native and non-native speaker performance on cloze tests. *Language Learning* 30 (1), 59–77. https://doi.org/10.1111/j.1467-1770.1980.tb00151.x

Anderson, J. (2022) The translanguaging practices of expert Indian teachers of English and their learners. *Journal of Multilingual and Multicultural Development*. https://doi.org/10.1080/01434632.2022.2045300

Anderson, J. and Lightfoot, A. (2018) Translingual practices in English classrooms in India: Current perceptions and future possibilities. *International Journal of Bilingual Education and Bilingualism* 24 (8), 1210–1231. https://doi.org/10.1080/13670050.2018.1548558

Bialystok, E. (2017) The bilingual adaptation: How minds accommodate experience. *Psychological Bulletin* 143 (3), 233–262. https://doi.org/10.1037/bul0000099

Boruah, P. (2017) Learning English in a low-cost semi-urban English-medium school in India: Challenges, interaction patterns and domains of use. In H. Coleman (ed.) *Multilingualisms and Development* (pp. 289–306). British Council.

Bourdieu, P. (1993) *The Field of Cultural Production: Essays on Art and Literature*. Polity Press.

Cain, K. and Oakhill, J. (2007) *Children's Comprehension Problems in Oral and Written Language: A Cognitive Perspective*. The Guilford Press.

Cenoz, J. and Santos, A. (2020) Implementing pedagogical translanguaging in trilingual schools. *System* 92. https://doi.org/10.1016/j.system.2020.102273

Cenoz, J. and Gorter, D. (2022) Pedagogical translanguaging and its application to language classes. *RELC Journal* 53 (2), 342–354. https://doi.org/10.1177/00336882221082751

Charamba, E. (2020) Pushing linguistic boundaries: Translanguaging in a bilingual science and technology classroom. *Journal of Multilingual and Multicultural Development* 43 (10), 1–15. https://doi.org/10.1080/01434632.2020.1783544

Chung-Fat-Yim, A. and Bialystok, E. (2022) Language and thought in multilingual children. In A. Stavans and U. Jessner (eds) *The Cambridge Handbook of Childhood Multilingualism* (pp. 113–140). Cambridge University Press.

Cox, T.L., Brown, J. and Bell, T.R. (2019) In advanced L2 reading proficiency assessments, should the question language be in the L1 or the L2?: Does it make a difference?. *Faculty Publications* 5886. https://scholarsarchive.byu.edu/facpub/5886

Cummins, J. (2008) Teaching for transfer: Challenging the two solitude assumptions in bilingual education. In J. Cummins and N.H. Hornberger (eds) *Encyclopedia of Language and Education: Bilingual Education* (2nd edn, Vol. 5, pp. 65–75). Springer. https://doi.org/10.1007/978-0-387-30424-3_116

Cummins, J. (2017) BICS and CALP: Empirical and theoretical status of the distinction. In B. Street and S. May (eds) *Literacies and Language Education. Encyclopedia of Language and Education* (3rd edn, pp. 59–71). Springer. https://doi.org/10.1007/978-3-319-02252-9_6

Cummins, J. (2019) The emergence of translanguaging pedagogy: A dialogue between theory and practice. *Journal of Multilingual Education Research* 9 (13). https://fordham.bepress.com/jmer/vol9/iss1/13

Cummins, J. (2021) Translanguaging: A critical analysis of theoretical claims. In P. Juvonen and M. Källkvist (eds) *Pedagogical Translanguaging: Theoretical, Methodological and Empirical Perspectives* (pp. 7–36). Multilingual Matters. https://doi.org/10.21832/9781788927383-004

Cushing, S.T. and Tywoniw, R. (2020) Validating a holistic rubric for scoring short answer reading questions. In G.J. Ockey and B.A. Green (eds) *Another Generation Of Fundamental Considerations in Language Assessment: A Festschrift in Honor of Lyle F. Bachman* (pp. 113–128). Springer. https://doi.org/10.1007/978-981-15-8952-2_8

De Houwer, A. (2007) Parental language input patterns and children's bilingual use. *Applied Psycholinguistics* 28 (3), 411–424. https://doi.org/10.1017/S0142716407070221

DeKeyser, R. (2020) Skill acquisition theory. In B. VanPatten, G.D. Keating and S. Wulff (eds) *Theories in Second Language Acquisition* (pp. 83–104). Routledge.

Desmond, V. and Makalela, P.L. (2013) The effects of translanguaging on the bi-literate inferencing strategies of fourth grade learners. *Perspective in Education* 34 (3), 86–97. https://doi.org/10.18820/2519593X/PIE.V34I3.7

Gagarina, N., Klop, D., Kunnari, S., Tantele, K., Välimaa, T., Bohnacker, U. and Walters, J. (2019) MAIN: Multilingual assessment instrument for narratives – Revised. *ZAS Papers in Linguistics* 63. https://doi.org/10.21248/zaspil.63.2019.516

García, O. and Li, W. (2014) *Translanguaging: Language, Bilingualism, and Education*. Palgrave MacMillan.

García, O. and Lin, A.M.Y. (2018) English and multilingualism: A contested history. In P. Seargent (ed.) *Routledge Handbook of English Language Studies* (pp. 77–92). Routledge.

Gough, P. B. and Tunmer, W. E. (1986) Decoding, reading, and reading disability. *Remedial and Special Education* 7 (1), 6–10. https://doi.org/10.1177/074193258600700104

Hamilton, J., Lopes, M., McNamara, T. and Sheridan, E. (1993) Rating scales and native speaker performance on a communicatively oriented EAP test. *Language Testing* 10 (3), 337–353.

Hsin, L. and Snow, C. (2017) Social perspective taking: A benefit of bilingualism in second language writing. *Reading and Writing: An Interdisciplinary Journal* 30, 1193–1214. https://doi.org/10.1007/s11145-016-9718-9

Huang, B. and Bailey, A. (2022) Assessing multilinguals. In A. Stavans and U. Jessner (eds) *The Cambridge Handbook of Childhood Multilingualism* (pp. 441–471). Cambridge University Press. https://doi.org/10.1017/9781108669771.024

Hungwe, V. (2019) Using a translanguaging approach in teaching paraphrasing to enhance reading comprehension in first-year students. *Reading and Writing* 10 (1), 216. https://doi.org/10.4102/rw.v10i1.216

Jisa, H. (2000) Language mixing in the weak language: Evidence from two children. *Journal of Pragmatics* 32, 1363–1386.

Kadam, V.A. and Mukhopadhyay, L. (2023) Using translingual mediated revisions to develop micro-linguistic abilities in writing argumentative essays: A study of Indian ESL learners. In K. Raza, D. Reynolds and C. Coombe (eds) *Handbook of Multilingual TESOL in Practice* (pp. 111–128). Springer. https://doi.org/10.1007/978-981-19-9350-3_8

Kalyanpur, M., Bhuyan Boruah, P., Chugani Molina, S. and Shenoy, S. (2023) *The Politics of English Language Education and Social Inequality: Global Pressures, National Priorities and Schooling in India* (1st edn). Routledge. https://doi.org/10.4324/9781003125488

Lanauze, M. and Snow, C.E. (1989) The relation between first- and second-language skills: Evidence from Puerto Rican elementary school children in bilingual programs. *Linguistics and Education* 1, 323–340.

Laufer, B. (2020) Lexical coverages, inferencing unknown words, and reading comprehension: How are they related? *TESOL Quarterly* 54 (4), 1076–1085. https://doi.org/10.1002/tesq.3004

Lightbown, P.M. and Spada, N. (2020) Teaching and learning L2 in the classroom: It's about time. *Language Teaching* 53, 422–432. https://doi.org/10.1017/S0261444819000454

Lightfoot, A., Mathew, R., Mukhopadhyay, L. and Tsimpli, I. (2022) Multilingual practices in Indian classrooms: Exploring and supporting teacher awareness and classroom strategies. In L. Adinolfi, U. Bhattacharya and P. Phayak (eds) *Multilingual Education in South Asia: At the Intersection Between Policy and Practice* (pp. 26–49). Routledge. https://doi.org/10.4324/9781003158660-3

Lowe, C.J., Cho, I., Goldsmith, S.F. and Morton, J.B. (2021) The bilingual advantage in children's executive functioning: A meta-analytic review. *Psychological Science* 32 (7), 1115–1146. https://doi.org/10.1177/0956797621993108.

Malkoff, M.E. (1992) Translation ability: A natural bilingual and metalinguistic skill. *Advances in Psychology* 83, 515–529. https://doi.org/10.1016/S0166-4115(08)61514-9

May, S. (2017) Bilingual education: What the research tells us. In O. García, A.M.Y. Lin and S. May (eds) *Encyclopedia of Language and Education* (3rd edn, pp. 81–100). Cham.

Mohanty, A.K. (2019) *The Multilingual Reality: Living with Languages*. Multilingual Matters.

Mohanty, A. and Panda, M. (2017) Language policy and education in the Indian Subcontinent. In T. McCarty and S. May (eds) *Language Policy and Political Issues in Education, Encyclopedia of Language and Education* (3rd edn, pp. 507–518). Springer. https://doi.org/10.1007/978-3-319-02320-5_37-1

Mohanty, A. and Skutnabb-Kangas, T. (2022) Growing up in multilingual societies: Violations of linguistic human rights in education. In A. Stavans and U. Jessner (eds) *The Cambridge Handbook of Childhood Multilingualism* (pp. 578–602). Cambridge University Press. https://doi.org/10.1017/9781108669771.031

Mukhopadhyay, L. (2020) Translanguaging in primary level ESL classroom in India: An exploratory study. *International Journal for English Language Teaching* 7 (2), 1–14. https://doi.org/10.5430/ijelt.v7n2p1

Mukhopadhyay, L., Tamboli, V., Das, K. Balasubramanian, A. and Tsimpli, I. (2020) What guides inference generation? A study of young Hindi learners studying in challenging contexts in India. *Indian Educational Review, NCERT Journal* 58 (1), 41–66. https://doi.org/ 10.13140/RG.2.2.16030.56645

Mukhopadhyay, L., Patil, V. and Selvan, C. (2022a) Indian multilingual education: Reviewing translanguaging pedagogy for reading. In E. Charamba (ed.) *Handbook of Research on Teaching in Multicultural and Multilingual Contexts* (pp. 245–261). IGI Global Publisher. https://doi.org/10.4018/978-1-6684-5034-5

Mukhopadhyay, L., Patil, V. and Selvan, C. (2022b) Developing a translanguaging reading model for Indian ESL learners. In E. Charamba (ed.) *Handbook of Research on Teaching in Multicultural and Multilingual Contexts* (pp. 262–286). IGI Global Publisher. https://doi.org/10.4018/978-1-6684-5034-5

Mukhopadhyay, L., Loganathan, S., Patil, V.K., Qamri, S., Ravindran, M.R., Balasubramanian, A., Vogelzang, M. and Tsimpli, I. (2023) Exploring opportunities and challenges using translanguaging pedagogy to develop reading comprehension: A study of Indian Multilingual Classrooms. In E. Charamba and P. Aloka (eds) *Special Issue on Creating Inclusive Classrooms in Multicultural Contexts: Opportunities and Challenges for the 21st Century, Journal of Educational Studies* (si1), 262–292. https://doi.org/10.59915/jes.2023.special.1.14

Mukhopadhyay, L., Tsimpli, I.M., Patil, V.K., Loganathan, S., Qamri, S., Ravindran, M.R., Balasubramanian, A. and Vogelzang, M. (2025) *Reading for Comprehension in Primary School Children in India: A Teacher-Training Programme*. British Council. https://doi.org/10.57884/C5SM-TD20

Muysken, P. (2013) Language contact outcomes as the result of bilingual optimization strategies. *Bilingualism: Language and Cognition* 16 (04), 709–730.

Ouellette, G. and Beers, A. (2010) A not-so-simple view of reading: How oral vocabulary and visual-word recognition complicate the story? *Reading and Writing: An Interdisciplinary Journal* 23 (2), 189–208. https://doi.org/10.1007/s11145-008-9159-1

Ortega, L. (2020) The study of heritage language development from a bilingualism and social justice perspective. *Language Learning* 70 (1), 15–53. https://doi.org/10.1111/lang.12347

Ozuru, Y., Briner, S., Kurby, C.A. and McNamara, D.S. (2013) Comparing comprehension measured by multiple-choice and open-ended questions. *Canadian Journal of Experimental Psychology* 67 (3), 215–227. https://doi.org/10.1037/a0032918

Phyak, P., Sah, P.K., Ghimire, N.B. and Lama, A. (2022) Teacher agency in creating a translingual space in Nepal's multilingual English-medium schools. *RELC Journal* 53 (2), 431–451. https://doi.org/10.1177/00336882221113950

Poplack, S. (1980) Sometimes I'll start a sentence in Spanish y termino en espanol: Toward a typology of code-switching. *Linguistics* 18 (7–8), 581–618.

Reyes, I. (2022) Literacy development in the multilingual child: From speaking to writing. In A. Stavans and U. Jessner (eds) *The Cambridge Handbook of Childhood Multilingualism* (pp. 376–392). Cambridge University Press. https://doi.org/10.1017/9781108669771.021

Rupp, A.A. and Choi, H. (2006) How assessing reading comprehension with multiple-choice questions shapes the construct: A cognitive processing perspective. *Language Testing* 23, 441. https://doi.org/10.1191/0265532206lt337oa

Sah, P.K. (2022) English medium instruction in South Asian multilingual schools: Unpacking the dynamics of ideological orientations, policy/practices, and democratic questions. *International Journal of Bilingual Education and Bilingualism* 25 (2), 742–755.

Sah, P. and Li, G. (2018) English medium instruction (EMI) as linguistic capital in Nepal: Promises and realities. *International Multilingual Research Journal* 12 (2), 109–123, https://doi.org/10.1080/19313152.2017.1401448

Sah, P. K. and Kubota, R. (2022) Towards critical translanguaging: A review of literature on English as a medium of instruction in South Asia's school education. *Asian Englishes* 24 (2), 132–146. https://doi.org/10.1080/13488678.2022.2056796

Sanchez-Alonso, S. and Aslin, R.N. (2022) Towards a model of language neurobiology in early development. *Brain and Language* 224, 105047. https://doi.org/10.1016/j.bandl.2021.105047

Savage, R. (2022) Teaching children to read. In M.J. Snowling, C. Hulme and K. Nation (eds) *The Science of Reading: A Handbook* (2nd edn). Wiley. https://doi.org/10.1002/9781119705116.ch10

Shepherd-Carey, L. (2020) Making sense of comprehension practices and pedagogies in multimodal ways: A second-grade emergent bilingual's sensemaking during small-group reading. *Linguistics and Education* 55. https://doi.org/10.1016/j.linged.2019.100777

Singleton, D. and Leśniewska, J. (2021) The critical period hypothesis for L2 acquisition: An unfalsifiable embarrassment? *Languages* 6 (149), 1–15.

Skutnabb-Kangas, T. and Dunbar, R. (2010) Indigenous children's education as linguistic genocide and a crime against humanity? A global view. *Gáldu Čála. Journal of Indigenous Peoples' Rights*, 1.

Tong, X., Kwan, J.L.Y., Xiuli Tong, S. and Deacon, S.H. (2022) How Chinese–English bilingual fourth graders draw on syntactic awareness in reading comprehension: Within- and cross-language effects. *Read Res Q* 57 (2), 409–429. https://doi.org/10.1002/rrq.400

Treffers-Daller, J. (2019) The measurement of bilingual abilities: Central challenges. In A. De Houwer and L. Ortega (eds) *The Cambridge Handbook of Bilingualism* (pp. 289–306). Cambridge University Press. https://doi.org/10.1017/9781316831922.016

Treffers-Daller, J. (2022) Code-switching among bilingual and trilingual children. In A. Stavans and U. Jessner (eds) *The Cambridge Handbook of Childhood Multilingualism* (pp. 190–204). Cambridge University Press. https://doi.org/10.1017/9781108669771.011

Treffers-Daller, J. (2024) Code-switching and translanguaging: Why they have a lot in common. *ELT Journal* 78 (1), 82–87. https://doi.org/10.1093/elt/ccad059

Treffers-Daller, J., Mukhopadhyay, L., Balasubramanian, A., Tamboli, V. and Tsimpli, I. (2022) How ready are Indian primary school children for English Medium Instruction? An analysis of the relationship between the reading skills of low-SES children, their oral vocabulary and English input in the classroom in government schools in India. *Applied Linguistics*. https://doi.org/10.1093/applin/amac003

Tsimpli, I.M., Balasubramanian, A., Marinis, T., Panda, M., Mukhopadhyay, L., Alladi, S. and Treffers-Daller, J. (2020b) *Research Report of a Four-Year Study of Multilingualism, Literacy, Numeracy, and Cognition in Delhi, Hyderabad, and Patna*. The University of Cambridge. https://www.britishcouncil.in/sites/default/files/multilila_project_overview_report_final_-_web.pdf

Upton, T. and Thompson, L. (2001) The role of the first language in second language reading. *Studies in Second Language Acquisition* 23, 469–495. https://doi.org/10.1017/S0272263101004028

UNESCO Global Monitoring Report (2016) *If You Don't Understand How Can You Learn*? Policy paper 24. UNESCO. https://unesdoc.unesco.org/ark:/48223/pf0000243713

Vaish, V. and Subhan, A. (2015) Translanguaging in a reading class. *International Journal of Multilingualism* 12 (3), 338–357. https://doi.org/10.1080/14790718.2014.948447

5 A Translanguaging Pedagogical Design for Reading Comprehension Development and Implications for Bilingual Classrooms

Abu Saleh Mohammad Rafi

Introduction

Translanguaging is the full range of linguistic performances of multilingual users regardless of the boundaries of politically constructed named languages and translanguaging pedagogies are the critical, creative and strategic ways of utilising these linguistic performances in the learning process (García & Kleyn, 2016; Rafi & Morgan, 2021, 2022a). While the former is a common practice in multilingual societies (See Sultana et al., 2015; Sultana, 2022), the latter has been widely researched for its pedagogical and social benefits in diverse global classroom contexts, including a few studies in South Asian settings (e.g. Rafi & Morgan, 2021, 2022a, 2022b, 2022c, 2022d, 2022e; Rafi, 2023a, 2023b; Panezai et al., 2022). I situate the current investigation within the pedagogical paradigm of translanguaging and present a pedagogical design that I applied in the English language teaching (ELT) classrooms of two Bangladeshi public and private universities as part of a larger project. While this section outlines the foundational theoretical constructs, the chapter moves beyond mere application to critically examine and extend translanguaging pedagogies in light of the empirical realities of Bangladeshi higher education.

Translanguaging as a pedagogical approach has gained considerable momentum, with positive outcomes in the fields of literacy and second language acquisition. As a pedagogical approach, translanguaging can move 'beyond traditional notions of linguistic creativity and creative pedagogy to formulate new ways of imagining creativity in language learning based on encouraging learners to make use of the full range of their semiotic resources and social experiences when communicating' (Jones, 2019: 3). The pedagogical benefits of translanguaging have been celebrated to the extent that recent research has begun to view ELT classrooms as sites for translingual interaction (Anderson, 2017). Other than English, linguistic resources were previously 'left at the door' of English-only classroom learning environments; there is now an acknowledgement that abilities in many languages can be used in ways previously not considered in ELT classrooms (Rafi & Morgan, 2021, 2022a; Rafi, 2023a).

ELT practitioners are increasingly looking for pedagogical designs that can foster a translingual environment for their students (Hirsu *et al.*, 2021). This study presents a translanguaging pedagogical design that enabled ELT students in Bangladeshi universities to explore, through two interventions using a range of texts and classroom discussions and activities, the implications of the colonial construction of beauty in their communities and beyond. The interventions were conducted in the English reading skill development classrooms of one public university and one private university in Bangladesh. The findings of these interventions demonstrate how the pedagogical design incorporating texts in both Bangla and English and activities designed to utilise students' full range of linguistic and semiotic skills through translanguaging assisted students in embracing a more active and collaborative role in the ELT classrooms. The activities enhanced their comprehension of complex English texts and provided opportunities for students to transform their racial ideologies about the construction of beauty through the challenge of colonial norms made possible through translanguaged discussion.

Research Background

Bangla (or Bengali, in colonial parlance) is the national language and the lingua franca of Bangladesh. Pre-tertiary education in Bangladesh comprises three major streams: Bangla medium, English medium and Madrassa education (Islamic school) and the newly introduced 'English version'. The English version teaches the same national curriculum as the Bangla medium, but through the medium of English. In contrast, the mainstream English medium teaches a different curriculum following the University of London's General Certificate of Education (GCE) or the Senior Cambridge curriculum and O/A-level examinations (Rafi & Morgan, 2022c). While several parallel education streams operate, the majority of the student population in Bangladesh learns to read, write and understand subject content in Bangla throughout their 12 years of schooling before seeking admission to Bangladeshi universities (Rafi & Morgan, 2022b).

Bangladeshi higher education (BHE) is primarily divided into two sectors: public and private. Bangladesh has 54 government-funded public universities, among which four operate as autonomous entities. In response to the increasing demand for higher education that public universities were unable to accommodate, the Bangladesh government enacted 'The Private University Act' in 1992. This legislation aimed to facilitate the registration of private higher education institutions. Bangladesh currently has 112 private universities approved by the University Grants Commission (UGC) of Bangladesh (UGC, 2023). Three international universities have been established and funded by international organisations, namely the Organisation of Islamic Cooperation, the South Asian Association for Regional Cooperation (SAARC) and the Goldman Sachs Foundation and the Bill & Melinda Gates Foundation. These three universities are not under government management and were not established according to the Private University Act (1992). This study concentrates primarily on public and private universities, rather than the three international universities because public and private universities attract the majority of the student population in Bangladesh and offer a clearer distinction between instructional approaches.

Two dominant policy discourses exist in the medium of instruction (MOI) landscape of public and private universities, according to research based on traditional conceptualisations of monolingualism and bilingualism. Public universities have implemented language policies, including the use of Bangla, a bilingual approach or a combination of Bangla and English. In contrast, private universities have predominantly adopted English as the MOI, using it for both content instruction and assessment across all academic disciplines (Akareem & Hossain, 2012; Hamid *et al.*, 2013; Rahman *et al.*, 2020). These studies indicate that public university MOI policy decision is influenced by linguistic nationalism, protectionism and additive bilingualism. On the other hand, MOI policy decision in private universities is influenced by internationalisation, globalisation and the perceived economic benefits of English.

English departments in both types of universities maintain an English-only environment despite the macro-level divide in the MOI landscape. The English departments in Bangladesh are said to be influenced by the English department at the University of Dhaka. This department, established in 1921, is the first of its kind in East Bengal and can be traced back to the 'Minute on Indian Education' proposed by Thomas Babington Macaulay, a British historian and politician. Macaulay's 'Minutes' sought to create 'a class of persons Indian in blood and colour, but English in tastes, in opinions, in morals, and intellect' (Macaulay, 1835: para. 34). This objective was pursued by prioritising English literature over English language teaching, as British administrators believed it would facilitate language acquisition, cultural assimilation and the humanising (*sic*) the local population (Rafi, 2023d).

The persistence of colonial influence is evident in Bangladesh, where English departments in Bangladeshi universities are commonly referred to as 'Royal Departments'. These departments mandate the study of English literary texts written in archaic, old, early-modern and modern English by writers from the early modern era to the present day. However, these texts do not align with the cultural backgrounds of students nor correspond to their linguistic abilities for comprehension (Rafi, 2023d). Existing research demonstrates that students struggle to understand English lectures and fail to perform well in English assessments in this monolingual environment (Sultana, 2014; Rafi, 2023a). Teachers in Bangladeshi university English departments also lack the training to utilise the students' bilingual (or multilingual) abilities to create interactive, learner-centred and activity-based classrooms (Rafi, 2020; Rafi & Morgan, 2024). Despite the intended English-only policies, recent studies have demonstrated a disconnect between institutional/macro-level language policy and actual practices across departments and courses in both public and private universities (Rafi & Morgan, 2022b). An observational study of two public and two private universities revealed that six out of eight classrooms accommodated translanguaging as the norm or separated language practices in the teachers' and students' pedagogical discourses, that is, English in teachers' and translanguaging in students' discourses, at least in oral activities. These classrooms demonstrated excellent opportunities for utilising naturally occurring (as well as planned) translanguaging practices to design coherent pedagogical approaches that could transform the existing policies and practices in Bangladeshi higher education for increased learner benefit (Rafi & Morgan, 2022a).

Literature Review

Recent sociolinguistic research reports that teachers and learners frequently draw on more than one language for a range of functions in the classroom, including language alternation, translation and other bilingual skills to strengthen the sophistication and effectiveness of bilingual learners' thinking in bi/multilingual classrooms (García, 2009; Probyn, 2006; Rafi, 2023d). García and Kano (2014: 261) have framed these practices in terms of 'translanguaging in education', which refers to:

> ... a process by which students and teachers engage in complex discursive practices that include ALL the language practices of ALL students in a class to develop new language practices and sustain old ones, communicate and appropriate knowledge, and give voice to new sociopolitical realities by interrogating linguistic inequality.

Translanguaging in instruction is not arbitrary or haphazard in this process; instead, it is purposeful, ensuring that bilingual students are thoroughly educated by systematically utilising their whole language repertoire and bilingual ways of knowing (García & Kleyn, 2016; Rafi, 2020). The value of translanguaging in providing bilingual students with the opportunity to compare and mesh languages when participating in different literacy activities while concurrently developing their language and conceptual knowledge has been recently documented (Daniel *et al.*, 2019; Karlsson *et al.*, 2019). With reference to literacy benefits, this study situates itself within the broader scholarship of translanguaging literature that mainly focuses on reading comprehension development. García (2020) argued that the act of reading is not dependent on the language of the written text nor the concept of a named language. It depends on how bilingual readers assemble all their meaning-making resources and act on them to read. As a pedagogical approach, 'translanguaging focuses attention toward the real action of bilingual readers with their full semiotic repertoire and away from what is perceived to be the monolingual/monoglossic language of the text' (García, 2020: 558).

In a Singaporean context, Vaish (2019) trialled a translanguaging approach to teach reading skills in English to 2nd graders in three schools and qualitatively analysed teachers' pedagogical strategies and individual students' responses from 14 hours of video data. This study presented an analysis of five exchanges, in which Exchanges 1 to 4 demonstrated how teachers judiciously and systematically translanguaged in Chinese and Malay to teach lexical items (vocabulary), grammar and comprehension in English. In these exchanges, translanguaging stimulated students' metalinguistic awareness to notice nuances in punctuation, orthography, grammatical structures and meaning. However, in Exchange 5, the teacher translanguaged to focus on Chinese vocabulary in a class where the target language was English. According to Vaish (2019), translanguaging was not required in this exchange, which recommends teacher training so that the teachers can understand where and when translanguaging may or may not be useful for learning the target language.

Maseko and Mkhize (2019) adopted translanguaging as a theoretical lens to study the reading literacy practices of multilingual Grade 3 learners and their teachers during the English and isiZulu reading lessons in a South African school, where English is offered at a First Additional Language Level and isiZulu at a Home Language Level. In this study, translanguaging promoted active engagement with the texts to the benefit of the learners, irrespective of their levels of competence in either language. Translanguaging enabled them to connect other dimensions of their cultural and social worlds and modern life to older times in making sense of the texts. However, the authors observed constant conflicts and tensions in teachers' discourses. The teacher believed in the promises of translanguaging to enhance the learners' abilities to make meaning of the texts, but seemed uncertain whether translanguaging was the right thing to do. Maseko and Mkhize (2019) recommended the official recognition of translanguaging practices (to remedy this dilemma for teachers). They advocated for multilingual policies that value learners' and teachers' multilingual practices to enhance effective learning and teaching in general, particularly in reading.

Chu (2017) explored literal, inferential and evaluative levels of reading comprehension and considered the possibility of enacting translanguaging as an alternate testing method. This study created two versions of assessments for 123 6th-graders in Taiwan. Both versions provided the same reading text in English, but the first version used English multiple-choice questions and options and the second one used a Chinese translation for the same questions and options. A comparative analysis of the findings demonstrated that assessment with the second version could assess students' knowledge more accurately. The integration of translanguaging into reading comprehension assessment allowed students to perform significantly better in all three comprehension levels with Chinese questions. This assessment method enabled students to access their entire linguistic repertoire while promoting reflexive, nuanced and high-order thinking, drawing on critical elements and background knowledge in other languages. Chu (2017) recommended this assessment method when the purpose is to determine how well English learners comprehend the text, but do not know how to express their understanding in English.

Song and Cho (2018) used think-aloud protocols to examine how Korean-English bilingual middle school students accessed their two languages during online reading. This study revealed that 37% of online reading strategies utilised translanguaging and served different functions such as facilitating planning, monitoring, revising their search and improving comprehension processes during online reading. Since little attention has been paid to bilingual adolescents' reading literacy practices on the multilingual internet, this study provides pedagogical evidence supporting how translanguaging during online reading can enhance students' learning from multilingual texts.

These studies collectively demonstrated the benefits of translanguaging in terms of improving students' comprehension processes in onsite and online classrooms, stimulating their metalinguistic awareness, promoting active engagement regardless of their level of linguistic competence and integrating translanguaging into reading comprehension assessment in pre-tertiary education. Additionally, scholars argued for the official recognition of translanguaging practices and the implementation of teacher training; however, translanguaging approaches in tertiary reading classrooms remain largely unstudied. Among the scant available studies, Rafi and Morgan (2022a) examined the influence of translanguaging pedagogy on first-year students' reading comprehension in an English-medium classroom at a Bangladeshi private university. This study demonstrates that translanguaging pedagogies can maximise students' linguistic and semiotic resources, put them at ease and improve their epistemic access to and comprehension of complex English texts. Mbirimi-Hungwe's (2019) study on summary writing as a measure of reading comprehension among university students corroborates these findings. This study aimed to determine the effectiveness of translanguaging in assisting students in comprehending texts. The results indicated that students better understood the main idea and overall meaning of texts, as evidenced by the summaries they produced. In addition to the targeted outcome of improving and balancing reading comprehension in target and home languages, Rafi and Morgan's (2022a) study also demonstrated how the intentional pedagogy of translanguaging transformed the colonial construction of beauty standards for the focal students into a more inclusive concept.

The current study adds to the small body of literature devoted to improving bilingual students' reading skills in university contexts from translanguaging pedagogical perspectives. Furthermore, it contributes to the Bangladeshi educational setting, which is underrepresented in translanguaging literature, by offering feasible and tangible answers to the challenges encountered in a teacher-centred classroom at a Bangladeshi public university.

The Study

This study is part of a larger project that collected four sets of data, including classroom observation, pedagogical interventions, focus group discussions with students and semi-structured interviews with teachers (Rafi, 2022). The current study mainly addressed the data collected from two pedagogical interventions in the classrooms of two reading comprehension development courses. These courses were offered in the first year of the undergraduate programs of one public and one private university, respectively pseudonymised as the Medha University of Bangladesh (MUB) and the Fariha University of Excellence (FUB). Approximately 100 students, that is, 70 MUB and 30 FUB students and two teachers, one at each university, participated in the interventions. Both interventions adopted the same translanguaging design, using one Bangla and two English stimulus texts, exploring the construction of beauty across languages and cultures. A brief thematic discussion of the texts is as follows:

> English text 1: This is an online article that explores how celebrity images influence the concept of beauty among young boys. It argues that these images project an inflated idea of beauty that contradicts the notion of beauty that these boys experience with a close female friend, family member or aunt.
>
> English text 2: Written from a black woman's perspective, this text explores the role of skin colour, body shaming and social media in the dating culture of American youth.

Bangla text: This blog post critically explores and challenges the role of colonisation in the construction of beauty in Bangladeshi culture and girls' subsequent suffering if they perceive they do not fit that colonial standard. It provides examples from the first Bengali Nobel laureate Rabindranath Tagore's literary works that arguably accepted colonial norms as the beauty standard. For example, Tagore appreciated dark skin in a song, but none of the female protagonists was dark-skinned in his novels.

The following table, reproduced from Rafi (2023a), demonstrates how the intervention was designed.

The intervention presented in Table 5.1 was designed not merely to apply translanguaging pedagogies but also to critically examine how such pedagogies operate in the distinct sociolinguistic and institutional contexts of Bangladeshi higher education. By drawing on named language texts in Bangla and English that interrogate sociocultural ideologies such as colourism and the colonial construction of beauty standards, the design foregrounds students' linguistic repertoires as cognitive, cultural and critical resources. Through the purposeful use of Bangla and other languages

Table 5.1 Intervention design

Phases	Activities
Phase 1: Translanguaging theory and pedagogical approaches	• Introduced the translanguaging theory of education • Briefed on the strategies of translanguaging pedagogy
Phase 2: Tell me now activity	• An activity comprising a picture of five young people and three questions
Phase 3: Reading the first English text	• Provided an English definition of beauty • Explored cognates of the proverb 'Beauty is in the eye of the beholder' across languages and cultures • Bangla scaffolding for difficult words in the text • Used a photo of a Bangladeshi actress to connect with English text • Completed the reading of the first English text • Researcher-students interaction: (1) What is this text about? (2) Do you agree with this author? Why/Why not?
Phase 4: Reading a Bangla text	• Used the Bangla text as a guided reading • Reflected on the struggle of Bangladeshi parents to get their dark-skinned daughters married off • Asked students' opinions on the messages of the text
Phase 5: Reading the second English text	• Providing scaffolding for difficult words • Paraphrasing to enhance students' access • Researcher-students interaction: (1) What is this passage about? (2) Do you agree with this author? If so, please share. (3) What do you think beauty is?
Phase 6	• Two sets of multiple-choice questions

such as Hindi from these repertoires as a scaffold and meaning-making tool alongside English, the intervention challenges the dominant language separation ideologies of English-only instruction while offering students opportunities to articulate complex perspectives in culturally resonant ways.

After the intervention, I organised two focus groups with 10 students and two semi-structured interviews with the teachers to elicit participant responses on each translanguaging intervention. Transcripts of these datasets were imported into the NVivo data management program for several rounds of inductive coding. A thematic analysis of these codes was conducted to generate a perspective on the role of translanguaging in enhancing reading comprehension in two ELT classrooms. As later sections of this chapter will show, the intervention provoked diverse responses from students, including affirmation of their linguistic agency, negotiation of identity and occasional resistance responses, which in turn shed light on the constraints and possibilities of implementing translingual approaches within exam-oriented, English-dominant institutional settings. In this way, the study not only localises but also extends the translanguaging framework by situating it within the pedagogical realities and postcolonial politics of Bangladeshi ELT classrooms.

Findings and Discussion

Both pedagogical interventions produced homogenous findings, that is, there was consistency across both groups in public and private universities. Results were grouped into two broad themes: the 'Face-value' component and engagement as one theme and enhancing comprehension and transforming the students' subjectivities as the other.

'Face-value' component and student engagement

Translanguaging pedagogies allowed the students to compare the intervention with their regular classes. Students consistently indicated that they discovered a sanctioned 'comfort zone' in the intervention class, which they had not previously experienced in a stated (if not always enforced) English-only environment. Most students were from Bangla medium pre-tertiary education, in both groups. Most do not possess the English language proficiency required in the English departments and hence, these students are routinely subjected to an environment of structured linguistic inequality. English medium and English version background students always outperform and, consciously or unconsciously, subjugate the Bangla medium students in such an environment, rewarded by a system that allows for such inequality despite Bangla nationalist sentiment and purported pride in the national language and culture. Furthermore, these students are young adults who develop a 'Face value' component of self-esteem in the transition period from pre-tertiary to tertiary education, as reflected in the comment of a MUB student:

> We are university students now. We could accept if people made fun of our mistakes in our childhood, but it's not the same anymore. We're very conscious of our face value now.

Under those circumstances, the enforcement to adhere to EMI policy and practices sour and even emotionally wound these students. Little or no attention has been paid to young adults' reputational or status value, but this component of their education has significant consequences on their psychosocial and academic development. For example, two FUB students revealed that many students suffer from low self-esteem and chronic depression arising from their sense of failure and inability to achieve good results. These universities offer 'remedial English courses' for identified (publicly known) 'weaker' students. However, this approach considers students from a deficit perspective and, further, does not necessarily serve the needs of all students whose English language abilities fall across a wide range and with different language knowledge 'gaps' (Sultana, 2014). Under such circumstances, many students struggle to remain motivated in ELT classrooms, are reluctant to seek assistance and eventually drop out of the courses that strictly adhere to the English-only policy (Rafi, 2023a).

In contrast, the purposeful design of translanguaging pedagogy created an academic space that valued bilingual students' natural and characteristic languaging practices and the diversity of experience, accommodating differing proficiencies without shame or loss of face value. The systematic incorporation of varied semiotic and multilingual resources in the interventions maximised the students' participation in the classroom. For example, the 'Tell me now' activity, designed on an image of five multicultural young adults, invited students to interact with content immediately from the beginning of the intervention. Students at MUB could not provide a Bangla cognate of 'Beauty lies in the eyes of its beholder', unlike their counterparts at FUB, who came up with a famous Bangla saying: যার চোখে যাকে লাগে ভালো, a metaphorical expression that does not translate well in English but perfectly captures the essence of the English cognate. Nonetheless, 'permission' to translanguage allowed the MUB students to initiate a conversation effectively, in which four students spontaneously participated and contributed to the discussion.

The purposeful inclusion of both Bangla and English texts on the same topic enabled students to go back and forth between languages and cultures while maintaining their attention and engagement and developing ideas throughout the intervention period. In terms of dealing with advanced English texts, students spontaneously joined the researcher in paraphrasing each sentence and translanguaging to express their understanding of the topic under discussion. Students who had never had a voice in English-only classrooms felt encouraged to talk in the intervention and possibly for the first time in their university study, experienced a sense of self-esteem as what they brought to the class was both valued by others and assisted their meaning-making. For example, a MUB student commented on the performance of her classmates who previously had hardly participated in regular class discussions:

> I noticed the boy, Imtiaz, who sat on the last bench, provided an excellent definition of beauty. I liked Mou's definition too. They were able to organise their thoughts because they were allowed to translanguage.

Analysis of the observation data characterised the MUB classroom as lecture-focused, featuring only one translanguaging moment of teacher-student interaction. The FUB classroom teacher described her course, which could also be characterised as didactic and teacher-focused, as 'boring' and held a lack of student engagement and participation responsible for this description. In contrast, the pedagogical design of the translanguaging intervention brought multiple voices, languages and modes of contribution from the students. Having witnessed the researcher's interventions, both teacher participants acknowledged the benefits of translanguaging pedagogies. For example, the FUB teacher said the students were more engaged in the intervention than in her regular classes. The MUB teacher explained such high engagement, arguing that translanguaging created a 'congenial classroom environment since the students were under less stress and anxiety regarding the use of language'. What is implicit in these teacher statements is that teacher enjoyment could also be enhanced through the increased engagement opportunities provided by a translanguaging pedagogical approach, avoiding the development of teacher cynicism (and comments on her class as 'boring') and potential burnout. In short, the analysis of four datasets demonstrated an interactive learning experience for teachers and students in ELT classrooms, with benefits for all (Rafi, 2023a).

Enhancing Comprehension and Transforming Subjectivities

This section discusses the second thematic category finding, related to the functions of intervention steps in enhancing English text comprehension while harnessing students' critical and high-order thinking and reasoning skills about the historical and cultural constructs of beauty. Each intervention activity comprised several translanguaging strategies, including vocabulary introduction in two languages using semantic attributes of the words, cognate expressions across languages, context clues and semiotic resources as learner-centred objects. Students were instructed to use bilingual dictionaries on their phones to look up the meanings of difficult English words alongside the researcher's multilingual vocabulary support.

They learnt the academic Bangla meaning of difficult English words such as 'inflated', 'subjective', 'wondered' and also the contextual meaning of the English word 'haunted'. Semiotic resources, such as using a picture of a Bangladeshi actress, helped students explore how the entertainment and media industry projects the concept of beauty from their respective cultural backgrounds.

The first activity, 'Tell me now', comprised viewing a picture of five young people from different ethnic origins and skin colours, followed by a discussion around three questions. In answer to the first question, 'Who is the most beautiful person here?', most of the students considered the white people as the most beautiful, providing a simplified explanation: 'because they are white'. They even laughed when the researcher suggested the possibility of considering a black person as the most beautiful. Nevertheless, one student resisted her classmates' racist remarks or conditioning, with a one-word response, 'No!'. The second question, 'What is the concept of beauty in your culture?', required the students to take a step back and provide a more in-depth look into their reality and question the feasibility of such colonial beauty standards in their context. They suggested that, despite having brown skin colour, most Bangladeshis consider fair skin the dominant defining feature of being beautiful. The third question, 'How much money and time do you spend on beauty and appearance?', challenged the gender-based stereotypes related to the beautification process. For instance, a male classmate inadvertently acknowledged that he spent more time than his female classmate on beauty preparation.

The first English text included the proverb, 'Beauty is in the eye of the beholder', which enabled the researcher to engage the students in exploring its cognates across languages and cultures. Interestingly, a private university student knew the Hindi cognate of that proverb as well, which is खब सुरति देखनेवालो की औखों में होति है, meaning 'Individuals have different beauty standards' in English. The example demonstrates how the pedagogic design of translanguaging actively resists the structured environment of Western ideologies in the EMI classroom, maximising the scope of understanding of the English text, including languages that were not even taught in Bangla schools – a situation common in most classrooms around the world, given the diversity of backgrounds of students in a superdiverse world (Vertovec, 2010).

The Bangla text enabled the students to examine the impact of the colonial beauty standard, drawing evidence from Bangla literature and common practices of the Bangladeshi people. They understood how the colonial standard discriminates against Bangladeshi women in marriage based on their dark skin colour. After reading the text, the students became socially and cognitively engaged, as reflected in their immediate expressions such as 'oh my God', 'terrible', 'bitter truth' and so on. Both cohorts agreed with the message that the text conveyed about challenging colonial stereotypes. The researcher then asked if similar discrimination prevails in the US context. Interestingly, both cohorts disagreed, given that the US is a developed country where people should have a more generous attitude towards skin tones. The second English text allowed students to compare and contrast the concept of beauty and discrimination from an American context. This text dealt with how skin colour and body shaming discriminate against many young people in the American dating culture. This text was written in advanced English; hence, the students struggled to access it. As soon as the researcher elected to paraphrase the text, students immediately joined him in paraphrasing each line, using both Bangla and English. They are translanguaged to think and speak seamlessly across languages to navigate language-intensive and cognitively demanding real-life inquiries. This phenomenon of active collaboration of students with the researcher to understand a complex phenomenon was prevalent in both interventions.

The question 'What do you think beauty is?' posed in the intervention placed the students as co-constructors of meaning. The following examples demonstrate how students orally produced their own definitions of beauty:

FUB student-1: Beauty is a concept that changes people's perceptions.
FUB student-2: I think beauty is not only your physical appearance but also your inner beauty.
MUB student-1: The things that make us feel better are beauty.
MUB student-2: A beautiful person is (one) who is comfortable in his/her own skin. Colours or body type, hair colours or whatever s/he has naturally; that is beauty.

Interestingly, the students spontaneously produced these definitions in English, indicating that translanguaging pedagogy served the school's English language requirement. Furthermore, it added a strong educational focus on nurturing the individualism (agency) of English major students, which the English departments promote by exploring explicitly targeted content on the subjective psychological and social consciousness of the literary characters. A MUB student noticed this unintended positive outcome of translanguaging pedagogy. She said:

We all are seeing physical beauty from different angles. This is individualism. Translanguaging gave us the platform to express our different perspectives.

Contrary to the English-only environment, translanguaging fostered students' bilingual ways of knowing the world and reaching their own conclusions about such a complicated topic as beauty. Upon completing the intervention, a FUB student said, 'We learned something fantastic today!'. His teacher did not overlook the joy of learning something new that transformed an age-old belief for the students. She praised the pedagogic design of the intervention, saying: 'It was marvellous! They clapped for you at the end!!' In the same fashion, a MUB student expressed her excitement in the focus group discussion, saying, 'This is the type of class we want more of'. Given the restrictions the students had previously been under, this very first encouragement to use all their resources revealed how this initial change could lead to greater possibilities in the longer term. The findings indicate several things, such as a natural release of previously pent-up feelings/understanding and an instant resistance to/flouting the (unjust) rules, which did not require much encouragement. Furthermore, the pedagogical design has the potential for much deeper engagement when students are more used to working in this way and can come prepared for lessons, think about things overnight, ponder on their way home and live their lives. The personal sides explored in the study are crucial, since they undeniably allow for richer academic and personal outcomes.

In an EMI classroom, students might get away with answering questions with responses they have drawn from the Internet, adapted from a textbook or repeating the teacher's dictation without really understanding the meaning (Baker, 2011). In contrast, students in this intervention used the Bangla text as a guide and utilised their metalinguistic and metacognitive resources to process the English texts more deeply. Most importantly, even in a short intervention, students moved away from the preconceived colonial beauty standard and produced their definitions that challenged the stereotypes and prejudices for a better world.

Conclusion and Implications

This study explored the potential of a translanguaging pedagogical design in two ELT classrooms of Bangladeshi higher education. The design enhanced student participation and ensured higher cognitive engagement in the reading classrooms. Students mobilised their metalinguistic resources, metacognitive skills and prior knowledge to make meaning of English texts. The instructional design offered students opportunities to be authorities on the concepts explored in the materials, made them feel confident, fostered their individualism and placed them as co-producers of meanings. Alongside the targeted outcome of enhancing reading comprehension in the ELT classroom, a robust design of translanguaging pedagogy can help students break racial stereotypes, tackle inequalities and fight for social justice (Rafi & Morgan, 2022a).

These findings have crucial pedagogical implications for the international context and 'Centres' of ELT, where classes tend to be multilingual (Phillipson, 1992 in Anderson 2017), as well as for conducting translanguaging research in classroom contexts in the Global South. The translanguaging pedagogical design discussed in this chapter addresses various challenges in higher education reading classrooms in the Global South. These challenges include but are not limited to a lack of emphasis on reading and writing in English during pre-tertiary education, which results in students being admitted to universities without the necessary foundational skills for academic reading (Hungwe, 2019; Probyn, 2006), difficulties faced by students in adjusting to English-only environments in 'remedial' English courses (Sultana, 2014; Rafi, 2023a) and students' tendency to focus on surface-level understanding of texts rather than seeking deeper explanations and understanding of language use (Hungwe, 2019; King, 2007; Rafi & Morgan, 2021).

As previously discussed, translanguaging is a prevalent practice in classrooms in the Global South, at least in Bangladeshi universities, regardless of the implementation of English medium instruction policies. Nevertheless, it is important to acknowledge that simply recognising translanguaging as a bilingual behaviour, without incorporating the essential principles of translanguaging pedagogies, may not guarantee optimal educational success (Rafi, 2020). I advocated elsewhere for distinguishing between naturally occurring translanguaging practices and translanguaging pedagogies to highlight the advantages of translanguaging pedagogies in the Global South (Rafi & Morgan, 2024). This distinction is important because each of these dimensions produces different outcomes in educational settings, given the context-specific nature of translanguaging (Rafi & Morgan, 2024).

In Vaish (2019) and Maseko and Mkhize (2019) reviewed the study, the teacher translanguaged to focus on Chinese vocabulary in a class where English was the target language and the teacher in Maseko and Mkhize (2019) appeared uncertain as to whether translanguaging was the best approach. In contrast, the teacher participants in the current study acknowledged the benefits of translanguaging pedagogical interventions in terms of creating a linguistically welcoming classroom atmosphere, alleviating language-related stress and anxiety, promoting active student involvement with study materials and fostering teacher satisfaction while mitigating the risk of teacher cynicism and potential burnout commonly observed in traditional English Language Teaching (ELT) classrooms. The findings collectively illustrate the significance of distinguishing between naturally occurring translanguaging practices and the deliberate, innovative and structured development of translanguaging pedagogies. This distinction is crucial to effectively address the objectives of all stakeholders in classroom settings within the Global South.

Crucially, this chapter advocates for a recalibration of English language education policy and practice in South Asia. The findings support a move beyond rigid, English-only remedial models and instead recognise multilingualism as a rich resource, not a problem to be fixed. Translanguaging pedagogical design offers a scalable, equity-focused framework that is not only attuned to the sociolinguistic realities of students but also aligned with wider goals of inclusion and justice. As I have argued elsewhere (Rafi, 2025), English in Bangladesh is best understood as a hybrid, locally owned resource, and translanguaging provides a more context-sensitive response to ELT crises than top-down reforms or over-hyped methodologies such as CLT. These insights may guide meaningful changes in how we design curricula, prepare teachers and shape policy, paving the way for a more humane, culturally grounded and socially just model of English language education.

References

Akareem, H.S. and Hossain, S.S. (2012) Perception of education quality in private universities of Bangladesh: A study from students' perspective. *Journal of Marketing for Higher Education* 22 (1), 11–33. https://doi.org/10.1080/08841241.2012.705792

Anderson, J. (2017) Reimagining English language learners from a translingual perspective. *ELT Journal* 72 (1), 26–37. https://doi.org/10.1093/elt/ccx029

Baker, C. (2011) *Foundations of Bilingual Education and Bilingualism* (5th edn). Multilingual Matters.

Chu, C.S.S. (2017) Translanguaging in reading comprehension assessment: Implications on assessing literal, inferential, and evaluative comprehension among ESL elementary students in Taiwan. *NYS TESOL Journal* 4 (2), 19–35.

Daniel, S.M., Jiménez, R.T., Pray, L. and Pacheco, M.B. (2019) Scaffolding to make translanguaging a classroom norm. *TESOL Journal* 10 (1), e00361. https://doi.org/10.1002/tesj.361

García, O. (2009) Education, multilingualism and translanguaging in the 21st Century. In T. Skutnabb-Kangas, R. Phillipson, A.K. Mohanty and M. Panda (eds) *Social Justice through Multilingual Education* (pp. 140–158). Multilingual Matters.

García, O. (2020) Translanguaging and Latinx bilingual readers. *The Reading Teacher* 73 (5), 557–562. https://doi.org/10.1002/trtr.1883

García, O. and Kano, N. (2014) Translanguaging as process and pedagogy: Developing the English writing of Japanese students in the US. In J. Conteh and G. Meier (eds) *The Multilingual Turn in Languages Education: Opportunities and Challenges* (pp. 258–277). Multilingual Matters. https://doi.org/10.21832/9781783092246-018

García, O. and Kleyn, T. (eds) (2016) *Translanguaging with Multilingual Students: Learning from Classroom Moments*. Routledge.

Hamid, M.O., Jahan, I. and Islam, M.M. (2013) Medium of instruction policies and language practices, ideologies and institutional divides: Voices of teachers and students in a private university in Bangladesh. *Current Issues in Language Planning* 14 (1), 144– 163. https://doi.org/10.1080/14664208.2013.771417

Hirsu, L., Zacharias, S. and Futro, D. (2021) Translingual arts-based practices for language learners. *ELT Journal*. https://doi.org/10.1093/elt/ccaa064

Hungwe, V. (2019) Using a translanguaging approach in teaching paraphrasing to enhance reading comprehension in first-year students. *Reading & Writing* 10 (1), 1–9. https://doi.org/10.4102/rw.v10i1.216

Jones, R. (2019) Creativity in language learning and teaching: Translingual practices and transcultural identities. *Applied Linguistics Review*. https://doi.org/10.1515/applirev-2018-0114.

Karlsson, A., Larsson, P.N. and Jakobsson, A. (2019) The continuity of learning in a translanguaging science classroom. *Cultural Studies of Science Education* 14, 1–25. http://doi.org/10.1007/s11422-019-09933-y

King, A. (2007) Beyond literal comprehension: A strategy to promote deep understanding of text. In D. McNamara (ed.) *Reading Comprehension Strategies: Theories, Interventions, and Technologies* (pp. 267–290). Lawrence Erlbaum Associates.

Macaulay, T.B. (1835) Minute on education. In H. Sharp (ed.) (1920) *Selections from Educational Records, Part I (1781-1839)* (pp. 107–117). Superintendent, Government Printing. Retrieved from http://www.columbia.edu/itc/mealac/pritchett/ 00generallinks/macaulay/txt_minut e_education_1835.html

Maseko, K. and Mkhize, D.N. (2019) Translanguaging mediating reading in a multilingual South African township primary classroom. *International Journal of Multilingualism* 38 (2), 1–20. https://doi.org/10.1080/14790718.2019.1669608

Mbirimi-Hungwe, V. (2019) Stepping beyond linguistic boundaries in multilingual science education: Lecturer's perceptions of the use of translanguaging. *Southern African Linguistics and Applied Language Studies* 37 (1), 15–26. https://doi.org/10.2989/160 73614.2019.1598877

Panezai, A., Channa, L.A. and Bibi, B. (2022) Translanguaging in higher education: Exploring interactional spaces for meaning-making in the multilingual universities of Pakistan. *International Journal of Bilingual Education and Bilingualism*. https://doi.org/10.1080/13670050.2022.2124842

Probyn, M. (2006) Language and learning science in South Africa. *Language and Education* 20 (5), 391–414. https://doi.org/10.2167/le554.0

Rafi, A.S.M. (2020) Shortcomings of validating translanguaging without pedagogic focus in bilingual classroom. *TESOL Bilingual-Multilingual Education Interest Section (B-MEIS)*. http://dx.doi.org/10.5281/zenodo.4539753

Rafi, A.S.M. (2022) Pedagogical benefits, ideological and practical challenges and implementational spaces of a translanguaging education policy: the case of Bangladeshi higher education. PhD thesis, James Cook University. https://doi.org/10.25903/k2bf-7s18

Rafi, A.S.M. (2023a) Students' uptake of translanguaging pedagogies and translanguaging-oriented assessment in an ELT classroom at a Bangladeshi university. In R. Khan, A. Bashir, L.B. Basu and E. Uddin (eds) *Local Research and Glocal Perspectives in English Language Teaching: Teaching in Changing Times* (pp. 31–45). Springer Nature.

Rafi, A.S.M. (2023b) Creativity, criticality and translanguaging in assessment design: Perspectives from Bangladeshi higher education. In L. Hirsu, M. Nitecka Barche and D. Futro (eds) *Assessment and Creativity Through a Translingual Lens* [Special issue]. *Applied Linguistics Review* 15 (5), 1831–1859. https://doi.org/10.1515/applirev-2023-0086

Rafi, A.S.M. (2023c) Language weaponization, missed opportunities, and transformational spaces in Bangladeshi English departments: A biographical perspective. In K.C. Bryan and L.J. Pentón Herrera (eds) *Weaponising Language in the Classroom and Beyond* (pp. 13–34). De Gruyter.

Rafi, A.S.M. (2023d) The invention of multilingualism (David Gramling) and multilingual perspectives on translanguaging (Jeff MacSwan). *Applied Linguistics* 46 (2), 367–372.

Rafi, A.S.M. (2025) Bogged down ELT, bailed-out CLT?: Translanguaging steps in a context-sensitive response to Bangladesh's ELT crisis. *English Today*, 1–8. doi:10.1017/S0266078425000148

Rafi, A.S.M. and Morgan, A.M. (2021) Translanguaging and academic writing in English-only classrooms: Possibilities and challenges in English-only classrooms. In W. Ordeman (ed.) *Creating a Transnational Space in the First Year Writing Classroom* (pp. 17–40). Vernon Press.

Rafi, A.S.M. and Morgan, A.M. (2022a) Translanguaging as a transformative act in a reading classroom: Perspectives from a Bangladeshi private university. *Journal of Language, Identity & Education*. https://doi.org/10.1080/15348458.2021.2004894

Rafi, A.S.M. and Morgan, A.M. (2022b) Linguistic ecology of Bangladeshi higher education: A translanguaging perspective. *Teaching in Higher Education* 27 (4), 512–529. https://doi.org/10.1080/13562517.2022.2045579

Rafi, A.S.M. and Morgan, A.M. (2022c) Translanguaging and power in academic writing discourse. *Classroom Discourse.* https://doi.org/10.1080/19463014.2022.2046621

Rafi, A.S.M. and Morgan, A.M. (2002d) Blending translanguaging and CLIL: Pedagogical benefits and ideological challenges in a Bangladeshi classroom. *Critical Inquiries in Language Studies.*

Rafi, A.S.M. and Morgan, A.M. (2022e) A pedagogical perspective on the connection between translingual practices and transcultural dispositions in an anthropology classroom in Bangladesh. *International Journal of Multilingualism.* https://doi.org/10.1080/14790718.2022.2026360

Rafi, A.S.M. and Morgan, A.M. (2024) Translanguaging in instruction and pedagogic design: Promoting learner-centredness in a teacher-centred reading classroom of a Bangladeshi university. *Critical Inquiry in Language Studies* 21 (4), 447–470. https://doi.org/10.1080/15427587.2024.2425355

Song, K. and Cho, B.Y. (2018) Exploring bilingual adolescents' translanguaging strategies during online reading. *International Journal of Bilingual Education and Bilingualism* 24 (4), 577–594. https://doi.org/10.1080/13670050.2018.1497008

Sultana, S. (2014) 'Young adults' linguistic manipulation of English in Bangla in Bangladesh. *International Journal of Bilingual Education and Bilingualism* 17 (1), 74–89. https://doi.org/10.1080/13670050.2012.738644

Sultana, S. (2022) Translingual practices and national identity mediated in the semiotized digital spaces. *Australian Review of Applied Linguistics.* https://doi.org/10.1075/aral.21051.sul

Sultana, S., Dovchin, S. and Pennycook, A. (2015) Transglossic language practices of young adults in Bangladesh and Mongolia. *International Journal of Multilingualism* 12 (1), 93–108. https://doi.org/10.1080/14790718.2014.887088

Vaish, V. (2019) Translanguaging pedagogy for simultaneous biliterates struggling to read in English. *International Journal of Multilingualism* 16 (3), 286–301. https://doi.org/10.1080/14790718.2018.1447943

Vertovec, S. (2010) Towards post-multiculturalism? Changing communities, conditions and contexts of diversity. *International Social Science Journal* 6 (1), 83–95. https://doi.org/10.1111/j.1468-2451.2010.01749.x

6 Translanguaging as a Decolonial Pedagogy in English Medium Classrooms: Reclaiming Epistemic Identities in an Unequal Language Policy in Nepal

Prem Phyak and Nani Babu Ghimire

Introduction

Translanguaging has received growing attention as a pedagogical approach in multilingual contexts (Seals, 2021; Vaish, 2020). The existing knowledge indicates that teachers are adopting translanguaging pedagogy to support multilingual students in learning both languages (heritage, second and foreign) and academic content subjects (Creese & Blackledge, 2010; Cummins, 2019; Rajendram, 2023). As a dynamic, simultaneous and fluid language practice, translanguaging pedagogy refers to the deployment of students' total linguistic repertoire in learning spaces, activities and processes (García & Li, 2014; Li, 2018). Recent studies have focused on how translanguaging offers affordances for multilingual students to learn effectively by investing their diverse linguistic and semiotic resources and knowledge (Rajendram, 2023). However, how teachers resist oppressive EMI policies and reclaim their epistemic identities through translanguaging has not been much investigated, particularly in the Global South context. In other words, how teachers implement translanguaging to make their own and students' epistemic identities, grounded in diverse linguistic and cultural resources and knowledge, has not received much attention in the existing literature. The purpose of this chapter is to discuss how translanguaging serves as a 'decolonial pedagogy' (Wane & Todd, 2018) for multilingual teachers and students in EMI classrooms. We draw on the case of Nepal to examine how translanguaging not only creates interactional spaces for multilingual students and teachers but also serves as a decolonial response to reclaim their epistemic identities.

Building on the theories of decoloniality (Mignolo & Walsh, 2018) and translanguaging pedagogy (García & Kano, 2014; Li, 2020), we discuss how translanguaging offers affordances to multilingual teachers and students for reclaiming their epistemic identities in the pedagogical space of the classroom. We define epistemic identity as a discursively co-constructed positionality that recognises multilingual teachers and students as knowers in a learning space. Epistemic identities are locally situated and constructed through dialogical engagement with members of learning communities, representing diverse linguistic and cultural backgrounds. In this chapter, we discuss how multilingual learners and teachers reclaim their epistemic identities as knowers through a translanguaging pedagogy. We argue that translanguaging pedagogy should not be taken only as an approach for accessing knowledge in a dominant language, but rather be understood as a decolonial pedagogy that contributes to reclaiming the epistemic identities of multilingual teachers and students in pedagogical engagement. We begin this chapter with the theorisation of translanguaging as a decolonial pedagogy.

Translanguaging as a Decolonial Pedagogy

Building on the work of Cen Williams, educational linguists have defined translanguaging as multilingual speakers' 'flexible use of their linguistic resources to make meaning of their lives and their complex worlds' (García, 2015: 1). Translanguaging as a 'practical theory of language' focuses on how fluid and dynamic language practices 'transcend socially constructed language systems and structures to engage diverse multiple meaning-making systems and subjectivities' (Li, 2018: 27). Li Wei further argues that translanguaging problematises and extends beyond boundaries between linguistic and non-linguistic, as well as cognitive and semiotic systems (2018: 27). Rather than seeing multilingual abilities as a sum of separate named languages, translanguaging considers them as a holistic and integrated system of language practices that breaks linguistic boundaries, supporting the hegemonic dominance of standard language ideology. Lippi-Green (1994) defines standard language ideology as 'a bias toward an abstracted, idealized, homogeneous spoken language which is imposed from above and which takes as its model the written language' (1994: 166). Lippi-Green (1994) argues that the most salient feature of this ideology is 'the goal of suppression of variation of all kinds' (1994: 166). This ideology promotes a monoglossic mindset that misrecognises fluid and heteroglossic language practices of multilingual speakers as a 'legitimate language' (Bourdieu, 1991).

At the centre of translanguaging as a decolonial pedagogy lies its power to challenge the 'colonial matrix of power' (Quijano, 2007) constructed by standard language ideology. We understand decoloniality as a praxis of lifeways that challenges and transforms the coloniality of Western modernity, universalism and ideological homogeneity (Mignolo & Walsh, 2018). As a continual struggle to resist 'deficit ideology' (Gorski, 2011) against diverse epistemic practices of bi/multilingual speakers, decoloniality involves 'border thinking' (Mignolo & Walsh, 2011) that problematises the long-standing epistemic racism that Western modernity has constructed against the people in and from the Global South. From this perspective, a decolonial pedagogy is the pedagogy of respect and recognition, but not one of fear and deficit judgment based on standards, targets and rules that reproduce boundaries, domination and homogeneity. Translanguaging as a decolonial pedagogy first challenges the ideological construction of linguistic separatism for bi-/multilingual speakers, opening up spaces for diverse language and semiotic practices in pedagogical processes (Phyak *et al.*, 2023). Considering translanguaging as 'a transformative pedagogical tool', Yilmaz (2021) discusses how translanguaging pedagogy promotes bi/multilingualism, affirms identities and helps multilingual speakers to combat structural inequalities. Similarly, Sánchez *et al.* (2018) scrutinised three major purposes of translanguaging pedagogies: scaffolding instruction, checking students' knowledge and action and transforming inferior beliefs about multilingual practices.

While translanguaging contributes to students' understanding of lessons, Sah and Kubota (2022) have discussed how liberal translanguaging practices in EMI classes, in which teachers ideologically and politically select certain languages while avoiding others, can reproduce dominant languages, primarily English and the national language, in South Asia. In another study, drawing on Nepal's context, Sah and Li (2018) take a 'multilingual perspective' of translanguaging to discuss how language practices in EMI classes are not equal. In other South Asian countries, translanguaging in education has been discussed as a transformative and meaning-making pedagogy. In India, Anderson (2022) examined how teachers' and students' translingual practices in ELT classrooms resist and transform the 'English-only mantra' by creating fluid spaces for local languages. In Bangladesh, particularly in tertiary education, Saha and Jahan (2023) discuss how translanguaging allows ethnic minority students to construct a 'trans-identity'. Rafi and Morgan (2024) found that translanguaging serves as a 'transformative act' to engage university students in critical reading. Rafi and Fox (2021) illuminate the use of translanguaging as 'culturally responsive pedagogy' in Pakistan, while Mohamed (2020) considers translanguaging as a language practice that transcends linguistic and cultural boundaries in the Maldives. Focusing on teaching writing, Nihmathulla (2024) investigates the 'scaffolding role' of translanguaging in developing competency in writing in Sri Lanka. However, the use of translanguaging in the classroom is often constrained by oppressive systems. For example, Sharma (2018), in Nepal's context, observes that teachers may not embrace translanguaging fully in an institutionalised system (e.g. private EMI school) where 'openly using or advocating local languages in the classroom can jeopardise a teacher's employment' (2018: 81). While the structure is always a shaper of language practices to be used in schools, teachers can also exercise their agency to break monolingual linguistic boundaries (Phyak et al., 2022). Our focus in this chapter is to discuss how teachers who use translanguaging to make sense of their teaching-learning processes in a hegemonic EMI policy context counter a deficit ideology, thereby affirming their epistemic identity as knowers.

At the centre of translanguaging as a decolonial project lies the issue of 'epistemic access' (Makalela, 2015) and the engagement of learners with epistemic diversities. Makalela's (2015) work in South Africa demonstrates that translanguaging enables students to access school/official knowledge by bridging the gap between community/home and school epistemologies. He argues that by allowing students to bring their home language into the learning process, translanguaging pedagogy contributes to addressing epistemic inequalities created by monolingual policies. Heugh (2015) also argues that translanguaging as a pedagogical approach responds to schools' systemic failure to address the learning challenges of multilingual students. These scholars argue that translanguaging pedagogies bridge the gap between home and school epistemologies. In this chapter, we extend the role of translanguaging pedagogy beyond epistemic access to examine how teachers and students reclaim their epistemic identities through translanguaging pedagogies. This stance is informed by the decolonial theories that question the coloniality of hegemonic language ideologies, pedagogies and epistemologies.

Decolonial theories question the long-standing political and epistemological domination of Western colonial ideologies. Quijano (2007) conceptualises the notion of 'colonial matrix of power' to unpack how coloniality serves as a tool to reproduce Western European epistemologies and ideologies. Western modernity, capitalism, racism and epistemologies (the production of knowledge) are the major colonial matrices of power that invisibilise the other (non-Western and Indigenous) ways of thinking, knowing and doing. Decoloniality is unmasking, resisting and transforming the coloniality of Euro-Western ideologies and power relations they have constructed. In this chapter, we build on Walsh et al.'s (2021) idea of decoloniality as 'a kind of posture, attitude and an action' to theorise translanguaging and a decolonial pedagogy. Posture involves resistance, while attitude is related to one's ideological stance. Focusing on decoloniality as a political-epistemological project, Walsh et al. (2021) argue that decoloniality 'points to a kind of resistance and refusal, an insurgence and a resurgence, but also a re-existence' (2021: 341). Moreover, decoloniality is an action that creates space for alternative ways of knowing, being and doing. Action with an ideological stance forms a decolonial praxis that resists and transforms colonial ideologies, promoting new ways of thinking, knowing and being. Walsh *et al.* (2021) consider decolonial praxis as:

> the creation of ways of thinking, of ways of knowing, of ways of sensing, being, and living outside coloniality—outside or despite coloniality, and in its borders, its fissures, and its cracks. (2021: 341–342)

Building on this standpoint of decoloniality, we adopt translanguaging as a decolonial pedagogy: *a pedagogy that resists the coloniality of a monolingual ideology and a deficit perspective* and *engages both teachers and students in the creation and promotion of alternative ways of knowing, being* and *doing in learning spaces*. A decolonial pedagogy extends beyond epistemic access, focusing on resisting and transforming the long-standing ideological domination of monolingual pedagogies. It offers members of a learning community the agency to reclaim their epistemic identities by utilising diverse ways of learning, doing and being through language practices (Phyak *et al.*, 2022). In other words, translanguaging as a decolonial pedagogy not only helps students and teachers to engage with dominant languages and epistemologies but also and more importantly, engages them in reclaiming their identities as knowers (Phyak, 2023).

Context and Method of the Study

The data for this study are drawn from two public schools – Light and Dharmachakra (pseudonyms) – in Nepal. Both schools have introduced an English medium of instruction (EMI) policy from the 1st grade. The head teachers from both schools told us that they introduced the policy to compete with private schools and attract more students. Public schools are supposed to adopt a multilingual policy to address the linguistic, educational and cultural needs of students coming from diverse linguistic and cultural backgrounds. However, there is a growing tendency among public schools to adopt EMI policy (e.g. Phyak & Sah, 2022; Sah & Li, 2018). This tendency emerges mainly to compete with private schools and increase student enrollment (e.g. Ghimire, 2019, 2021). Light School, located in a rural village in eastern Nepal, is a primary school. More than 80% of students are bilingual Yaakthung indigenous. Their language practices are fluid – they predominantly speak Yaakthung at home and Nepali in the community and public places. Dharmachakra School is another public school included in this study. The school is situated in one of the rural municipalities in the hills of a mid-eastern district. The majority of the students are from the Tamang indigenous community. Some students are from Magar, Sunuwar, Thami and Dalit communities. Very few students are from the dominant caste group (Brahmins and Kshetri) whose mother tongue is the dominant language, Nepali. Among indigenous students, Tamangs predominantly speak Tamang at home and in the community.

Neither school have ever introduced a mother tongue education policy, nor do they have any plans to implement it in the future. The head teachers of both schools reproduce deficit views about students' mother tongues and support their decision to implement the EMI policy for 'a quality education' (Ghimire, 2024). They told us that parents are 'not interested in mother tongue education' and believe that 'mother tongues' are learned at home, but not in school. As key language policy actors for schools, both head teachers reveal that they are 'forced' to implement the EMI policy due to the private schools' EMI policy. In a series of informal conversations, they shared with us that they are not aware of how mother tongue-based multilingual education is implemented in a multilingual classroom, such as in their schools.

We collected the data from both schools using an ethnographic method. We observed language practices in the classroom. We observed ten classes each, taught by two teachers – Chandra and Dilman (pseudonyms), who teach both English and one of the content subjects, such as social studies, science and environmental studies. We audio-recorded all the classes we observed and took field notes to supplement the recorded data. Additionally, we interviewed both teachers to gather their perspectives on the use of translanguaging practices. The three interviews with each teacher, conducted in Nepali, were audio-recorded and transcribed. We also translated the interview data into English. However, we have not translated classroom data to show the naturally occurring translanguaging practices. We have used regular Roman script for Nepali and Roman bold with italics for Yaakthung and Tamang, respectively. The classroom data sets are presented and analysed as anecdotes and organised under two major themes: becoming and resistance and breaking the silence. These themes emerged from close readings of the data sets (observations, field notes and interviews) for each teacher. We treated each teacher as a unique case due to differences in their sociolinguistic backgrounds. First, we discuss how the teachers and students reclaim their epistemic identities through translanguaging pedagogy. Then, we focus on how the teachers justify the use of translanguaging, with an emphasis on the translanguaging stance.

Becoming a translingual teacher: Chandra's resistance against English monolingual pedagogy

Chandra has been teaching at Light School for more than two decades. As a primary-level teacher, he has taught almost all subjects. As a Yaakthung Indigenous teacher, he predominantly speaks Yaakthung at home and in the community. His language practices are fluid and cross the boundaries of three named languages, Yaakthung, Nepali and English.

After having a series of informal conversations with Chandra and his head teacher, the first author observed seven of his Grade 2 classes.

Lesson 1: Listen and say

In one of his classes, Chandra began his lesson on daily activities by asking two questions: *what time do you wake up? What do you do in the morning?* Most students remained silent because they did not understand the questions in English. Then, he asked students to look at the pictures in the textbook (Figure 6.1) and describe what's happening there. The entire class remained silent again, as students were unable to describe the pictures in English. They were talking about the pictures in Nepali. But when asked to express their understanding in English, they remained silent. After that, Chandra read the sentences from the textbook and asked students to reproduce each sentence after him, explaining the meanings of each word and sentence translingually. He asked them a series of questions in both Nepali and English. He began doing so by asking questions translingually:

- bihaan uthera ke garchau? What do you do in the morning?
- timiharu daant brush garchau? Do you brush your teeth?

Figure 6.1 Listen and say
Source: Curriculum Development Center

- kapaal korchau? Do you comb your hair?
- nuhaauchau? Do you take bath?

Chandra's translanguaging practice creates a space for students to position themselves as multilingual epistemic subjects. Breaking the silence created by monolingual English instructions, his translanguaging pedagogy allows students to bring their diverse knowledge about the topic of the discussion into the classroom. Chandra not only translated English texts into Nepali but also created epistemic spaces for students to diversify their understanding of the topic. For example, in their translingual practices, Yaakthung indigenous students shared their divergent knowledge about the activities they do in the morning while discussing the picture description activities as follows (bolded words are Yaakthung in Chandra's case and Tamang in Dilman's case):

Student 1: bihaan uthera **aangaa muraa haptung**. I wash my face after in the morning.
Student 2: ma ta kehee gardina. I do not do anything.
Student 3: mero maa burush chaina? I do not have a brush.
Student 4: teeth bhaneko **he:bobbaa**. Teeth are he:bobba.
Student 5: **pareele thekpaan kho:maa**. Comb hair with a paree.
Student 6: bath bhaneko **urumsingma**. chiso hunchha bihaan. Bath means urumsingmaa. It's cold in the morning.

Chandra's translanguaging practice in his questions serves as an invitation for students to diversify their knowledge about their morning activities. The above excerpt shows that the Yaakthung students invest their total linguistic repertoire to make their diverse sets of knowledge visible in the process of learning about the topic. The use of 'muraa' (face), 'haptung' (wash), 'he:bobbaa (teeth), 'paree' (comb), 'thekpaan' (hair), 'kho:maa' (comb) and 'urimsingma' (bathe) in the process of describing morning activities represents their epistemic identity as a knower of different concepts translingually. As seen in the above excerpt, Yaakthung students have invested their entire linguistic repertoire in understanding the meaning of the pictures by utilising their existing knowledge about their daily activities. Throughout the lesson, Chandra did not impose monolingual English instruction; instead, he motivated students to discuss their everyday knowledge in a translingual manner. By shifting away from a monolingual speakerhood, he moves between languages to facilitate students' diverse ways of knowing about the lesson topic.

After helping students describe their everyday activities, he engaged them in discussing how they would take care of their bodies. First, Chandra read aloud the question from the textbook and asked students to share how they would 'take care' of their body. He explained the question in Nepali and instructed them to express their understandings in Nepali and Yaakthung. Indeed, he encouraged them to utilise their comprehensive linguistic knowledge to describe the methods of caring for their bodies. Chandra knew that forcing students to use monolingual English would not help them to express and organise their knowledge about taking care of their bodies. So, he began by telling his own story translingually: *I take care of my body. ma mukh wash garchu (I wash my face). I brush my teeth daily. ma daant maahchu. I take bath. Bath bhaneko nuhaaunu. timiharu ke garchau? (Bath means nuhaaunu. What do you do?).* These examples encouraged students to naturalise their translanguaging practices in the classroom, thereby diversifying their knowledge about the topic. Initially, students struggled to understand what 'taking care of the body' meant. Chandra explained the concept by providing examples of how to maintain the body's 'cleanliness' and 'health' through a translingual approach. He talked about eating 'good food' and wearing 'clean clothes' translingually, including the features of Yaakthung, Nepali and English. Then, students shared the activities they would do to take care of their bodies as follows:[1]

Student 1: ma ta paani khaanchu. I drink water.
Student 2: ma **tak** ra **pi:nu** khaanchu. I eat rice and milk.
Student 3: ma **faaksaa** khaanchu. I eat pork.
Student 4: safaa lugaa laauchu. I wear clean clothes.

While Student 1 talked about drinking 'paani' (water), Students 2, 3 and 4 used **'tak** ra **pi:nu'** (rice and milk), **'faaksaa'** (pork) and 'safaa lugaa' (clean clothes), respectively.

The use of knowledge of all languages (Yaakthung, Nepali and English) converts Chandra's English language classroom into a 'translanguaging space' (Li, 2011), where students from both Indigenous and non-Indigenous backgrounds can invest their diverse epistemologies to make sense of the topic of discussion. Building on students' existing knowledge, Chandra encouraged students to participate in classroom activities translingually by scaffolding their interactions and existing knowledge translingually. For example, he engaged students in discussing about **'tak'** (rice), **'pi:nu'** (cow milk) and **'faaksaa'** (pork) (all Yaakthung words) to understand the importance of healthy food for a healthy body. For example, he told students that 'pi:nu' (cow milk) provides vitamins and makes you strong in Nepali, Yaakthung and English simultaneously. Chandra concluded the lesson by asking students to write down three good things they do at home to take care of their bodies, using a translational approach that mixed and alternated the features of Nepali and English.

Lesson 2: Before going to school

The next day, Chandra focused on engaging students in describing what they would do before going to school. He started the lesson by asking students to look at the pictures (Figure 6.2) and describe what

Figure 6.2 Before going to school
Source: Grade 2 textbook of Curriculum Development Center

'Bunny' was doing. He first described who Bunny was in English, followed by Nepali and read the following text from the book:

> This is Bunny, a little rabbit. Bunny gets up in the morning. He takes breakfast and drinks a glass of milk. He reads books for an hour. Then, he eats his morning meal. He dresses him up around nine. At nine thirty, he goes to school.

Chandra asked students to read aloud after him and described the meaning of each word and sentence in Nepali. As he helped students understand the meanings of each word and the whole text by using translanguaging, he linked the major words to their personal and social contexts. For example, 'breakfast' was described as 'khaajaa' (snack) and 'meal' was interpreted as 'khaanaa'. He also used Yaakthung words such as '**tak**' (meal) and '**pok**' (gets up) as an invitation to students to bring their diverse knowledge while using translanguaging in the classroom. Chandra's translanguaging created the classroom as a space of diverse knowledge where students and teachers reclaim their epistemic identities. While describing the pictures, students not only shared their own knowledge from their everyday life but also asked several questions about the concepts that did not make sense to their personal and social life:

> **Student 1:** Sir, breakfast bhaneko gaajar ho? (Sir, is breakfast a carrot?)
> **Chandra:** No. Breakfast bhaneko bihaan ko khaaja. (Breakfast is morning snacks.)

Student 2: ma ta breakfast khaadina. ma bhaat maatra khaanchu. (I don't eat breakfast. I eat luch only.)
Student 3: Sir, esto table chaina haamro gharmaa. haamee ta piraa ma baser khaanchau. (Sir, we do not have such a table at our home. We eat sitting on a handmade mat.)
Student 4: Sir, ghaanti ma ke laako cha? (Sir, what's on the neck?)
Chandra: That's a tie.

In Chandra's class, translanguaging offers a critical space for students to question the relevance of the knowledge in the textbook. They not only asked questions to understand the meanings of key words such as 'breakfast' but also contributed to the discussion by bringing their diverse knowledge into the classroom. For example, Student 2 shared that she does not eat 'breakfast'; rather, she eats 'bhaat' (rice/meal). In Nepal, the major meals in the morning and evening are called 'bhaat/khaanaa' (a meal which usually includes rice, curry, lentil soup, etc.). The first author's observation shows that students cannot make epistemic diversity visible in the classroom if English-only instructional strategies are adopted. The concern of Student 3 about the material condition of the home, as displayed in the pictures in the textbook, shows the power of translanguaging to challenge the relevance of formal knowledge in students' lives. The student compared the materials on the images with those available in his own house and shared with the class that he does not have a 'table', so he has meals sitting on a 'peeraa' (a handmade mat). Most houses in the local community do not have a dining table. Unlike what is displayed on the figure in the textbook, people in the local community do not have a separate study room for their children. Most students do not have a room with a table, they do their homework sitting on a handmade long mat, locally known as a *gundri*.

After helping students to describe their morning activities, Chandra focused on explaining the menu of a school (Figure 6.3). He began by asking students to look at the pictures and describe the food items. Chandra allowed them to use all languages. Here are some responses from the students:

pi:nu, dudh, **tak**
kola, keraa, **telaase**
kheer, ciuraa, **saambek**,
andaa, juice, apple

Students used Nepali, English and Yaakthung simultaneously to describe the images in the textbook. Chandra translated Nepali and Yaakthung words into English and asked students to use all of them, not only to make sense of the images but also to contribute to the construction of knowledge. Yaakthung students described milk, rice, banana and beaten rice as 'pi:nu', 'tak', 'telaase' and 'saambek', respectively. Other students

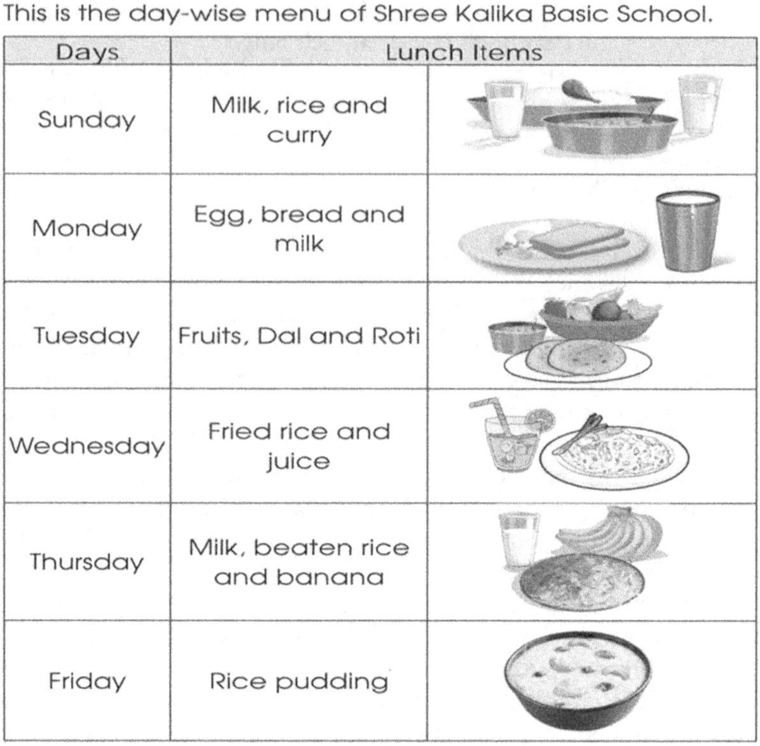

This is the day-wise menu of Shree Kalika Basic School.

Days	Lunch Items	
Sunday	Milk, rice and curry	
Monday	Egg, bread and milk	
Tuesday	Fruits, Dal and Roti	
Wednesday	Fried rice and juice	
Thursday	Milk, beaten rice and banana	
Friday	Rice pudding	

Figure 6.3 Menu
Source: Grade 2 textbook of Curriculum Development Center

used 'dudh', 'kolaa', 'keraa', 'kheer', 'ciuraa' and 'andaa' for milk, banana, rice pudding, beaten rice and egg, respectively, in Nepali. Rather than using their knowledge about Yaakthung and Nepali to understand the food items in the menu given in the textbook, students diversify their knowledge about the topic (menu) through translanguaging. The use of Yaakthung and Nepali words is not just a translation of English words given in the textbook, but rather they represent students' existing knowledge and worldviews about food items.

In Chandra's class, both teacher and students reclaim their epistemic identities through translanguaging pedagogy that offers affordances for trans-semiotic practices. They were building on the images from the textbook to incorporate diverse knowledge about food items from their homes and communities. Rather than worrying about the textual meanings of the food items in English, they co-constructed knowledge by investing their translanguaging competencies. In the process of positioning themselves as translingual speakers, students also questioned what the food items were in the textbook. For example, one student asked what 'lunch' was and some other students asked what a 'menu' meant. Chandra responded to each question translingually and allowed students to ask further questions:

Chandra: lunch bhaneko deusko ko khaanaa. (Lunch means afternoon meal.)
Student 1: tara hamee deuso kei khaadauna ta sir. (But we do not have an afternoon meal.)
Student 2: Haamro school ma menu chaina ta sir. (We do not have a menu, sir.)
Chandra: Hamro ma chaina. Tiffin lyaaunu parcha. (We do not have one. You bring tiffin.)
Student 2: Sir, hamee ta gharmai khaayera auchaau lunch (Sir, we eat lunch at home.)
Chandra: What do you eat? Ke khanchau? (What do you eat? What do you eat?)
Student 2: Bhaat (rice)
Student 3: [pointing to the picture of juice] Sir, yo ke ho? (What is this, sir?)
Chandra: Juice.
Student 3: Hoina sir yo pipe jasto? (No sir, this, like a pipe?)
Chandra: tyo juice chusne pipe ho? (Is this a pipe to drink juice?)
Student 4: Sir, pipaa ho. (Sir, that is a pipaa)

In the above excerpt, the language practices of both the teacher and the students break monolingual linguistic boundaries to co-construct their identities as experts on the topic. In the process of learning about a 'menu' and 'lunch items', students asked Chandra several questions in a translingual manner. Their translanguaging practices were primarily mediated by the images presented in the textbook. Students' questions about what 'lunch' means and their sharing that they would eat 'lunch' at home, not in school, challenge the epistemology of 'lunch' as an 'afternoon meal' as described by Chandra and the textbook. They also questioned the meaning of a 'menu' and why their school did not have a menu. Then, Chandra used the words from both Nepali and English to help students make sense of the food items in the menu.

Chandra's translanguaging approach allowed students to become interactive, not just for understanding the food items in English but also for the diversification of knowledge. For example, Student 4 used the term 'pipaa' (used for both Nepali and Yaakthung) for a straw in the picture (which is described as a pipe by Chandra). During classroom discussion, students also talked about how a 'pipaa' is made by using their personal lived experiences translingually. Student 4 talked about the use of a bamboo 'pipaa' to drink **'tongbaa'** (a jar to drink a local wine) in their family. Tongbaa is one of the main drinks that the Yaakthung Indigenous people in Nepal make and drink. It is a locally fermented wine made from a blend of rice, millet, corn and wheat. Similarly, students also discussed how the 'bread' that Chandra described as a 'roti' did not make sense to them. In the village, students have never seen such bread. Chandra finally used 'paauroti' that helped them make sense of the bread in the image. In the local community, English 'bread' is known as 'paauroti'. What was interesting was that some Yaakthung students could not associate the 'roti' in the picture with the roti in their daily lives. One student from the example said, 'Sir, yo ta **loto** ho?' In Yaakthung, a flat bread, as mentioned in the picture, is called '**loto**'. For Yaakthung students, 'roti' is a 'selroti', a ring-shaped deep-fried bread.

Breaking the silence: Dilman's translanguaging resistance

Dilman has been teaching in Dharmachakra schools for two decades. He is known as a 'good teacher' by his students. His students told the second author that Dilman is 'friendly' and helps them understand the lesson as much as he can. As a local, Dilman has a deeper understanding of students' linguistic, cultural and social backgrounds. Most of his students are from the Tamang indigenous community. He is a multilingual Tamang. At the primary level, he teaches social studies, science and the environment. Before the implementation of the EMI policy, his school had introduced Nepali textbooks, so he used Nepali predominantly in his classes. However, he told the second author that he should also use Tamang to help most of his students learn effectively. The second author observed seven classes. We have analysed two of his classes to understand how he and his students use translanguaging to reclaim their epistemic identity as knowers of diverse sets of knowledge.

Lesson 1: Kitchen & Utensils (I)

After some informal discussions, the second author observed Dilman's class in the 1st grade. As the school has now implemented the EMI policy, Dilman is asked to teach Social Studies in English. All students are given an English textbook. Like in other days, Dilman checked whether his students had brought the textbook with them and asked them to open the page to find the topic of the lesson 'Kitchen & Utensils'. He then wrote the topic on the board and asked students to read it aloud. But students remained silent. They could not read the words. How could they read such difficult words in the 1st grade? They had just started learning English in school. To help students pronounce the topic, Dilman spelt both 'kitchen' and 'utensil' and asked them to follow him.

Dilman: K-I-T-C-H-E-N U-T-E-N-S-I-L
Students: K-I-T-C-H-E-N U-T-E-N-S-I-L
Dilman: What does utensil mean? Utensil bhaneko ke ho?
Students: thaahaa chhaina. (We do not know.)
Dilman: Bhaansaamaa use hune things such as thaal, batuko, karaahi, kasaudi aadi. Now, read with me.

Students:	Ok, sir.
Dilman:	P-L-A-T-E, B-O-W-L
Students:	P-L-A-T-E, B-O-W-L

Dilman would have to teach the spelling and pronunciation of each word throughout the lesson. He used translanguaging to provide diverse knowledge of the items associated with the kitchen and utensils. Rather than translating 'utensil' into Nepali, Dilman diversified the concept by using items such as thaal, batuko, karahi and kasaudi (all kitchen items) in Nepali. He then gave examples of some utensil items in English. Dilman did not require his students to describe utensil items in English first. He provided examples of different items in Nepali and English and asked a series of questions about each item. His goal was to help students associate each item with 'utensil'. His translanguaging strategy not only breaks students' silence in the classroom but also creates a safe space for Tamang indigenous students to visibilise their knowledge in their mother tongue.

Dilman:	What is a plate? What is a bowl?
Students:	[Silent]
Dilman:	Plate means thaal. **dimri.**
Dorje:	**Hyanglaa dimri khaarbaa mulaa.** Haamro gharamaa thaala chha (There is a plate in our house).
Dilman:	Ok. plate bhaneko bujhyau? (What do you mean by plate?)
Students:	Yes, sir. **Hyangli khaarbaari kaan chaalaa.** Haami thaalmaa bhaat khaanchhau (We eat rice in plate).
Dilman:	Listen to me. Bowl means batuko. **manjya.**
Dolma:	**Ngaalaa manjya jaajaa mulaa.** Mero batuko saano chha (My bowl is small).
Dilman:	Batukomaa ke garchhau? (What do you do in a bowl?)
Students:	**Ngaam manjyari daal thunglaa.** Batukomaa daal khaanchhau. We eat daal in a bowl.
Tilak:	Ma ta batukomaa khaajaa khaanchhu. (I eat breakfast in a bowl.)

When Dilman asked questions in English, students remained silent. Their silence, however, does not reveal their deficit identity; rather, it expresses their resistance to the monolingual ideology reproduced by the school. Students did not respond to Dilman's questions in English. However, when he translanguaged (e.g. plate means thaal, dimri), students began to respond to him. Dilman's use of 'plate', 'thaal' (Nepali) and 'dimri' (Tamang) simultaneously invited students to contribute to the discussion by drawing on their diverse knowledge of each utensil item in Tamang, Nepali and English. Dorje described 'dimri' (plate) as an item in their kitchen. When Dilman asked students whether they understood what a plate was in both English and Nepali, the students replied, 'Yes, sir'. What was interesting was that a group of students said, **'Hyangli khaarbaari kaan chaalaa. Haami thaalmaa bhaat khaanchhau'** (we eat rice in a plate) in both Nepali and Tamang. While using translanguaging in his class, Dilman positioned himself and his students as multilingual knowers with diverse ways of learning and knowledge about the topic of discussion.

Dilman's translanguaging approach creates a space for Tamang students to make their linguistic and cultural knowledge, as well as their diverse ways of learning, visible in the classroom. Dilman translates purposely to diversify the knowledge construction process in the school. For example, he added **'dimri'** and **'manjya'** (both Tamangs) for plate and bowl, respectively, to the discussion to give students the impression that their knowledge of Tamang would be recognised as a legitimate language in the classroom. Consequently, Tamang students contributed to the discussion by linking their existing knowledge about 'plate' and 'bowl' in their home language, Tamang. Dolma used both **'manjya'** (Tamang) and 'batuko' (Nepali) to make sense of 'bowl' by bringing her knowledge into the discussion. She used **'jaajaa'** (small) to describe the size of the bowl in the family. Towards the end of the lesson, Dilman focused on engaging students in a discussion about the use of each item in their personal lives. Rather than asking questions in English only, he adopted a translanguaging approach to engage students in discussions. This approach helped students position themselves as multilingual epistemic subject that does not reproduce knowledge but co-construct it. Using a translanguaging approach, students said that they would eat 'daal' and 'khaajaa' in a batuko translingually. Dilman concluded his lesson by asking students to write about the different utensil items they are used for as homework.

Lesson 2: Kitchen and utensils (II)

The next day, Dilman focused on students' understanding of different utensil items. He began by checking whether they had done the homework. Students had not finished their homework. They told Dilman that they did not know how to do the homework translingually. Then, he asked them to answer his questions:

Dilman:	What is a pan?
Students:	(Silent)
Dilman:	P-A-N bhaneko ke ho? (What do you mean by a pan?)
Students:	(Silent)
Dilman:	Do not know? Listen! Pan means karaahi. Do you have a pan at your home?
Students:	Yes, sir.
Dilman:	Karaahimaa haami ke garchhau? (What do we do in a pan?)
Students:	tarkaari pakaauchhau. (We cook vegetables in a pan.)
Dilman:	What is a pot?
Dorje:	**Pumbaa. Ghyaampaa.** Thulo bhaandaa.
Dilman:	Yes. But here, P-O-T means kasaudi. Kasaudimaa ke garinchha ni? (What do you do in a kasaudi?)
Students:	Bhaat pakaainchha. (We cook rice in a pot.)

Bhuwan:	**Haamro gharamaa thulo kasuadi chha** (There is a large pot at my house).
Dorje:	Kasaudiri **hyanglaa maamse baab daailaa silaa.** haamro hajuraamaale kasaudimaa jaand pakaaunu hunchha. (Our grandmother usually cooks jaand in a large pot.)
Mina:	**aamse kasaudiri sewaa daailaa.** Mero aamaale kasaudimaa bhaat pakaaunu hunchha. (My mother cooks rice in a pot.)
Dilman:	Ok. timiharulaai yi words ko artha aauchha ta? (Do you know the meaning of these words?)
Students:	aauchha.
Dilman:	Now, read and write these words in your notebook. Aba padhera lekhata.
Students:	Ok, sir.

Dilman first checked whether his students knew the meaning of 'pan' in both English and Nepali. But they remained silent, not because they did not understand the question, but because they had never heard 'pan' as one of the utensil items. Then, he gave an equivalent word 'karaahi' and asked whether they had a 'pan' in the home. Most students reported having one. Dilman's translanguaging approach allowed students to describe the use of each utensil item. Throughout the lesson, students feel comfortable contributing to the discussions translingually. As seen in the above excerpt, students diversify their knowledge of various utensil items by investing their existing knowledge beyond the textbook. For example, Dorje used 'pumbaa' (Tamang) and 'ghyaampaa. Thulo bhaandaa' (Nepali) and Dilman used 'kasaudi' for pot. The diverse knowledge and ideas in the class made it productive and engaging. As seen above, Dilman and his students co-construct their identities as the knowers of diverse knowledge of the topic. Most students said that a pot is used to cook rice, but some students, such as Dorje, shared that her grandmother cooks 'jaand' (local booze) in a pot. Dilman recognises all knowledge as a pedagogical resource in his class. He ended his lesson by ensuring that students had understood the concept of utensil and asked them to read and write the words in their notebooks.

Reclaiming Epistemic Identities Through a Translanguaging Stance

We discussed with Chandra and Dilman to understand how they would justify the use of translanguaging in the classroom. Both consider translanguaging as a relevant approach to support students in understanding the lesson and allow them to utilise their existing knowledge in the learning process. In a series of discussions, they have shown their 'translanguaging stance' (García *et al.*, 2017; Menken & Sánchez, 2019) and multilingual awareness in their pedagogies. Their ideological position resists the long-standing coloniality of monolingual English as the most appropriate pedagogical approach in multilingual schools. In defending the relevance of his own pedagogical approach, Chandra argued:

> I don't see the relevance of teaching English in English. How can my students in the first grade learn only in English? I am a local teacher. I know the problems and needs of students. Students speak different languages. We need to start from what students know. We need to create an environment where they can speak. If they are allowed to speak, they do not learn [English]. So, I always use students' mother tongues in my class. Students are happy and enjoy the class.

Chandra claims that the method of 'teaching-English-in-English' has no relevance in his context. Rather than seeing students' existing knowledge of mother tongues as a problem, Chandra embraces them as a resource for creating a learning environment where they feel free to speak. Most importantly, Chandra claims that students are unable to learn content in English if they are not allowed to talk in the classroom. Chandra recognises students' 'right to speak' (Norton, 1997) as a principal requirement for a happy and joyful class. He maintains that using multiple languages in the classroom helps students become 'confident' in their learning and 'makes classes diverse in terms of knowledge, languages and cultures'. What is more striking in his translingual stance is that Chandra positions himself as a knower of the topic of the discussion. During informal interactions with the first author, Chandra consistently argued that translanguaging practices in the classroom position him as 'a person with the knowledge of multiple languages, communities and cultures'. Giving the example of **'tak'** (meaning 'rice' in Limbu), he mentioned that he purposely uses Yaakthung, along with Nepali, to demonstrate his knowledge about languages and cultures and encourage students to apply their existing knowledge in the learning process. For him, translanguaging allows both teachers and students to co-construct knowledge 'by recognising diverse sets of knowledge and perspectives as an integral aspect of an effective pedagogy'.

Translanguaging pedagogy transforms Dilaman's students' silence into engaging classes where diverse knowledge and ways of learning are acknowledged and valued. In a series of interactions with the second author, Dilman criticised the relevance of the EMI policy in his school. For him, the EMI policy has created 'multiple challenges' for both teachers and students. He recounted that the EMI policy has positioned teachers as 'weak' and 'helpless' in teaching content subjects such as Social Studies. He told the second author that since he and other teachers in the school were not hired to teach content subjects in English, it is now 'unfair' to force them to do so. Justifying the relevance of translanguaging pedagogy, he argued that 'both teachers and students need to use home languages in the classroom to utilise their knowledge about topics related to community fully'. His translanguaging stance reflects 'critical multilingual language awareness' (García, 2015).

> Our community is multilingual. So, our pedagogies cannot be monolingual. Students of speak their mother tongues [Nepali and Tamang] in class because they are dominant languages in their everyday life. So, I teach them in Nepali and the Tamang language. I don't have to waste time learning in English. Students easily understand what I say in both Tamang and Nepali. They can share their knowledge and experiences about the topic in their mother tongues.

Dilman's justification for the relevance of translanguaging pedagogy recognises the importance of students' home languages in his social studies class. He contends that imposing a monolingual policy of instruction is a waste of time, as it bars students and teachers from sharing their knowledge and experiences in the learning process. Dilman's stance highlights the importance of translanguaging pedagogy in reclaiming the identities of both students and teachers as a source of knowledge, rather than as a deficit subject as constructed in EMI policy (Phyak & Sah, 2022).

Discussion and Conclusion

Translanguaging pedagogies in Dilman's and Chandra's classes question, resist and transform the hegemonic domination of monolingual English pedagogy. The ideology of monolingual English instruction is historically linked with the coloniality of English as an international language. Critical applied linguists have examined how the monolingual supremacy of English both as a subject of teaching and a medium of instruction reproduces colonial ideologies that support capitalism and Western cultures (Canagarajah, 1999; Pennycook, 1994; Phillipson, 1992; Phyak, 2024; Sah & Li, 2018). Both Chandra and Dilman resist the supremacy of monolingual English pedagogy, which their schools have legitimised through their translanguaging pedagogies. Their translanguaging pedagogies are not only used to help students interact with their classmates and teachers, but also to diversify knowledge and ways of knowing in the classroom. Both students and teachers visibly invest their identities as a source of knowledge in the school due to the naturalisation of translanguaging pedagogies. Both teachers and students co-construct their epistemic identities as knowers, but not just the reproducers of official/textbook knowledge. Translanguaging pedagogies in Chandra's and Dilman's classes go beyond interactional space and construct the classroom as a diverse epistemological space where students and teachers bring their home, community and cultural knowledge into discussions.

The translanguaging pedagogy discussed in this chapter can be interpreted as a 'decolonial pedagogy' (Odugu, 2022) on two principal grounds. First, as Li Wei and García (2022) have argued, Chandra's and Dilman's pedagogies 'abandon the focus on named standard languages and engage fully with their students' full repertoire of features and meanings' and allow teachers to use their 'agency and autonomy to develop effective and inclusive pedagogical practices for the classroom' (2022: 322). Translanguaging as a decolonial pedagogy does not characterise teachers and students as deficit subjects based on their abilities in separate named languages (Odugu, 2022). As Li Wei and García (2022) argue, translanguaging pedagogy is not about 'adding more named languages into the classroom practice but is fundamentally reconstitutive and transformative of the power relations between the named languages in society' (2022: 322). The cases of translanguaging pedagogy discussed in this chapter add another dimension of a decolonising pedagogy – epistemic identity – to the existing knowledge in translanguaging pedagogy. Rather than positioning students as deficit subjects, both Dilman and Chandra recognise them as epistemic subjects with diverse sets of knowledge (linguistic, cultural and societal) and skills that can offer a space for building an inclusive learning environment, mainly for Indigenous students. Phyak (2023) has discussed how translanguaging pedagogy allows Indigenous youth to show their identity as epistemic subjects in the context of unequal language education policy. Both Yaakthung and Tamang students in Chandra and Dilman's classes not only feel safe interacting with their classmates and teachers but also position themselves as sources of knowledge in the translanguaging classroom space. Rather than focusing on access to knowledge codified in dominant languages (Nepali and English), translanguaging pedagogies in both cases have afforded Indigenous youth with the opportunities to share and promote their knowledge about Indigenous cultures, beliefs, environment and languages.

Second, translanguaging pedagogy, as discussed in the chapter, is also a 'decolonial praxis' (Walsh et al., 2021). Walsh et al. (2021) discuss 'decolonial praxis as theory, in other words, theorising practice' disrupts and cracks the 'colonial matrix of power' (Quijano, 2007) and promotes 'other ways of learning, of knowing, of thinking, of sensing, of being, of doing that are interconnected' (2021: 343). Decolonial praxis involves an action for change, one that recognises linguistic and epistemological diversities as integral to inclusive, equitable and transformative education. Translanguaging pedagogy is an action for resistance and transformation, but not just a random use of fluid language practices to address specific learning problems. Another dimension of decolonial praxis in translanguaging pedagogy involves critical multilingual awareness of teachers. Both Chandra and Dilman have justified the relevance of their translanguaging pedagogies in their classroom. They do not view their translanguaging practices as an indicator of deficit ability, but rather as a source of knowledge to diversify the process of co-constructing knowledge in the classroom. Teachers have shown their multilingual awareness through their 'translanguaging stance' (Menken & Sánchez, 2019). Reflecting on their own translanguaging pedagogies, both Chandra and Dilman take a strong translanguaging stance to resist monolingual ideologies in teaching English as a subject and using it as a medium of instruction. Their translanguaging stance demonstrates their knowledge of local linguistic ecology and the learning needs of their students. Translanguaging as decolonial pedagogy, as discussed in this chapter, resists the hegemonic power matrix of English monolingualism and the narrow official knowledge circulated through textbooks.

We conclude by arguing that translanguaging, particularly in content subject classrooms, acknowledges teachers' struggles to create a space for bi-/multilingual students to reclaim their identity as multilingual epistemic subjects. This implies that translanguaging pedagogies in EMI classrooms should focus on diversifying epistemologies to recreate the classroom as a safe and inclusive space for multilingual students.

References

Anderson, J. (2022) *Learning from Indian Teacher Expertise: A Policy and Practice Report for Educational Organisations in India*. University of Warwick.

Bourdieu, P. (1991) *Language and Symbolic Power*. Harvard University Press.

Canagarajah, A.S. (1999) *Resisting Linguistic Imperialism in English Teaching*. Oxford University Press.

Creese, A. and Blackledge, A. (2010) Translanguaging in the bilingual classroom: A pedagogy for learning and teaching? *The Modern Language Journal* 94 (1), 103–115. https://doi.org/10.1111/j.1540-4781.2009.00986.x

Cummins, J. (2019) The emergence of translanguaging pedagogy: A dialogue between theory and practice. *Journal of Multilingual Education Research* 9 (13), 19–36. https://files.eric.ed.gov/fulltext/EJ1310558.pdf

García, O. (2015) Critical multilingual language awareness and teacher education. In J. Cenoz, S. May and D. Gorter (eds) *Language Awareness and Multilingualism: Encyclopedia of Language and Education* (pp. 263–280). Springer.

García, O. and Kano, N. (2014) Translanguaging as process and pedagogy: Developing the English writing of Japanese students in the US. In J. Conteh and G. Meier (eds) *The Multilingual Turn in Languages Education: Opportunities and Challenges* (pp. 258–277). Multilingual Matters.

García, O. and Li, W. (2014) *Translanguaging: Language, Bilingualism, and Education*. Palgrave MacMillan.

García, O., Johnson, S.I., Seltzer, K. and Valdés, G. (2017) *The Translanguaging Classroom: Leveraging Student Bilingualism for Learning*. Caslon.

Ghimire, N.B. (2019) English as a medium of instruction: Students' discernment in Nepal. *Education and Development* 29, 146–160.

Ghimire, N.B. (2021) Teacher identity in English Medium Instruction schools of Nepal. *Journal of NELTA Gandaki* 4 (1–2), 42–56.

Ghimire, N.B. (2024) Unravelling the dynamics of English Medium Instruction (EMI) policy in community schools: A critical ethnographic exploration of teacher ideology, identity and agency. Unpublished doctoral dissertation, Tribhuvan University, Faculty of Education, Kathmandu.

Gorski, P.C. (2011) Unlearning deficit ideology and the scornful gaze: Thoughts on authenticating the class discourse in education. *Counterpoints* 402, 152–173. http://www.jstor.org/stable/42981081

Heugh, K. (2015) Epistemologies in multilingual education: Translanguaging and genre – companions in conversation with policy and practice. *Language and Education* 29 (3), 280–285.

Li, W. (2011) Moment analysis and translanguaging space: Discursive construction of identities by multilingual Chinese youth in Britain. *Journal of Pragmatics* 43 (5), 1222–1235.

Li, W. (2018) Translanguaging as a practical theory of language. *Applied Linguistics* 39 (1), 9–30. https://doi.org/10.1093/applin/amx039

Li, W. and García, O. (2022) Not a first language but one repertoire: Translanguaging as a decolonizing project. *RELC Journal* 53 (2), 313–324.

Lippi-Green, R. (1994) Accent, standard language ideology, and discriminatory pretext in the courts. *Language in society* 23 (2), 163–198.

Makalela, L. (2015) Translanguaging as a vehicle for epistemic access: Cases for reading comprehension and multilingual interactions. *Per Linguam: A Journal of Language Learning Per Linguam: Tydskrif vir Taalaanleer* 31 (1), 15–29. https://hdl.handle.net/10520/EJC170988

Makalela, L. (2022) *Not Eleven Languages: Translanguaging and South African Multilingualism in Concert*. Walter de Gruyter.

Makoni, S. and Pennycook, A. (2007) *Disinventing and Reconstituting Language*. Multilingual Matters.

Menken, K. and Sánchez, M.T. (2019) Translanguaging in English-only schools: From pedagogy to stance in the disruption of monolingual policies and practices. *TESOL Quarterly* 53 (3), 741–767. https://doi.org/10.1002/tesq.513

Mignolo, W.D. and Walsh, C.E. (2018) *On Decoloniality: Concepts, Analytics, Praxis*. Duke University Press.

Mohamed, N. (2020) Transcending linguistic and cultural boundaries: A case study of four young Maldivians' translanguaging practices. In B. Paulsrud, Z. Tian and J. Toth (eds) *English-Medium Instruction and Translanguaging* (pp. 77–93). Multilingual Matters.

Ndhlovu, F. and Makalela, L. (2021) *Decolonising Multilingualism in Africa: Recentering Silenced Voices from the Global South*. Multilingual Matters.

Nihmathulla, M.C.B. (2024) Translanguaging influenced writing in different languages: A case of multilingual students at secondary education in Sri Lanka. *The English Teacher* 53 (2), 73–90.

Norton, B. (1997) Language, identity, and the ownership of English. *TESOL Quarterly* 31 (3), 409–429.

Odugu, D.I. (2022) Translanguaging as decolonial praxis: Pedagogic and epistemic thrusts in the politics of official knowledge. *Journal of Multilingual Theories and Practices* 3 (1), 27–52. https://doi.org/10.1558/jmtp.21483

Pennycook, A. (1994) *The Cultural Politics of English as an International Language*. Longman.

Phillipson, R. (1992) *Linguistic Imperialism*. Oxford University Press.

Phyak, P. (2023) Translanguaging as a space of simultaneity: Theorizing translanguaging pedagogies in English medium schools from a spatial perspective. *The Modern Language Journal* 107 (1), 289–307.

Phyak, P. (2024) Producing the disciplined English-speaking subjects: Language policing, development ideology, and English medium of instruction policy. *Language in Society* 53 (2), 321–343.

Phyak, P. and Sah, P.K. (2022) Epistemic injustice and neoliberal imaginations in English as a medium of instruction (EMI) policy. *Applied Linguistics Review*. https://doi.org/10.1515/applirev-2022-0070

Phyak, P.B., Sah, P.K., Ghimire, N.B. and Lama, A. (2022) Teacher agency in creating a translingual space in Nepal's multilingual English-medium schools. *RELC* 53 (2), 431–451. https://doi.org/10.1177/00336882221113950

Phyak, P., Sánchez, M.T., Makalela, L. and García, O. (2023) Decolonizing multilingual pedagogies. In C. McKinney, P. Makoe and V. Zavala (eds) *The Routledge Handbook of Multilingualism* (pp. 223–239). Routledge.

Quijano, A. (2007) Coloniality and modernity/rationality. *Cultural Studies* 21 (2–3), 168–178. https://doi.org/10.1080/09502380601164353

Rajendram, S. (2023) Translanguaging as an agentive pedagogy for multilingual learners: Affordances and constraints. *International Journal of Multilingualism* 20 (2), 595–622. https://doi.org/10.1080/14790718.2021.1898619

Rafi, M.S. and Fox, R.K. (2021) Translanguaging as a culturally responsive pedagogy for teaching English to multilingual Pakistani university students. *SPELT Quarterly* 36 (1), 2–17.

Rafi, A.S.M. and Morgan, A.M. (2024) Translanguaging as a transformative act in a reading classroom: Perspectives from a Bangladeshi private university. *Journal of Language, Identity & Education* 23 (4), 543–558.

Sah, P.K. and Li, G. (2018) English medium instruction (EMI) as linguistic capital in Nepal: Promises and realities. *International Multilingual Research Journal* 12 (2), 109–123.

Sah, P.K. and Kubota, R. (2022) Towards critical translanguaging: A review of literature on English as a medium of instruction in South Asia's school education. *Asian Englishes* 24 (2), 132–146.

Sah, P.K. and Li, G. (2022) Translanguaging or unequal languaging? Unfolding the plurilingual discourse of English medium instruction policy in Nepal's public schools. *International Journal of Bilingual Education and Bilingualism* 25 (6), 2075–2094.

Saha, M. and Jahan, A. (2023) Translanguaging as trans-identity: Insights from ethnic minority students in Bangladesh. In S. Sultana, M. Naushaad Kabir, Z. Haider, M. Moninoor Roshid, and M. Obaidul Hamid (eds) *Language in Society in Bangladesh and Beyond: Voices of the Unheard in the Global South* (pp. 157–175). Routledge.

Sánchez, M.T., García, O. and Solorza, C. (2018) Reframing language allocation policy in dual language bilingual education. *Bilingual Research Journal* 41 (1), 37–51.

Seals, C.A. (2021) Benefits of translanguaging pedagogy and practice. *Scottish Languages Review* 36, 1–8. https://tinyurl.com/3pf28k9k

Sharma, S. (2018) Translanguaging in hiding: English-only instruction and literacy education in Nepal. In X. You (ed.) *Transnational Writing Education* (pp. 79–94). Routledge.

Vaish, V. (2020) *Translanguaging in Multilingual English Classrooms*. Springer.

Walsh, C., Mignolo, W., Herrero, F. and Tinker, T. (2021) What do we mean by "decoloniality"? *Journal for Cultural & Religious Theory* 20 (3), 341–360.

Wane, N.N. and Todd, K.L. (eds) (2018) *Decolonial Pedagogy: Examining Sites of Resistance, Resurgence, and Renewal*. Springer.

Yilmaz, T. (2021) Translanguaging as a pedagogy for equity of language minoritized students. *International Journal of Multilingualism* 18 (3), 435–454. https://doi.org/10.1080/14790718.2019.1640705

7 Equity, Awareness, and Engagement: Translingual Practices in the Linguistic Landscape of Early Childhood Classrooms in the Maldives

Naashia Mohamed

Introduction

Research into the visible language of public signage, or the study of Linguistic Landscapes (LL), highlights the linguistic diversity of societies and the translingual nature of our semiotic repertoires (Gorter *et al.*, 2021). The LL of a place signals which languages are prominent and valued in that space, and influences people's language ideologies and linguistic behaviour (Gorter, 2018). It can be expected that the majority language of a language community will be represented more prominently in public signage, in alignment with any official language policies (Cenoz & Gorter, 2006). Since the original framework proposed by Landry and Bourhis (1997), LL research has expanded to explore the implicit ideologies and the linguistic hierarchies promoted through the visible, audible and otherwise textualised languages in the public sphere (Shohamy & Gorter, 2009). A growing trend within the LL field has been to focus on the LL of educational spaces, or schoolscapes. The concept of schoolscape is defined by Brown (2012: 282) as being a 'school-based environment where place and text, both written (graphic) and oral, constitute, reproduce and transform language ideologies'. While the schoolscape can be a source of input for language learning (Malinowski *et al.*, 2020), it can also index the social positioning of people based on their relationships with the languages represented in the space (Dagenais *et al.*, 2008) Although the school context should be a place where students can see themselves semiotically represented, enabling them to feel a sense of belonging, studies (e.g. Brown, 2018; Huebner, 2006) in this emerging field suggest that dominant societal languages overshadow others, exacerbating linguistic and social inequalities.

Much of the early research on LL focused on the characteristics or meanings of signs and a quantitative analysis of linguistic representation in the public sphere. More recently, there have been calls to move beyond this and to examine the interrelationships between policies that lead to the production of signage, how people engage with signs and the actions that result from this (Seargeant & Giaxoglou, 2020). Others have proposed the use of LL as a site for critical, social justice-oriented pedagogies to boost multilingual practices (Malinowski et al., 2020) and valorise students' languages and cultures (Zapata & Laman, 2023). Responding to these calls, the proposed chapter focuses on the schoolscapes in the context of early childhood education (ECE) in the Maldives and aims to explore:

- The extent to which early childhood schoolscapes reveal linguistic and social equities.
- Learners' awareness of the languages represented in classrooms.
- How teachers and learners engage with the visible language of the classroom.

Early Childhood Education

ECE provides young children with strategies to develop the social, cognitive and emotional skills needed to become lifelong learners. Language and literacy skills are foundational at this stage, as children learn to communicate, express and understand feelings. Language skills are linked not only to children's cognitive and conceptual development but are also vital for their social, emotional and cultural awareness and understanding (Finders et al., 2023) and are a reliable indicator of future academic achievement (Brown, 2014). Additionally, ECE settings play a crucial role in developing children's identities and safeguarding their belonging – two important aspects of a child's social and personal development that support children in achieving a positive sense of who they are and feeling that they are valued and respected as part of a community (Erwin et al., 2022).

In linguistically diverse societies, ECE providers have an important role to play in supporting childhood multilingualism. These learning spaces should support language acquisition in the official language(s) of the society, while being responsive to the children's home languages (Barac et al., 2014; Cummins, 2001; De Houwer, 2021). Children draw on the language and literacy practices of their families to make sense of their lives and their connectedness to other people. These funds of knowledge (Moll et al., 1992) are indispensable sources of rich cultural and social learning that teachers should draw on to provide linguistically and culturally responsive education (Alim et al., 2020; Hedges, 2022). A wealth of research evidence confirms that incorporating children's home languages in educational settings in culturally sustaining ways supports their learning experiences and language development (Peleman *et al.*, 2022; Sierens & Van Avermaet, 2013), improves their self-esteem, nurtures positive identities and develops learners' abilities to navigate discrimination (Alim & Paris, 2017; Crisfield, 2021).

English Dominance in Education

Despite the benefits of multilingualism, monolingual practices continue to dominate in education, even in multilingual contexts, often privileging colonial languages and failing to recognise the value of linguistic diversity (Anderson, 2018; Fashanu *et al.*, 2020). The rise of English as a global language has intensified this mindset, with English becoming the favoured medium of instruction at all levels of education. Referring to the context of China, Hu (2008) characterises the phenomenon as 'a runaway juggernaut that is rattling across the country with fierce velocity' (2008: 195). Giri *et al.* (2024) describe the phenomenon of 'English mania' (2024: 24) as 'the greatest linguistic tsunami' (2024: 24) the world has ever seen. This 'English fever' (Choi, 2023: 670) or the fervent desire to become proficient in English at almost any cost arises from a belief that the global language represents modernity, progression and technology (Annamalai, 2004), thereby regarding it as a privileged form of linguistic capital (Bourdieu, 1986) that will provide a passport for upward social and economic mobility (Sah & Li, 2018). However, research suggests that the hasty adoption of EMI has declined the quality of education (De Witt, 2011), threatened to silence local languages (Mohanty, 2019; Shamim, 2024) and exacerbated social stratification (Sah, 2022). When children are subjected to learning a language that is unfamiliar to them, they acquire this language at the expense of their mother tongue, impoverishing their linguistic repertoire (Skutnabb-Kangas, 2010). As a result of this subtractive multilingualism, children begin to develop low self-esteem and regard their languages and cultures as being inferior (Mohanty, 2017).

Translingual Practices

Sidelining home languages may have originally been based on the false notion that full immersion in English and the prohibition of other languages from the classroom would hasten language acquisition, as it would prevent other languages from interfering with the learning of English (Spada, 2015). However, translingual practices have always been a natural part of multilingual societies (Canagarajah, 2013; Sugiharto, 2015) and despite English-only educational policies, there often arose a state of 'guilty multilingualism' (Coleman, 2017: 31), where home languages were secretly drawn upon to supplement English. The foregrounding of multilingualism and translingual practices in recent educational approaches has highlighted how multilinguals draw flexibly on all of their linguistic resources and use them as appropriate to context, interlocutor and interaction (Anderson & Lightfoot, 2021). The concept of translingualism recognises that language users engage in 'fluid and creative adaptation of a wide array of semiotic resources' (Hawkins & Mori, 2018: 2) as they communicate in 'complex layers of entangled and intertwined repertoires' (Dovchin et al., 2024: 1). As a result, there has been a revival of support for the use of home languages in the classroom, even by Western scholars, with the recognition that learning may be enhanced through translingual practices (Macaro, 2015) as it legitimises students' linguistic identities and valorises their agency (Dovchin et al., 2015; Sah & Kubota, 2022).

This study is framed by a weak translanguaging theoretical lens (García & Lin, 2017; Turner & Lin, 2020), which acknowledges the existence and sociopolitical weight of named languages while advocating for pedagogical flexibility that softens these boundaries in practice. Rather than viewing languages as completely fluid or ignoring their distinctiveness, this approach recognises the importance of strategic, purposeful use of home and school languages to enhance learning, affirm identity and disrupt rigid language hierarchies. It positions translanguaging not simply as a spontaneous linguistic phenomenon, but as a deliberate pedagogical practice that supports inclusion and equity in multilingual classrooms.

While the strong version of translanguaging proposes that multilinguals do not operate within discrete languages at all, the weak version acknowledges these named categories while advocating for more porous and fluid boundaries between them. Turner and Lin (2020), for example, argue that the goal of translingual pedagogies should be to disrupt linguistic hierarchies, not to erase language identities. They contend: 'Rather than having translanguaging as a tool for learning a named language, we need to inverse this and see named languages as a tool for expanding our holistic linguistic repertoire' (2020: 431).

Through this lens, translanguaging is seen as a pedagogical stance that fosters deeper understanding by using students' home languages to support content learning in English (Lewis et al., 2012), building stronger home-school connections and enriching metalinguistic awareness. Yet, as Hornberger and Link (2012) point out, classroom practices often privilege standard or literary forms of language over vernacular, oral or multimodal forms. This study, therefore, recognises the need, as Mendoza (2022) argues, for teachers to be intentional and responsive, designing curricula that broaden linguistic horizons and index inclusion through the purposeful use of languages in the classroom.

Sociolinguistic Context

The Maldivian people are believed to have inhabited the Indian Ocean archipelago since the fifth century. Maldivians link their identity to their language. They call their nation *Dhivehi Raajje*, which literally means Dhivehi country and refer to themselves as *Dhivehin* – the people of Dhivehi. Dhivehi is an Indo-Aryan language, believed to have descended from Maharashtri Prakrit and is linguistically related to Marathi, Konkani and Sinhalese languages, although not mutually intelligible with them (Fritz, 2002). Although many languages have left their mark on Dhivehi over time, it has remained the dominant language of the people, although there is a clear language shift taking place among the younger generations, in favour of English (Mohamed, 2020). Other languages that have a significant role to play in the community are Arabic, due to its religious significance for this Muslim nation and Hindi, due to the impact of popular media from neighbouring India. Anecdotal evidence suggests that in recent years, the languages associated with the growing number of expatriate workers (e.g. Bengali, Malayalam, Nepali) are beginning to impact societal language use.

To protect the nation's linguistic heritage and raise its status, the Constitution of 2008 declared Dhivehi as the official language of the Maldives. Subsequently, in 2011, the Dhivehi Language Act stipulated that Dhivehi must be prioritised over other languages across all domains. It required prioritising Dhivehi in all forms of communication, including public signage. Among its stipulations was that when public signs are multilingual, the Dhivehi script should be written first and should be the more prominent one.

In the educational domain, English as a medium of instruction (EMI) was introduced in the early 1960s, initially in selected government schools. This created a dual system of education where Dhivehi-medium schools were seen to be less prestigious than their EMI counterparts (Lutfi, 2011). The demand for EMI grew to the extent that gradually all schools adopted EMI and since 2000, there have been no schools that provide education in the national language. From the time children start preschool at the age of three till they graduate from secondary school at 18 years, they are educated through EMI. Recognising the importance of starting a child's education in a language that they are familiar with, in 2012, the Preschool Management Act stipulated that at the preschool level, Dhivehi would be the language of instruction. Nevertheless, empirical evidence from preschools suggests that enactment of the mandated policy has been less than ideal (Mohamed, 2019) and that translanguaging practices that limited the use of Dhivehi were the norm in teachers' discourse (Mohamed, 2016). This chapter aims to extend current knowledge of the context by exploring the LL of preschool classrooms to uncover the implicit ideologies and the linguistic hierarchies promoted through the visible environment and examine how children and teachers engage with the languages in these spaces.

Method

I draw on material gathered for an earlier project, which took place between January–September 2017 in a preschool in Maale, the capital city. The project was inspired by linguistic ethnography (Copland & Creese, 2015), focusing on the relationship between language policy and language practice and gathering data through observations in classrooms supplemented by interviews with key stakeholders. While formal interviews with teachers were not part of the analysis for this chapter, I do draw on the information gathered from informal talks with teachers, while I took photographs and made field notes about the placement of signs in the classrooms. As Blommaert (2013) notes, this is an important part of the fieldwork of ethnographic observation.

In this preschool, children were exposed to three languages through its curriculum. Dhivehi was expected to be the language of instruction, but children would also learn English and Arabic as additional languages. The preschool operated in three sessions of three hours each. The oldest children (aged 5–6 years) attended the first session in the morning. The second group of children (aged 4–5 years) attended the next session, which ran from late morning to early afternoon. The youngest children (3–4 years) attended the late afternoon session. Children spent most of their time in their assigned classrooms, following a very structured timetable, but had designated times when they could enjoy unstructured play outdoors. Data for this study focused on two classrooms: one for children aged 5–6 years old and one for children aged 4–5 years old.

Data and Participants

There were 22 children enrolled in each of the classes. They were all of Maldivian ethnicity and were roughly equally divided in terms of gender. The teachers were both Maldivian, female, in their 20s and were qualified and experienced early childhood educators. I visited the classrooms at various points during the study period, each visit lasting approximately three hours. During these visits, data were gathered in three ways. I photographed all the displays and signage in each classroom. This included displays on the classroom walls, which were generally permanent or semi-permanent during the duration of the study. I also photographed whiteboards and children's workbooks, which, although more transient, were important ways children were exposed to language. I video-recorded whole-class teaching sessions that typically occurred at the start of each day. I also had conversations with children as they were engaged in learning and playing and recorded these through audio recordings on my phone or as fieldnotes that were written immediately after each conversation. These conversations are typically aimed to understand children's awareness of vocabulary-related key concepts taught or displayed in the learning space. I spoke to children in Dhivehi and asked them questions such as 'What's this poster about?', 'Can you tell me the colours here?', 'What do you see here?'. If children responded with the keywords in English (which they typically did), I would ask them to say it in Dhivehi, with a question like 'Do you know what it's called in Dhivehi?'. I focused on key concepts displayed in the classrooms: days of the week, colours, animals, parts of the body, shapes, emotions and numbers. In this chapter, I will focus on 250 photographs that were gathered from these two classrooms: 12 recordings of whole-class teaching, which were on average 18 minutes in duration; 10 recordings of interactions with children, which were between 5–12 minutes in length; and my fieldnotes from the observations.

Analysis Procedures

The first step in analysing the data was to decide on the unit of analysis for the photographed images. I followed Backhaus (2007: 66) in this regard, taking 'any piece of text within a spatially definable frame' as the unit of analysis. This included signs that labelled different parts of the classroom (e.g. 'Creative Corner'); collective displays of student work, where each child had a named space where a selective piece of work was displayed; posters of alphabets and key vocabulary; child-created work based on their current focus of learning; classroom routines and reminders; a notice board summarising topics of focus for each learning area for the week; and a single or double page spread of children's workbooks. Each unit was categorised for linguistic code, semiotic value and function. Inspired by the work of Cenoz and Gorter (2006) on analysing language hierarchy and relationships; Kress and Van Leeuwen's (2006) analysis of multimodal data; and Tran's (2022) use of semiotics to make meaning of signs based on their placement, I developed the coding scheme summarised in Figure 7.1 for analysing the photographic data. Each image was then analysed for its linguistic code, semiotic value and function. This meant that each image was analysed for the visible languages in them, their order, appeal and saliency; how the placement, composition and material of the sign impacted intended and implied meaning; as well as what the intended function of each sign was meant to be. Based on this, a holistic judgment was made on the equitable representation of languages within each unit of analysis and more broadly, in each classroom.

To illustrate this process, consider the two images in Figure 7.2. Both contain images and multilingual text (linguistic code) and both are displayed on the wall (location). The image on the left was shown in a place of prominence at the front of the classroom (position). The image on the right was placed on a side wall (location), fairly high up on the wall, so that it was eye level to an adult, but not easily readable by children (visibility). The image on the left is an example of a summary of weekly learning areas. We see two languages, Dhivehi and English, represented here (linguistic code: multilingual). The labels in yellow suggest that both languages are given equal prominence in terms of size, colour and placement (saliency). However, we see that the learning for Maths is the concepts of *tall* and *short* and the focus of Environmental Studies (ES) is *My Family*

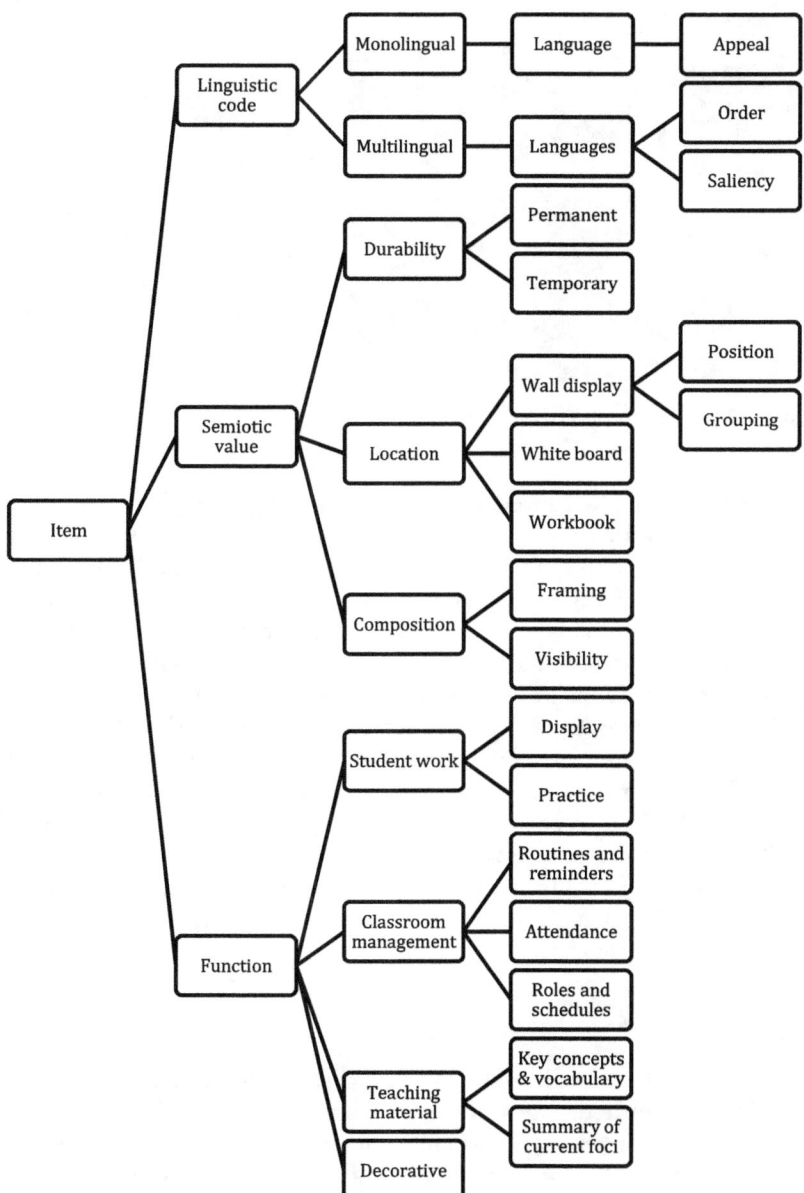

Figure 7.1 Coding scheme for photographic data

(function: teaching material). These concepts are presented solely in English (monolingual), suggesting that they will be taught with that focus. The linguistic saliency in this image is biased towards English.

The image on the right shows a reminder of prayer (function: classroom management: reminder). It is printed on regular white printing

 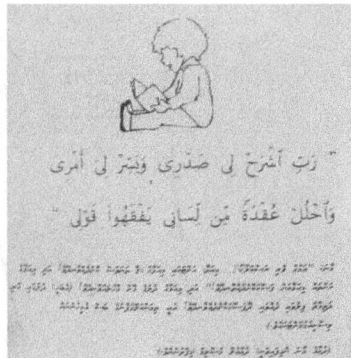

Figure 7.2 Two examples of wall displays

paper and not on coloured card like most other displays (durability, appeal). It is multilingual (linguistic code), with the actual prayer in Arabic text written in a larger font and presented first (order). The Dhivehi translation is arguably too small to draw the attention of children (visibility), making it less likely to be read. The visual image is that of an outline of a child reading a book. These characteristics make this item less appealing and show evidence of Dhivehi being represented inequitably.

The video recordings were transcribed with non-verbal data (such as items being drawn on the board, actions of the children, etc.) recorded within the transcription. These, along with documentation of my interactions with children, recorded through fieldnotes, were analysed for language choice, function, translingual patterns and linguistic salience. Interactions with children were also coded for language awareness to determine if they were able to name concepts in each of the three languages being taught.

Findings

In this section, I will first provide a distributional description of the multilingual characteristics of the photographs. I then present findings related to teacher and student engagement with the LL and children's awareness and understanding of languages used in this context.

Representation of multiple languages

The quantitative analysis of the photographs showed that the two classrooms were translingual spaces with three languages – English, Dhivehi and Arabic – visibly represented, albeit to varying degrees (see Figure 7.3). Both classrooms had teaching materials such as alphabet charts in all three languages. Classroom routines and reminders were

Figure 7.3 The multilingual landscape of the classroom

primarily in English, with some bilingual displays. Often (as seen in Figure 7.3), the English text preceded both Dhivehi and Arabic and in some cases, was presented in larger/more prominent ways. Each classroom had a 'Reading Corner' where children could help themselves to a small selection of picture books. The books were all in English.

Of the 250 photographs in the sample, 205 included English, 67 included Dhivehi and 14 included Arabic. In 151 cases, only one language was present on an individual item. This was typically English. Figure 7.4 shows two examples of monolingual displays in the classrooms. On the left, you see the space where children mark their attendance every day. As they walk into their classroom, they pick their name and place it on the board. The image on the right-hand side of Figure 7.4 is a display created by children of the human body, labelling the parts in Dhivehi.

In 32 of the 250 photographs, both English and Dhivehi were used. The English-Dhivehi translingual images were typically wall displays of routines and reminders or teaching materials depicting key concepts being learned. Figure 7.5 shows an example of classroom displays which were in English and Dhivehi. This image shows a teacher-created display made on

Figure 7.4 Two examples of monolingual displays

a poster board focusing on the weather that was placed at the front of the class, giving it prominence in terms of positioning. The use of mixed media, including colourful glitter paper and cotton wool, made it appealing for children. While the size of the lettering in both languages is comparable, in three of the four quarters, the English text is placed first and the Dhivehi text is placed below the image.

As noted earlier, the photographs were taken of wall displays and student workbooks. In comparison to the 32 Dhivehi-English images, only nine of the photographs showed Dhivehi-Arabic translingualism. This included mostly reminders of prayers that were or workbook activities completed by the children. Figure 7.6 illustrates the translingual use of Dhivehi and Arabic in a child's workbook, where instructions are given in Dhivehi for a task where children are practising their Arabic words and letters.

However, most of the work that children did in their workbooks was in English. Figure 7.7, for example, shows three examples focusing on the concepts of colour, good habits in practising personal hygiene and emotions, where only English is used.

When children illustrated a concept (such as my family, or my favourite person), they then explained their drawing to the teacher, who wrote down the verbatim of their description of the picture. Figure 7.8 captures

Equity, Awareness, and Engagement   133

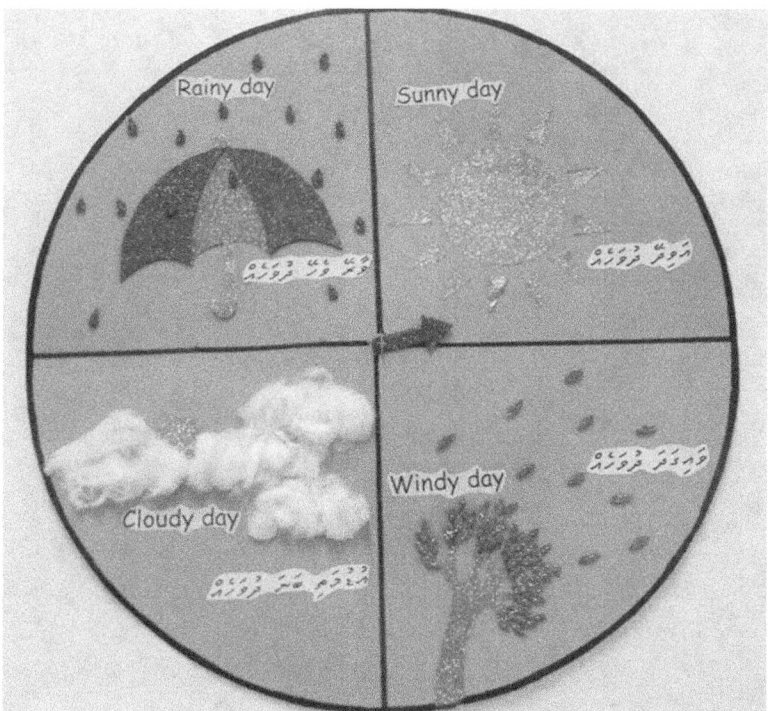

Figure 7.5 An example of a Dhivehi-English display

Figure 7.6 An example of the translingual use of Dhivehi and Arabic in children's workbook

Figure 7.7 English-only activities in workbooks

four examples where both English and Dhivehi are used. The double-page spread shows that the child has written the date and title of each work in English. The teacher's transcribed description, based on the child's explanation, is written in Dhivehi. The three smaller examples of teachers' transcriptions show the translingual nature of descriptions, using words such as 'daddy' and 'beach', as well as statements such as 'he is my c[o]usin' within the Dhivehi utterance.

Both classrooms had a large space dedicated to showcasing student work. As Figure 7.9 shows, in these spaces, children's names were displayed in English and any attempt at writing on the children's work was also typically in English.

In other instances where children's names were displayed (e.g. attendance board), the names were mostly in English. Where the displays were

Figure 7.8 Translingual descriptions of drawings

Figure 7.9 Display of children's work

Figure 7.10 Bilingual attendance board

bilingual, the writing in Dhivehi was much smaller and less salient than the English, as seen in Figure 7.10.

Engagement with classroom displays

I select two extracts from classroom interactions to present how teachers and learners interacted with the LL of the classroom. In Extract 1, the teacher (T) is going through the process of eliciting the date and day of the week before starting to discuss the plan for the day. The teacher repeatedly uses the English word 'date' rather than the Dhivehi equivalent 'thaareekh' and says the numbers to write the date ('13.2.2017') in English, interestingly using the number of the month, rather than the name to do this. Despite the obvious opportunity to provide both forms of the day of the week ('Monday' and 'Hoama'), she only uses the English form. Going through the schedule for the day, again, the English is prioritised over the Dhivehi.

Extract 1

	Transliteration (Dhivehi; English)	Observed action	Translation (Dhivehi; English)
T	Miadhu mee kon dhuvaheh? Kobaa miadhuge date akee?	T stands facing semi-circle of children gathered in front of white board.	What day is it today? What is today's date?
Cs	Thirteen.	Children chorus date	Thirteen.
T	Rangalhu. Hingaa liyelan dho **date**.	T walks to white board and starts writing.	Good. Let's write the date.

	Transliteration (Dhivehi; English)	Observed action	Translation (Dhivehi; English)
	Kihineh liyaanee miadhuge **date**? Thirteen. Dot. Two. Dot. Two thousand seventeen.	Begins writing the date, talking as she does this.	How do we write today's **date**? Thirteen. Dot. Two. Dot. Two thousand seventeen.
	Aan. Esha bunebala miadhu ge **date** akee kobaa?	T turns towards children.	Yes. Esha tell me, what is today's **date**?
C1	Thirteen. Dot. Two. Dot. Two thousand seventeen.	Child repeats date.	**Thirteen. Dot. Two. Dot. Two thousand seventeen.**
T	Aan Nabeel bunebala miadhu mee kon dhuvaheh. Mithanun.	T selects another child. T points to wall display of day of the week, as she asks C2 the question.	Yes. Nabeel can you tell me which day it is, from here.
C2	Monday		Monday
T	Aan varah rangalhu. Miadhu mee **Monday**. Hingaa liyelan. **Spelling** kiyaalachchey thikudhin **Aunty** liyaa iru.	Turns towards white board and begins writing 'Monday'	Yes, very good. Today is **Monday**. Let's write that. You should all call out the **spelling** while **Aunty** [I] write it.
Cs	M-O-N-D-A-Y	Children call out spelling of Monday	M-O-N-D-A-Y
T	Aan then hingaa miadhuge dhuvas **plan** kollan. Mihaaru aharemen mi **assembly** in ais, **sharing time** mioh nimenee. Dhen dhaanee kon kameh kurah, Izaan?	Points to wall display titled 'our day' as she talks through the plan for the day.	Yes. Now let's **plan** today. We have come back from **assembly** and we are now finishing **sharing time**. What will we now go to do, Izaan?

The teacher also elicits the day of the week from one child, referring her to the chart on the wall (Aan Nabeel bunebala miadhu mee kon dhuvaheh. Mithanun) and encourages the class to spell out the word as she writes on the board. This was another lost opportunity to teach the same concept in Dhivehi, as the chart she was referring to had both languages on it.

In Extract 2, the teacher is practising children's knowledge of shapes and colours through an illustrated storytelling task. The teacher consistently uses English words for all shapes and colours (e.g. square, blue) and the children use English names of animals (e.g. elephant, giraffe) to try to guess what the teacher is drawing on the board. At the end of the extract, we also see that the teacher begins to use parts of the body in English. This extract is illustrative of the translingual nature of classroom language. The children follow the translingual pattern set by the teacher. Despite the language policy stipulating that Dhivehi is the language of instruction and the linguistic landscape of the classroom being largely monolingual, the ease with which both the children and the teacher engage in translanguaging indicates that this was the norm for them. It is concerning, however, that key concepts are consistently introduced and practised in English. The teacher makes no attempt to teach the colour and shape words in Dhivehi. Neither does she teach nor elicit names of animals in Dhivehi. While translingual practices may be the norm in interactions between multilinguals, teachers should be introducing concepts and key vocabulary in the language of instruction and encouraging children to use their full linguistic repertoire, rather than prioritising one linguistic form.

In this extract, we also see the teacher referring to herself in the third person, calling herself Aunty, the label used for preschool teachers in the Maldives, rather than using the personal pronoun. As will be evident in later extracts, the children also do this when interacting with me. The use of illeism is expected in parental language with very young children, but unusual with children at preschool.

Extract 2

	Transliteration (Dhivehi; **English**)	Observed action	Translation (Dhivehi; **English**)
T	Balaa kuchen miothee kon **shape** eh? Varah kuda **shape** eh miothee miadhu. Mee kon **shape** eh?	T stands facing semi circle of children gathered in front of white board. She is holding up a small orange square of cardboard.	Look children, what **shape** is this? Today we have a very small **shape**. What **shape** is it?
Cs	Square		Square
T	Rayyan kon **shape** eh mee?	Points to boy who is standing up	Rayyan, what **shape** is this?
C1	Square		Square
T	Kon kula egge **square** eh mee?	Asks whole class	What colour is this **square**?
Cs	Orange		Orange
T	Ammar kon kula eh mee?	Points to boy who is distracted	Ammar, what colour is this?
C2	Orange		Orange
T	O.K. Mee kon kula eh?	Holds up a blue rectangle	O.K. What colour is this?
Cs	Blue		Blue
T	**Blue** kula dho. **Blue** kulaige koacheh?		**Blue**, right? **Blue** what?
Cs	Rectangle.		Rectangle.

	Transliteration (Dhivehi; **English**)	Observed action	Translation (Dhivehi; **English**)
T	Rectangle.		Rectangle.
	Mee kon **shape** eh?	Holds up pink triangle	What **shape** is this?
Cs	Triangle		Triangle
T	Kon kulaegge?		What colour?
Cs	Pink		Pink
T	Mee kon kula eh?	Holds up red circle, along with the triangle	What colour is this?
Cs	Triangle		Triangle
T	Mee **triangle** tha?	Puts away triangle and holds up circle only	Is this a **triangle**?
Cs	Circle		Circle
T	Kon kulaegge?		What colour?
Cs	Red		Red
T	Aan **Aunty** miulhenee **shape** thah **board**uga thaikollaigen **story** eh kiyaidheyn ingey. Kon kujjeh **story listen** kollaanee madu madun indhegen?		Yes. **Aunty** [I] am going to attach the **shape**s to the **board** and tell you a **story**. Who is going to sit quietly and **listen**?
	Thikudhin bune bala **Aunty** mi kurahanee koacheh?	Begins drawing on the board	Can you tell me what **Aunty** [I] am drawing?
Cs	**Elephant** eh **Giraffe** eh **Elephant** eh noon **Dinosaur** eh **Monster** eh Aan **monster** eh	Children calling out various guesses, talking over each other	An **elephant** A **giraffe** Not an **elephant** A **dinosaur** A **monster** Yes, a **monster**
T	Mee **monster** eh ingey? **Monster body**ga mihiree koacheh? Balaa **monster** ge **nose**? **Monster** ge **nose**.	Points to the triangular shaped nose of the monster	This is a **monster**, okay? What is on the **monster**'s **body**? Look at the **monster**'s **nose**. **Monster**'s **nose**.

Awareness of key language

As stated earlier, I engaged with children during my observations, primarily to see their language awareness and use. Extract 3, shows an interaction between me (R) and a child (C) called Amr. He was colouring in shapes and I tried to get him to name some of the shapes and the colours he was using. As is evident from the extract, his default language in naming shapes and colours was English and he seemed to be unaware of the Dhivehi terms. He did later go on to name some colours in Dhivehi (not included in this extract), but was unable to name any shapes in Dhivehi, while he was confident about naming both concepts in English.

Extract 3

	Transliteration (Dhivehi; **English**)	*Translation* (Dhivehi; **English**)
R	Koachegga this kula jassanee?	What are you colouring?
C	**Shape** thakeh mee	These are **shapes**.
R	Eki kahala battan dho? Mithanun kon battameh Amr ah emme kamudhanee?	All kinds of shapes, right? Which of these shapes is your favourite, Amr?
C	Thibunee?	What do you mean?
R	Mi bunee mi thanuga huri hurihaa battan thakuge therein Amr ah emme kamudhanee, Amr ah amme reethee kon battameh hey?	I'm asking you, of the many shapes here, which ones are your favourite, which ones do you like the best, Amr?
C	Amr ah emme reethee **circle, no, star**.	Amr [I] like **circle** the best, **no, star**.
R	Ehentha? Ahannah ves varah kamudhey **star**. Amr ah engey tha **star** ah Dhivehin kiyanee kon nameh kan?	Really? I also like the **star** a lot. Amr, do you know what **star** is called in Dhivehi?
C	(shakes head)	(shakes head)
R	Thari dho?	Star, right?
C	(nods)	(nods)
R	Kon kulaeh thi jassanee thareega?	What colour are you using for the star?
C	**Star** ga? Mee **white** kula. E ee **stars** hunnanee **white** kulaiga nun. Reygandu feneynun **night sky** ga **twinkle twinkle** koh.	On the **star**? This is **white** colour. Because **stars** are **white**, right? [You] see them in the **night sky**, going **twinkle twinkle**.

Extract 4 is an interaction between myself and a girl called Lua. We were sitting near a poster which displayed numbers 1–20, with corresponding numbers of different animals, to encourage counting. I asked Lua to count and she began straightaway in English. I asked her to then count in Dhivehi and she did do so, but slipped into English to claim that there were 'three rabbits'. Even though I used the term 'musalhu', she did not pick up the Dhivehi term and continued using the English name. She described her rabbit at home as being pink and when prompted to say the colour in Dhivehi, she gave the incorrect name ('fehi' rather than 'fiyaathoshi').

Extract 4

	Transliteration (Dhivehi; **English**)	Translation (Dhivehi; **English**)
R	Lua ah engey dho gunan?	Lua, you know how to count, right?
C	Aan.	Yes.
R	Alhe gunaala bala mi than (points to numbers chart with animals)	Try counting these
C	**One, two, three. Three rabbits.**	**One, two, three. Three rabbits.**
R	Varah molhu. Mifaharu hingaa Dhivehin gunaalan.	Very clever. This time, let's count in Dhivehi.
C	Ekeh, dhey, thineh.**Three rabbits.**	One, two, three. **Three rabbits.**
R	Aan. Thin musalhu.	Yes. Three rabbits.
C	Lua geyga onnaane **pink rabbit** eh.	Lua [I] have a **pink rabbit** at home.
R	Hama aslu musalheh?	A real rabbit?
C	Aan. Bappa genai rashakun.	Yes. Father brought [it] from an island.
R	(points to colour chart) kobaa mithan **pink**?	(points to colour chart) where is **pink** from here?
C	(points to pink)	(points to pink)
R	**Pink** ah Dhivehin kiyanee keekay?	What is **pink** called in Dhivehi?
C	Fehi	Green.

These extracts are illustrative of all the interactions I had with the children in these two classrooms. They were able to confidently use key concepts using English terms and were either hesitantly able to recall the Dhivehi equivalents when prompted, or were unable to do so.

Summary

The findings show how the ECE spaces in this study privileged English, despite the status of Dhivehi in educational policies. English dominated the LL of the classrooms in terms of the quantity and salience of signage in the language, while teachers' language use affirmed their monolingual biases. The children followed the patterns set by the teachers, with their language use and awareness clearly in favour of English.

Discussion

This study draws on the *weak version of translanguaging* as its theoretical lens (García & Lin, 2017; Turner & Lin, 2020), which acknowledges national and state language boundaries while advocating for their softening to foster more flexible, inclusive linguistic spaces. This lens provides a useful starting point for examining classroom language practices in the Maldivian early childhood context, where multilingualism is a societal norm. However, the findings of this study suggest that even the weak translanguaging stance may be insufficiently attuned to the realities of post-colonial, hierarchised language ecologies in which deeply ingrained ideologies elevate English above national and Indigenous languages. While the framework calls for disrupting linguistic hierarchies, the classroom practices observed often reinforced them, revealing the limits of the theory's applicability when systemic constraints and internalised linguistic biases are not adequately addressed. Thus, this study not only applies but also expands the weak translanguaging lens by highlighting the need for its further localisation: one that makes visible the persistent effects of coloniality, attends to structural inequalities and empowers educators to engage with multilingualism as a decolonial and justice-oriented practice.

This study has provided valuable evidence concerning translingual practices in the schoolscape of a post-colonial ECE context. Both teachers and children drew from an integrated semiotic communicative repertoire, using speech in multiple languages and responding through gesture, gaze and engagement with artefacts. Prior research in translingual pedagogy has largely been advocated and implemented in predominantly English-dominant societal contexts. When applied to societally multilingual contexts, like the Maldives, where local and national vernaculars are competing for status and prestige with the forces of English as a global language, it can be observed that pedagogical approaches will have to be adapted to best cater to linguistic needs. What we see from the context of this study is that rather than achieving the decolonising aims of translanguaging (Li & García, 2022) and valorising pride in students' identities as multilingual speakers (García & Li, 2014), neocolonial ideologies are being perpetuated. Reminiscent of Hornberger and Link's (2012) claim, we see there that even with the flexible blurring of language boundaries, the classroom discourse privileged literary over vernacular language and textual over oral and multimodal literacy. The clear bias towards English over the national and Indigenous languages suggests that the instrumentalist approach to language teaching has not been successful in creating transformative change.

Evidence from the visible, audible and textualised languaging practices in this study highlighted tensions between monolingual biases and translingual practices. Observational data showed an imbalanced engagement with the languages in this translingual space and a corresponding effect on children's language development. Rather than engage in translanguaging as a systematic pedagogical strategy to promote the learning of both language systems (Cenoz & Gorter, 2020), teachers' language use indicated their deeply held view that English was the only language of consequence. This goes against what Turner and Lin (2020) argue to be the aim of translingual pedagogies: the disruption of linguistic hierarchies. Rather than engage in a state of 'guilty multilingualism' (Coleman

2017: 31), the findings of this study suggest the reverse. Teachers were resorting to teaching content in English even when they were expected to do so in Dhivehi, thereby betraying their ideologies regarding which languages deserved to be taught. Even when the language policy explicitly states that Dhivehi needs to be prioritised over other languages, findings suggest that this is not implemented. This is reminiscent of the privileging of English in other South Asian contexts due to lingering legacies of colonialism (Canagarajah & Ashraf, 2013; Hamid & Rahman, 2019). Rather than utilise multilingualism as a resource and a pedagogy, key concepts were often being taught and reinforced in only English, delegitimising Dhivehi as the medium of instruction and the dominant societal language. The lack of visibility of Dhivehi and Arabic in the LL symbolically conveys a closer allegiance and positive identity towards English, given its saliency in this space (Cenoz & Gorter, 2006). The ease with which children engaged in translanguaging by privileging English and lacking awareness of key concepts in Dhivehi suggests that urgent attention is needed to redress the pedagogical approach to encourage a solid foundation in the home language that they can then draw on in the acquisition of subsequent languages (Cummins, 2001) and positively impact individual and collective development of identity (Dovchin et al., 2015; Sah & Kubota, 2022).

As acknowledged by Wiley and García (2016: 58), in such situations where minoritised languages must compete against powerful global languages, there is a need 'to allocate separate spaces for the named languages' while creating 'an instructional space where translanguaging is nurtured and used critically and creatively'. The fault lies not in the teachers themselves, but in society's seemingly blind acceptance of linguistic hierarchies and the educational system's lack of teacher preparation to counter the linguistic asymmetry (Mendoza, 2022). Teacher education programmes must address how to utilise languages inclusively in culturally sustaining ways.

Conclusion

This study of the schoolscapes of ECE has made clear how power relationships among languages and competing ideologies affect the contexts of teaching and learning. The insistence on privileging English has caused the suppression of the national and home language of the children within the educational space, raising concerns that it may eventually lead to language loss and attrition. To counter the linguistic asymmetry evident here, two actions appear to be essential. Policymakers need to evaluate the implementation of the medium of instruction policies and consider whether English language education needs to be reframed to nurture a more equitable multilingual focus. Importantly, teachers' capacity to offer an additive multilingual experience, not a subtractive one, needs to be bolstered. Teacher education programmes must explicitly address the crucial need to protect societal languages and provide guidance on adopting culturally sustaining pedagogies that can oppose neoliberal ideologies. While translingual pedagogies have the potential to create transformative change, if teachers are inadequately prepared, caution must be taken in promoting them as a liberatory approach.

References

Alim, H.S. and Paris, D. (2017) What is culturally sustaining pedagogy and why does it matter? In D. Paris and H.S. Alim (eds) *Culturally Sustaining Pedagogies: Teaching and Learning for Justice in a Changing World* (pp. 1–22). Teachers College Press.

Alim, H.S., Paris, D. and Wong, C.P. (2020) Culturally sustaining pedagogy. In N.S. Nasir, C.D. Lee, R. Pea and M. McKinney de Royston (eds) *Handbook of the Cultural Foundations of Learning* (Chapter 15). Routledge.

Anderson, J. (2018) Reimagining English language learners from a translingual perspective. *ELT Journal* 72 (1) 26–37. https://doi.org/10.1093/elt/ccx029.

Anderson, J. and Lightfoot, A. (2021) Translingual practices in English classrooms in India: Current perceptions and future possibilities. *International Journal of Bilingual Education and Bilingualism* 24 (8), 1210–1231. https://doi.org/10.1080/13670050.2018.1548558

Annamalai, E. (2004) Medium of power: The question of English in education in India. In J.W. Tollefson and A.B.M. Tsui (eds) *Medium of Instruction Policies: Which Agenda? Whose Agenda?* (Chapter 9). Taylor & Francis Group.

Backhaus, P. (2007) *Linguistic Landscapes: A Comparative Study of Urban Multilingualism in Tokyo*. Multilingual Matters.

Barac, R., Bialystok, E., Castro, D.C. and Sanchez, M. (2014) The cognitive development of young dual language learners: A critical review. *Early Childhood Research Quarterly* 29 (4), 699–714. https://doi.org/10.1016/j.ecresq.2014.02.003

Blommaert, J. (2013) *Ethnography, Superdiversity and Linguistic Landscapes: Chronicles of Complexity*. Multilingual Matters.

Bourdieu, P. (1986) The forms of capital (R. Nice, Trans.). In J. Richardson (ed.) *Handbook of Theory and Research for the Sociology of Education* (pp. 241–258). Greenwood.

Brown, C.S. (2014) Language and literacy development in the early years: Foundational skills that support emergent readers. *The Language and Literacy Spectrum* 24, 35–48.

Brown, K. (2012) The linguistic landscape of educational spaces. In D. Gorter, H. Marten and L. van Mansel (eds) *Minority Languages in the Linguistic Landscape* (pp. 281–298). Palgrave Macmillan.

Brown, K. (2018) Shifts and stability in schoolscapes: Diachronic considerations of southeastern Estonian schools. *Linguistics and Education* 44, 12–19.

Canagarajah, S. (2013) *Translingual Practice: Global Englishes and Cosmopolitan Relations*. Routledge.

Canagarajah, S. and Ashraf, H. (2013) Multilingualism and education in South Asia: Resolving policy/practice dilemmas. *Annual Review of Applied Linguistics* 33, 258–285. https://doi.org/10.1017/S0267190513000068

Cenoz, J. and Gorter, D. (2006) Linguistic landscape and minority languages. *International Journal of Multilingualism* 3 (1), 67–80. https://doi.org/10.1080/14790710608668386

Cenoz, J. and Gorter, D. (2020) Teaching English through pedagogical translanguaging. *World Englishes* 39, 300–311. https://doi.org/10.1111/weng.12462

Choi, T. (2023) English fever: Educational policies in globalised Korea, 1981–2018. *History of Education* 52 (4), 670–686. https://doi.org/10.1080/0046760X.2020.1858192

Coleman, H. (2017) Development and multilingualism: An introduction. In H. Coleman (ed.) *Multilingualisms and Development: Selected Proceedings of the 11th Language and Development Conference* (pp. 15–34). British Council.
Copland, F. and Creese, A. (2015) *Linguistic Ethnography: Collecting, Analysing and Presenting Data*. SAGE.
Crisfield, E. (2021) *Bilingual Families: A Practical Language Planning Guide* (1st edn) Multilingual Matters. https://doi.org/10.21832/9781788929356
Cummins, J. (2001) *Negotiating Identities: Education for Empowerment in a Diverse Society* (2nd edn). California Association for Bilingual Education.
Dagenais, D., Moore, D., Sabatier, C., Lamarre and Armand, F. (2008) Linguistic landscape and language awareness. In E. Shohamy and D. Gorter (eds) *Linguistic Landscape: Expanding the Scenery* (pp. 253–269). https://doi.org/10.4324/9780203930960
De Houwer, A. (2021) *Bilingual Development in Childhood*. Cambridge University Press.
De Witt, H. (2011) *Trends, Issues, and Challenges in Internationalisation of Higher Education*. Centre for Applied Research on Economics and Management.
Dovchin, S., Sultana, S. and Pennycook, A. (2015) Relocalizing the translingual practices of young adults in Mongolia and Bangladesh. *Translation and Translanguaging in Multilingual Contexts* 1 (1), 4–26. https://doi.org/10.1075/ttmc.1.1.01dov
Dovchin, S., Oliver, R. and Li, W. (2024) Introduction: Translingual practices: Playfulness and precariousness. In S. Dovchin, R. Oliver and Li Wei (eds) *Translingual Practices: Playfulness and Precariousness* (pp. 1–16). Cambridge University Press.
Erwin, E.J., Valentine, M. and Toumazou, M. (2022) The study of belonging in early childhood education: Complexities and possibilities. *International Journal of Early Years Education*. https://doi.org/10.1080/09669760.2022.2128307
Fashanu, C., Wood, E. and Payne, M. (2020) Multilingual communication under the radar: How multilingual children challenge the dominant monolingual discourse in a super-diverse. *English in Education* 54 (1), 93–112. https://doi.org/10.1080/042504 94.2019.1688657
Finders, J., Wilson, E. and Duncan, R. (2023) Early childhood education language environments: Considerations for research and practice. *Frontiers in Psychology* 14, 1202819–1202819. https://doi.org/10.3389/fpsyg.2023.1202819
Fritz, S. (2002) *The Dhivehi Language: A Descriptive and Historical Grammar of Maldivian and its Dialects*. Beitraige zur Südasienforschung: Heidelberg.
García, O. and Li, W. (2014) *Translanguaging: Language, Bilingualism and Education*. Palgrave Macmillan. https://doi.org/10.1057/9781137385765
García, O. and Lin, A.M.Y. (2017) Translanguaging in bilingual education. In O. García, A.M.Y. Lin and S. May (eds) *Bilingual and Multilingual Education* (pp. 117–130). Springer International Publishing.
Giri, R., Padwad, A. and Kabir, M.M.D. (2024) EMI in South Asia. Ideological underpinnings and practical considerations. In R. Giri, A. Padwad and M.M.D. Kabir (eds) *English as a Medium of Instruction in South Asia: Issues in Equity and Social Justice* (Chapter 2). Routledge.
Gorter, D. (2018) Linguistic landscapes and trends in the study of schoolscapes. *Linguistics and Education* 44, 80–85. https://doi.org/10.1016/j.linged.2017.10.001
Gorter, D., Cenoz, J. and van der Worp, K. (2021) The linguistic landscape as a resource for language learning and raising language awareness. *Journal of Spanish Language Teaching* 8 (2), 161–181.
Hamid, O. and Rahman, A. (2019) Language in education policy in Bangladesh. In A. Kirkpatrick and A.J. Liddicoat (eds) *The Routledge International Handbook of Language Education Policy in Asia* (Chapter 27). Routledge. https://doi.org/10.4324/9781315666235
Hawkins, M.R. and Mori, J. (2018) Considering 'trans-' perspectives in language theories and practices. *Applied Linguistics* 39 (1), 1–8. https://doi.org/10.1093/applin/amx056
Hedges, H. (2022) *Children's Interests, Inquiries and Identities: Curriculum, Pedagogy, Learning and Outcomes in the Early Years*. Routledge.

Hornberger, N.H. and Link, H. (2012) Translanguaging and transnational literacies in multilingual classrooms: A biliteracy lens. *International Journal of Bilingual Education and Bilingualism* 15 (3), 261–278.

Hu, G. (2008) The misleading academic discourse on Chinese–Chinese-English bilingual education in China. *Review of Educational Research* 78 (2), 195–231.

Huebner, T. (2006) Bangkok's linguistic landscapes: Environmental print, codemixing and language change. *International Journal of Multilingualism* 3 (1), 31–51.

Kress, G.R. and Van Leeuwen, T. (2006) *Reading Images: The Grammar of Visual Design* (2nd edn). Routledge, Taylor & Francis Group.

Landry, R. and Bourhis, R. (1997) Linguistic landscape and ethnolinguistic vitality: An empirical study. *Journal of Language and Social Psychology* 16 (1), 23–49. https://doi.org/10.1177/0261927X970161002

Lewis, G., Jones, B. and Baker, C. (2012) Translanguaging: Developing its conceptualisation and contextualisation. *Educational Research and Evaluation* 18 (7) 655–670. https://doi-org.ezproxy.auckland.ac.nz/10.1080/13803611.2012.718490.

Li, W. and García, O. (2022) Not a first language but one repertoire: Translanguaging as a decolonizing project. *RELC Journal* 53, 313–324. https://doi.org/10.1177/00336882221092841.

Lutfi, M. (2011) *Dhivehi Raajjeyge School Manhajaai Thauleem* [School curriculum and education in the Maldives]. (n.p.)

Macaro, E. (2015) English medium instruction: Time to start asking some difficult questions. *Modern English Teacher* 24 (2), 4–8.

Malinowski, D., Maxim, H.H. and Dubreil, S. (2020) *Language Teaching in the Linguistic Landscape. Educational Linguistics.* Springer. https://doi-org.ezproxy.auckland.ac.nz/10.1007/978-3-030-55761-4_1

Mendoza, A. (2022) What does translanguaging-for-equity really involve? An interactional analysis of a 9th grade English class. *Applied Linguistics Review* 13 (6), 1055–1075. https://doi.org/10.1515/applirev-2019-0106

Mohamed, N. (2016) Language of instruction and the development of biliteracy skills in children: A case study of a pre-school in the Maldives. In V. Murphy and M. Evangelou (eds) *Early Childhood Education in English for Speakers of Other Languages* (pp. 187–194). British Council.

Mohamed, N. (2019) From a monolingual to a multilingual nation: Analysing the language education policy in the Maldives. In A. Kirkpatrick and A. Liddicoat (eds) *The Routledge International Handbook of Language Education Policy in Asia* (Chapter 29). Routledge.

Mohamed, N. (2020) First Language loss and negative attitudes towards Dhivehi among young Maldivians: Is the English-first educational policy to blame? *TESOL Quarterly* 54 (3), 743–772. https://doi.org/10.1002/tesq.591

Mohanty, A.K. (2017) Multilingualism, education, English and development: Whose development? In H. Coleman (ed.) *Multilingualism and Development* (pp. 261–280). British Council.

Mohanty, A.K. (2019) *The Multilingual Reality: Living with Languages*. Multilingual Matters.

Moll, L.C., Amanti, C., Neff, D. and Gonzalez, N. (1992) Funds of knowledge for teaching: Using a qualitative approach to connect homes and classrooms. *Theory into Practice* 31 (2), 132–141.

Peleman, B., Van Der Wildt, A. and Vandenbroeck, M. (2022) Home language use with children, dialogue with multilingual parents and professional development in ECEC. *Early Childhood Research Quarterly* 61, 70–80. https://doi.org/10.1016/j.ecresq.2022.05.007

Sah, P.K. (2022) Language ideologies, symbolic power, and social stratification: An ethnographic exploration of English medium instruction policy in Nepal's public schools. In L. Adinolfi, U. Bhattacharya and P. Phyak (eds) *Multilingual Education in South Asia: At the Intersection Between Policy and Practice* (pp. 50–68). Routledge. https://doi.org/10.4324/9781003158660-4

Sah, P.K. and Li, G. (2018) English medium instruction (EMI) as linguistic capital in Nepal: Promises and realities. *International Multilingual Research Journal* 12 (2), 109–123. https://doi.org/10.1080/19313152.2017.1401448

Sah, P.K. and Kubota, R. (2022) Towards critical translanguaging: A review of literature on English as a medium of instruction in South Asia's school education. *Asian Englishes*. https://doi.org/10.1080/13488678.2022.2056796

Seargeant, P. and Giaxoglou, K. (2020) Discourse and the linguistic landscape. In A. De Fina and A. Georgakopoulou (eds) *The Cambridge Handbook of Discourse Studies Cambridge Handbooks in Language and Linguistics* (pp. 306–326). Cambridge University Press. https://doi.org/10.1017/9781108348195.015

Shamim, F. (2024) EMI, ELT, and social justice: Case of Pakistan. In R. Giri, A. Padwad and M.M.D. Kabir (eds) *English as a Medium of Instruction in South Asia: Issues in Equity and Social Justice* (pp. 94–111). https://doi.org/10.4324/9781003342373-7

Shohamy, E. and Gorter, D. (2009) *Linguistic Landscape: Expanding the Scenery*. Routledge.

Sierens, S. and Van Avermaet, P. (2014) Language diversity in education: Evolving from multilingual education to functional multilingual learning. In D. Little, C. Leung and P. Van Avermaet (eds) *Managing Diversity in Education: Languages, Policies, Pedagogies* (pp. 204–222). Multilingual Matters. https://doi.org/10.21832/9781783090815-014

Skutnabb-Kangas, T. (2010) Education of indigenous and minority children. In J.A. Fishman and O. García (eds) *Handbook of Language and Ethnic Identity* (pp. 186–206). Oxford University Press.

Spada, N. (2015) SLA research and L2 pedagogy: Misapplications and questions of relevance. *Language Teaching* 48 (1), 69–81. https://doi.org/10.1017/S026144481200050X.

Sugiharto, S. (2015) The multilingual turn in applied linguistics? A perspective from the periphery. *International Journal of Applied Linguistics* 25 (3), 414–421. https://doi.org/10.1111/ijal.12111

Tran, T.T. (2022) Language ideology in the linguistic landscape of Hanoi. In S. Mirvahedi (ed.) *Linguistic Landscapes in South-East Asia: The Politics of Language and Public Signage* (pp. 9–29). Routledge. https://doi.org/10.4324/9781003166993-3

Turner, M. and Lin, A.M.Y. (2020) Translanguaging and named languages: Productive tension and desire. *International Journal of Bilingual Education and Bilingualism* 23 (4), 423–433. https://doi.org/10.1080/13670050.2017.1360243

Wiley, T. and García, O. (2016) Language policy and planning in language education: Legacies, consequences, and possibilities. *The Modern Language Journal* 100 (1), 48–63.

Zapata, A. and Laman, T.T. (2023) Reconditioning a new linguistic normal for children's classrooms through critical translingual literacies. *Language Arts* 100 (3), 245–253. https://doi.org/10.58680/la202332269

8 Translanguaging in English Language Education in Sri Lanka: Social and Academic Gains

Harsha Dulari Wijesekera

Introduction

With its deep-rooted coloniality, learning a language like English (Kubota, 2020) is not a neutral activity for many learners. It is a value-laden and political process that subordinates other languages with less capital value in a linguistic marketplace. At times, it may threaten one's self-concept, resulting from the fear of making mistakes, being laughed at and being excluded, where the 'right to speech' or 'power to impose reception' determines a legitimate or illegitimate speaker (Bourdieu, 1977: 651). For example, who can speak and who is destined to be the listener can also be decided by the proficiency level of the speaker. The metaphor for English in Sri Lanka, 'kaduwa' (double-edged sword), that guillotines those who cannot speak English mirrors the positionality of many ESL learners in Sri Lanka. Monolithic 'English Only' classroom language policy (LP) may have heightened this disdain and resulting stigma. Spolsky (2007) argues that irrespective of formally stipulated macro-level policies, LP operates at lower levels also, that is, within a speech community such as classrooms and family, which are called domain-specific LP. These domain-specific LPs may be dynamic, immanent and emergent in relation to the domain's linguistic ecology and its underlying sociopolitical aspects.

In multilingual classroom environments, the emergent domain-specific LPs may be characterized by heteroglossia, where students and teachers intrinsically pull from the diverse range of linguistic and other semiotic resources available to them to accomplish their communication needs in achieving educational goals. Here, students' mother tongue becomes an asset, not a deficit (Lin, 2020) and 'provides a rightful space for the students' mother tongue' (Sah & Kubota, 2022: 143). Furthermore, recognizing one's mother tongue/s is bonded to identity, enhances students' self-concept, self-esteem and agency. Exploited wisely, linguistic heterogeneity may set students' and teachers' *unthinking thoughts and actions* towards social and educational profits such as the right to participation/expression, inclusivity, engagement in activities and deep learning. Such heteroglossic policies also help students who grapple with learning English due to inhibition resulting from Foreign Language Classroom Speaking Anxiety (Horwitz et al., 1986).

This chapter explores how heteroglossic LPs in ESL and BE/EMI classrooms can shape students' right to expression and participation in activities, thereby achieving academic gains and social gains such as equity and inclusion. To discuss the above, I utilize data from two studies. One is a qualitative study in BE/EMI classrooms to demonstrate how ethnolinguistic inclusion and social cohesion are emancipated while enhancing both content and language learning through a heteroglossia policy. The second study is teacher-interventionist action research in an ESL classroom, to discuss how ESL classrooms can enable low-proficient students' right to expression and participation in educational activities through heteroglossic LP (particularly the use of L1). I begin by delineating the context of Sri Lanka's education system.

The School System and Exclusions

On par with the main aspects of the present volume, it is worth elaborating on the highly segregated Sri Lankan school system. Sri Lanka has a strong free public education system (10,146 schools) that helps report the highest literacy rate among the youth in the region. Nevertheless, the schools are highly polarized along language and hence ethnicity, which may again be segregated by religion – Buddhist, Christian (Christian schools again split along different denominations), Hindu and Islam. The Sri Lankan Constitution decrees that the medium of instruction (MOI) shall be either the National Language – Sinhala or Tamil (Article 21 (1). This very progressive act of mother tongue instruction (MTI), which was in place even before the independence, recognized the right to education in the mother tongue that facilitated social mobility for the rural poor, irrespective of ethnicity. Unfortunately, this is the main reason for ethnically exclusive schools: only Sinhala medium (6323) and only Tamil medium (3026). A few schools have both Sinhala and Tamil media (40 + 36 = 75) as per the Annual School Census 2021 (MOE, 2021 – see Table 8.1). Even in such schools, Sinhala-medium and Tamil-medium students learn in separate sections and classrooms, usually without or with very little interaction. The absence of shared experiences and resulting alienation foster mistrust among diverse ethnolinguistic groups, contributing to the formation of narrow ethnocentric identities. This ethnocentric socialization within schools has partially fuelled the ethnic unrest

Table 8.1 Schools by Language medium/s of instruction

Medium/s	No. of schools	%
Sinhala medium	6323	62.3
Tamil medium	3026	29.8
Sinhala and Tamil mediums	40	0.4
Sinhala and Bilingual (S/English) mediums	552	5.4
Tamil and Bilingual (T/English) mediums	170	1.7
Trilingual (Sinhala, Tamil & Bilingual (S/E and/or T/E) mediums)	35	0.3

experienced by the country from time to time (Wickrema & Colenso, 2003; Wijesekera, 2018).

EMI is available only in 35 bi-media (Sinhala and Tamil media) schools. Only in the EMI classes of these 35 schools, Sinhala and Tamil-speaking students can learn together. Even so, the LP in their classrooms is vague in the absence of a legitimate classroom domain-specific LP on BE or ESL. However, immanent LP emerging at these domain levels may depend on their sociolinguistic contexts.

English Language Education in Sri Lanka

The students have formal exposure to English language learning in two ways: ESL and EMI through BE (English and Sinhala/Tamil). ESL is a core subject in the national curriculum from Grades 3 to 13, which has continued to fail to yield its expected outcomes (NEC, 2022; Wijesekera, 2012a). Moreover, the Activity-Based Oral English (ABOE) component was introduced in Grades 1–2 in 2005. ABOE requires primary-trained teachers (not English-trained teachers) to introduce oral English, including vocabulary and phrases related to Environmental Studies. However, this program was not successful 'owing to lack of preparation of primary teachers for the purpose' (NEC, 2022: 141).

The disparities in access to English, either as ESL or EMI, are explicit between the rich and the poor or the urban and the remote, irrespective of ethnicity. The public schools are granted permission to implement BE/EMI only if teachers who can teach content through English are available. ESL teacher availability is also an issue in remote areas. The limited BE availability in the public system is due to the government's failure to expand its implementation as initially promised. Though very limited, the availability of BE in public schools (727) addresses this disparity, as it allows EMI for those who cannot afford fee-levying English Medium international schools. However, even in schools where BE is available, school authorities are compelled to hold selection tests, since the demand is very high. Schools are permitted to deliver up to six subjects (including ICT) in the curriculum through EMI from grade six, depending on teacher availability. This again excludes some children from English education since teachers who can teach content in English may not be available in rural schools. Thus, gatekeeping for English education happens in three main ways: the non-availability of ESL teachers in rural schools, the lack of BE availability in schools and the limited opportunities for EMI in schools where BE is available. The achievement disparities at the two main public examinations reflect low achievement in remote, low socio-economic, under-privileged schools/provinces, whereas the best-performing schools on the island are privileged schools located in urban areas (cf. https://www.doenets.lk/statistics).

English is not merely another language in postcolonial and conflict-affected countries like Sri Lanka; 'it is also intricately tied with aspirations, identities and sociocultural status of people, resulting in a quite complex role it plays in the nations' lives' (Padwad *et al.*, 2023: 192). It sometimes divides people between those who know English and do not. At other times, it becomes the 'neutral' language between the two competing national languages – Sinhala and Tamil (Wijesekera, 2018). I use the word 'neutral' with caution because English still maintains an elite status in Sri Lanka, a social marker symbolizing power and prestige (Kandiah, 1984; Lo Bianco, 1999, 2010; Wijesekera, 2018; Wijesekera & Hamid, 2022; Wijesekera *et al.*, 2019), given its imperial legacy and present neo-imperialism. The gatekeeping mechanism through English and its influential role in perpetuating discrimination is not a new phenomenon in Sri Lanka. NEC (2022) points out that 'those educated in Sinhala and Tamil have been disadvantaged in access to remunerative employment and pursuing higher studies. To a great extent, this has caused social polarization' (2022: 150). English's hegemony and hence linguistic injustice are perpetuated due to the government's failure to provide equitable access to English education both as ESL and EMI.

The discussions thus far demonstrate the supremacy of the English language and its systematic and tenacious inequalities in education through ESL and EMI. Even when English is accessible and taught, 'English-only' monolithic classroom policies may deepen these exclusions of the low-proficient children from participation and expression. These classrooms become '*site[s]*' (original emphasis) for perpetuating unequal relations among' students, producing 'unfair and disparate educational outcomes' (Johnson & García, 2023: 1). Regardless of these overarching inequalities, immanent actions may be necessitated due to classroom communication requirements. Here, the students and teachers may opt for the best pedagogic tool they have, that is, translanguaging for meaning-making, not necessarily deliberately. This may provide 'a rightful space for the students' mother tongue for pedagogic purposes' (Sah & Kubota, 2022: 143) where all voices may be equally valued and heard, resisting hegemonies without succumbing to anxieties and stigma emanating from 'English-only' oppressive LP conditions.

Translanguaging

Translanguaging considers languages and other semiotic resources as constituent elements of a single system or unitary repertoire of resources that the bi/multilinguals possess (García & Li, 2014) 'without regard for watchful adherence to the socially and politically defined boundaries of named (and usually national and state) languages' (Otheguy *et al.*, 2015: 281). This brings a fluidity to identities bounded by languages such as Sinhala and Tamil ethnicities (Chandra, 2006; Wijesekera, 2018). Translanguaging in a given multilingual space forms unique idiolects and sociolects of individuals/communities – one's own way of what they do with language, which Kohn (2022) terms 'MY language', one's own version of English (2022: 121) and 'disrupts the socially constructed language hierarchies' (Otheguy *et al.*, 2015: 283). This may provide the low-proficient children with belongingness to English and may shed socially inherited linguicism (Skutnabb-Kangas, 1989) and ethnolinguistic divisions embodied by language, hence transformative. Use of L1 also reduces Foreign Language Classroom Speaking Anxiety: FLCA (Horwitz *et al.*, 1986; Wijesekera, 2012b), inequalities and brings linguistic justice to low-proficiency students, securing their ability to participate in the ESL and EMI classrooms. The recognition and value given to L1 in classrooms may decolonize and democratize English language education, reducing its elitism and salvation from the oppressed linguistic habitus. It will also liberalize linguistic marketplaces in EMI and ESL multilingual classrooms and 'protect the language culture, and identity of those who have received marginalization' (Sah & Kubota, 2022: 143).

Theoretically, translanguaging or navigating to L1 emerges through *illusion* – the sensation that comes instinctively and unthinkingly. It is a natural occurrence resulting from a 'feel for the game' – an intuitive and practical sense of what is to be done best in any given situation (Bourdieu, 2000), coming from the desire to achieve educational and social targets in classrooms. On the contrary, there may be inner and outside resistance from monolithic colonial dispositions that habituate teachers' and students' linguistic habitus and make them feel the use of L1 is 'bad' and deficit (Wijesekera, 2018). Though the circumstances in the classroom drive them to use L1 in classrooms, they do it with guilt, anxiety and shame (Liyanage & Canagarajah, 2019) because teachers (and students) think that the use of L1 is illegitimate. They fear being judged as substandard English teachers who do not know English well (Wijesekera, 2018). This would have been avoided if an explicit policy were available recommending heteroglossia classroom LP.

SLA Theories

Translanguaging and Second Language Acquisition (SLA) theories such as Input (Krashen, 1985), Interaction (Long, 1981), Output (Swain,

1985), IIO and ecological stance of language learning (van Lier, 2010) may be located under the meta theory of constructivism, both cognitive and social constructivism. The ecological perspective of language learning foregrounds quality (learning opportunities, classroom interaction and educational experience), relationships and agency. Interaction provides the learner with consciousness-raising, noticing gaps, negative/positive/corrective feedback, negotiation of meaning and comprehended input essential for language learning. These happen when the learners (and teachers) are constructing new knowledge through interaction and participation, where they build up relationships and agency. These knowledge constructions are traceable in metatalk or Language-Related Episodes (LREs – metalinguistic episodes) in interactions during group work (Swain & Lapkin, 2001). They help externalize knowledge/thoughts that reinforce and reconstruct messages to convey in the target language.

Learners tend to engage in metatalk through L1. L1 emerges as their metalanguage for knowledge construction and the group's social interaction. Further, navigating to L1 in ESL/EMI is a valuable cognitive and psychological tool that helps reduce nervousness (Larsen-Freeman, 2000). L1 mediates both interpersonal and intrapersonal aspects of language learning and externalizes the learner's inner speech that regulates mental processes (Antón & DiCamilla, 1998). Letting the struggling ESL/EMI students use L1 empowers them and creates an agency-rich environment. In such learning environments, students' subjectivity and 'inner lives' (Chen & Lin, 2023) are not ignored. Notably, their self-concepts, inhibitions and social stigma are taken care of and a sense of inclusion, justice and equity is felt. Research in Sri Lanka also shows a positive contribution of translanguaging in both ESL and BE classes (Perera, 2022; Ratwatte, 2015; Wijesekera, 2018). For instance, a cross-sectional case study in a BE classroom where EL is learned confirms translanguaging support to acquire the targeted language, challenge language hierarchies and promote social justice (Perera, 2022). Her study further shows the importance of the meta-skill aspect of translanguaging. She posits that experienced users of translanguaging use 'it for complex inner and intrapersonal sociolinguistic and metalinguistic activities' and that this exploratory talk increases understanding of content (Perera, 2022: 83). This is where explicit heteroglossic LP is vital, so learners and teachers legitimately do it without fear and shame.

On the whole, the discussion thus far provides paybacks of heteroglossic LP and translanguaging in different perspectives, particularly, sociolinguistic and psycholinguistic. It proposes that translanguaging as a pedagogy, particularly navigating to L1, can facilitate self-expression and participation in classrooms, empower students, create agency and therefore increase engagement in activities/tasks, bringing inclusion, justice and equity while yielding interethnic/cultural interdependence. The findings of the two studies I conducted are discussed below to explicate further and reaffirm these arguments.

The studies

Study 1: This qualitative study employed classroom observations followed by focus-group discussions (FGDs) and interviews with stakeholders such as BE students, BE teachers, parents, principals and officials at the Ministry of Education. Classroom observations were conducted in four schools attended by Sinhala, Tamil and Muslim students. For this chapter, I draw on data collected in two schools. The study's overarching aim was to explore how the ethnolinguistic identities of these Sinhala, Tamil and Muslim students are shaped when they start working together in a heteroglossic linguistic context (i.e. in multiethnic BE classrooms) to achieve their educational targets. This study was framed and interpreted through the Logic of Practice (Bourdieu, 1990) and translanguaging. The research question that guides the study reported in this chapter is: How might the 'socially situated conditions' (Bourdieu, 1990: 55) of these classrooms, that is, heteroglossia, enable students' restricted and stereotypical ethnolinguistic dispositions that are sourced and framed by languages to become fluid and flexible?

Study 2: This teacher interventionist action research was conducted in an overcrowded ESL classroom attended by 58 Sinhalese students with highly heterogeneous English language proficiency. These students had done only one individual writing activity for two terms, as evidenced in their writing books. Before the intervention, they had not done any group activity during these two terms, as students reported and their ESL teacher confirmed. The intervention was Dictogloss[1] Activities in Cooperative Groups. The main aim of this intervention was to increase the accuracy of writing by noticing the gaps, raising consciousness, providing corrective input, scaffolding by peers and initiating a cooperative learning community. It was based on SLA theories, mainly Input, Interaction and Output: IIO (Mitchell & Myles, 2004) and translanguaging, the overarching Social Constructivism Theory (Vygotsky, 1978). It analyzes students' meta-talk through LREs during group activities. Additionally, the students wrote reflections on this experience, which many of them wrote in their mother tongue.

Findings and Discussion

In this section, I first present the main findings of Study 1 on shaping ethnolinguistic identities towards inclusivity in BE classrooms when the logic of the classroom language practice is heteroglossia. To explicate this, I bring excerpts from FGDs with students. The excerpts presented in the article did not undergo any corrections or modifications to reflect their genuine expressions and linguistic styles. Next, the findings of Study 2 are presented to illustrate how translanguaging benefits ESL learning, participation and social inclusivity. In brief, both studies show how translanguaging can enhance social outcomes of learning – inclusivity, justice and equity, by ensuring the right to participate and, therefore, learning.

Translanguaging, ethnolinguistic integration and language of scaffolding

Study 1 demonstrates how previously ethnolinguistically alienated students can build a network of relationships through shared lived experiences in ethnolinguistically diverse BE classrooms. Earlier, they were segregated in mother-tongue-only Sinhala medium and Tamil medium classrooms. These students had been socialized into ethnocentric individuals due to ethnically alienated environments in their schools/classrooms and societies where they underwent primary socialization (Wijesekera, 2018). The following excerpts (see Excerpt A and Excerpt B) are from FGDs with BE students in two schools in response to the question about their preferred group composition – whether their own ethnicity or diverse. During group work, students flexibly navigate among all three languages, as evidenced in Excerpt C.

Excerpt A:

Sinhala student	We like to be with all the students. It is helpful because we can learn from each other. <u>If we don't understand or we find it difficult to understand something they [Tamil-speaking students] also explain us in Sinhala.</u>
Sinhala student	<u>We also explain them in Sinhala.</u> In some group activities, we need each other's help. If our civics teacher asks us to write in all three languages.
Sinhala student	=knowledge sharing, we can talk with and share knowledge.
Tamil student	We like working together. We can collect many information because each other have many ideas on the=
Tamil student	=different ideas [we get different ideas] because of their environment ... when comparing our environment with their environment, it is <different> no. now not only that. There are all three languages there, so if we don't know Sinhala, we can ask from Sinhala colleagues, likewise Sinhala friends can know Tamil when there are Tamil students in the class, also, we can learn their culture and their customs which is also reason.
Tamil students	we can learn so many things in Sinhala, and we can study the second (2NL) language also, for our O <level exam so we can learn <so many things> <yes so many things>

Muslim student	When all are there, <u>there will be different ideas we can share</u>. When doing group work one's ideas are different from others because <u>we can know some sentences in other languages</u>.
Muslim student	We can practice the Sinhala language. Yeah, yeah [other Muslim students in chorus]
Muslim student	We can share our experiences and personal ideas with them now earlier we didn't do it because we had only Muslim friends and sometimes a few Tamil friends also. But now we have them equally in this class.

Excerpt B:

Muslim student	<u>Mix of all.</u> *If we are in a mixed group we have Sinhala, Tamil and English students* So if someone doesn't know Sinhala hard words, we can ask Sinhala medium students and like that. And by doing everything together is a good opportunity for us to be friendly with all, all groups.
Muslim student	<u>It's like studying in all three languages</u>. According to the textbook, the lesson is in English but when he is explaining in Sinhala, we can get the idea. And when we do group work in all three languages like writing definitions in all three languages, we can get the idea of that lesson in our mother tongue also.

These excerpts demonstrate a growing sense of interdependence, knowledge sharing and appreciation of diversity. These are the key aspects of mutual bonding and inclusivity. Students' views demonstrate the increasing familiarity and acknowledgement of each other's language and culture. They acknowledge the advantages of sharing knowledge, learning from each other's experiences, especially '*work in all three languages*' and getting the content of a lesson in '*our mother tongue also*' (B). By pooling their talents, ideas and resources facilitated by L1, students learn and consolidate the content of a lesson, build mutual trust and foster a sense of connection and shared purpose.

A student in Excerpt A suggests: 'When all are there, there will be different ideas we can share. When doing group work, one's ideas are different from others, also we can know some sentences in other languages'. Another student expressed, 'We can learn so many things in Sinhala, and we can study the second (2NL) language' – the language of the 'other'. These illustrate that students are beginning to accept diversity and respect the ideas of others and develop a willingness to learn the language of the 'other'. These educational spaces appear to facilitate a shift from ethnocentric dispositions towards inclusivity. They seem to have embarked on a new identification process that is flexible and inclusive, encompassing all ethnicities. As another student notes, 'Doing everything together is a good opportunity for us to be friendly with all, all groups.' This demonstrates that students have now begun to appreciate and value ethnolinguistically heterogeneous inclusive social groups, as opposed to previously held negative dispositions towards other ethnolinguistic groups.

Theoretically, this exemplifies Bourdieu's concept of group membership (Bourdieu, 1985), wherein each member benefits from collectively owned resources, allowing them to pursue common educational objectives collectively. The most important thing is that they can achieve all these when there is a heteroglossia space that accommodates navigation between all three languages to achieve educational and social targets of the classroom. In these linguistically and socially democratic spaces, everyone's ideas are expressed, heard and recognized, removing ideological barriers, such as native speakerism, anxieties, shame and shaming. Therefore, participation and engagement in learning are encouraged, including English low-proficiency students, which is doubtful if a monolithic 'English only' LP is artificially imposed. Student engagement in learning using all three languages is well reflected in the excerpts below.

Excerpt C: Excerpts from FGDs

Tamil student: human activities
Sinhala student: <L1> *ekiyanne mokakakda demalen*<L1> {A Sinhala student asks in Sinhala – 'What is it in Tamil'}
Tamil student: <L1> *Enna? Athu enna?* <L1> {A Tamil student also doesn't know the Tamil equivalent and he asks in Tamil another Tamil student}
Muslim Tamil speaking student: <L1> *nadavadikkaikal* <L1> *(activities)* {other Tamil students give a try – translating word by word in phrase – unfavourable human activities}
Sinhala student: human activities? {A Sinhala student thinks that a Tamil friend has given a Tamil translation of only one word and hence repeats the whole phrase in English to stress the missing words}
Tamil student: <L1> *Manitha nadavadikkaikal, Manitha Nadavadikkaikal*</L1> *(It is human activities. it is human activities)* {This student answers, i.e., the equivalent for the phrase, but incomplete}
Tamil student: <L1> *Enna?* <L1> <NL2>*Ahithakara minis Kriya*<NL2> *(What is it? unfavourable human activities?)* {This student notices that the word 'unfavourable' is missing in the translation and therefore highlights the absence of the same and simultaneously tries to elicit the word from his peers}
Sinhala student: *unfavourable human activities* <L1>*ahithakara minis kriyakarakam*</L1> *(unfavourable human activities)* {Sinhala student repeats the whole phrase both in English and Sinhala to bring Tamil students' attention so that it would be easy for his Tamil-speaking peers to get the Tamil equivalents}

In the previous excerpt, Sinhala and Tamil-speaking students attempt to find equivalent terms in their respective languages for English terms. The activity requires students to write the definitions of natural disasters, their root causes and outcomes in all three languages. To accomplish this, they seek peer support: Sinhala-speaking students from Tamil-speaking students and vice versa. In these interactive dialogues, students use the group's complete linguistic repertoire, where boundaries between Sinhala, Tamil and English begin to blur and become a unitary meaning-making system (García & Li, 2014) of their group speech community. As evident in the above excerpts, translanguaging becomes the group's metalanguage that facilitates academic knowledge comprehension and completion of cognitively and academically demanding tasks because they use it as their metalanguage. The comprehensible language input and output (Swain, 1985) needed to complete these tasks is also constructed through this metalk/metalanguage. For instance, in the last line of Excerpt C, the Sinhala-speaking student repeats/recasts the entire phrase in both English and Sinhala, aiming to capture the attention of Tamil students who, then, pool the missing input in Tamil, while encouraging Sinhala students' understanding of the Tamil equivalents. By recasting, the Sinhala student engages in consciousness-raising among his Tamil counterparts, drawing their attention to potential gaps in their understanding. Furthermore, in the subsequent excerpt from Excerpt C, the Sinhala student doubts the Tamil phrase's completeness. It appears that he is leveraging his pragmatic competence along with his global and textual knowledge of his own language, as he lacks knowledge of Tamil. This prompts the Tamil students to notice the gap that the word 'unfavourable' is missing in the translation, prompting them to provide the missing term.

> **Sinhala student:** Human activities? {A Sinhala student thinks that a Tamil friend has given a Tamil translation of only one word and hence repeats the whole phrase in English to stress the missing words.}
> [...]
> **Tamil student:** <L1> *Enna?* <L1> <NL2> *Ahithakara minis Kriya*<NL2> (What is it? unfavourable human activities?) {This student notices that the word 'unfavourable' is missing in the translation and therefore highlights the absence of the same and simultaneously tries to elicit the word from his peers}

In summary, the preceding excerpts illustrate how translanguaging functions as the metalanguage that is indispensable for accomplishing academic tasks in an EMI classroom. The flexible utilization of all available languages enhances both language comprehension and the successful execution of academic activities. It also appears that the students get exposure to the language of the other and ideas about the other language.

Next, I dig into comparable processes within the ESL classroom, drawing insights from the findings of Study 2.

Translanguaging as 'metalanguage' in the ESL classroom

The excerpts below are LREs from student interaction during cooperative group writing in a Dictogloss activity. This was followed by students' reflections on the activity. The LREs mirror how learners solve their linguistic problems with peer input when they talk, argue and agree to complete the writing activity. Concerning target language, peer consciousness-raising, noticing the errors and providing corrective feedback are apparent in the above interactive metatalk.

S1: Okay *hari* <L1>write (Okay, well, let's write)
S2: Rugby is a game played by round shape ball
S3: Round *nemei* <L1>oval (Not round it is oval) [This low proficient student corrects round to oval]
S4: Played with *enna ona* <L1> *(it should be played with)*
S4: *Methanata 'a' enna ona.* <L1> Rugby is a game played with a ... ah... 'a' *nemei* <L1> 'an'... oval ('a' should come here – he repeats the sentence with 'a'- then realizes it should be 'an') PS: O.K. Rugby is a game played with an oval shape ball.
PS: shaped... shaped... oval shaped
S2: *ovne* <L1> oval-shaped ball. (Yes, oval-shaped ball)
S1: dan liyanna playersla ke denek innavada kiyala<L1> (now write no. of players)
S2: There are... ke denek innawada<L1> (How many are there?) [This proficient student does not know the number of players in a rugby team – he poses the question to low proficient students since he knew that this one knows]
S6: ekohalai... ekohalai...<L1>eleven (eleven... eleven... eleven) [This low proficient student who is also a rugby payer provides the answer]
S4: There are eleven players in a team.

Noticed in these episodes is are raising consciousness on grammatical errors, hence noticing the gap and providing corrective feedback/input (Krashen, 1985; Long, 1981; Swain, 1985). As explicit, all these are facilitated by L1. Especially, it also illustrates how a low L2 proficient student (S6) pools his content knowledge in L1, which is essential content input for the task. This will not happen if L1 is banned from the class. In the LRE above, the low-proficient students use L1 to exteriorize their knowledge, especially the facts/content that the group required to complete the writing task. The use of L1 during the task facilitates expressing one's self (especially those who are not proficient and hence in fear of talking). This fosters active participation and thereby learner autonomy, empowerment and self-esteem. These conditions also bring 'more unity' and team spirit, as evident in excerpt E below.

Changing viewpoints: Proficient vs. low-proficiency students

The reflective notes of students in the ESL class provide evidence that the distance between those 'who know English' and 'who do not' is now reduced and thus, the relegation of the latter group by the former relaxes. The fears and stigma of the latter group, that is, low- proficient students, seem to be starting to reduce. Also illuminated is low-proficient students' raised confidence and motivation for participation, as seen in Excerpt E. Excerpts D and E below are from students' reflections in Study 2. Though what they mainly and explicitly talked about is cooperative group work and how it helps them participate, their views demonstrate how low proficient students are now recognized by proficient students, which was not the case earlier. The excerpts also demonstrate a growing willingness among low-proficient students to engage in ESL activities. Traceable in both excerpts is growing team spirit and interdependence, reducing exclusion.

Excerpt D: From proficient students' reflections

'I am *learning to listen to others now.*'
'In the past, weak students never worked, but now everyone works.'
'When I don't have facts and ideas, my friends give.' 'I earlier thought those who don't know English can't do anything, now I know they can give important facts in Sinhala.'

Excerpt E: Low-proficient students' reflections

'Earlier during the English period, all were shouting; those days, we did not do group work.'
'Frankly, I started to like English after the teacher started group work. I'm not scared when I do group work.'
'Now I feel there is **more unity** in the class.'

The proficient ESL students now seem to recognize their low-proficient peers and their contributions to group work, disrupting the elitism of English and exclusion. Statements such as 'I am learning to listen to others now' and 'I earlier thought those who don't know English can't do anything...' imply their growing respect and recognition towards their low-proficient peers and their repentance about how they thought about low-proficient students earlier. The excerpts from low-proficient ESL students' reflections in Excerpt E illustrate how low-proficient students can gain confidence because now they can participate and contribute to the task.

Conclusion and Implications

Overall, the heteroglossic linguistic ecologies help students grappling with English language learning due to inhibition and stigma in

'English-only' environments. Translanguaging 'disrupts the socially constructed language hierarchies' (Otheguy *et al.*, 2015: 283), fostering inclusive and democratic social spaces that transcend proficiency levels and ethnolinguistic differences. It challenges the symbolic power and dominance of English and other powerful languages (Sah & Kubota, 2022), as was evident in learners' translanguaging not only into the majority's language (Sinhala) but also the minority language (Tamil) alongside English. In heteroglossic social spaces, the hierarchical positioning of languages, including varieties such as 'good' and 'bad' English, seems to lose validity. Within these spaces, students seem to confront socially inherited stereotypical negative attitudes towards other ethnic groups and low-proficient speakers, fostering a newfound recognition and respect for the language of the 'other'. This helps neutralize and democratize the deep-rooted coloniality (Kubota, 2020), facilitating students to shed previously internalized 'apartheid' linguistic habitus. In essence, translingual practices do some 'pedagogic work' (Bourdieu & Passeron, 1977: 31) that re-socializes students towards diversity responsiveness, paving the way forward for inclusion and social cohesion.

As was evident in the above analysis, translanguaging, as a metalanguage, scaffolds gaps in content knowledge construction. It facilitates engagement/participation and, hence, deep learning. Likewise, the analysis of LREs during ESL group work highlights how translingual practices facilitate L2 acquisition via metatalk that uses L1. Heteroglossic metatalk also provides recognition to English low-proficiency students, enabling their active participation and essentially providing scaffolding in content input for ESL writing. This would be impossible under a strict monolithic English-only LP in force where these low-proficiency students are suppressed and deprived of the 'right to speech.' The analysis also provides evidence for various aspects of language production/output, such as noticing the gaps, consciousness-raising, recasting, translation, offering advice, providing input and text-interpreting facilitated through metatalk in L1 when translanguaging in both EMI and ESL classrooms.

In the two classroom spaces discussed in this chapter, translanguaging and L1/L1s therein seem to be the 'linguistic currency' of the time determined by users 'for meeting the needs of' the group in the given 'time and setting' (Lo Bianco, 2021: 7). In such linguistic ecologies, students are empowered ensuring their right to participate in educational activities, linguistic justice/democracy and equity. Who has the 'right to speech' and 'power to impose reception' or who is the legitimate and illegitimate speaker (Bourdieu, 1977: 615) becomes no more relevant. The once anxious learners who suffered from Foreign Language Classroom Speaking Anxiety – FLCSA (Horwitz *et al.*, 1986) and whose self-concept was threatened in the monolithic English-only learning spaces are now relieved from being laughed at and fear of making mistakes.

It is reiterated that teachers allow these heteroglossic conditions to *happen* because they understand the practical advantages of teaching and learning. However, they navigate to L1 and let the students do the same in ESL or BE/EMI classrooms with hesitance, fearing potential accusations and being labelled as incompetent teachers of English/EMI by parents, peers and authorities (Wijesekera, 2018). In contrast, if a heteroglossic policy is established with clear instructional guides as the legitimate domain-specific (classroom-specific) LP (Spolsky, 2007) in ESL and EMI domains, it would encourage both teachers and students to utilize translanguaging as a pedagogical tool. Moreover, EMI and ESL teacher education curricula should incorporate critical pedagogy and include components such as hegemony of English, translanguaging, linguistic human rights and global Englishes, to name a few. Finally, it is essential to note that though these recommendations are principally focused on Sri Lanka, they hold equal relevance and applicability to countries with comparable experiences and challenges. Looking ahead, the insights of this chapter are expected to contribute to policy and praxis. The persisting educational inequalities in the postcolonial South Asian milieu, resulting from complex sociolinguistic diversity and linguistic hierarchies, require a critical reimagining of EMI and ESL at policy and practice levels.

Acknowledgement

I express my sincere gratitude to the School of Literature, Languages and Linguistics of the Australian National University for generously providing facilities and resources for writing this article during my Visiting Fellowship.

Note

(1) This is a classroom dictation activity, in which learners listen to a text, note down keywords/phrases and then use them to reconstruct the text. This involves multiple skills and is usually done in groups.

References

Antón, M. and DiCamilla, F. (1998) Socio-cognitive functions of L1 collaborative interaction in the L2 classroom. *Canadian Modern Language Review* 54 (3), 314–342.
Bourdieu, P. (1977) *Outline of a Theory of Practice* (R. Nice, Trans.). Cambridge University Press. (Original work published 1972, Switzerland: Equisse D'une Théorie de la Pratique, Librairie Driz).
Bourdieu, P. (1985) The social space and the genesis of groups. *Theory and Society* 14 (6), 723–744. http://www.jstor.org.ezp01.library.qut.edu.au/stable/657373
Bourdieu, P. (1990) *The Logic of Practice*. Stanford University Press.
Bourdieu, P. (2000) *Pascalian Meditations*. Stanford University Press.
Bourdieu, P. and Passeron, J.-C. (1977) *Reproduction in Education, Society and Culture*. Sage Publications.

Chandra, K. (2006) What is ethnic identity and does it matter? *Annual Review of Political Science* 9, 397–424. https://doi.org/10.1146/annurev.polisci.9.062404.170715

Chen, Q. and Lin, A.M. (2023) Social structures, everyday interactions, and subjectivity – Where (and how) does decolonizing begin? Attending to desires, fears, and pains. *Critical Inquiry in Language Studies* 20 (2), 105–126. https://doi.org/10.1080/15427587.2023.2219059

García, O. and Li, W. (2014) *Translanguaging: Language, Bilingualism and Education*. Palgrave Macmillan.

Horwitz, E.K., Horwitz, M.B. and Cope, J. (1986) Foreign language classroom anxiety. *Modern Language Journal* 70 (2), 125–132.

Ibarra Johnson, S. and García, O. (2023) Siting biliteracy in New Mexican borderlands. *Journal of Latinos and Education* 22 (5), 1913–1928.

Kandiah, T. (1984) Kaduva: Power and the English language weapon in Sri Lanka. In P. Colin-Tome and A. Halpe (eds) *Honouring EFC Ludowyk* (pp. 117–154). Tisara Prakasakayo.

Kohn, K. (2022) Global Englishes and the pedagogical challenge of developing one's own voice. *Asian Englishes* 24 (2), 119–131.

Krashen, S.D. (1985) *The Input Hypothesis: Issues and Implications*. Longman.

Kubota, R. (2020) Confronting epistemological racism, decolonizing scholarly knowledge: Race and gender in applied linguistics. *Applied Linguistics* 41 (5), 712–732.

Larsen-Freeman, D. (2000) *Techniques and Principles in Language Teaching*. Oxford University Press.

Lin, A. (2020) From deficit-based teaching to asset-based teaching in higher education in BANA countries: Cutting through 'either-or' binaries with a heteroglossic plurilingual lens. *Language, Culture and Curriculum* 33 (2), 203–212.

Liyanage, I. and Canagarajah, S. (2019) Shame in English language teaching: Desirable pedagogical possibilities for Kiribati in neoliberal times. *TESOL Quarterly* 53 (2), 430–455.

Lo Bianco, J. (1999) Sri Lanka's bi-lingual education plan. Interview by Jill Kitson. *Lingua Franca*, 10 July [Radio broadcast]. http://www.abc.net.au/radionational/programs/archived/linguafranca/sri-lankas-bi-lingual-education-plan/3563390.

Lo Bianco, J. (2010) The importance of language policies and multilingualism for cultural diversity. *International Social Science Journal* 61 (199), 37–67. https://doi.org/10.1111/j.1468-2451.2010.01747.x

Lo Bianco, J. (2021) Literacy learning and language education: Dominant language constellations and contemporary multilingualism. In L. Aronin and E. Vetter (eds) *Dominant Language Constellations Approach in Education and Language Acquisition* (pp. 1–16). Springer Nature.

Long, M.H. (1981) Input, interaction and second language acquisition. *Native Language and Foreign Language Acquisition. Annals of the New York. Academy of Sciences* 379, 259–78.

Ministry of Education (2021) *Annual School Census of Sri Lanka – Summary Report 2021*. Ministry of Education Sri Lanka. https://moe.gov.lk/wp-content/uploads/2023/02/School_Census-2021_Summary-Tables-Final-Report1.pdf

Mitchell, R. and Myles, F. (2004) *Second Language Learning Theories* (2nd edn). Hodder Arnold.

National Education Commission (2022) *National Education Policy Framework (2020–2023)*. National Education Commission. Sri Lanka.

Otheguy, R., García, O. and Reid, W. (2015) Clarifying translanguaging and deconstructing named languages: A perspective from linguistics. *Applied Linguistic Review* 6 (3), 281–307.

Padwad, A., Wijesekera, H., Phyak, P., Manan, S. and Mohamed, N. (2023) EMI in South Asia. In C. Griffiths (ed.) *The Practice of English as a Medium of Instruction (EMI) Around the World* (pp. 190–210). Springer.

Perera, C. (2022) An exploration on translanguaging in Sri Lankan bilingual education secondary classrooms during ESL cooperative group activities: Forms, functions and learner perceptions. MA Dissertation, Open University of Sri Lanka.

Ratwatte, H.V. (2015) Conditions for second language learning: Translanguage meta-talk in peer interaction: The Sri Lankan experience. In B. Spolsky and K. Sung (eds) *Conditions for English Language Teaching and Learning in Asia* (145–166). Cambridge Scholars Publishing.

Sah, P.K. and Kubota, R. (2022) Towards critical translanguaging: A review of literature on English as a medium of instruction in South Asia's school education. *Asian Englishes* 24 (2), 132–146. https://doi.org/10.1080/13488678.2022.2056796

Skutnabb-Kangas, T. (1989) Multilingualism and the education of minority children. *Estudios Fronterizos* 18, 36–67.

Sri Lanka Janalēkhana hā San'khyālēkhana Depārtamēntuva (2012) *Census of Population and Housing 2012: Provisional Information Based on 5% Sample*. Colombo, [Sri Lanka]: Population Census and Demography Division, Department of Census and Statistics.

Spolsky, B. (2007) Towards a theory of language policy. *Working Papers in Educational Linguistics (WPEL)* 22 (1), 1–14

Swain, M. (1985) Communicative competence: Some roles of comprehensible input and comprehensible output in its development. In S.M. Gass and C.G. Madden (eds) *Input in Second Language Acquisition* (pp. 235–253). Newbury House.

Swain, M. and Lapkin, S. (2001) Focus on form through collaborative dialogue: Exploring task effects. In M. Bygate, P. Skehan and M. Swain (eds) *Researching Pedagogic Tasks. Second Language Learning, Teaching and Testing* (pp. 99–118). Longman.

van Lier, L. (2010) The ecology of language learning: Practice to theory, theory to practice. *Procedia: Social and Behavioral Sciences* 3 (2–6), 2–6.

Vygotsky, L.S. (1978) *Mind in Society: The Development of Higher Psychological Processes*. Harvard University Press.

Wickrema, A. and Colenso, P. (2003) Respect for diversity in education publication – The Sri Lankan experience. Unpublished paper presented at the World Bank Colloquium on Education and Social Cohesion, Washington, D.C., March 23–25.

Wijesekera, H. (2012a) Dreams deferred: English language teaching in Sri Lanka. *Vistas Journal of Humanities and Social Sciences* 7/8, 16–26.

Wijesekera, H.D. (2012b) Opening tight lips: Improving oral participation of the low proficiency ESL learners by reducing anxiety – Action research. Master of Arts in TESOL dissertation, Postgraduate Institute of English, Open University of Sri Lanka.

Wijesekera, H.D. (2018) Students' ethnolinguistic identities in multiethnic, bilingual education classrooms in Sri Lanka. Doctoral dissertation, Queensland University of Technology. https://eprints.qut.edu.au/119217/

Wijesekera, H.D. (2021) Recognizing diversity: Multiethnic Sinhala and Tamil-medium schools in Sri Lanka. In C. Davis and C. LaDousa (eds) *Language, Education, and Identity: Medium in South Asia* (pp. 182–205). Taylor & Francis.

Wijesekera, H.D. and Hamid, M.O. (2022) The dynamics of bilingual education in post-conflict Sri Lanka. In L. Adinolfi, U. Bhattacharya and P. Phyak (eds) *Multilingual Education in South Asia: At the Intersection of Policy and Practice* (pp. 4–25). Routledge.

Wijesekera, H.D., Alford, J. and Mu, M.G. (2019) Forging inclusive practice in ethnically-segregated school systems: Lessons from one multiethnic, bilingual education classroom in Sri Lanka. *International Journal of Inclusive Education* 23 (1), 23–41.

9 Translanguaging and Assessment in English Language Learning in Pakistan: Exploring the Affordances and Challenges

Tanzeela Anbreen and Pramod K. Sah

Introduction

While the use of multiple languages in English language classrooms in South Asian contexts is not a new phenomenon, the recent shift in focus towards examining this practice from a translanguaging perspective (Anderson & Lightfoot, 2018; Sah & Kubota, 2022) is a novel and intriguing development. In South Asia, translanguaging has been an unconscious yet persistent strategy for language teaching and learning for decades (Sah & Kubota, 2022), offering an effective teaching approach that promotes linguistic inclusivity and encourages language users to challenge conventional academic boundaries in their language practices. Despite the linguistic diversity of the region, with 660 languages spoken, there is a dearth of research on translanguaging practices in English language education classrooms (Panda & Mohanty, 2015). For instance, Pakistan alone is home to 69 active languages (Pakistan Ethnologue Free, 2023), making it a fascinating case study for examining translingual practices in education. English, as the dominant language of instruction in Pakistan's higher education (Anbreen & Ayub, 2024; Ashraf et al., 2021; Canagarajah & Ashraf, 2013; Galante, 2020; Panda & Mohanty, 2015), sees the frequent use of translanguaging practices within English language classroom discourses. However, the assessment practices are primarily conducted in monolingual English (Ashraf, 2018). The extent to which students use monolingual English and/or multilingualism in the assessment practices remains unclear.

This creates a gap between what is taught and what is assessed, which needs to be addressed carefully. In this regard, this chapter will focus on translanguaging in Pakistan's higher education. This chapter is an effort to critically inspect the disconnect between multilingual classroom practices and monolingual assessments using the translanguaging theory (García & Li, 2014; Li, 2017). Translanguaging is taken here not simply as a classroom strategy but as a lens that reconceptualizes language practices beyond the language boundaries. It is through this lens that we interrogate the tensions between multilingual learning spaces and monolingual assessment regimes in Pakistan's higher education context. To understand this phenomenon comprehensively, we first explored languaging practices in classroom interactions and then examined the context of translingual assessment. Since the goal of assessment is to measure teaching and learning achievements, we decided to focus on the translanguaging process from classroom interactions to assessment practices. This study aimed: (1) to explore students' and teachers' purpose of utilizing translanguaging in the classroom; (2) how such practices challenge students in their writing-based assessment; and (3) how students handle those challenges. Based on the findings, this chapter provides some policy suggestions and recommendations on how translanguaging can be incorporated into assessment.

Translanguaging in Higher Education

Translanguaging is defined as a dynamic language practice of bi/multilingual speakers that draws on their bi/multilingual knowledge to make meanings (García, 2011). Translanguaging does not simply mean the use of different languages but rather a complete reconceptualization of the languages used by an individual where knowledge of multiple languages forms a single repertoire; as García (2011) stated, 'Bilingualism is not monolingualism times two' (2011: 71). Translanguaging has been discussed as an educational theory (Lewis *et al.*, 2012) and a useful pedagogical strategy (García, 2011). Translanguaging practices are frequently used in various contexts, and they can potentially help language learners use their home language(s) or most familiar languages to learn the target language (Tian *et al.*, 2020). In other words, translanguaging is a process bi/multilingual students use during their target language lessons to create a space to use their home and/or community language(s) and target language.

The majority of translanguaging research has mainly focused on classroom teaching and learning (Canagarajah, 2011; Cenoz, 2017; Creese & Blackledge, 2010, 2015; García & Li, 2014; Jones, 2017; Lasagabaster & García, 2014; Lewis *et al.*, 2012; Moriarty, 2016), while limited attention has been paid to how translanguaging is used in assessment practices. Moreover, these studies highlighted how translanguaging is used or can be used to enhance learners' L2 learning, keeping a limited discussion on how it imposes challenges on assessment practices. In important studies like García and Li (2014), the researchers portrayed the teacher's perspective by summarizing several goals of teachers' use of translanguaging. These goals included (1) differentiating students' existing level (e.g. monolingual, bilingual and emergent bilinguals) and adapting instructions according to their level; (2) developing background knowledge so that students can understand the content and the ways of languaging in the lesson; (3) enhancing understanding and sociopolitical engagement for cross-linguistic metalinguistic awareness to strengthen learners' ability to cater the communicative needs in the socioeducational situation for cross-linguistic flexibility, identity investment and positionality; and (4) questioning linguistic inequality to disrupt linguistic hierarchies and social structures. However, translanguaging practices and their alignment with assessment are yet to be explored. Thus, the current study maps students' challenges in relation to assessment due to translingual practices in English language classrooms in Pakistan.

Translanguaging has been found to serve different purposes in higher education. For instance, some universities in Puerto Rico permit teachers to apply their own policies (micro-level policies) in their classrooms, despite the absence of a clear language policy. This approach promotes translanguaging, which these teachers used to manage resistance from the local language and culture (Mazak & Carroll, 2017). Translanguaging was promoted in a Japanese university context to show more language learning diversity (Adamson & Coulson, 2015). In a Rwandan university, where English was the medium of instruction, students used translanguaging to overcome the challenges of learning content knowledge (Marie, 2013). Translanguaging is also becoming popular in South Asian higher education contexts (Panda & Mohanty, 2015). The case of Pakistan is fascinating as the Higher Education Commission (HEC) encourages public and private sector universities to adopt English as the medium of instruction (EMI) (Panezai *et al.*, 2022). Despite promoting EMI, translanguaging is common in these universities (Saleem *et al.*, 2023). The language policy, however, does not provide any statements or guidelines in terms of translanguaging during classroom teaching and learning.

The literature also suggests that monolingual English is utilized in higher educational institutions for writing purposes (Tamim & Lee, 2021) in the absence of limited guidance available on it in the language policy. Translanguaging remains a continuous phenomenon in other South Asian countries' higher education, such as Nepal, Bangladesh and India (Adhikari & Poudel, 2023; Rafi & Morgan, 2022). Though there is a dearth of research on translanguaging in South Asia in comparison with some other EMI higher education contexts, despite being a multicultural and multilingual region of the world (Anderson, 2022; Mohamed, 2021; Paulsrud *et al.*, 2021; Sah & Kubota, 2022; Sah & Li, 2022, 2024), there are some evidences which suggests that there is a collective resistance to monolingual assessment systems. For example, Adhikari and Poudel's (2023) study reflects that university students used translanguaging in responding to the assessment tasks, thus demarcating the expectations of English-only boundaries. Further exploration of translanguaging in various assessment contexts is vital for a broader understanding of the phenomenon, as it would highlight how translanguaging in assessment works in various educational settings and across various cultures and linguistics landscapes. Also, it would help identify various translanguaging practices, types and strategies, which would expand our overall understanding of the phenomenon, which may help devise policies for multilingual assessment realities.

Bi/Multilingual Assessment Practices in Higher Education

It has been observed that the current language assessment practices lack sufficient attention towards multilingual assessment (Baker & Hope, 2019). As Cenoz and Gorter (2017) and Shohamy et al. (2022) suggested, the existing language assessment theory is primarily based on a monolingual perspective. However, translanguaging is gaining recognition as a useful and inclusive teaching method for bi/multilingual students. Schissel et al. (2021) and Saville (2019) question the principles of traditional language assessment practices, which promote monolingual constructs and practices, as the multilingual realities in applied linguistics compel us to reconsider these principles. In response, researchers have emphasized the need to consider this approach in assessments, as demonstrated by the works of García (2011), Shohamy et al. (2022) and Steele et al. (2022). Language proficiency and content knowledge are two critical facets of assessment that exist together and cannot be disjointed (García, 2011; Shohamy, 2011); prioritizing one facet over the other cannot bring meaningful results (Baker, 2011; García, 2011; García & Li, 2014). Recognizing the potential of translanguaging in assessment should be given high priority according to various studies (García, 2011; Schissel et al., 2021; Shohamy et al., 2022; Steele et al., 2022).

For instance, Shohamy et al. (2022) raised concerns about the fairness of monolingual tests for bilingual test takers. According to their study, presenting a test in both the test takers' first and target language can help them utilize both languages, thereby assisting them in demonstrating and enhancing their academic knowledge. The study conducted on Russian immigrant students showed that bilingual students who received questions in two languages (Russian and Hebrew) performed better than those who received questions only in monolingual Hebrew. As a result, Shohamy et al. (2022) suggested shifting from monolingual to multilingual assessment.

Over the past five years, numerous studies have drawn attention to translanguaging in assessment. For instance, Wolf (2020) discussed several validation challenges faced by young language minority learners. These challenges relate to assessment and include integrating the concepts of translanguaging, scaffolding among language minority children, the role of teachers in language assessment and the intended impact and consequences on students. Other studies, such as those by Otheguy *et al.* (2015) and García and Ascenzi-Moreno (2016), have also explored this topic. Otheguy *et al.* (2015), in this regard raised the assessment concern that 'schools confuse the assessment of general linguistic proficiency, which is best manifested in bilinguals while translanguaging, with the testing of proficiency in a named language, which insists on inhibiting translanguaging' (2015: 281). García and Ascenzi-Moreno (2016) also found that monolingual language practices penalize students even though translanguaging expands their linguistic repertoire. In contrast, monolingual practices limit students' language use by forcing them to use the features of only one dominant language of assessment.

Recently, testing organizations and researchers started to incorporate translanguaging features in the assessment content (e.g. exam questions and instructions are written in test takers' first and target language) with the assumption that, through such practices, a complete language repertoire will be available to them and students would better respond (Baker & Hope, 2019; Cenoz & Gorter, 2017; López *et al.*, 2017; Shohamy *et al.*, 2022). Dendrinos' (2013) study reiterated the usefulness of translanguaging in her experiments with test-takers in the Greek context, where she used source texts in the test takers' first language (i.e. Greek) and test-takers responded to the tasks in the form of summary or commentary in the target language (English). This study further asserts that students often translate test tasks into their first language to better understand them; this makes a stronger case for translanguaging in assessment.

Although there is a good amount of theoretical research on translanguaging practices, more studies are needed to analyze their effects in different contexts. It is essential to view translanguaging practices holistically in language classroom research, particularly in contexts where students must pass monolingual writing assessments to advance to certain levels (e.g. Pakistan). A dynamic translanguaging model should be considered as the world becomes more globalized and inclusive.

Multilingual Classrooms in Pakistan's Higher Education

As a post-colonial society in Pakistan, English remained a dominant language, continuing the colonial legacy (Haider, 2019; Haider & Fang, 2019; Haroon *et al.*, 2023; Hussain & Khan, 2021). Pakistan's linguistic landscape is diverse and complex, with 69 actively spoken languages. However, English holds a dominant position in the higher education context despite Urdu being one of the official languages. English is associated with more prestige and dominates Urdu in the education system. Pakistan's national education policy promotes English language teaching and learning from the beginning years of education. However, it has been criticized for promoting English over the national language, Urdu, and neglecting the regional languages. This policy's repercussions include creating a divide between elites and the masses and causing socioeconomic division. Pakistan's Education Policy (2019) acknowledged the importance of bilingual education and focused on striking a balance between English and Urdu in schools, yet due to the political instability in 2022 in the country, this policy could not be implemented in its spirit as planned, and the earlier education policy (Government of Pakistan, 2009) continues to operate. The Education Policy (Government of Pakistan, 2009) emphasizes that the Ministry of Education, along with other relevant departments, would develop a comprehensive plan for the implementation of the English language in the shortest possible time and would keep special attention to the disadvantaged groups and less developed regions in promoting English (Government of Pakistan, 2009; Mahboob, 2017). This policy promotes the implementation of English, first as a subject in schools and then promoting EMI. However, it is important to note that this policy does not discuss EMI or monolingual English in the assessments in Higher Education. It is commonly understood that English is the dominant language; therefore, conventional assessments in English will continue to be used (Mahboob, 2017; Rassool & Mansoor, 2007). As per this policy and previous policies, course materials and assessments should follow this monolingual English policy. Notably, some contexts, such as Pakistan, promote monolingual assessment policies and language segregation, which requires further research.

However, there is limited mention that this policy lacks in setting direction at the university level, but for universities to use English as a medium of instruction remains acceptable and is undebatable (Mahboob, 2017). Thus, like some other South Asian countries, Pakistan struggles to develop an equitable and effective language policy for several reasons, particularly due to political and ideological factors that favor English and bestow it with more power. In Pakistan, students attend private English medium schools, public-funded Urdu medium schools, or religious schools (locally called Madrassahs), which also offer Urdu medium instruction (Anbreen & Ayub, 2024). Generally, students' English language fluency largely depends on the type of school they attend. Pakistan's elites are usually fluent English speakers, unlike the common masses (Rahman, 2001). When students with low proficiency in English join universities, they tend to adopt translanguaging, often codemixing between Urdu and English codes (Hussain & Khan, 2021). Although English is the recommended medium of instruction in university programs, translanguaging between English and Urdu is frequently observed (Panezai et al., 2022).

Several studies conducted in Pakistan have highlighted the use of translanguaging in classrooms (Ashraf, 2018; Saleem et al., 2023; Saleem &

Khan, 2023; Shah *et al.*, 2019; Syed, 2022). However, there has been limited discussion on assessment practices in this context. Formal assessments in Pakistani universities rely heavily on writing exams, which are primarily conducted in English. This approach to assessment is challenging for students, as it follows a monolingual perspective (Panezai *et al.*, 2022). In light of this, the current research aims to explore how translanguaging is practiced during lessons and tests, its purpose and how students cope with these challenges. Building on García's (2011) concept of translanguaging as a dynamic, fluid use of the entire linguistic repertoire and Canagarajah's (2011) ideas on translingual negotiation in academic spaces, the current study employs translanguaging theory as a critical lens to reveal how Pakistani students navigate and challenge monolingual ideologies embedded in assessment. Li's (2017) view of translanguaging as a practical theory of language that enables meaning making and identity performance further informs our interpretation of the students' agency in resisting the monolingual demands.

Research Methodology

The research context

This study was conducted in a Pakistani university located in Punjab province, where most students come from an Urdu or Punjabi language background. However, Urdu is frequently spoken in the university context. The university context chosen in this study had both elite and middle-class students. Students who attended English medium schools in the local context had better English fluency and those who attended Urdu medium schools had limited fluency in English. However, additional factors also impact students' language skills and fluency (e.g. individual circumstances related to learning and social opportunities, such as private tutoring).

The current study employed sequential qualitative research methods to gain a deeper understanding of the impact of translanguaging on the assessment of higher education students. Understanding the process of translanguaging during lessons was important to establish a link between students' practices and challenges, so the research was designed to focus on understanding the current translanguaging practices in English language classrooms, their purpose, how such translanguaging practices challenge students in their assessment and how students handle those challenges.

Data collection

Data collection started with classroom observations. The observations were taken during compulsory English language classes at a university in Lahore, followed by semi-structured interviews with teachers and students. The compulsory English lessons focused on developing students' academic English skills. In their interviews, the teachers discussed the instances of translanguaging practices in students' written scripts. Some written test (N = 10) scripts were collected. Interviews with students also focused on exploring their translanguaging practices during lectures and tests, particularly their reasons and purposes for translanguaging, challenges and strategies to handle them. This section discusses the methodology in detail.

Participants

This study's participants included teachers and students pursuing the Bachelor of Studies (also called BS) degree (undergraduate level). Table 9.1 presents their brief profiles.

Each participating teacher taught compulsory English in various departments of the university. Passing compulsory English is a requirement for undergraduate students to obtain an undergraduate degree. Thus, 10 different classes were observed.

The data sets

Three data sets included (i) semi-structured interviews with 10 teachers, each interview lasting for approximately 20–30 minutes, (ii) semi-structured interviews with 20 students, each approximately between 10–20 minutes and (iii) written exam scripts. Data collection started with the observation sessions. Lessons of 10 teachers (N = 10) who taught in various Social Sciences and Humanities departments were observed. In the observed classes, teachers taught compulsory English anthology/essay books. The reading comprehension activity required the students to comprehend the text and answer the related questions. They also had to perform language-related tasks such as writing synonyms for given vocabulary and completing grammar exercises. During the observation, the researcher noted the classroom's current translanguaging practices, documenting incidents of translanguaging in the class. The notes were used as evidence of translanguaging and further explored in the interview. The researcher also recorded the observations. All translanguaging occurred in Urdu-English.

Table 9.1 Participants' profiles

Participants	Number (N)	Departments where observations conducted (N = 10)	Experience level	Class taught/ attended
Lecturers (full-time), all females, taught English in different departments	10	(1) Economics, (2) Political Science, (3) History, (4) Business Studies, (5) Education, (6) Mass Communication/Journalism, (7) English Literature, (8) Persian, (9) Islamic Studies, (10) Sociology	5 years	BS Undergraduate 1st Semester compulsory English
Students (full-time), all females, studying in various departments	10	(1) Economics, (2) Political Science, (3) History, (4) Business Studies, (5) Education, (6) Mass Communication/Journalism, (7) English Literature, (8) Persian, (9) Islamic Studies, (10) Sociology	13 years of education	BS Undergraduate 1st Semester compulsory English

Immediately after each session, the researcher conducted semi-structured interviews with the teachers and students to get their insights into why they used translanguaging. The interviews were guided by questions such as: What were the purposes for doing so? Did it help them achieve their purpose? How far can students may/will be successful in using translanguaging in their mid-term/final-term tests?

During each session, the researcher selected two students (N = 2) based on their engagement in translanguaging during the lesson. These students were willing to participate in semi-structured interviews. They talked about their purpose and reasons for using translanguaging practices and how they can help or challenge them during their examination. The researcher made sure to follow the ethical requirements of the institution and the participation of both teachers and students was voluntary.

During the interview, teachers and students pointed out that translanguaging occurs unplanned in the classroom and on written tests, and they showed the students' scripts. Twenty scripts (N = 20) were reviewed, following all relevant ethical requirements.

All data were qualitative, and the researchers analysed them using Braun and Clarke's (2006) five-step thematic analysis. The first author collected the data herself, which gave her a good understanding of it. However, she further read and discussed the data with fellow researchers. Both researchers looked at instances of translanguaging, students' and teachers' ideas in the interviews and the written examples of translanguaging in the exam scripts. They read and discussed the data carefully and repeatedly, which helped them understand the data well. They generated initial codes and reviewed them. Finally, they defined the themes and interpreted them in writing. They found four key themes from the data. Two themes were related to students' academic needs: one, translanguaging for clarification purposes during lectures and two, its use in assessment situations where students employ translanguaging to cover a gap between their available English language knowledge/skills and the required knowledge/skills. The third theme was its culture-related use, where translanguaging is practiced as a vehicle of identity. The fourth theme reflected students' strategies to handle tests.

Findings

Translanguaging practices in the classroom: From learning contents to affirming identities

The classroom observation data was used to explore the current translanguaging practices, which suggested that (i) frequent translanguaging occurs in verbal communication during lectures and (ii) Urdu and English languages were used for translanguaging. An example of spoken translanguaging is presented here with its English translation in the parentheses:

Student: Excuse me madam, does it mean that it is inappropriate for a woman *kai* money earn *karnay ko apna* main goal *bana lai*? (Excuse me madam, does it mean that it is inappropriate for a woman **to make** earning **money her** main goal?)

Teacher: Yes, bilkul that's true. You must decide carefully aur *apni Akhlaqi Quadro ko* compromise *na karay*. (Yes, *absolutely* that's true. You must decide carefully *and do not* compromise your *moral boundaries*.)

Student: But madam, what do you say about Mr Rochester *wo lalchi nahi tha kai* young *majboor* woman *sai shadi ki* who was of her daughter's age? (But madam what do you say about Mr Rochester, *wasn't he greedy that he married* a young *helpless* woman who was of her daughter's age?).

Translanguaging from both sides (i.e. the teacher and student) is seen during an exchange of dialogue in the classroom lecture. This means that both parties use their own language to communicate, including terms and phrases related to their culture. Students may have a limited vocabulary in the language being taught, so they use their first language to understand the concepts better. This approach aligns with Cummins' theory that using a student's home language can be beneficial for them to understand the material. In this particular example, translanguaging worked positively for the teacher and student despite English being the primary language of instruction. It is worth noting that conducting classroom activities entirely in English can be challenging, as the literature suggests (Phyak *et al.*, 2022). Perhaps another reason for the use of translanguaging is to express cultural identity. Therefore, using both their home language and English can help achieve a better understanding of the material.

During class observations, it was noticed that translanguaging was taking place in note-taking and class tests. Some examples of notes taken by students are presented here:

Example 1: Amjad explained *waldain kai haqooq* to the class (Amjad explained *parents' rights* to class).

Example 2: Parents are the most important people in our life because *wo hamari bunyad rakhtay hain* (Parents are the most important people in our life because *they set our foundation*.)

Example 3: In a girl's marriage *Jahaiz sab sai bari rokawat hai*. We cannot stop people and this is increasing *bahaseeat* aik social **laanat** (*In a girl's marriage, dowry is the biggest hurdle. We cannot stop people and this is increasing as a social curse*).

This example shows that students used culture-related concepts in Urdu, such as 'waldain kai haqooq', 'bunyad' and 'Jahaiz', while translanguaging.

During lectures, note-taking requires quick coordination between the mind and hand. Using Urdu terms and phrases suggests that they may have used it to compensate for a lack of suitable vocabulary or to express complex ideas that cannot be written in monolingual English quickly.

The observed instances of translanguaging among students and teachers in the classroom after the Eid festival holidays vividly illustrate how language serves as a conduit for expressing a strong Pakistani identity. We noticed a fluid mixing of English and Urdu codes during the conversation, indicating a natural integration of both languages in their communicative interactions. As can be seen in the classroom vignette below, the exchange between the teacher and students began with greetings in both languages, using phrases like 'Assalam o Alikum' and 'Eid Mubarak,' which effortlessly merged English and Urdu. The conversation further unfolded with the teacher using a mix of Urdu and English to inquire about the students' holiday experiences, illustrating the students' activities during Eid and the teacher's attempt to link festivities with the impending exams.

Students:	Assalam o Alikum teacher, Eid Mubarak (Hello/God bless you teacher, Eid greetings)
Teacher:	Waalikum Assalam and Khair Mubarak (Hello/God bless you and greetings to you too)
Teacher:	How was your weekend **baccho (children)**
Students:	**Bohat accha (very good)** sir
Teacher:	Did you enjoy the Eid holidays **ya parhai bhi** ki? (Did you enjoy the Eid holidays **or did you also study?**)
One student (# 4):	Sir Bakra Eid **par** no one studies, **Qurbani karni** (slaughtering animal), meat dishes **banana (cook) aur (and)** distribution of meat to the poor and relatives were our main tasks. **Hamaray ghar walon nai chorna nahi tha (Our family would not spare us from work)** if we would not give them a hand.
Teacher (# 2):	Beta (dear) all is acceptable **par (but)** exams **aap hi ko dena hai (you will undertake exams)**, make your family understand **har waqay guddi guddi nahi ho sakta (every time is not a fun time)**.

When the researcher asked why they translanguaged, the student said, 'Pakistani students often do like this.' Another student stated, 'We all know Urdu and there is no problem if we use Urdu and English codes; this is our language; when a teacher speaks in Urdu with English, we feel she is our own.' Another student replied, 'We love speaking Urdu and English to express our feelings and emotions, as culture-bound discussions like the Eid festival are well presented in our language. It gives ownership.' The students expressed a sense of cultural belonging and familiarity. They highlighted that using a mix of Urdu and English is a common practice among Pakistani students. Their responses reflected a deep-rooted comfort with both languages, viewing this amalgamation as an expression of their cultural identity. They expressed feelings of belonging and ownership when teachers communicate using this hybrid language, making them feel more connected and understood.

The analysis underscores that language serves as a powerful tool for communicating and constructing identity. The multilingual capabilities of both teachers and students facilitate the expression and negotiation of their identities through the choice and blend of languages. This further emphasizes the contextual nature of identity display and the intrinsic link between language and the representation of one's identity.

Translanguaging in Assessment

During one of the classroom observations, the researcher entered a class with the teacher and all the students greeted them, 'Good morning, madam.' The teacher reminded them that it was a class test and they needed 'to write a letter of application to the Head of the Department to seek permission to go on a recreational trip.' She wrote the task on the board. However, the students asked clarity questions where translanguaging was evident.

Student: *Miss, kitnay words write karnay hain?* (Translation: Teacher, **how many** words **must we write?**)
Teacher: You can write about 250 to 300 words, *ya kuch ziada bhi ho saktay hain,* no problem, you focus on the content. (Translation: You can write about 250 to 300 words, some more can be acceptable, no problem, you focus on the content.)
Student: Miss, 'recreational' *ka kiya matlab*? (Translation: Teacher, what does 'recreational' mean?)
Teacher: *Sair o tafreeh par jana* (Translation: to go on leisure)

This scenario highlighted that the students used translanguaging to understand the test task. Reflecting on the classroom practices, the teacher shared her strategies and beliefs about translanguaging in assessment.

Teacher: In day-to-day classroom learning, they frequently use Urdu-English codes [translanguaging], which is fine for us. You might have noticed that I sometimes used Urdu because students would not know complete English. However, this practice [translanguaging] is unacceptable in writing exams.
The researcher: If they cannot translanguage in a test, then why did you use it in the class?
Teacher: I answered their questions and explained them in Urdu and English because they would understand the task better; already, they are challenged in writing monolingual English codes. If I do not explain in Urdu, they will not handle and fail.

The teacher was familiar with the requirement of monolingual English in writing tests. However, she was aware of the actual student needs and used translanguaging as a tool to explain the test task. The teacher led us to confirm what Phyak *et al.*'s (2022) study highlighted in Nepal's context: translanguaging is an essential pedagogical tool for engaging students in class. Ashraf (2018) rightly stated that educational needs should be considered holistically in countries like Pakistan, where there is high linguistic diversity and spontaneous translanguaging. Our analysis suggested that translanguaging has the potential to be used as a strategy during tests.

In another class test, the teacher provided the questions on the whiteboard, and students had to write answers based on their earlier reading (without having access to the text). Again, the translanguaging was noticed in students' writing work.

Question:	What was the most disliked thing for King Rassalu?
Student answer:	According to Rassalu, the third most *laanti* (cursed) thing is a daughter with a **Ghussa Wali** (fierce) and unfriendly *shakal* (appearance).
Question:	What did the girl decide about Rassalu?
Student answer:	The girl decided Rassalu to go because they were impressed by his **acchi shakal** (good looks).
Question:	When was King Honn of Delhi defeated?
Student answer:	Raja Honn of Delhi has been defeated by **dosra Raja** (another king) in a great **Jang** (battle).

Students use translanguaging to increase their space for the local epistemologies, which focus on the monolingual use of English in writing. In this example, the student seems to be increasing her space through translanguaging while describing the case of a king from a folk story.

The analysis shows that teachers often use translanguaging to achieve diverse pedagogical goals, including improving task clarity, giving instructions and helping students understand the material. Moreover, this practice is not limited to classroom instruction but extends to written tests, indicating that students also utilize translanguaging continuously. Although Shah *et al.* (2019) observed the unconscious use of translanguaging in class discussions involving Pashto and Urdu in Pakistan, our study shows that students intentionally and knowledgeably use translanguaging to bridge gaps in their learning during written exams. One student expressed,

> If I struggle with English vocabulary in exams, I sometimes write in Urdu because writing something is better than not writing.

Interestingly, while teachers acknowledge the usefulness of translanguaging for learning purposes, they highlight a significant gap between learning practices and assessment methods. They recognize that students frequently resort to using Urdu-English codes for explanations and notes, which aids their learning process. However, this multilingual practice becomes unacceptable during timed writing exams, where monolingual codes, specifically in English, are mandated. As one teacher pointed out,

> In day-to-day classroom learning, they frequently use Urdu-English codes [translanguaging] to write the explanations, instructions, and notes, which help them in better learning. But this practice is unacceptable in timed writing exams where they must answer in monolingual codes requiring all English. Translanguaging challenges them in independent writing tasks during exams.

This discrepancy between multilingual classroom practices and monolingual assessment methods is not unique to Pakistan. García and Li (2014) lamented the prevalence of standardized assessments administered in a single language, disregarding the potential benefits of multilingual tests. Similarly, Pakistan's language policy (Government of Pakistan, 2009) emphasizes monolingual assessments, neglecting the practical needs of students proficient in multiple languages. Teachers, recognizing the limitations of solely using English codes in teaching, find it impossible to implement in classrooms, especially for students with limited English proficiency. Consequently, students habitually rely on Urdu-English codes, which become a hurdle when they must adhere strictly to monolingual English codes during exams. As one teacher discussed,

> Using monolingual English codes in class is impossible for students with limited English language skills, and they habitually use Urdu-English codes as an alternative to 'all English codes', which is fine. But the real problem comes when they are required to write in monolingual English codes.

Thus, this finding underscores the practical necessity of adopting a multilingual approach in educational settings, particularly in Pakistan. It exposes the discrepancy between classroom realities, where multilingualism supports learning and assessment requirements that demand monolingualism, highlighting the need for reforms in assessment policies. Addressing this mismatch is crucial to ensure equitable and effective evaluation methods, considering students' linguistic diversity and supporting their academic success.

Students' strategies to handle monolingual English writing tests

The interview findings unveil a spectrum of strategies students employ to navigate monolingual English tests, indicating their struggles and adaptive measures within the assessment framework. One prevalent approach involves memorization, notably focusing on textbook exercises, as these exercises often constitute a significant portion of the exam. Students resort to cramming solved exercise books available in the market, leveraging their memory prowess to reproduce these exercises during tests. Though effective in securing minimum passing grades, this method highlights the reliance on rote learning and memorization techniques. Teacher # 2 highlighted,

> There are several solved exercise books available in the market that students would use to memorize the end-of-chapter exercises. Those with good memory will cram it and produce it in exams. These exercises have reasonable weighting; at least, they help them to pass the exam with a minimum grade.

Moreover, students express the challenges of memorizing extensive content, including letters, applications and essays on various topics. While time-consuming, this approach becomes necessary for them to ensure proficiency during English exams, reflecting the pressure they face to excel within the given constraints. Student # 3 stated:

> I memorise content like end exercises from the textbook and sometimes letters, applications, and essays on general exam-relevant topics. It takes long hours to memorise, but otherwise, I cannot make sure to pass the exam.

Moreover, students express the challenges of memorizing extensive content, including letters, applications and essays on various topics. While time-consuming, this approach becomes necessary for them to ensure proficiency during English exams, reflecting the pressure they face to excel within the given constraints. A student stated:

> I sometimes write vocabulary or ideas in Urdu when I do not remember their English because writing something is better than nothing. Maybe the teacher understand and give me some marks.

However, the reliance on memorization and translanguaging poses concerns about students' genuine development of English language skills. The emphasis on memorizing large volumes of content might hinder their ability to acquire language proficiency for practical use in real-life scenarios beyond examination contexts. In line with Chalhoub-Deville's (2019) insights, there is a pressing need to shift from monolingual testing constructs to multilingual ones. Multilingual testing constructs would better align with the increasingly diverse linguistic demographics, allowing students to demonstrate their knowledge and skills more authentically. This shift could redirect the focus from cumbersome strategies like rote memorization towards more meaningful and comprehensive learning experiences.

Reconsidering the current multilingual assessment policy becomes imperative. A re-evaluation could pave the way for a more inclusive and adaptive assessment framework that acknowledges and accommodates students' multilingual abilities. Such a shift could not only ease the testing burden on students but also foster genuine language development and a deeper understanding of the English language in diverse real-life contexts.

Discussion

The analysis of classroom observation, interviews and exam papers in this study illuminates that translanguaging is a natural part of teaching, learning and assessment in Pakistan's higher education context, which has a significant potential to enhance the writing abilities and assessment outcomes of multilingual language users. Our findings indicate that translanguaging enables students to express complex ideas more efficiently, including in timed writing examinations where students must articulate sophisticated arguments within a limited time frame. As García and Li (2014) asserted, translanguaging expands students' expressive and interpretative capacities. The findings of this study show that students can convey their thoughts more clearly and confidently by leveraging their entire linguistic repertoire. Moreover, translanguaging practices in classrooms and assessments should be aligned, as they may increase students' engagement and confidence; this study found that students felt comfortable and less restricted when allowed to use their linguistic range. This comfort, in turn, may often result in improved performance, echoing Shohamy *et al.*'s (2022) finding that translanguaging in assessment needs to be given high priority as it positively impacts students' performance. Also, students often use their first language to grasp complex ideas and translate them into English. This process appears to help in internalising and understanding the content more profoundly; thus, translanguaging seems to facilitate deeper cognitive processing, which can help them avoid memorising the content. The findings from this study extend translanguaging theory by highlighting its role not only in pedagogical engagement but also as a resistance strategy within strict monolingual assessment systems. While García and Li (2014) focus on classroom learning, our findings suggest that students strategically employ their full linguistic repertoires during high-stakes assessment, despite institutional discouragement. This explains how translanguaging can function as a subversive act in contexts where linguistic hierarchies are reinforced through assessment.

Interestingly, the findings of this study remind us of the sociocultural theories of language and identity, which focus on where a language is used and how and for whom it is used (e.g. Creese & Blackledge, 2015; García & Li, 2014; Norton, 2013). As teachers and students in this study were familiar with Urdu and English, they used these languages flexibly. This analysis of the identity of multilingual Pakistani students and teachers is located on the idea that identities involve a discursive positioning of self and others. Since language is a mode of communicating an identity, it stands to reason that the identity of multilingual people is fluid and the display of their identity depends upon the context (Cabo & Rothman, 2012). The language users in this study were familiar with both Urdu and English and they used them to display their identity.

This study reveals that translanguaging is not limited to verbal communication during classroom teaching and learning, but rather it extends to assessments, the ultimate aim of students' learning in the local context, as they must pass these assessments to graduate. Since assessments have serious implications for students in our chosen context and there is evidence of translanguaging in assessment, translanguaging in assessments needs policy attention. Translanguaging in exams can bridge the gap between students' linguistic and cultural backgrounds and the predominantly English-centric academic environment. For example, writing the test tasks or instructions in both learners' native language and the target language, allowing learners to use course terms or culture-bound terms in their native language, and even allowing some specific proportion of writing where they can use their native language, for example, one third to half of the total work. Such steps will foster a more inclusive and equitable educational atmosphere by validating students' home languages and cultures. However, realistically speaking, the implementation of translanguaging in assessment is not without challenges in Pakistan's context, where there is resistance from traditional assessment paradigms that prioritize monolingual teaching and assessment, often equating it with academic rigor and quality. Additionally, instructors must be mindful, proficient and trained in students' first language use and determine to what extent translanguaging should be acceptable in the classroom and assessments.

Conclusion

This study extended beyond merely exploring translanguaging practices in assessment; it examined a continuum, spanning from classroom interactions to assessment. By highlighting the mismatch between translanguaging-rich pedagogy and monolingual assessment, the current study challenges deeply rooted institutionalized ideologies of linguistic purity and proposes translanguaging as a legitimate tool for both learning and evaluation. In conclusion, this study contributes to the growing body of research advocating translanguaging as a pedagogical and assessment tool. In Pakistan, where there is significant linguistic diversity, translanguaging can bridge the gap between students' linguistic realities and English learning demands.

Translanguaging challenges traditional monolingual ideologies and proposes a more inclusive approach that values the linguistic repertoires of all students. The findings of this study hold significant implications for language policy and educational practice in Pakistani universities. The study indicates that adopting translanguaging can enhance writing assessments and promote the academic success of multilingual students. It also highlights the need to shift towards more inclusive language policies that cater to students' social and cultural needs and acknowledge their linguistic diversity. In this regard, official recognition of the multilingual needs of Pakistani students may be the first step that would provide space for translanguaging strategies in national language policies. On practical grounds, a comprehensive review of the existing language policies is needed as a priority, followed by teacher training and institutional recognition of translanguaging as a means to support linguistic equity, especially for students from marginalized educational backgrounds, and developing new guidelines to promote multiple language use and translanguaging in teaching and assessment. In doing so, the chapter offers a framework for reconciling language education with the multilingual, postcolonial realities of South Asia, fostering more just and context-responsive English language learning environments.

References

Adamson, J. and Coulson, D. (2015) Translanguaging in English academic writing preparation. *International Journal of Pedagogies and Learning* 10 (1), 24–37. https://doi.org/10.1080/22040552.2015.1084674

Adhikari, B.R. and Poudel, P.P. (2023) Countering English-prioritised monolingual ideologies in content assessment through translanguaging practices in higher education. *Language and Education* 38 (2), 155–172. https://doi.org/10.1080/09500782.2023.2217804

Anbreen, T. and Ayub, S. (2024) EAP practitioners' identity in Pakistan: From social class to social capital. In A. Ding and L. Monbec (eds) *Practitioner Agency and Identity in English for Academic Purposes* (pp. 91–107). Bloomsbury Publishing.

Anderson, J. (2022) The translanguaging practices of expert Indian teachers of English and their learners. *Journal of Multilingual and Multicultural Development*. https://doi.org/10.1080/01434632.2022.2045300

Anderson, J. and Lightfoot, A. (2018) Translingual practices in English classrooms in India: Current perceptions and future possibilities. *International Journal of Bilingual Education and Bilingualism* 24 (8), 1210–1231. https://doi.org/10.1080/13670050.2018.1548558

Ashraf, H. (2018) Translingual practices and monoglot policy aspirations: A case study of Pakistan's plurilingual classrooms. *Current Issues in Language Planning* 19 (1), 1–21. https://doi.org/10.1080/14664208.2017.1281035

Ashraf, H., Turner, D.A. and Laar, R.A. (2021) Multilingual language practices in education in Pakistan: The conflict between policy and practice. *SAGE Open* 11 (1), 215824402110041. https://doi.org/10.1177/21582440211004140

Baker, B. and Hope, A. (2019) Incorporating translanguaging in language assessment: The case of a test for university professors. *Language Assessment Quarterly* 16 (4–5), 408–425. https://doi.org/10.1080/15434303.2019.1671392

Baker, C. (2011) *Foundations of Bilingual Education and Bilingualism* (5th edn). Multilingual Matters.

Braun, V. and Clarke, V. (2006) Using thematic analysis in psychology. *Qualitative Research in Psychology* 3 (2), 77–101. https://doi.org/10.1191/1478088706qp063oa

Cabo, D. P. Y. and Rothman, J. (2012) The (Il)logical problem of heritage speaker bilingualism and incomplete acquisition. *Applied Linguistics* 33 (4), 450–455. https://doi.org/10.1093/applin/ams037

Canagarajah, S. (2011) Translanguaging in the classroom: Emerging issues for research and pedagogy. *Applied Linguistics Review* 2 (2011), 1–28. https://doi.org/10.1515/9783110239331.1

Canagarajah, S. and Ashraf, H. (2013) Multilingualism and education in South Asia: Resolving policy/practice dilemmas. *Annual Review of Applied Linguistics* 33, 258–285. https://doi.org/10.1017/s0267190513000068

Cenoz, J. (2017) Translanguaging in school contexts: International perspectives. *Journal of Language Identity and Education* 16 (4), 193–198. https://doi.org/10.1080/15348458.2017.1327816

Cenoz, J. and Gorter, D. (2017) Minority languages and sustainable translanguaging: Threat or opportunity? *Journal of Multilingual and Multicultural Development* 38 (10), 901–912. https://doi.org/10.1080/01434632.2017.1284855

Chalhoub-Deville, M. (2019) Multilingual testing constructs: Theoretical foundations. *Language Assessment Quarterly* 16 (4–5), 472–480. https://doi.org/10.1080/15434303.2019.1671391

Creese, A. and Blackledge, A. (2010) Translanguaging in the bilingual classroom: A pedagogy for learning and teaching? *The Modern Language Journal* 94 (1), 103–115. https://doi.org/10.1111/j.1540-4781.2009.00986.x

Creese, A. and Blackledge, A. (2015) Translanguaging and identity in educational settings. *Annual Review of Applied Linguistics* 35, 20–35. https://doi.org/10.1017/s0267190514000233

Dendrinos, B. (2013) Testing and teaching in mediation: Input from the KPG exams in English. *Directions in Language Teaching and Testing*. http://rcel.enl.uoa.gr/directions/issue1_1f.htm

Ethnologue (2023) Pakistan ethnologue. https://www.ethnologue.com/country/PK/

Galante, A. (2020) Pedagogical translanguaging in a multilingual English program in Canada: Student and teacher perspectives of challenges. *System* 92, 102274. https://doi.org/10.1016/j.system.2020.102274

García, O. (2009) *Bilingual Education in the 21st Century: A Global Perspective* (1st edn). John Wiley & Sons.

García, O. (2011) *Bilingual Education in the 21st Century: A Global Perspective* (2nd edn). John Wiley & Sons.

García, O. and Li, W. (2014) *Translanguaging: Language, Bilingualism and Education*. Palgrave Macmillan.

García, O. and Ascenzi-Moreno, L. (2016) Assessment in school from a translanguaging angle. In S. Ptashnyk, R. Beckert, P. Wolf-Farré and M. Wolny (eds) *GegenwärtigeSprachkontakte im Kontext der Migration* (pp. 119–130). Universitatsverlag WINTER Heidelberg

Government of Pakistan (2009) *National Education Policy*. Govt of Pakistan. https://itacec.org/document/2015/7/National_Education_Policy_2009.pdf

Haidar, S. (2019) Access to English in Pakistan: Inculcating prestige and leadership through instruction in elite schools. *International Journal of Bilingual Education and Bilingualism* 22 (7), 833–848. https://doi.org/10.1080/13670050.2017.1320352

Haidar, S. and Fang, F. (2019) Access to English in Pakistan: A source of prestige or a hindrance to success. *Asia Pacific Journal of Education* 39 (4), 485–500. https://doi.org/10.1080/02188791.2019.1671805

Haroon, S., Aslam, M. and Saleem, T. (2023) Exploring the cross-linguistic functioning of the Principles of WH-Movements: The case of Pakistani ESL learners. *Cogent Arts & Humanities* 10 (1). https://doi.org/10.1080/23311983.2023.2174518

Hussain, S. and Khan, H.K. (2021) Translanguaging in Pakistani higher education: A neglected perspective. *Journal of Educational Research & Social Science Review* 1 (3), 16–24. https://ojs.jerssr.org.pk/index.php/jerssr/article/view/12

Jones, B. (2017) Translanguaging in bilingual schools in Wales. *Journal of Language Identity and Education* 16 (4), 199–215. https://doi.org/10.1080/15348458.2017.1328282

Lasagabaster, D. and García, O. (2014) *Translanguaging*: Towards a dynamic model of bilingualism at school/Translanguaging:*hacia un modelo dinámico de bilingüismo en la escuela*. *Culture and Education* 26 (3), 557–572. https://doi.org/10.1080/11356405.2014.973671

Lewis, G., Jones, B. and Baker, C. (2012) Translanguaging: Developing its conceptualisation and contextualisation. *Educational Research and Evaluation* 18 (7), 655–670. https://doi.org/10.1080/13803611.2012.718490

Li, W. (2017) Translanguaging as a practical theory of language. *Applied Linguistics* 39 (1), 9–30. https://doi.org/10.1093/applin/amx039

López, A.A., Türkan, S. and Guzman-Orth, D. (2017) Conceptualizing the use of translanguaging in initial content assessments for newly arrived emergent bilingual students. *ETS Research Report Series* 2017 (1), 1–12. https://doi.org/10.1002/ets2.12140

Mahboob, A. (2017) English medium instruction in higher education in Pakistan: Policies, perceptions, problems, and possibilities. In B. Fenton-Smith, P. Humphreys and I. Walkinshaw (eds) *English Medium Instruction in Higher Education in Asia-Pacific* (pp. 71–92). Springer.

Marie, K.A. (2013) Coping with English as language of instruction in higher education in Rwanda. *International Journal of Higher Education* 2 (2), 1–12. https://doi.org/10.5430/ijhe.v2n2p1

Mazak, C.M. and Carroll, K.S. (2017) *Translanguaging in Higher Education: Beyond Monolingual Ideologies*. Multilingual Matters.

Mohamed, N. (2021) Transcending linguistic and cultural boundaries: A case study of four young Maldivians' translanguaging practices. In B. Paulsrud, Z. Tian and J. Toth (eds) *English-Medium Instruction and Translanguaging* (pp. 77–93). Multilingual Matters.

Moriarty, M. (2016) Developing resources for translanguaging in minority language contexts: A case study of rapping in an Irish primary school. *Language, Culture and Curriculum* 30 (1), 76–90. https://doi.org/10.1080/07908318.2016.1230623

Norton, B. (2013) *Identity and Language Learning: Extending the Conversation* (2nd edn). Multilingual Matters.

Otheguy, R., García, O. and Reid, W. (2015) Clarifying translanguaging and deconstructing named languages: A perspective from linguistics. *Applied Linguistics Review* 6 (3), 281–307. https://doi.org/10.1515/applirev-2015-0014

Parho Pakistan (2019) Education Policy 2019 - Punjab school education department. *Parho Pakistan*, 7 March. https://www.parhopak.com/education-policy-2019-punjab/#

Panda, M.P. and Mohanty, A.K.M. (2015) Multilingual education in South Asia: The burden of the double divide. In W.E. Wright, S. Boun and O. García (eds) *The Handbook of Bilingual and Multilingual Education* (1st edn, pp. 542–553). John Wiley & Sons, Inc. https://doi.org/10.1002/9781118533406

Panezai, A., Channa, L.A. and Bibi, B. (2022) Translanguaging in higher education: Exploring interactional spaces for meaning-making in the multilingual universities of Pakistan. *International Journal of Bilingual Education and Bilingualism*. https://doi.org/10.1080/13670050.2022.2124842

Paulsrud, B., Tian, Z. and Toth, J. (eds) (2021) *English-Medium Instruction and Translanguaging*. Multilingual Matters.

Phyak, P., Sah, P.K., Ghimire, N.B. and Lama, A. (2022) Teacher agency in creating a translingual space in Nepal's multilingual English-medium schools. *RELC Journal* 53 (2), 431–451. https://doi.org/10.1177/00336882221113950

Rafi, A.S.M. and Morgan, A. (2022) Linguistic ecology of Bangladeshi higher education: A translanguaging perspective. *Teaching in Higher Education* 27 (4), 512–529. https://doi.org/10.1080/13562517.2022.2045579

Rahman, T. (2001) English-teaching institutions in Pakistan. *Journal of Multilingual and Multicultural Development* 22 (3), 242–261. https://doi.org/10.1080/01434630108666435

Rassool, N. and Mansoor, S. (2007) Contemporary issues in language, education and development in Pakistan. In N. Rassool (auth) *Global Issues in Language, Education and Development: Perspectives from Postcolonial Countries* (pp. 218–241). Multilingual Matters.

Sah, P.K. and Kubota, R. (2022) Towards critical translanguaging: A review of literature on English as a medium of instruction in South Asia's school education. *Asian Englishes* 24 (2), 132–146. https://doi.org/10.1080/13488678.2022.2056796

Sah, P.K. and Li, G. (2022) Translanguaging or unequal languaging? Unfolding the plurilingual discourse of English medium instruction policy in Nepal's public schools. *International Journal of Bilingual Education and Bilingualism* 25 (6), 2075–2094. https://doi.org/10.1080/13670050.2020.1849011

Sah, P.K. and Li, G. (2024) Toward linguistic justice and inclusion for multilingual learners: Implications of selective translanguaging in content-based English-medium instruction classrooms. *Learning and Instruction* 92, 101904. https://doi.org/10.1016/j.learninstruc.2024.101904

Saleem, T. and Khan, B. (2023) Exploring the efficacy of children's media use in enhancing L2 vocabulary acquisition. *International Journal of Early Years Education*. https://doi.org/10.1080/09669760.2023.2261501

Saleem, T., Latif, S., Khan, A.A., Javaid, M.K. and Khan, B. (2023) Bridging linguistic divides in higher education: An exploration of translanguaging practices in Pakistan. *Ampersand* 11, 100160. https://doi.org/10.1016/j.amper.2023.100160

Saville, N. (2019) How can multilingualism be supported through language education in Europe? *Language Assessment Quarterly* 16 (4–5), 464–471. https://doi.org/10.1080/15434303.2019.1676246

Schissel, J.L., De Korne, H. and López-Gopar, M.E. (2021) Grappling with translanguaging for teaching and assessment in culturally and linguistically diverse contexts: Teacher perspectives from Oaxaca, Mexico. *International Journal of Bilingual Education and Bilingualism* 24 (3), 340–356. https://doi.org/10.1080/13670050.2018.1463965

Shah, M., Pillai, S. and Sinayah, M. (2019) Translanguaging in an academic setting. *Lingua* 225, 16–31. https://doi.org/10.1016/j.lingua.2019.05.001

Shohamy, E. (2011) Assessing multilingual competencies: Adopting construct valid assessment policies. *The Modern Language Journal* 95 (3), 418–429. https://doi.org/10.1111/j.1540-4781.2011.01210.x

Shohamy, E., Tannenbaum, M. and Gani, A. (2022) Bi/multilingual testing for bi/multilingual students: Policy, equality, justice, and future challenges. *International Journal of Bilingual Education and Bilingualism* 25 (9), 3448–3462. https://doi.org/10.1080/13670050.2022.2062665

Steele, C., Dovchin, S. and Oliver, R. (2022) 'Stop measuring black kids with a white stick': Translanguaging for classroom assessment. *RELC Journal* 53 (2), 400–415. https://doi.org/10.1177/00336882221086307

Syed, H. (2022) "I make my students' assignments bleed with red circles": An autoethnography of translanguaging in higher education in Pakistan. *Annual Review of Applied Linguistics* 42, 119–126. https://doi.org/10.1017/s026719052100012x

Tamim, T. and Lee, J. (2021) Language, class, and education: Deconstructing the centre to rethink inclusivity in education in Pakistan. *Cogent Education* 8 (1). https://doi.org/10.1080/2331186x.2021.1897933

Tian, Z., Aghai, L., Sayer, P. and Schissel, J.L. (2020) *Envisioning TESOL Through a Translanguaging Lens: Global Perspectives*. Springer Nature.

Weber, J. (2009) Bilingual education in the 21st century: A global perspective by Ofelia García. *Journal of Sociolinguistics* 13 (4), 569–573. https://doi.org/10.1111/j.1467-9841.2009.00423_7.x

Wolf, M.K. (2020) Assessing young language-minority students: Validation challenges and future research directions. *Language Assessment Quarterly* 17 (5), 559–567. https://doi.org/10.1080/15434303.2020.1826488

10 Translanguaging Pedagogy and Democratizing Higher Education in Bangladesh: Possibilities and Challenges

Rowshon Ara and Shaila Sultana

Introduction

While neoliberal capitalism has supported and promoted English as a medium of instruction (EMI) across the world (Phyak & Sah, 2022; Sultana, 2023a) and ontological and epistemological logo-centrism in applied linguistics has been critiqued in recent research studies (Pennycook, 2018), academia has been inundated with research studies on EMI, on the one hand, and translanguaging, on the other. English, specifically in resource and research-deficient contexts and class-based societies, has become a source of linguistic hegemony and imperialism and causes conflicted feelings for students in South Asia (Bolander & Sultana, 2019; Sultana, 2021; Sultana & Bolander, 2022). English seems to enjoy greater support in all South Asian countries (Sah & Kubota, 2022), such as Afghanistan (Ahmed et al., 2023; Orfan & Seraj, 2022), Bangladesh (Rahman et al. 2020), Bhutan (Dukpa, 2019, 2021), India (Bhatia, 2022), Pakistan (Baig & Ahmad, 2022; Manan, 2024), Maldives (Meierkord, 2018), Nepal (Phyak & Sah, 2022; Sah, 2021, 2022) and Sri Lanka (Jayathilake et al., 2021; Rameez, 2019; Wijesekera & Hamid, 2022). Phyak and Sah (2022) and Sultana (2014), on a graver note, identified linguistic imperialism (as practiced at schools) and indicated the top-down imposition of the medium of instruction. Mohanty (2010) ideates a 'double divide' in this regard that reveals how the relationship between a hegemonic language like English and a national/official language being hierarchically placed causes the Indigenous languages to suffer negligence twice: once, because of the two hierarchically placed languages, and then for the national/official language of the land. In Bangladesh, for example, language policies and language-in-education policies have encouraged Bangla in the domain of education but have failed to create a healthy linguistic ecology where English, Bangla and ethnic minority and Indigenous languages should have equal rights.

Research shows that translanguaging ensures a better learning opportunity for students with an equal emphasis on the mother tongue as a medium of instruction. Accepting multilingual and multimodal measures as valid pedagogic resources allows a democratic linguistic ecology for students from different ethnolinguistic and indigenous backgrounds (Li, 2018; Li & García, 2022). Researchers define translanguaging as a decolonial approach (Wijesekara, ch. 8 in this book) which, while being transformative (Li & García, 2022; Tyler, 2023), holds promise within itself to promote social justice as well as equity in EMI (Phyak et al., 2022; Rafi & Morgan, 2022a). However, critics have already shown concerns, and the transformative potential of translanguaging has been challenged (Sah & Kubota, 2022).

In Bangladesh, translanguaging is a fairly under-researched concept, even though translingual practices and transglossia have been extensively covered. Translingual practice is an umbrella term that highlights the fluidity of languages and their ability to transcend their boundaries in meaning-making processes in communication. Translingual practices include different semiotic resources along with other linguistic features. Transglossia refers to how languages transform and transcend to fit into communication with heterogeneous meanings. These research studies concerning different trans-approaches in sociolinguistics are done about popular culture (Dovchin et al., 2015, 2016, 2018; Sultana & Dovchin, 2015), youth languages and identities (Sultana, 2015, 2018, 2022b; Sultana & Duemert, 2022; Sultana et al., 2015;), nationalism and religionism and social media (Sultana, 2018, 2020, 2022a).

There are, possibly, various reasons why translanguaging has not received appropriate attention in Bangladesh. For one thing, translanguaging, as a term, has not been widely used in or known to academia, even though it has been given focus in recent research on higher education in Bangladesh (Rafi & Morgan, 2022a, 2022b, 2022c, 2022d, 2021; Sultana & Fang, 2023). For example, translanguaging is generally observed in classroom practices, but translanguaging pedagogies are not adopted systematically as such in higher education in Bangladesh. Teachers and students in Bangladesh are unaware of translanguaging pedagogies that are planned and deliberately devised to help students use and enhance their multilingual faculties in the classroom and help them learn languages and content. Moreover, the immense emphasis given to English as an international language and Bangla as a national language, the presence of monolingual biases and the perception of language as a demarcated entity do not create translanguaging as a prescribed mode of teaching in Bangladesh at any level of education (Sultana, 2024). In addition, politically, socially and culturally, any sort of mixing of languages, specifically with Bangla, is considered the 'corruption of languages' (Sultana, 2024). Hence, translanguaging seems to be an impossible option for pedagogic resources in the context of Bangladesh.

To exacerbate the issue, EMI has always existed as a type of elite reality throughout the history of Bangladesh (Sultana & Roshid, 2021). The outcome of the eliticization of English as the most prestigious foreign language and as a medium of instruction has been grave. For example, EMI in higher education seems unsuccessful because EMI is promoted without any constructive consideration of various individual and social dynamics that may impact students' learning and negotiation of identity. Akter and Mitul (2020) identified that students in higher education in Bangladesh had various levels of competence in English; they differed in their learning styles. They also struggled to understand the content delivered in English. Based on a qualitative study that explored the effect of EMI in private universities in Bangladesh, Sultana (2023a) revealed that students failed to understand lectures and textbooks, interact with teachers and other students, express their opinions in English and develop sound knowledge of their disciplines. Consequently, they started depending on rote memorization for classroom presentations and higher grades in exams. Pedagogic practices with an emphasis on EMI, in other words, severely impeded students' possibilities of constructing knowledge and becoming critically aware, which were desirable. Pedagogic practices based on EMI disempowered students, on the one hand, by forcing them to adopt limited learning strategies and, on the other, by crippling their prospects of better life chances in future. EMI created an undemocratic learning environment in classrooms for students, compromising the ethos of human rights and social justice. However, neither the government nor the educational institutions have taken any constructive steps.

A similar picture is observable in other South Asian countries (Sultana, 2023b). A common mechanism guiding EMI policy is the broad objectives of human capital development based on performance and national and international competition, consistent with national development plans to strengthen the economy (Sah & Fang, 2023). Milligan (2022: 4) echoes and advocates for political stability along with these. Vulli (2014: 2) reports that English in India is 'seen not just as a skill language, but as a means of a better life, a pathway out of exclusion and suppression from the unequal society'. As a result, neoliberal language discourse and practices have viewed higher education as a tool for building wealth at the local, national and individual levels, which in turn fosters language hierarchies, language minoritization, social stratification and the commodification of English-Bangla bilingualism (Sultana, 2023a).

Hence, it seems important to explore translanguaging in higher education, specifically as a pedagogic resource and means to linguistic human rights and social justice. Focusing on the concept that translanguaging is highly beneficial for learners in acquiring content knowledge by using their native tongue while being in an emotionally supportive environment in an EMI classroom, this study addresses the following questions:

- In what ways is translanguaging used in EMI classrooms in higher education in Bangladesh?
- What are the perceived benefits of translanguaging according to teachers and students?
- How does translanguaging ensure linguistic human rights and social justice in higher education in Bangladesh?

Trans-Movement in Applied Linguistics: Translanguaging as a Pedagogical Tool for Educational Equity

In recent research studies, terms such as 'bilingualism' and 'multilingualism' have been problematized. With reference to the language practices of late-modern urban youth groups, Jorgensen (2008) showed that they simultaneously borrow features from a wide range of linguistic resources, and it is difficult to demarcate linguistic features according to their languages. The layers of integration that occur within a language and across languages also do not reflect speakers' linguistic competence. The notion of 'bi-lingualism' or 'multilingualism', in contrast, was developed with a reference to speakers' competence in two or more languages, showing that they borrow the linguistic and cultural repertoire from varied sources for diverse purposes. In addition, for some multilingual speakers, the code-mixing and code-switching is so smooth that they do not notice the transition from one language to another. Consequently, these notions, such as, bilingualism and multilingualism, somewhat fall short in addressing the newer linguistic phenomenon observed in late modern societies in which individuals prefer to use forms of linguistic and global cultures as their linguistic repertoire. Jorgensen (2008) and others (Jorgensen, 2010; Jorgensen *et al.*, 2011) promote newer terms, such as 'polylingualism', 'polylanguagers' and 'polylanguaging' instead.

On a similar note, Otsuji and Pennycook (2009, 2011) suggested to move beyond the accepted terms, such as 'multilingualism' and 'multiculturalism' to make room for 'metrolingualism' that addresses the urban interaction in which people from different and mixed backgrounds engage in communication and the process, come up with emerging languages and identities. According to them, addressing the fixity and fluidity in urban linguascape required us to go beyond the notions of 'bi-lingualism' and 'multilingualism' in which, by default, we considered discreet linguistic features of the language as norm. Sultana (2015), Sultana and Dovchin (2015), Sultana *et al.* (2015) and Mehrin (2023) suggested 'transglossia', on the one hand, to describe the language with reference to the individual meaning, intentions, aspirations and socioideological conflicts, and contradictions; and on the other hand, to bring forth the autonomous and unmerged voices of the speaker that throb underneath the neat symmetric amalgamation of different languages. This notion of language is mainly used to explore the young adults' transgressive mixture of various codes, modes, features, styles and genres within and beyond their cultural/linguistic boundaries and how they occur within the explicit and implicit sociocultural and historical relationships.

While all these notions in relation to trans-movement in applied linguistics share a similar ethos, translanguaging seems to be widely accepted for its association with language practices in classrooms and the domain of education. Based on an educational as much as a sociolinguistic imperative, *translanguaging* is 'firmly rooted in the multilingual and multimodal language and literacy practices of children in schools in the 21st century' (García, 2009: 8). Translanguaging has been defined as 'the deployment of a speaker's full linguistic repertoire without regard for watchful adherence to the socially and politically defined boundaries of named ... languages' (Otheguy *et al.*, 2015: 281). García (2009) also mentioned that it is 'the act performed by bilinguals of accessing different linguistic features of various modes of what are described as autonomous languages to maximize communicative potential' (2009: 140). Williams' (1996, as cited in Lewis *et al.* 2012: 40) original use of the Welsh term 'trawsieithu' expresses translanguaging as a pedagogical method that supports the users to have the liberty to utilize various communicative tools from their linguistic repertoire. Because of the freedom of using varied linguistic and non-linguistic resources, students can plan, draft and produce new ideas necessary for effective learning. If teachers allow students to use multiple languages, the classroom environment creates interest among students and encourages them to learn even though they may have different levels of communicative competence (this volume: Rafi, Chapter 5; Anbreen & Sah, Chapter 9; Manan *et al.*, Chapter 11). In other words, translanguaging enables students of different linguistic abilities to participate equally in classroom activities.

In Canagarajah's (2013) view, pedagogy needs to 'be refashioned to accommodate the modes of performative competence and cooperative disposition we see outside the classroom. Rather than focusing on a single language or dialect as the target of learning, teachers have to develop a readiness in students to engage with the repertoires required for transnational contact zones' (2013: 191). Likewise, based on their studies of the mixed language practices of heritage language classes, Blackledge and Creese (2010) advocate 'teaching bilingual children using a bilingual pedagogy', and argue for a 'a release from monolingual instructional approaches' (2010: 201) through translanguaging. Consequently, this term seems appropriate to adopt for conducting the research in classrooms of higher education in Bangladesh.

Empirical studies in recent years have focused on the benefits of translanguaging. It has been identified that translanguaging helps learners transfer the features of literacy of one language to the other. Students, this way, feel more flexible in simultaneously producing multiple languages and, eventually, end up speaking and writing more sophisticated texts in their mother tongue and target language. Additionally, translanguaging focuses on creating an unbiased learning environment in the classroom (Agathokleous, 2020). Thus, it is expected that translanguaging in higher studies has great use if appropriately planned in lessons (Sands, 2018).

Translanguaging on its own redetermines the language status determined by national-state and racial and linguistic ideologies; it reconstructs language structures by dynamically combining elements and styles of named languages, language varieties, or genres; and it restructures the power relations among groups of language users with varying access to symbolic capital through claims of native speakership and non-native speakership. Moreover, through pedagogical translanguaging, educators can promote social change (García & Leiva, 2014), setting students of ethnic minority groups free from the confines of monolingual practices and fostering a plurilingual environment where all students can make sense of their own learning experiences in their own languages.

Translanguaging creates opportunities for spontaneous interaction, which may serve greater purposes going beyond language learning. For example, Rajendram (2019) stated that the focus of translanguaging is supposedly a sustainable language practice which is beyond language maintenance. She found that collaborative learning is an enthusiastic way of collective practicing. Translanguaging engages both students and teachers, and hence, they communicate without any hesitation, gathering multiple linguistic repertoires. However, it is expected that this cooperation strategy of both languages will eventually ensure target language proficiency. Translanguaging also ensures 'content' teaching in the elementary stage and moves on towards holistic learning at the advanced level. For translanguaging to succeed, teachers need to create flexible and common translanguaging spaces for the students (Li, 2011).

When classrooms are strongly biased towards monolingual ideologies, the exam and assessment systems nurture and promote monolingual literacy, and teachers are hired based on and trained in monolingual literacy, the education system seems to require a strong, suitable translanguaging model – a model that includes the use of native languages and other semiotic resources. Rowe and Miller (2016) suggest that a strong translanguaging model in the classroom needs ample writing practices to encourage students' use of their native language. Moreover, students need additional support and opportunities for 'multilingual correspondence', 'two-way understanding' encouragement, conveying 'dual-language messages', and 'interfacing' with bilingual or multilingual speakers to make translanguaging effective. Daniel *et al.* (2017) suggest that instructors may just 'eclectically' use translanguaging by simply introducing it in class. 'Principled eclecticism' ensures the authority of the instructor in deciding on the instructional activities in class based on a holistic understanding of the student's needs and the objectives of learning in the classroom (Gao, 2011). Gao (2011) added, 'eclectic approach was not a concrete, single method, but a method, which combined listening, speaking, reading, and writing and included practice in the classroom' (2011: 56). Padmini Boruah (Chapter 3) suggests a 'constructivist' approach and 'contextually appropriate translingual pedagogy' which may serve to preserve the minority languages along with serving English learning.

However, translanguaging has had its share of criticism recently, while being romanticized for its effectiveness for learning. Stakeholders need to consider the warnings of the critics on the use of translanguaging. Jaspers (2018) advised that this may be 'inflated expectations about the effects of language learning' (2018: 5). Students also may not find it appealing and liberating. Teachers also seem to have conservative views of translanguaging when they engage in it frequently in classrooms. Sah and Kubota (2022) critiqued the 'elite bilingualism' in the name of translanguaging, which seems to dominate the Nepalese classrooms. In the process, the Nepalese indigenous languages seem to be marginalized and eventually neglected in the collective psyche.

Based on the discussion above, the chapter intends to explore the efficacy of translanguaging in higher education in Bangladesh.

Methodology

Type of research, data collection, population and sampling

The focus of the research is to find out the effectiveness of using translanguaging in teaching disciplinary knowledge in higher studies. Qualitative as well as quantitative data are gathered for this study by amalgamating a mixed methods approach into action research. Data collected from several sources is put to use to provide more authentic and reliable findings, projecting a thorough and coherent set of conclusions for the research. The action research design model is used for this project because it is a collaborative research approach that brings researchers and stakeholders together to address real-world problems and enhance language teaching techniques. At each of the four steps of action research, namely, planning, acting, observing and reflecting, integrity and ethical standards are practiced. While setting the hypotheses, designing the questionnaires and interviews, conducting the survey and interviews and analyzing data, the researchers take the utmost care to remain neutral to ensure the reliability and validity of the study.

Primary data for this study were collected from students and teachers through online questionnaires. The questionnaires are designed with closed-ended and open-ended questions so that both qualitative and quantitative data may be collected. Classroom observations and teacher interviews are conducted to find out real-life practices and expert opinions of the teachers. There is a focus group discussion with the students to find out more data to solidify and strengthen the transparency of the collected data. These resources help to understand the ideologies associated with Bangla, the national language of Bangladesh and English, the language of prestige, status, and lingua franca in the private sector and international communication and the medium of instruction in private education in Bangladesh, and the benefits of translanguaging in the domain of education.

A private university is the research context, which is the focus of the case study presented in this chapter.

Demographic background of the student participants

One hundred and two students and 10 teachers from four different departments (Business administration, Law, English and Computer science) from the private university volunteered to participate in the research. Ten students participated in the focus group discussion. Three of them are from the Department of Law and English, and two are from the Department of Business and Computer Science. Among the 102 students, 45 are females and 57 are males. However, in the focus group discussion, four are females and six are males. These students come to study here from almost all over Bangladesh, such as Dinajpur, Rangpur, Bogra, Rajshahi, Gazipur, Dhaka, Brahmanbaria, Faridpur, Barisal, Jessore, Jhinaidah, to Mymensingh, Jamalpur, Habiganj, Sylhet, Cumilla, Lakshmipur, Noakhali, Chadpur, Vola, Feni, to Khagrachari, Chattogram, Cox's Bazar and other locations. They completed their higher secondary level of education from educational institutions located in the geographical locations mentioned above. With them, they bring their mother tongue or dialect embedded with all the cultural attributes. Based on the ranking of the university and the fee structure, it can easily be discerned that these students belong to economically and socially middle-class families, as understood in the context of Bangladesh. Students from four different disciplines participate in the research (cf. Figure 10.1).

Demographic background of the teacher participants

Ten teachers from the private university participated in the interview and gave their opinions through a questionnaire. There are five male and five female teachers. Of them, three are from the Department of English and the Department of Law and two each from the Department of Business Administration and Computer Science. These teachers have teaching experiences ranging from 8 years to 16 years and 9 months. They are from Dhaka, Chattogram, Feni, Rajbari, Rajshahi and Shariatpur.

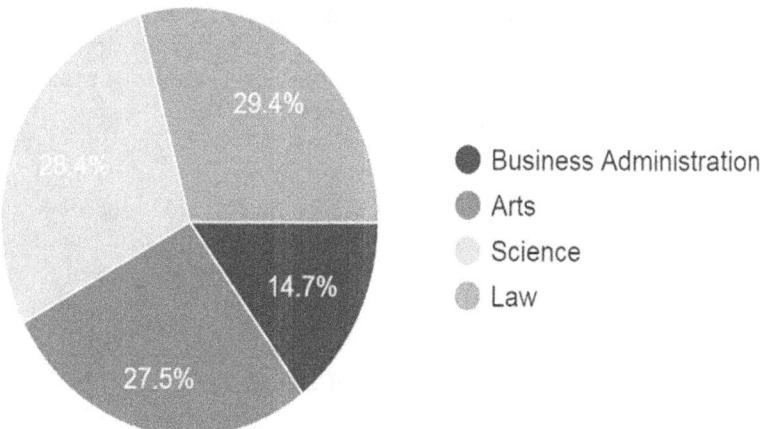

Figure 10.1 Fields of study of 102 student participants

Table 10.1 Personal and professional information of the teacher participants

Teacher	Teaching experience (in years)	Education	Demographical locations	Department
1	16+	PhD from Italy	Dhaka	CSE
2	12+	MA	Chattogram	Law
3	14	MCom	Chattogram	BBA
4	14	MSc	Rajbari	CSE
5	13	MA	Feni	English
6	12+	MCom from China	Shariatpur	BBA
7	10	MA in International Law, Germany	Dhaka	Law
8	13+	MA	Dhaka	English
9	8+	MA	Chattogram	English
10	17+	MA	Rajshahi	Law

Nine of them have Master's level (MA, MCom, MSc, MEd) degrees, and one has a PhD. Three of them have their degrees from Sweden, China and Italy.

Data analysis

The Quantitative data are gathered through a questionnaire survey, and the questionnaire is disseminated using Google Forms. When analyzing student data from four departments, a sample size of 102 is used, and 10 teachers from the same departments are included in the sample. Descriptive analysis is carried out for hypothesis testing. The researchers review and analyze the qualitative data obtained from interviews and focus group discussions of the teachers and students. Additional qualitative data were collected from two classroom observations of the Business and Computer Science departments. After collection, the data are analyzed through descriptive and content analysis. The identity of the respondents is kept confidential. Teacher and student opinions are analyzed, and after that, all the data are summarized and interpreted. The focus group discussion and interview data are analyzed qualitatively and thematically to align with the research questions. Hypotheses are also tested.

Results

Translanguaging at private higher education in Bangladesh

The data drawn from the research participants indicate that various forms of translanguaging are used in private higher education in Bangladesh.

Possible code-meshing in class

Canagarajah (2013) differentiated between code-meshing and code-switching and mixing to demonstrate the non-hierarchical relationship among languages in translingual practices. In its approach, code-meshing comes out as a mode of communication where all the languages involved are considered equal in terms of their status, values and complexity. When codeswitching refers to switching to different languages and codemixing to the mixture of different languages based on the context or audience (Fromkin *et al.*, 2003), code-meshing is a deliberate use of multiple languages that allows individuals to exercise agency and identity in their language use (Lee & Handsfield, 2018). Code-meshing in this regard is a fairly novel term to specifically define the nuances of the use of two or more languages in the same utterance that are considered equal and agentive.

Ten teachers respond to the research; 90% of the teachers prefer to use both languages in class (Figure 10.2); 70% of the teachers said they were allowed to use both languages in class (Figure 10.3); only 30% of them respond negatively. In an ideal classroom practice in Bangladesh, these three teachers (Teachers 5, 8 & 9) are presumably in their positive role following the prescribed mode of teaching (EMI). In practice, however, a greater number of teachers are following a form of code meshing.

The following graph shows the perception regarding their use of code-meshing in the classroom.

On the other hand, student responses to teachers' use of English as the mode of communication varied, ranging from 11% to 34% of the class duration (cf. Figure 10.4).

In terms of the use of Bangla in class, students respond that from around 8% to 44% of the class time, teachers use Bangla as the mode of

10 responses

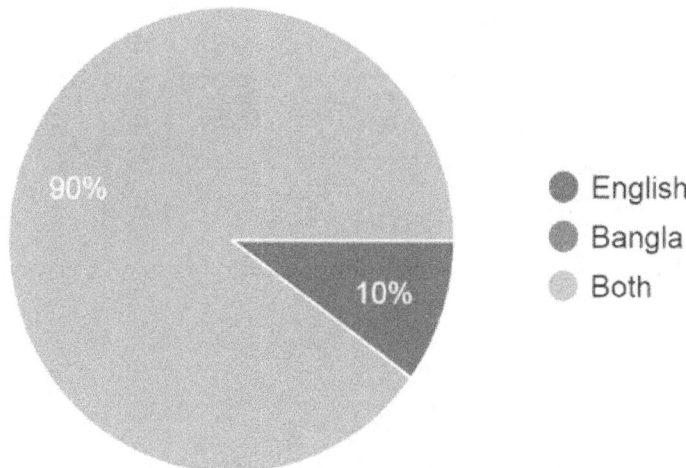

Figure 10.2 Teachers' response on their language preference in class

10 responses

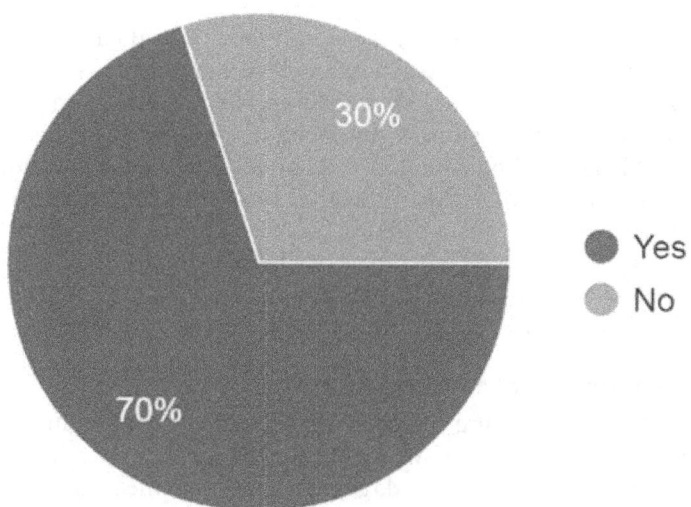

Figure 10.3 Are teachers allowed to use both Bangla and English in class?

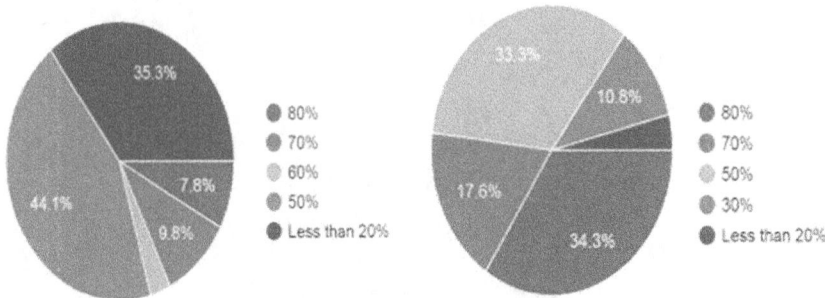

Figure 10.4 Student opinion on Teachers' use of Bangla & English in class

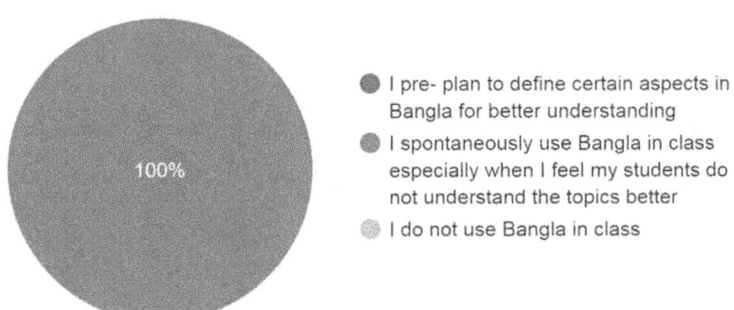

Figure 10.5 Teachers' responses on how Bangla is used in class by them

communication. The data shows that both Bangla and English are simultaneously used by the teachers in class, denying the mandatory mode of communication in English. However, there is a huge margin visible here that creates confusion. It has been observed by the researcher that in STEM classes, English is less used by both teachers and students. Data for the research is collected uniformly. Hence, this gap could not be addressed properly. This leaves a trail for further research in this regard.

In the questionnaire survey, teachers unanimously responded that they administer translingual techniques in class 'spontaneously'. None of them mentioned a pre-planned use of the techniques (cf. Figure 10.5).

The techniques of translanguaging in class

Translanguaging indicates the efficacy of the linguistic repertoire of different languages, as well as other semiotic devices like gestures, symbols and metaphors, as pedagogic resources in meaning-making processes in classrooms. The following charts show the modes of translanguaging in class alongside the application of different semiotic devices.

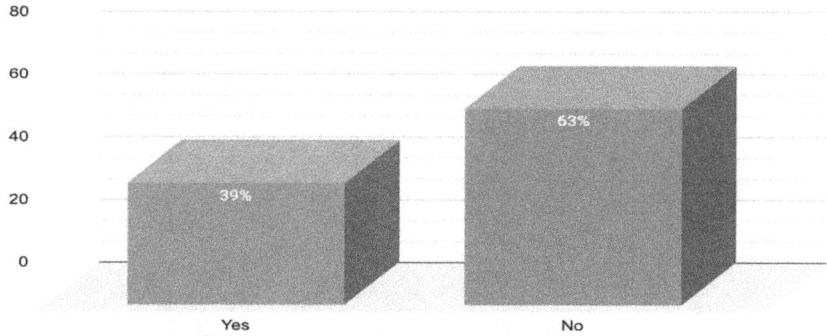

Figure 10.6 Student response on the teachers' use of other resources than switching between languages

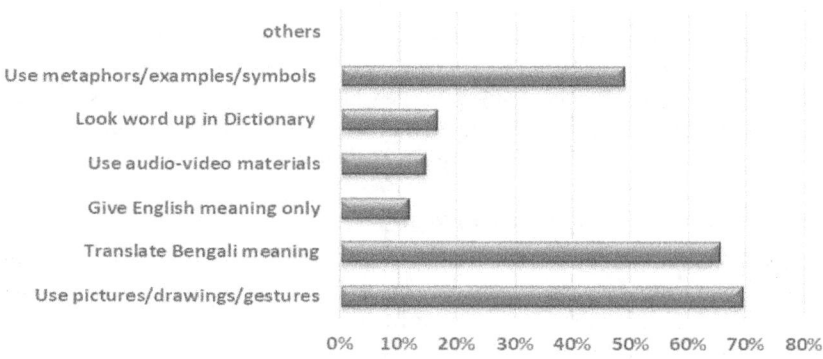

Figure 10.7 Student response on teachers' use of different techniques and semiotic resources

Sixty-three percent of students respond positively to the use of semiotic devices and 39% reply negatively (cf. Figure 10.6). The information in Figure 10.7 shows the modes of translanguaging along with the use of different semiotic resources in class.

Pictures, whiteboard drawings and gestures are used by most of the teacher participants (70%). Sixty-six percent respond that teachers translate to explain difficult terms. Metaphors, examples, symbols, pictures, drawings, gestures, etc., that help students understand the spatial and temporal aspects through the use of language come next (48%). Only 11.8% of students agree that teachers give the meanings of difficult words in English while teaching; 14.7% respond that teachers use audio and video materials in class. Use of other devices (not specified) is negligible, only 10.8%.

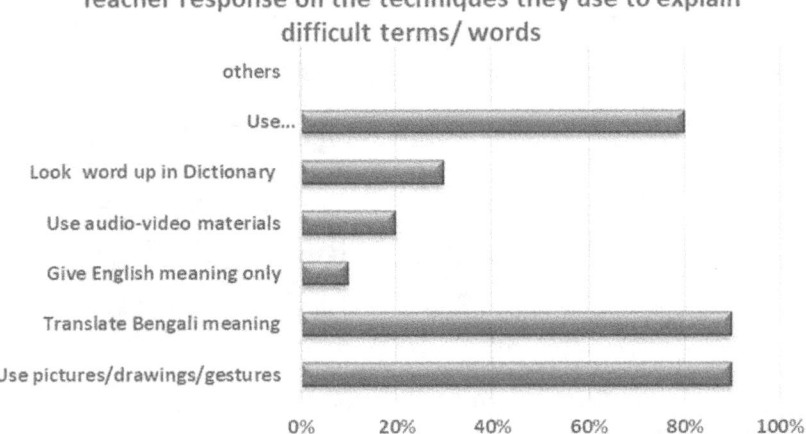

Figure 10.8 Teacher techniques and use of semiotics in effective classroom teaching

Nine teachers agree on the use of different semiotic devices like pictures, whiteboard drawings, gestures and translating from English to Bengali to provide meaning in class (cf. Figure 10.8).

Eight teachers use metaphors, examples and symbols in class. Three teachers supported asking students to look up the words in the dictionary. Only one teacher supported giving English meanings for English terms.

Possible reasons behind translanguaging

All teacher participants agree that both languages used in classrooms help students understand the topics in focus and eventually learn better. Translanguaging ensures lucid and innovative communicative practices to help users make effective meaning of the linguistic as well as semiotic resources (Sah & Li, 2020). In this case, the focus is on transferring content knowledge through translanguaging.

Teachers also believe that students can remain confident about their abilities, even when they are weak in English. T7 said,

It allows exceptionally weak students in English a better footing to showcase their actual capacity.

T5 stated,

By creating a friendly, more communicative, interactive and conducive environment, the mother tongue always helps to understand (better) everything. There are opportunities to have interactions about languages and cultures. Sometimes, when indigenous or minority languages or cultures are explained by students, it creates an opportunity to learn something new.

However, teachers do not seem to constructively consider translanguaging as a pedagogic resource. For example, translanguaging may be administered in class in a pre-planned manner, or it could be done spontaneously based on the demands of the lesson.

Linguistic human rights and social justice
Assessment supporting translanguaging

Assessment in higher education institutions in Bangladesh is divided into formative assessment and summative assessment. In translanguaging pedagogy, during assessment, students are given the liberty and flexibility to demonstrate their entire linguistic repertoire to communicate their understanding of the taught knowledge. To estimate translanguaging practice in the formative and summative assessment, the following queries are made of the participants. However, the data shows that translanguaging is permissible only in classroom participation, but hardly in final and mid-term exams, assignments, presentations, or quizzes (cf. Figure 10.9).

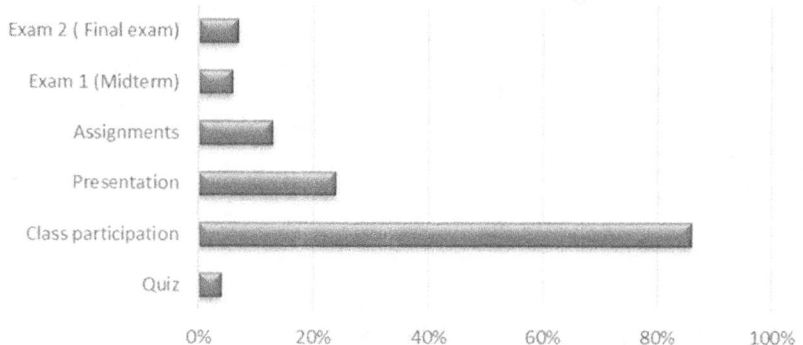

Figure 10.9 Student responses on code meshing in the assessment

Students are allowed to use Bengali in formative assessments (quizzes, class participation, presentations and assignments), which seems unbelievable from our own teaching experiences in private universities. According to students, most teachers allow the use of translanguaging in class participation. The second most supported translingual practice during assessment is presentation. In summative assessment, that is, the midterm examination and the final examination, little translanguaging is allowed. However, teachers' response denies any use of translanguaging in summative and little translanguaging in formative assessment (cf. Figure 10.10).

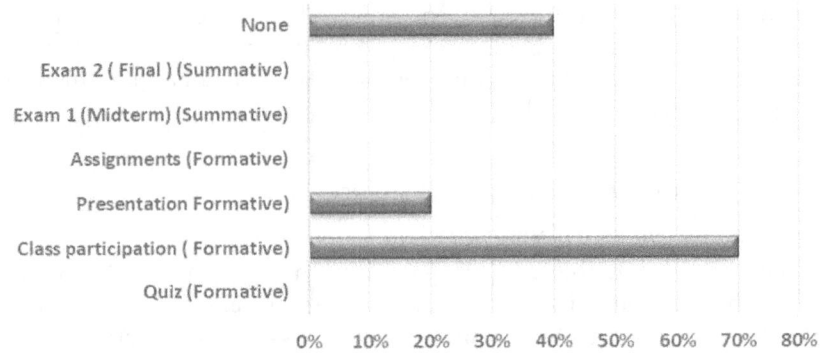

Figure 10.10 Teacher response on code meshing in assessment

The teacher response chart supports the finding in the student chart that most translanguaging is allowed in formative assessments in the form of class participation and presentation. Interestingly, 40% of teachers deny the use of translanguaging in any type of assessment. No support was given to translanguaging in quizzes, assignments or any sort of written assessment. Their responses confirm the empirical findings that language-in-education policies and practices at the private tertiary level of education promote the use of English and other languages beyond English, are not acceptable in formal assessments (Sultana, 2014).

Furthermore, when teachers are asked about the use of any minority-speaking or indigenous languages in assessments, their responses are unanimously negative (cf. Figure 10.11).

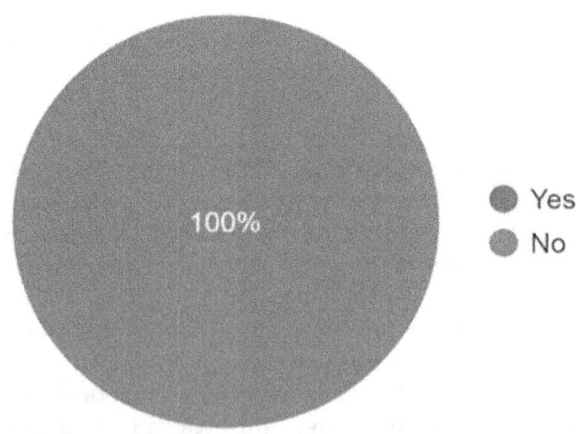

Figure 10.11 Teacher responses on the use of minority-speaking languages in assessment

No scope for using Indigenous and minority languages beyond English and Bangla

S1, an Indigenous student in the department of English, belongs to the Chakma Indigenous community and lives in Cox's Bazar. She speaks in the Chakma language and cannot use this language in class.

R (Researcher) 1:	Do you use the Chakma language in class?
S1:	(She smiles) No, I do not! Nobody understands my language! Sometimes, my teachers and my friends ask me to speak in that language just to hear how it sounds.
R1:	So, there is no chance of using your mother tongue in classroom interaction and assessments?
S1:	Absolutely not! It has never been used! In fact, my teachers do not use any Bangla in the exams. It is strictly done in English.
R1:	Do you think your learning would get easier if you had any chance to use Bangla and your mother tongue to write the answers?
S1:	(thinks for some time) I am not so sure about this. I think teachers will never allow this.

This response of S1 indicates the predicaments involved in translanguaging in the context of Bangladesh.

In the interview, teachers are asked if they allow indigenous or minority-speaking students to use their mother tongue in class. Seven of them put their responses showing their reasons for not allowing Indigenous languages in class:

Indigenous languages are also mother tongues and can contribute to the learning process. Often, their use clarifies different cultural aspects to the students, which they are unaware of. However, in this context, translanguaging involving the use of only two languages (Bangla and English) with no function of other languages in linguistic ecology is an example of 'elite bilingualism' (Sah & Karki, 2023). The Indigenous languages, which are silenced in policies and practices have no existence in any formal domains (cf. Ahmed *et al.*, 2023; Sultana, 2021; Sultana & Bolander, 2022; Sultana *et al.*, 2022) as well as in grassroots practices, indicating that translanguaging as practiced in Bangladesh may be limiting for indigenous language speakers.

Ways to Include Translanguaging in the Classroom

The assessment seems to be a big hurdle for the constructive use of translanguaging as a pedagogic resource. In the interviews, teachers clearly state their opinion in favor of restructuring the exam system. Ten responses were received from teachers regarding the use of Bangla, English and other

Table 10.2 Teacher responses on the use of Indigenous or minority languages in class

Teacher	Teachers' responses
1	I cannot understand Chakma language
2	No response
3	No one will understand their language unfortunately including the teacher
4	No, because I do not understand their language.
5	If they are discussing with their own people, then it is allowed. But they are not allowed when answering or in general discussion as no one will understand them.
6	Others do not understand indigenous languages.
7	Because other students do not know that language, there will be no communication ultimately

native languages. All 10 participating teachers responded, and three of the suggestions seem to summarize the opinions of the teachers about translanguaging and assessment systems. Teacher 5 mentions that,

> *Depending on the fluency of the teacher of a course, the use of any minority, native or any language other than English or Bengali for assessment in Bangladesh would probably end up defeating the purpose. Only excellent skills in the various Indigenous languages, along with the subject, can prevent that. Moreover, the existence, use, extent, form, etc., of the written version of those indigenous languages is also another issue to be considered before using them for assessment in exams.*

Teacher 3 mentions developing 'case study/situation-based questions that may allow the use of Bangla, English and/or other native languages in the exam scripts'. Teacher 10 focuses on the changes in the policies initiated by the 'regulatory authority', so that 'different languages in the in-course assessment, quiz, etc. will be permissible'.

Classroom observation

Two undergraduate classes, one from the Department of Computer Science and the other from the Department of Business Administration, are observed for the research. In both classes, Researcher 1 sits at the back and observes the use of English and Bangla by teachers and students. In both classes, there are no Indigenous students; hence, the classroom is occupied with Bangla-speaking students only. Throughout the 1 hour 20 minutes class, while teaching 'Basics of the Design of Algorithm', the teacher uses terms like 'optimization' and 'recursion tree'. She also defines them using Bangla. The teacher also frequently engages in code-meshing during the class hour.

Described below is the critical moment when the teacher writes the definition of the term 'recursion' on the whiteboard and starts defining it to students:

T: You see, recursion is an algorithm that reduces the complexity of the algorithm by reducing it into recurrences ... কোন algorithm যদি অনেক বড় হয়, recursion সেটাকে ছোট করে... less time-consuming করে. Recursion পুনরাবৃত্তি... মানে recurrence এর মাধ্যমে কাজ করে। (You see, recursion is an algorithm that reduces the complexity of the algorithm by reducing it into recurrences ... If an algorithm is too large, recursion makes it smaller... it becomes less time-consuming. Recursion means repetition... it works through recurrence).
S: Sir, example দেন please. (Sir, please give an example.)
T: $T(n) = \Theta(1)$; if $n = 1$
$2T(n/2) + \Theta(n)$; if $n > 1$ whose solution can be found as $T(n) = \Theta(n \log n)$

The teacher also explains how the 'recursion tree' works.

T: A recursion tree is a method where the algorithm is divided into smaller parts to make it easy to solve. গাছের ডালের মত শাখা প্রশাখা থাকে। উদ্দেশ্য হল to divide and conquer the problem. (A recursion tree is a method where the algorithm is divided into smaller parts to make it easy to solve. These parts are like the branches of a tree. The purpose is to divide and conquer the problem.)

The teacher then discusses terms like Cn and logn with the students by drawing a complex algorithm divided into different levels of shorter algorithms to find the value while solving the problem. All the while, students ask questions and the teacher responds using both Bangla and English.

In the course called 'Business Statistics', the teacher-student interaction reflects the ethos of translanguaging:

Teacher writes four terms on the board with their Bangla meanings 'sample' (নমুনা), 'population variable' (জনসংখ্যা অনিয়ত), 'weighted mean' (ভরযুক্ত কর) and 'standard deviation' (আদর্শ পরিবর্তনশীল).

T: Today, we will know how these four terms work. We have the following data set, which we will use in the table to understand them better.
S1: But Ma'am এই বাংলা terms কি মুখস্থ করতে হবে? These are very confusing. ভরযুক্ত করা Never heard. (But Ma'am, do I need to memorize these Bengali terms? These are very confusing. 'weighted mean'. Never heard.)
T: না। (No) You don't need to memorize, but you should be familiar with the Bangla terms.

Next, when the teacher is showing how to find the standard deviation from a table, a student asks:

> S2: Standard deviation যেন কি? Oh, আদর্শ পরিবর্তনশীল (she saw her notes). Ma'am, this is very difficult to remember. English terms are easier. বাঙলা term বোঝা যায় না। (What is standard deviation? Oh, 'standard deviation' (she saw her notes). Ma'am, this is very difficult to remember. English terms are easier. Bengali terms are hard to understand.)
> (All students: true, ma'am!)
> T: Procedure টা মনে রাখনে। terms মনে থাকবে। (Remember the procedure. You will remember the terms).

It is quite evident that the teacher here is deliberately and spontaneously code-meshing on the whiteboard and in the interaction with students. Once a part of the lesson is given in English, the teacher asks students whether they understand or not. Some of them reply in Bangla that they do not, and the teacher instantly starts explaining the terms in Bangla. The teacher wants the students to know the Bangla terms, but it does not work very well. No indigenous language is used in the class. Teachers use English but take refuge in Bangla while trying to clarify lessons or draw the students' attention.

Discussion

The research demonstrates that teachers use flexible language policies to support students in their learning through meaningful interactions. Teachers respond in favor of translanguaging. While translanguaging helps weaker students to have a better footing and be confident about their abilities, it also helps teachers to create a friendly, more communicative, interactive and conducive environment for students. Teachers also emphasize the positive contribution of the mother tongue to the comprehension of lessons for a student. This sort of supportive use of linguistic resources at students' and teachers' disposal is observed in different countries in Asia, too. Gu *et al.* (2019) also discovered that Chinese teachers frequently adhere to a pluralistic language philosophy about language use, acknowledging the advantages of students' home languages in mediating between heritage communities and modern society. Lin and He (2017) demonstrate that teachers and students in Hong Kong are eager to 'learn together' from each other's language and cultural resources (2017: 243). They discovered that translanguaging pedagogy has made room for more purposeful and inclusive learning. Their teaching is now more inclusive, equitable and effective because they have embraced an asset-based approach and have learned to value students' language and cultural repertoires.

The use of translanguaging at the tertiary level of education in Bangladesh seems limited. According to Wang (2019), there are three main types of pedagogical translanguaging: interpretive translanguaging, which is teacher-led and used to explain concepts, managerial translanguaging, which is teacher-led and used to establish rapport with students and interactive translanguaging, which is student-led and used to address a variety of learning needs. Teachers frequently and instinctively engage in instructional translanguaging, even in environments with the strictest regulations, thus practicing 'principled eclecticism' of translanguaging pedagogy. According to ethnographic research already conducted (e.g. Cenoz & Gorter, 2021), educational translanguaging has taken the place of other classroom interaction techniques. It seems that the first two types of pedagogical translanguaging, interpretative and managerial, are visible in higher education in Bangladesh. However, students do not seem to have any control over the choices of languages, specifically Indigenous students whose languages are non-existent in classes as well as in the linguistic ecology of Bangladesh. Cenoz and Gorter (2017) clarify that neglecting the 'sociolinguistic context' may harm the local 'minority languages'. This highlights the presence of 'elite bilingualism' in higher education in Bangladesh, similar to that of Nepal. Cenoz and Gorter (2017) also encourage to free use the indigenous languages in the classroom while ignoring any threat to other languages, develop metalinguistic awareness and link the indigenous linguistic aspects to pedagogical purposes. Thus, it will be possible to render the languages necessary in classroom communication.

Generally, in STEM (or technical) classrooms, translanguaging can collaborate in the making of meaning and sense through a planned use of codemeshing. In this context, it must be added that translanguaging is seen as the 'multiple discursive practices in which bilinguals engage to make sense of their bilingual worlds' (García, 2009: 45). In this study, teachers of the Computer Science and Engineering department respond to the importance of code meshing. Teacher 4 acknowledges using Bangla to define difficult Engineering terms, which he is unable to make students understand just by using English. It is easier for him to mesh Bangla with English to define terms, as Bangla is the mother tongue of students. His classroom practices and opinions justify the efficacy of translanguaging (cf. Mazak & Herbas-Donoso, 2015). In other words, there is a mismatch between EMI policies, the language ideologies of stakeholders and their actual language practices.

Rahman *et al.* (2020) showed that English-medium STEM teachers and students construct knowledge through translanguaging when university authorities promote EMI in their policies, policy management and language practices in Bangladesh. Hence, they raised serious concerns about the consequences of EMI practices. They drew attention to the fact that the policy adaptation requires further exploration of issues about admission requirements, the qualification of teachers, their professional development, curriculum content, pedagogic practices, teaching methods and program evaluation. In the context of Bangladesh, Rafi and Morgan (2022a) observed the efficacy of translanguaging strategies in classroom practices in higher education, but students and teachers showed reservations about translanguaging as a pedagogic resource. They displayed English-only biases when they expressed concerns about cross-contamination of the Bangla language and linguistic nationalism in Bangladesh. Hence, Hamid *et al.* (2013) stated that EMI makes students and teachers 'struggle as policy actors at the micro level'.

The role of English is quite ambiguous at the tertiary level of education in Bangladesh. Students prefer the use of Bangla to understand the difficult concepts in STEM, but show reluctance to learn the terms in Bangla. However, an opposing situation occurs in classroom observations when the researcher finds that students are not familiar with the Business terms explained in Bangla and find the English terms rather easier. They are well acquainted with terms in English. The widespread use of English in higher education in Bangladesh seems to make the use of native linguistic terms difficult for students. The discomfort demonstrates the dubious role of English as a medium of instruction and as a lingua academia in Bangladesh. This also supports the research findings, in which teachers at the private tertiary level of education show reservations about the introduction of Bangla as a medium of instruction and share skepticism about its efficacy in ensuring effective learning and teaching (Sultana & Fang, 2024).

The findings of this study leave doubt on the equal participation of minority students in classroom teaching-learning. Very few students from these minority groups come to study at the tertiary level. Since the languages are not widely used throughout the country for their absence in language policies and practices in Bangladesh, teachers and students do not have any literacy in any indigenous or minority languages (cf. Sultana, 2021; also Mehrin *et al.*, 2025). As a result, accommodating these languages in the classroom as translanguaging resources seems impossible. Hence, collaborative learning with the help of all linguistic and cultural resources of students is not an option for teachers and students. A similar reality is observable for other varieties of Englishes and Bangla. The use of only the varieties approximating Standard English and Standard Bangla is observed in classroom practices. Since dialectical differences are not addressed in classroom practice other than oral communication only, the use of any varieties and/or ethnic languages is not at all encouraged or allowed in written discourse in the quizzes or examinations.

The research indicates that assessment practices are solely monolingual at the tertiary level of education in Bangladesh. While research studies have equivocally encouraged translanguaging resources, no resources are available for teachers and stakeholders to understand how translanguaging may be accommodated in the assessment system, specifically in the education system, overburdened with monolingual biases. The research suggests the need for further investigation into educational policies and practices that may be reformulated and reimagined within assessment systems. Academics must pay special attention to assessment processes, specifically the formative ones, which are within the control of teachers, to make translanguaging a viable pedagogic resource. More study is needed to democratize assessment systems and procedures so that they do not push teachers and students to inappropriate and undesirable teaching styles. Professional teacher development programs should pay specific attention to this component so that teachers are equipped to meet the requirements of different students with varying language abilities in their pedagogical practices.

Conclusion

Translanguaging is uncharted in Bangladesh. Translanguaging, in the form of code-meshing, is frequently applied as a convenient classroom tool to convey meaning to students. However, it is also quite comprehensible that teachers are not aware that this could be done in a very meticulous and methodical way. It is indubitable that to ensure deeper multi-modal engagement of students in learning, to provide philosophical and cultural aspects of the content and to support the native tongue is always beneficial. Stakeholders should reconsider the 'indigenization of the language of instruction' (Shrestha & Khanal, 2016: 52) that values the self, identity, and the local and revives an ecological approach to teaching otherwise, there always is the possibility of 'structural realities of double-divided multilingual societies' (Mohanty, Afterword). For classroom interaction through translanguaging, different facts must be considered, specifically teachers' language proficiency, students' attitude towards their native language and most importantly, classroom participation norms (Daniel et al., 2017). While communicating in the target language, a speaker may use their mother tongue if stuck due to not being able to recall the necessary vocabulary and expressions. Moreover, often, due to cultural differences, the meaning-making process faces a gap. Native/mother tongue may help in this case to keep up the student's fluency in speaking.

Nevertheless, in the context of Bangladesh, it may be questioned whether translanguaging is effectively used at all. There is no existence of multimodal resources beyond PowerPoint slides and whiteboards for language teaching. Students are not encouraged to use varied semiotic resources for teaching and learning. The use of the national language, Bangla and the most prestigious commodified language with imperial legacies, English, is observed in the classroom. In other words, translanguaging exists with a minimal role in transformation and political activism. Empirical research worldwide suggested that translanguaging is both a transformative pedagogy and a political act since it provides language minority students with a voice and establishes a third place for them to discuss and address linguistic disparities (Flores & García, 2014). The status of all languages is equal (García & Leiva, 2014).

By questioning the dominance of English in the classroom, Showstack (2012) recognizes and draws on multilingual students' linguistic diversity and cultural knowledge resources (Gort & Sembiante, 2015). This enables bilinguals to express their distinctive identities in the classroom. Flores and García (2014) claim that any teacher (bilingual or monolingual) in any course may use translanguaging to successfully teach language-minority students who are at various levels of bilingualism in their classrooms. Translanguaging can be used as a pedagogy by everybody participating equally in an educational endeavor by making use of the linguistic repertoires of emerging bilinguals. In other words, teachers and students in Bangladesh must be aware of translanguaging as transformative pedagogies through utilizing 'students' full linguistic repertoire', along with their 'mother tongues', growing 'competence and pedagogic sophistications' upon 'students' multiple languages' and through reforming 'the examination system' (Sah & Li, 2022: 2092). Only then may they actively decolonize and de-eliticize English and democratize higher education in Bangladesh.

References

Agathokleous, E. (2020) Translanguaging in the education of young learners. https://www.grin.com/document/1007722 on 07.09.2023

Ahmed, T.N., Sultana, S., Huda, S. and Bhuiyan, F.N. (2023) Linguistic landscapes (LLs) of government primary schools in Khagrachari, Chattogram, Bangladesh: Peripheralisation of indigenous communities. In S. Sultana, N.M. Kabir, Z. Haider, M. Roshid and O. Hamid (eds) *Language in Society in Bangladesh and Beyond: Voices from the Global South* (pp. 211–233). Routledge.

Akter, S. and Mitul, S.M. (2020) English as a medium of instruction at Bangladesh university of Professionals: An investigation. *Journal of ELT and Education* 3, 58–70.

Baig, M.M.Z. and Ahmad, M.M. (2022) Not just MOI (medium of instruction): The ambivalent attitude towards English in the language education policy of multicultural Pakistan. *International Journal of Multiculturalism* 3 (1), 40–50.

Bhatia, K.T. (2022) English language policy in multilingual India. In Ee Ling Low and A. Pakir (eds) *English in East and South Asia: Policy, Features and Language in Use* (pp. 1–16). Routledge.

Blackledge, A. and Creese, A. (2010) *Multilingualism: A Critical Perspective*. Continuum.

Canagarajah, S. (2013) *Translingual Practice: Global Englishes and Cosmopolitan Relations*. Routledge.

Cenoz, J. and Gorter, D. (2017) Minority languages and sustainable translanguaging: Threat or opportunity? *Journal of Multilingual and Multicultural Development* 38 (10), 901–912. https://doi.org/10.1080/01434632.2017.1284855

Cenoz, J. and Gorter, D. (2021) *Pedagogical Translanguaging*. Cambridge Elements.

Daniel, S.M., Jimenez, R.T., Pray, L. and Pacheco, M.B. (2017) Scaffolding to make translanguaging a classroom norm. *TESOL Journal* 10 (1), 1–14. https://doi.org/10.1002/tesj.361

Dovchin, S., Sultana, S. and Pennycook, A. (2015) Relocalizing the translingual practices of young adults in Mongolia and Bangladesh. *Translation and Translanguaging in Multilingual Contexts* 1 (1), 4–26.

Dovchin, S., Sultana, S. and Pennycook, A. (2016) Unequal translingual Englishes in the Asian peripheries. *Asian Englishes* 18 (2), 92–108.

Dovchin, S., Pennycook, A. and Sultana, S. (2018) *A Popular Culture, Voice and Linguistic Diversity – Young Adults on - and Offline*. Palgrave Macmillan.

Dukpa, L. (2019) Language policy in Bhutan. In A. Kirkpatrick and A. Liddicoat (eds) *The Routledge International Handbook of Language Education Policy in Asia* (pp. 355–363). Routledge.

Flores, N. and García, O. (2014) Linguistic third spaces in education: Teachers' translanguaging across the bilingual continuum. In D. Little, C. Leung and P. Van Avermaet (eds) *Managing Diversity in Education: Key Issues and Some Responses* (pp. 243–256). Multilingual Matters

Fromkin, V., Rodman, R. and Hyams, N. (2003) *An Introduction to Language*. Thomson.

Gao, L. (2011) Eclecticism or principled eclecticism. *Creative Education* 2 (4), 363–369. https://doi.org/10.4236/ce.2011.24051

García, O. (2009) *Bilingual Education in the 21st Century: A Global Perspective*. Blackwell/Wiley.

García, O. and Leiva, C. (2014) Theorizing and enacting translanguaging for social justice. In A. Blackledge and A. Creese (eds) *Heteroglossia as Practice and Pedagogy* (pp. 199–216). Springer. https://doi.org/10.1007/978-94-007-7856-6_11

Gort, M. and Sembiante, S.F. (2015) Navigating hybridized language learning spaces through translanguaging pedagogy: Dual language preschool teachers' languaging practices in support of emergent bilingual children's performance of academic discourse. *International Multilingual Research Journal* 9 (1), 7–25.

Gu, M., Kou, Z. and Guo, X. (2019) Understanding Chinese language teachers' language ideologies in teaching South Asian students in Hong Kong. *International Journal of Bilingual Education and Bilingualism* 22 (8), 1030–1047. https://doi.org/10.1080/13670 050.2017.13320 00

Hamid, M.O. and Nguyen, H.T.M. (2016) Globalization, English language policy, and teacher agency: Focus on Asia. *International Education Journal: Comparative Perspectives* 15 (1), 26–44.

Hamid, M.O., Nguyen, H.T.M. and Baldauf, R.B. (2013) Medium of instruction in Asia: Context, processes and outcomes. *Current Issues in Language Planning* 14 (1), 1–15. https://doi.org/10.1080/14664208.2013.792130

Jaspers, J. (2018) The transformative limits of translanguaging. *Language & Communication* 58, 1–10. https://doi.org/10.1016/j.langcom.2017.12.001

Jayathilake, C., Hettiarachchi, S. and Pereira, S.S. (2021) 'EMI is a War': Lecturers' practices of, and insights into English medium instruction within the context of Sri Lankan higher education. *Journal of Language Teaching and Research* 12 (6), 864–874.

Jorgensen, J.N. (2008) Polylingual languaging around and among children and adolescents. *International Journal of Multilingualism* 5 (3), 161–176.

Jorgensen, J.N. (2010) The sociolinguistic study of youth language and youth identities. In N.J. Jorgensen (ed.) *Love Ya Hate Ya: The Sociolinguistic Study of Youth Language and Youth Identities* (pp. 1–14). Cambridge Scholars Publishing.

Jorgensen, J.N., Karrebaek, S.M., Jorgensen, S.M. and Madsen, M.L. (2011) Polylanguaging in superdiversity. *Diversities* 13, 23–37.

Lee, A.Y. and Handsfield, L.J. (2018) Code-meshing and writing instruction in multilingual classrooms. *The Reading Teacher* 72 (2), 159–168.

Li, W. (2011) Moment analysis and translanguaging space: Discursive construction of identities by multilingual Chinese youth in Britain. *Journal of Pragmatics* 43 (5), 1222–1235. https://doi.org/10.1016/j.pragma.2010.07.035

Li, W. (2018) Translanguaging as a practical theory of language. *Applied Linguistics* 39 (1), 9–30. https://doi.org/10.1093/applin/amx039

Li, W. and García, O. (2022) Not a first language but one repertoire: Translanguaging as a decolonizing project. *RELC Journal*. https://doi.org/10.1177/00336882221092841

Lin, A.M.Y. and He, P. (2017) Translanguaging as dynamic activity flows in CLIL classrooms. *Journal of Language, Identity & Education* 16 (4), 228–244.

Manan, S.A. (2024) 'English is like a credit card': The workings of neoliberal governmentality in English learning in Pakistan. *Journal of Multilingual and Multicultural Development* 45 (4), 987–1003.

Mazak, C.M. and Herbas-Donoso, C. (2015) Translanguaging practices at a bilingual university: A case study of a science classroom. *International Journal of Bilingual Education and Bilingualism* 18 (6), 698–714.

Mehrin, I. (2023) Transglossia and virtual role-play: Bangladeshi youths' virtual resistance against oppression. In S. Sultana, M.M.N. Kabir, M.Z. Haider, M.M. Roshid and M.O. Hamid (eds) *Language in Society in Bangladesh and Beyond* (pp. 176–191). Routledge.

Mehrin, I., Ahmed, T., Sultana, R. and Sultana, S. (2025) Indigenous ethnic students in the mainstream education of Bangladesh: Cultural misrecognition, linguistic inequality and social injustice. *Journal of Language, Identity & Education*. https://doi.org/10.1080/15348458.2025.2520429

Meierkord, C. (2018) English in paradise: The Maldives: English is rapidly establishing itself as a second language in a society transforming from fishing to tourism and trade. *English Today* 34 (1), 2–11.

Milligan, L.O. (2022) Towards a social and epistemic justice approach for exploring the injustices of English as a medium of instruction in basic education. *Educational Review* 74. https://doi.org/ 10.1080/00131911.2020.1819204

Mohanty, A.K. (2010) Language, inequality and marginalisation: Implications of the double divide in Indian multilingualism. *International Journal of the Sociology of Language* 205, 131–154.

Orfan, S.N. and Seraj, M.Y. (2022) English medium instruction in higher education of Afghanistan: Students' perspective. *Language Learning in Higher Education* 12 (1), 291–308.

Otheguy, R., García, O. and Reid, W. (2015) Clarifying translanguaging and deconstructing named languages: A perspective from linguistics. *Applied Linguistics Review* 6 (3), 281–307. http://dx.doi.org/10.1515/applirev-2015-0014.

Otsuji, E. and Pennycook, A. (2009) Metrolingualism: Fixity and fluidity in urban language mixing. *International Journal of Multilingualism* 7 (3), 240–254.

Otsuji, E. and Pennycook, A. (2011) Social inclusion and metrolingual practices. *International Journal of Applied Linguistics* 14 (4), 413–426.

Pennycook, A. (2018) Posthumanist applied linguistics. *Applied linguistics* 39 (4), 445–461.

Phyak, P. and Sah, P.K. (2022) Epistemic injustice and neoliberal imaginations in English as a medium of instruction (EMI) policy. *Applied Linguistics Review*. https://www.degruyter.com/document/doi/10.1515/applirev-2022-0070/html

Phyak, P., Sah, P.K., Ghimire, N.B. and Lama, A. (2022) Teacher agency in creating a translingual space in Nepal's multilingual schools. *RELC Journal* 53 (2), 431–451.

Rafi, A.S.M. and Morgan, A.M. (2022a) Translanguaging and power in academic writing discourse: The case of a Bangladeshi university. *Classroom Discourse* 14 (2), 1–23. https://doi.org/10.1080/19463014.2022.2046621

Rafi, A.S.M. and Morgan, A.M. (2022b) Translanguaging as a transformative act in a reading classroom: Perspectives from a Bangladeshi private university. *Journal of Language, Identity & Education* 21, 1–16. https://doi.org/10.1080/15348458.2021.2004894

Rafi, A.S.M. and Morgan, A.M. (2022c) Linguistic ecology of Bangladeshi higher education: A translanguaging perspective. *Teaching in Higher Education* 27 (4), 1–18. https://doi.org.10.1080/13562517.2022.2045579.

Rafi, A.S.M. and Morgan, A.M. (2022d) A pedagogical perspective on the connection between translingual practices and transcultural dispositions in an Anthropology classroom in Bangladesh. *International Journal of Multilingualism* 21 (1), 1–22. https://doi.org/10.1080/14790718.2022.2026360

Rahman, M.M., Singh, M.K.M., Johan, M. and Ahmed, Z. (2020) English medium instruction ideology, management and practices: A case study of Bangladeshi private university. *English Teaching & Learning* 44 (1), 61–79.

Rajendram, S. (2019) Translanguaging as an agentive, collaborative and socioculturally responsive pedagogy for multilingual learners. Doctor of Philosophy, The University of Toronto.

Rameez, A. (2019) English language proficiency and employability of university students: A sociological study of undergraduates at the Faculty of Arts and Culture, South Eastern University of Sri Lanka (SEUSL). *International Journal of English Linguistics* 9 (2), 199–209.

Rowe, D.W. and Miller, M.E. (2016) Designing for diverse classrooms: Using iPads and digital cameras to compose eBooks with emergent bilingual/biliterate four-year-olds. *Journal of Early Childhood Literacy* 16 (4), 425–472. https://doi.org/10.1177/1468798415593622

Sah, P.K. (2021) Reproduction of nationalist and neoliberal ideologies in Nepal's language and literacy policies. *Asia Pacific Journal of Education* 41 (2), 238–252.

Sah, P.K. (2022) English medium instruction in South Asian multilingual schools: Unpacking the dynamics of ideological orientations, policy/practices, and democratic questions. *International Journal of Bilingual Education and Bilingualism* 25 (2), 742–755.
Sah, P.K. and Li, G. (2018) English medium instruction (EMI) as linguistic capital in Nepal: Promises and realities. *International Multilingual Research Journal* 12 (2), 109–123.
Sah, P.K. and Li, G. (2020) Translanguaging or unequal languaging? Unfolding the plurilingual discourse of English medium instruction policy in Nepal's public schools. *International Journal of Bilingual Education and Bilingualism* 25 (6), 2075–2094. https://doi.org/10.1080/13670050.2020.1849011
Sah, P.K. and Li, G. (2022) Translanguaging or unequal languaging? Unfolding the plurilingual discourse of English medium instruction policy in Nepal's public schools. *International Journal of Bilingual Education and Bilingualism* 25, 2075–2094. https://doi.org/10.1080/13670050.2020.1849011
Sah, P.K. and Kubota, R. (2022) Towards critical translanguaging: A review of literature on English as a medium of instruction in South Asia's school education. *Asian Englishes* 24 (2), 132–146.
Sah, P.K. and Fang, F. (eds) (2023) *Policies, Politics, and Ideologies of English-Medium Instruction in Asian Universities: Unsettling Critical Edges*. Taylor & Francis.
Sah, P.K. and Karki, J. (2023) Elite appropriation of English as a medium of instruction policy and epistemic inequalities in Himalayan schools. *Journal of Multilingual and Multicultural Development* 44 (1), 20–34. https://doi.org/10.1080/01434632.2020.1789154
Sands, B. (2018) What every teacher should know about translanguaging [Blog]. https://study.com/blog/what-every-teacher-should-know-about-translanguaging.html
Showstack, R.E. (2012) Symbolic power in the heritage language classroom: How Spanish heritage speakers sustain and resist hegemonic discourses on language and cultural diversity. *Spanish in Context* 9 (1), 1–26.
Shrestha, I.M. and Khanal, S.K. (2016) Indigenization of higher education: Reflections from Nepal. In J. Xing and P. Ng (eds) *Indigenous Culture, Education and Globalization* (pp. 137–57). Springer. https://doi.org/10.1007/978-3-662-48159-2_8
Sultana, S. (2012) Young adults' linguistic manipulation of English in Bangla in Bangladesh. *International Journal of Bilingual Education and Bilingualism* 17 (1), 74–89. https://doi.org/10.1080/13670050.2012.738644
Sultana, S. (2014) English as a medium of instruction in Bangladesh's higher education: Empowering or disadvantaging students? *Asian EFL Journal* 16 (1), 11–52.
Sultana, S. (2015) Transglossic language practices: Young adults transgressing language and identity in Bangladesh. *Translation and Translanguaging in Multilingual Contexts* 1 (2), 68–98.
Sultana, S. (2018) Gender performativity in virtual space: Transglossic language practices of young women in Bangladesh. In S. Kroon and J. Swanenberg (eds) *Language and Culture on the Margins: Global/Local Interactions* (pp. 69–90). Routledge.
Sultana, S. (2020) TV advertisements in the mediascape of Bangladesh: A disjuncture between the realities of the emerging 'transsemiotic' arena and the language policies in practice. *Language, Digital Communication and Society* (pp. 39–72). Peter Lang.
Sultana, S. (2021) Indigenous ethnic languages in Bangladesh: Paradoxes of the multilingual ecology. *Ethnicities*. https://doi.org/14687968211021520.
Sultana, S. (2022a) Translingual practices and national identity mediated in the semiotised digital spaces. *Journal of Australian Review of Applied Linguistics* 45 (2), 175–197. https://doi.org/10.1075/aral.21051.sul
Sultana, S. (2022b) Young professional Bangladeshi women with rebel bones: Translingual practices and gender. *Journal of Multilingual and Multicultural Development*. https://doi.org/10.1080/01434632.2022.2063298

Sultana, S. (2023a) EMI in the neoliberal private higher education of Bangladesh: Fragmented learning opportunities. In P. Sah and G.F. Fang (eds) *English-Medium Instruction in Multilingual Universities: Politics, Policies, and Pedagogies in Asia* (pp. 83–103). Routledge.

Sultana, S. (2023b) English as a medium of instruction in the multilingual ecology of South Asia: Historical development, shifting paradigms, and transformative practices. In R.A. Giri, A. Padwad and M.M.N. Kabir (eds) *English as a Medium of Instruction in South Asia: Issues in Equity and Social Justice* (pp. 31–56). Routledge.

Sultana, S. (2024) English as a medium of instruction and translingual practices: Reality vs. dream for the South Asian education system. In H. Kayi-Aydar and L. Mahalingappa (eds) *Contemporary Perspectives on English as a Medium of Instruction* (pp. 77–96). Information Age Publishing.

Sultana, S. and Dovchin, S. (2015) Popular culture in transglossic language practices: Young adults in Bangladesh and Mongolia. *International Multilingual Research Journal* 12 (1), 93–108.

Sultana, S. and Roshid, M.M. (2021) English language and English language education in the multilingual ecology of Bangladesh: Past, present and future. In S. Sultana, M. Roshid, Z. Haider, N. Kabir and M. Hasan (eds) *The Routledge Handbook of English Education in Bangladesh* (pp. 1–14). Routledge.

Sultana, S. and Bolander, B. (2022) English in a multilingual ecology: "Structures of feeling" in South and Central Asia. *Multilingua Multilingua* 41 (4), 387–414.

Sultana, S. and Duemert, A. (2022) The ordinariness and extraordinariness of resistance: Young Bangladeshi professional women doing/undoing gender. *Discourse, Context, and Media* (Special Issue). https://doi.org/10.1016/j.dcm.2022.100664

Sultana, S. and Fang, F. (2024) English as the medium of instruction and mother-tongue-based translanguaging: Challenges and prospects for tertiary education in Bangladesh and China. *International Journal of Educational Development*. https://doi.org/10.1016/j.ijedudev.2023.102951

Sultana, S., Dovchin, S. and Pennycook, A. (2015) Transglossic language practices of young adults in Bangladesh and Mongolia. *International Journal of Multilingualism* 12 (1), 93–108.

Sultana, S., Ahmed, T.N., Bhuiyan, F.N. and Huda, S. (2022) Linguistic governmentality, neoliberalism, and communicative language teaching: Invisibility of Indigenous ethnic languages in the multilingual schools in Bangladesh. In S. Makoni and A. Bassey (eds) *Southernizing Sociolinguistics: Colonialism, Racism, and Patriarchy in Language in the Global South* (pp. 251–269). Routledge.

Tyler, R. (2023) *Translanguaging, Coloniality and Decolonial Cracks: Bilingual Science Learning in South Africa*. Multilingual Matters. https://doi.org/10.21832/9781800411999

Vulli, D. (2014) English and medium of instruction: Dalit discourse in Indian education. *Research Journal of Educational Sciences* 2 (2), 1–6.

Wang, D. (2019) *Multilingualism and Translanguaging in Chinese Language Classrooms*. Palgrave MacMillan. https://doi.org/10.1007/978-3-030-02529-8

Wijesekera, H.D. and Hamid, M.O. (2022) The dynamics of bilingual education in post-conflict Sri Lanka. In L. Adinolfi, U. Bhattacharya and P. Phyak (eds) *Multilingual Education in South Asia: At the Intersection of Policy and Practice* (pp. 4–25). Routledge.

Williams, C. (1996) Secondary education: Teaching in the bilingual situation. In C. Williams, G. Lewis and C. Baker (eds) *The Language Policy: Taking Stock* (pp. 39–78). CAI.

11 Rethinking EMI Through Equity and Inclusiveness Lens: Autoethnographic Insights into Anglophonic Norms in Pakistan

Syed Abdul Manan, Muhammad Yasir Khan and Liaquat Ali Channa

Introduction

Anglophonic linguistic norms dominate language policies and practices within the universities in Pakistan. Anglophonic norms refer to teachers' exclusive reliance on and the supposed celebration of the orthodox English-only policy and practice. The traditional monolingual approaches, such as the direct method, the natural approach and the communicative language teaching (CLT), are still upheld enthusiastically and maintained strictly in contexts such as universities where English is used as a medium of instruction. These policies and pedagogical approaches have implications for students from public schooling and lower-middle or working-class backgrounds, particularly those with lower English proficiency who find such teaching norms to their disadvantage as it silences their self-expression and results in reduced cognitive and otherwise engagement in the teaching, learning and testing processes. Previous studies in the context have described such compromise and compliance as a 'guilty multilingualism' (Manan et al., 2022). 'Guilty multilingualism' describes the 'negative perceptions of teachers, who feel guilty about local language use and hesitate to publicly recognize their pedagogical value, despite knowing the various benefits local multilingualism brings' (2022: 1). 'Guilty multilingualism' in the EMI context reinforces the English-only policy that leaves non-English speaking students vulnerable and disadvantaged and subjects them to discrimination (Dryden & Dovchin, 2022).

Complementary to this view is the ideological standpoint, also known as translanguaging, that actively acknowledges the value and instrumentality of drawing strategically on the languages of students in the classroom as a strategy to address linguistic disparities and inequalities (Dovchin, 2021). Xu and Fang (2024) contend that even though monoglossic English-only ideology is still prevalent, it is nevertheless 'failing to meet the current dynamic landscape of sociolinguistic and sociocultural diversity' (2024: 53). García (2009) describes translanguaging as 'the act performed by bilinguals of accessing different linguistic features or various modes of what are described as autonomous languages, in order to maximise communicative potential' (2009: 140). In educational settings, Van Viegen (2020) argues, translanguaging allows learners to flexibly utilize the languages they know to not only meet their communicative and learning needs but also enables them to draw on their existing funds of knowledge to enhance and facilitate their learning experiences. Embodying a decolonial and political stance, tranlanguaging can potentially serve as an inclusive strategy to promote equality and social justice within educational settings (Fang & Xu, 2022).

In this backdrop, we draw on autoethnographic insights and our own experiences within an EMI university in part of Pakistan to demonstrate how official institutional policies firmly enforce Anglophonic norms within the university and how those norms affect teaching and learning, especially for the English-disadvantaged students. We, the three authors with varying teaching experiences, share our narratives to show how we negotiate the official policy in favor of linguistically disadvantaged students, what triggers us to negotiate policies in contextually responsive ways and finally, how our agentive response to the policies and our appropriation strategies engender meaningful spaces for linguistic inclusivity, students' empowerment and equitable employment of translingual practices within the classrooms. Toward the end, we discuss the significance of our narratives from the viewpoint of theory, policies and practices. Theoretically, we draw on frames such as 'public sphere' paradigm (Menken & García, 2010), 'Postmethod conditions' (Kumaravadivelu, 2006) and 'Southern Epistemologies' (Makalela, 2018; Pennycook & Makoni, 2019).

The Theoretical Underpinnings

This study is underpinned by the 'public sphere' paradigm (Tollefson, 2013) and 'a new wave' (Hult, 2012; Menken & García, 2010a) of LPP inquiry. Menken and García (2010a) allude to it as an 'integrative and dynamic approach' to LPP research because these scholars posit that language education policies are socially constructed and dynamically negotiated on a moment-by-moment basis (Menken & García, 2010b). This new paradigm challenges the traditional ways of viewing policy from a 'technocratic perspective' (Johnson, 2013: 96), that is, to conceptualize LPP conventionally as a top-down process influenced exclusively by policymakers' intentions. As Johnson (2013) suggests, the traditional and technocratic perspective 'assumes the intentions of the policymakers are knowable and renders powerless those who are meant to put the policy into action since they are portrayed simply as "implementers" of a policy over which they have no control' (2013: 96). Some of the overarching premises of this new paradigm may be summarized as language policy has multiple layers and multiple actors (Hornberger & Johnson, 2007; Ricento & Hornberger, 1996); local educators can negotiate language policies and they can act as policymakers (Menken & García, 2010a); classroom is not a fixed space; it comes down to the teachers' to manipulate classroom as a negotiating space for the pedagogies of their choice in multilingual classrooms (Cummins, 2009).

Placing classroom practitioners at the heart of language policy, Ricento and Hornberger (1996) used the onion metaphor to theorize that language policy is a complex process where multiple layers work through and multiple players act their roles in developing language policies, in which most importantly, a teacher stands at the epicenter of the process and thus teacher becomes a crucial arbiter. Therefore, language policy research should shift focus from top-down government policies to bottom-up policy structures focusing on 'local school administrators, teachers, students, parents and community members' (Menken & García, 2010a: 1-3). According to Menken and García (2010a), this 'new wave of language education policy research' focuses on 'agency in implementation' (2010a: 2). Agency refers to an individual's capability to 'make a difference to a pre-existing situation or course of events. An agent ceases to be such if he or she loses the capability to make a difference, that is, to exercise some sort of power' (Giddens, 1986: 14). This sums up that teachers are not just policy implementers but policymakers too (Menken & García, 2010a). Hence, local educators and players at institutional levels can create substantial spaces for policy reinterpretation and manipulation.

Building on the above conceptual framework, we emphasize that while studying language policies from 'below' – and recognizing the agency exercised by local actors, particularly teachers, is essential. It is even more critical that these agents demonstrate translingual awareness. They must also develop pedagogies and practices that are translingually informed, as well as socioculturally and contextually responsive and inclusive (Manan *et al.*, 2021). Translingual practices and translingual competence can create meaningful instructional opportunities for students and teachers to learn languages, learn about languages and learn content through languages (Pacheco *et al.*, 2019). In the same view, research finds that translingual practices can significantly shape students' writing by encouraging linguistic and rhetorical sensitivity as well as a transcultural disposition. These practices enable the creation of flexible spaces for interaction, where students and teachers alike become more receptive to diverse semiotic resources, both linguistic and cultural. Such environments cultivate an appreciation for language diversity and creativity (Lee & Canagarajah, 2019).

Background Context

English was mandated to be the official language of multilingual Pakistan as the British left the subcontinent in 1947. Thus, all the official business was done in English. The Constitution of the Islamic republic, unanimously approved in 1973, too legalized English as the official language and Urdu as the national one (Rahman, 1996). Before 2009 when the most comprehensive language-in-policy was charted out in the National Education Policy (NEP, 2009), English was taught as a compulsory subject in government schools in Grade 6 and onward. English as the medium of instruction (EMI) for all subjects started in Grade 11 and onward. Later, with NEP 2009 implementation all over the country, English became the compulsory subject in Grade 1 and onward. In addition, it was proposed in the NEP 2009 that English be also used as the medium of instruction in Grade 4 and onward for content subjects such as Science and Mathematics (Channa, 2014, 2017). This proposal, although enacted in a few provinces, was made fully functional at the national level in the shape of Single National Curriculum (SNC), which is now called the National Curriculum of Pakistan (NCP). The NCP not only uses English as a compulsory subject in Grade 1 and onward but it also recommends EMI for the delivery of content subjects in Grade 1 and onward.

However, English has always been the medium of instruction in higher education. Given its colonial legacy and association with the globalization and internalization of higher education (Manan & Hajar, 2022), English is the most sought-after language in the country. Unlike other countries such as China, Germany, Japan and South Korea, where globalization and internationalization have resulted in an upsurge in the use of EMI in higher education (Doiz et al., 2013), in Pakistan, the spread of EMI has more to do with the colonial past. It is a continuation of colonialism in the Indian subcontinent (Mahboob, 2017). However, despite a strong penchant for the English language among the populations, a low proficiency level in English is a serious challenge among students hailing from Urdu medium public schools and rural areas (Haidar, 2021). With most of the schools using Urdu as a medium of instruction, the use of EMI in higher education is a major cause of discord between the actual needs and the aspirations of the students. Without having the required English proficiency to comprehend the instruction in English, students resort to rote learning instead of proper conceptual engagement (Irfan, 2019). 'Teachers also find themselves in a dilemma as to whether they should appease the policy makers or look after the interests of the students' (Manan et al., 2022). Besides the policy obligations, the prevalent view of the promotion of linguistic, ethnic and cultural diversity as being inimical to the national unity also encourages teachers and students to adhere to the strict English-only policy, simultaneously discouraging the use of local languages in the classrooms.

Methodology

This collaborative autoethnography draws on the teaching experiences, pedagogical transformation, ideological orientation and praxis of three EMI university teachers. The autoethnography in collaborative autoethnography refers to the qualitative method that 'utilizes the data about self and context to gain an understanding of the connectivity between self and others' (Ngunjiri et al., 2010: 2). However oxymoronic it might sound, collaborative autoethnography as a qualitative research method is at the same time collaborative, ethnographic and autobiographical in nature (Ngunjiri et al., 2010). For this purpose, we drew on our teaching journey, dwelling specifically on the experiences related to the phenomenon in question. Moreover, we all share our experiences of teaching at the same public sector university in Pakistan.

To keep the narratives consistent and structured, a set of preliminary questions guided the narrative. All those responses were shared among the authors and were subjected to discussion, comments and analysis.

A Reflective Response to the Prevailing Anglophonic Linguistic Norms

In this part, we present our autoethnographic accounts and personal narratives to highlight how the education system shaped us as English teachers and applied linguists over the years and how we experienced transformations to shape our own language policies and practices in the classrooms using negotiation and appropriation strategies. The narratives focus on three important themes: policy negotiation, appropriation (the triggers for policy negotiation and appropriation) and the impact of policy negotiation on linguistic equity and inclusivity.

Policy negotiations strategies

Author 1

I grew up in a society where linguistic hierarchy was/is sharply drawn and where the following sociolinguistic order is socially legitimated and normalized – English, Urdu and the rest of the native/indigenous languages. Given the normative superiority of the English language and the

Table 11.1 Demographic information

Name	EMI experience in years	Number of languages spoken
Author 1	14 Years	3
Author 2	7 Years	3
Author 3	18 Years	5

soft power it wields in society, many aspiring students and their families, especially from the lower strata and working classes, look up to English as a transformative tool, an empowering resource for socioeconomic mobility and a panacea for all their social and economic woes. English is believed to serve as a passport to privileges, power and prosperity (Haidar, 2018; Manan, 2019, 2021; Rahman, 2005). The manifestation of these aspirations becomes evident in the 'English-medium fever', that is, the public's heavy reliance and feverish pursuit of low-fee English-medium private schools, private English language academies and tutoring centers that have expanded exponentially and chaotically in recent years (Manan & Hajar, 2022; Manan et al., 2015).

Like many other youngsters from the lower strata of society, I also tied my career dreams with the English language and saw it as a 'passport' to some form of prosperity. Thus, in pursuit of these aspirations, I enrolled in MA English literature and linguistics program in an English-medium university. During the program, the professors systematically injected in me and all other students a monoglossic view, as they vehemently accentuated the glorification of the English language and English literature. Multilingualism was viewed as a problem and the native/indigenous languages were seen as impediments to English learning. The system instilled in us an orientation where we were made to strongly believe that English could best be learned through English instruction in the classrooms. As I recall, the system virtually turned me into a hard-core traditionalist and a blind subscriber to the school of thought that saw direct method and communicative language teaching as the ultimate approaches towards language teaching and learning, regardless of the teaching/learning context, the learners, learners' existing language repertoires and their socioeconomic or educational backgrounds. By this benchmark, one-size-fits-all approach premised language teaching and learning and the best teacher stood out as the one who would never switch between languages and the one who would strictly police their students not to switch codes during the class. What we now describe as translanguaging was a taboo practice and a sign of teachers' poor English proficiency/fluency. The idea of language purism was the essential premise that underpinned instructional practices.

Thus, having internalized this whole monoglossic baggage of language beliefs and purportedly best teaching practices, I, too, began to employ the same beliefs and practices when I embarked upon my teaching career in a public university. As a freshly recruited English teacher, I used to take great pride in suppressing any voices other than the ones in the English language and boasted about upholding linguistic purism during my teaching in the classroom while paying no regard to the local context, the local learner, their needs and the local language ecology (Kumaravadivelu, 2006). The university also took pride in using EMI and the management strongly emphasized employing an English-only approach, as it would presumably hit two birds with one shot – learning language and content simultaneously. I can remember that my rigidity and stubborn form of language policing would render many bright and brilliant students silenced in the classroom. If one kept the English language bias aside, those English-disadvantaged students would be equally competent and competitive in their content subjects. In a nutshell, the earlier days of my language teaching career were characterized by folk theorization and a deficit ideology, where I exuberantly pressed for the English-only policy. I erroneously believed that English could best be taught through English and understood monolingualism as a pathway to English learning. Perceived as barriers to English teaching and learning, I believed that local languages should be abandoned altogether within the formal classroom setting. Similarly, recourse to translanguaging was seen as a sign of low proficiency and competency. While I recall and recollect those memories, I can now trace the roots of my language shaming in the hegemonic effects of English (Gramsci, 1985), in the symbolic power of English (Bourdieu, 1991) and in the coloniality and colonial mindset (Maldonado-Torres, 2007; Thiong'o, 1986; Walter D. Mignolo, 2010). Thus, all that historical colonial baggage invoked in me and hundreds of other English teachers and applied linguists the feelings of what I now describe as 'guilty multilingualism' (Manan *et al.*, 2022).

Author 2

Teaching different courses of linguistics over the course of years, I have had plenty of opportunities to negotiate with the strict English-only policy in my classrooms. Since the students would come to the class with an internalized guilt associated with their mother languages, not only would they avoid using and drawing upon their first languages themselves, but they would also consider anyone else indulging in this practice as unacademic and would deem it against the spirit of the educational environment promised to them. Irrespective of their levels of English competencies and their varying needs, all the students would always talk highly of the teachers, who firmly adhered to the English-only policy in their classrooms. I used to be one of those teachers: I delivered lectures entirely in the English language only and I encouraged my students to do the same. This way I would reinforce unknowingly the notion that classrooms are 'reserved for the dominant language only' (Dobinson *et al.*, 2024: 307). A lot of students would come to visit me during my office hours and tell me how much they liked my lectures just because they were entirely in the English language.

The overall environment and policies contributed to the stigmatization of the local languages and actively shrank the spaces for them in academic settings because the use of first languages was a forbidden privilege (Dobinson *et al.*, 2020). As a teacher, I knew the first measure that ought to be taken was to initiate a destigmatization process – a process meant to bust the misplaced guilt associated with the local languages in general and their usage in the academic spaces in particular: the inspiration of this strategy was rooted in Ruiz's orientation, 'language as a resource'. Firstly, in every introductory class, I would ask my students to introduce themselves and share the number of languages that they could speak and, most importantly, their first languages. The rationale behind this activity was to give everybody a chance to realize that all of them were bilinguals and that it is something that ought to be celebrated. Secondly, as I mentioned earlier, the teaching of linguistic courses really facilitated the negotiation and furnished a lot of opportunities for me to make space for the local languages. For instance, while teaching them introductory courses on Semantics, Syntax and Phonetics, I would constantly encourage them to draw on their first languages and share examples with the rest of us even though the official course outline was just confined to the English language. I have a vivid recollection of a few instances when the students were overjoyed and super excited when they could identify certain linguistic phenomena in their first languages. For example, when they identified minimal pairs, drew syntactic tree diagrams or found out about different instances of word-formation processes in their mother languages. Such activities not only demystified the English language but also made them realize that their languages are equally complex and worth exploring.

Over the years, translanguaging became one of the essential elements of my pedagogical style. Though initially, I did not know that this practice of strategically using languages in the classroom is translanguaging, it was quite later that I came to know that it is a popular phenomenon within scholarly communities exploring EMI contexts. At some point in my teaching career – which I have discussed in detail in the following section of the findings – I realized that the potential for negotiating spaces vested in me by my agency as a policy implementer within the bounds of a classroom ought to be utilized to facilitate the students instead of guarding and endorsing the inimical English-only policy. Instantly, all the languages that I was competent in (Pashto and Urdu language) aided me in furnishing learning affordances for those students who hailed from a disadvantaged socioeconomic background. This, in general, created a safe space where each of us tried our best to make our classroom as inclusive as possible.

Author 3

I have been a teacher in the Department of English at a Pakistani university since 2005. Because English is the medium of instruction in Pakistani universities, all the teachers are required to conduct all the classroom transactions only in English. The ideology behind this institutional English-only policy has been to provide students, who have been studying English either as a compulsory subject in Grade 1 or 6 and onward or have been instructed in English medium education before coming to the university classes, with an exposure to an advanced level of English. The majority of the students who reach the university classes are not grade-level English proficient. The students are not taught English well in the lower grades. Either because they belong to the lower strata of society or because they do not have educated parents who can help them with their studies. Teachers, too, do not have adequate proficiency to teach English in grades lower than those in university education. On top of that, there is no viable and effective assessment and feedback system that could examine their progress and suggest future improvements.

When I have such students in my class who come from lower socioeconomic backgrounds and do not have enough English proficiency, it is simply not possible to conduct all my teaching in only English. I have, over the years, realized that my inclination to use only English in classes and not use the languages such as Urdu, the national language of Pakistan, or the ones that the students speak, has had the following repercussions: (a) it has made my classes less engaging and boring, (b) I have not been able to fully gauge if learning has occurred, (c) majority of the students has been silent in classes; the classes seem to be lifeless, and (d) students struggle in terms of their confidence when they interact with me in English or come to make PowerPoint presentations before other students.

As I realized these things and actively reflected, I found that I was at the extreme point in terms of teaching only monolingually. Although I was right as far as institutional English-only policy was concerned, I felt it made little to no impact in the context where I was teaching. I realized this English-only policy was divorced from my context. Deciding to move from the extreme position of using only English I started incorporating Urdu in my classroom transactions. Since I taught courses related to linguistics and applied linguistics, I drew upon these languages either for explanation or comparative analysis purposes. For instance, while lecturing, I translanguaged freely. I made sure that students understood the concepts that I taught. To ensure that learning occurred, I asked questions and gave feedback to them while translanguaging in both English and Urdu/Sindhi/other languages. As a whole, my English-only instruction changed from monolingual to multilingual. This agentive decision by me as a teacher created a space that made my teaching and classes meaningful. I could see meaning and life in my classes as the students understood, interacted; and, I felt satisfied.

The triggers for policy negotiation and appropriation

Author 1

The evolution of my scholarly outlook, from a rigid Anglophonic stance to becoming an advocate for linguistic flexibility, is a transformation worth reflecting upon. This shift occurred gradually as I progressed in my academic journey through my Masters and PhD studies, a process that spanned nearly a decade or so. With each academic milestone, my understanding deepened and my views began to change. Significant influences on this transformation included experiences abroad, where I had the opportunity to compare my previous experiences in Pakistan with those in countries like Malaysia, where local languages occupy a much more prominent space in education. This contrast was eye-opening. Additionally, engaging with professors specializing in multilingualism and language policies illuminated me about the intricate ways in which power, politics, ideologies and state interests intersect with language policies, language hierarchies and public perceptions. These interactions helped me critically reassess my previous idealized notions of English language teaching and the ways in which Native-speakerism and coloniality were embedded in these practices.

A key factor driving this change was my evolving sense of identity. Initially, I saw myself solely as an English teacher; however, over time, I recognized that I was also a sociolinguist, an applied linguist, a policymaker, a critical researcher and importantly, an agent of change. This realization empowered me to challenge Anglophonic norms with greater confidence. Moreover, publishing in top-tier journals, book contributions and networking with like-minded scholars worldwide further reinforced my conviction. These academic accomplishments allowed me to build my arguments on a solid foundation of empirical and theoretical knowledge, enabling me to critique monolingual practices with greater intensity. Through these scholarly contributions, I found both a voice and the energy to advocate for linguistic flexibility and multilingualism, advancing both my activism and agency in challenging normative practices.

I must admit that having read critical scholarship and research work of critical scholars on policies, practices and English language teaching had a massive influence on my outlook as a teacher, scholar, researcher and thinker. To be precise, a wide range of critical theoretical and philosophical concepts served as triggers to make me see things differently. These include *linguistic imperialism* (Phillipson, 1992), *linguistic human rights* (Skutnabb-Kangas, 2000), *critical applied linguistics* (Pennycook, 2001), *critical language policy* (Tollefson, 2006), *postmethod pedagogy* (Kumaravadivelu, 2006), *multilingual turn and translanguaging* (García & Li, 2013; May, 2014), *coloniality/decoloniality* (Maldonado-Torres, 2007; Thiong'o, 1986; Walter D. Mignolo, 2010), *language capital and symbolic power* (Bourdieu, 1991), *governmentality* (Foucault, 1991), *Global South and Southern Epistemology* (Connell, 2007; Makalela, 2018; Makoni et al., 2022; Pennycook & Makoni, 2019; Santos, 2014, 2016) and *agency* (Bouchard & Glasgow, 2019; Canagarajah, 1999; Johnson & Johnson, 2015; Liddicoat & Taylor-Leech, 2020; Menken & García, 2010b). This work was enlightening in many ways as it offered an alternative vision and an unconventional lens through which I could analytically scrutinize the limits of my previous beliefs and practices. It inculcated in me a critical niche and completely transformed the way I previously viewed the language teaching profession, the role and significance of native/indigenous languages, local multilingualism, language-mixing, policymaking and policy implementation and so on. So, greater theoretical awareness and ideological clarity emboldened me to question the normative assumptions, normative practices and normative policies (Manan *et al.*, 2021). As a result of theoretical awareness and ideological clarity, I was able to realize the power of my agency and agentive acts (Johnson & Johnson, 2015; Liddicoat, 2019; Menken & García, 2010a; Nguyen & Bui, 2016) and the impact my agentive power could create in the classroom and beyond. Over the years, I also realized the fact that teachers are the real implementers and negotiators of the policies and they can significantly reshape policies with the help of policy appropriation, interpretation and reinterpretation (Johnson & Johnson, 2015; Menken & García, 2010a). I also knew that language education policies are socially constructed and dynamically negotiated on a moment-by-moment basis (Menken & García, 2010b). Personally, I practiced and found that the classroom is not a fixed space and 'It really comes down to the teachers' to manipulate the classroom as a negotiating space for the pedagogies of their choice in multilingual classrooms (Cummins & Early, 2010; Manan, 2020).

Author 2

At the beginning of my teaching career, I saw myself as a representative of the organization (University) within the classroom. I was convinced that I owed my agency to the institute that employed me and that the only justified utility of that agency was to implement the policies of the university within its classrooms. As a direct consequence, stemming from this outlook, unbeknownst to me, my pedagogy actively otherized the students within the classrooms. In my head, adhering to and enforcing the English-only policy was basically a job well done: I took pride in it and my students, despite being disadvantaged, liked me for it as well. For quite a while, it was unknown to me that I have become a 'self-contained enterprise' (Friedrich & Shanks, 2021), otherizing my students with my pedagogy, committing violence, for 'violence ranges from the prohibition of the use of native languages in public spaces and the forcible adoption of Christian names to conversion and the destruction of ceremonial sites and symbols and to all forms of racial and cultural discrimination' (Santos, 2014: 123). My rationale at that time, however, was goaded by the embeddedness of success, economic prosperity, global mobility and upward social mobility in the English language. Associated with all these, the execution of my agency and pedagogy in upholding strict English-only policy and discouraging the use of other local languages within the classrooms always felt like a reasonable thing to do. Thinking about it in retrospect, it can better be explained through the notion of 'Whiteness as futurity' in the globalization of higher education (Shahjahan & Edwards, 2021) in the way it 'fashions mentalities, and is fashioned by those mentalities in return' (Marginson, 2011: 22) and its ability in creating 'conditions that make it harmful to not invest or continue the investment in Whiteness' (Shahjahan & Edwards, 2021: 3). Not immune to the trends of the global knowledge economy and colonial history, the assignment of the epistemic privilege to the English language seems like an inevitability in a country with a colonial past. 'The colonial is thus the blind spot upon which the modern conception of knowledge and law are built' (Santos, 2014: 22). However, over the course of time, I was able to reorient or, in many ways, reclaim my agency. Now, this was not an overnight and a sudden transition, nor was it a result of one radical theoretical paper or a book or an epiphany: it was a slow and gradual process that resulted from exposure to critical scholarship, observing unconventional teaching practices of colleagues (it reminds me of how two of my senior colleagues would defy the English-only policy of the university by giving their students the choice of attempting exams in Urdu language if they had any difficulty with English) and continuous reflection on my role as a teacher within the classroom. This reclamation involved the transition from considering myself as an agent of implementing the top-down policies to a classroom practitioner facilitating the needs of the diverse student body. Gradually, I saw the inimical nature of the English-only policy that denied space for a culturally responsive pedagogy. Moreover, the mismatch between the needs of the ultimate stakeholders – students – and the enforced top-down language policies furnished a gap that contributed to the reproduction of inequalities, marginalizing the already disadvantaged students. In the process of using my teacher agency to fill the gap in a bid to facilitate the needs of the linguistically diverse students, my understanding of what agency is also evolved: from it being 'the ability or potential to act' (Priestley *et al.*, 2015: 22) to it being as the 'resistance to and transformation of dominant power' (Lipponen & Kumpulainen, 2011: 813). In this vein, Santos (2016) argues that 'alternatives are not lacking in the world. What is indeed missing is an alternative thinking of alternatives' (2016: 20).

Author 3

As I continued teaching and grew, I knew that I did not make sense to a great extent to most of my students. Upon reflecting on finding an answer and improving, I could see that my classes had students who came from well-off families. Because they studied in English medium schools and had well-educated parents and families who supported them through various means, they did not have issues in my classes. However, they were only a few in number. I also had students who struggled in my classes due to their weak English proficiency. They came from government schools where they could not get effective English language education. They were in the majority.

What triggered me to rethink my stance on using only English as the medium of instruction of my classes for the majority of students were the applied linguistic debates on the role of mother tongue/first language in English medium education, content-based instruction (CBI)/content and language integrated learning (CLIL), code-switching/mixing/meshing, translanguaging and teachers' agency and identity in negotiating a language policy at the micro classroom level. Framed by diverse but conceptually aligned terminologies such as decolonizing education, culturally responsive pedagogy and the notion of teachers as policy agents – these debates focus on language policy, planning and bilingual education with the shared goal of humanizing education. These debates attempted to humanize education. After my master's degree in English in Pakistan, I had graduate studies abroad in the UK and the US. My exposure to these debates during my studying abroad opened my eyes and demystified many an idea that I had cherished for a long. I realized that no matter what language policymakers as language actors suggest at the macro level, it is the teacher who does policies at the micro level. Since a class teacher is the best judge to observe what is going on in their class, they may best be able to negotiate with the language policies by exercising their agentive behavior for the overall benefit of the student. Thus, ironically, it may sound that my master's and doctorate degrees, that I thought would help me as an EMI teacher to better teach in only-English in Pakistan, they took me to the world of bi/multilingual education. The courses that I took in the degrees showed me the models where English content was negotiated as per class culture. They sensitized me on how the UK and US teachers in their schools taught effectively to their students whose mother tongue/first language was not English by drawing upon their students' funds of knowledge. All these courses and their teaching material in the shape of books, research papers and other resources clearly invited me to critically reflect on my context. As the US and UK had non-native students in their schools, so did Pakistan. The question, then, was how Pakistani teachers can be successful in their pedagogical transactions. It oriented my teaching philosophy by upholding the belief that student's learning and comprehension should be the prime focus, not teaching in only-English and limiting the students' inclusion and equity.

The impact of policy negotiation on linguistic equity and inclusivity

Author 1

Drawing on my personal experiences and observations, one immediate effect of policy negotiation and appropriation has been a more inclusive, participatory and engaging classroom environment, where every student, be English-disadvantaged or others, has found classrooms more secure places for their 'power of self-expression' (Manan, 2018). Students no longer felt lower-level fluency in the English language as a sign of stigma or an inherent deficiency. Neither did I make them realize so. Crucially, the fear of negative evaluation no longer withheld them from expressing themselves in the 'languages of their choice' (Cummins, 2009), such as Pashto, Balochi, Brahvi or Urdu. In particular, the English-disadvantaged students began to feel a sense of more liberation and empowerment.

Due to space limitations, I am unable to provide a comprehensive account of the many instances, where allowing linguistic flexibility and openness to the use of languages other than the official medium, English, encouraged typically quiet students to speak, ask questions and actively participate in class. However, I will illustrate one such example. A student, Rafiullah (a pseudonym), a Pashto speaker from a remote town in the province, was notably more silent and reserved compared to other students. Initially, I perceived him as disinterested in his studies, perhaps even a lazy student who shirked his responsibilities. One day, I assigned a classroom activity and asked one member from each group to present their work. This time, however, I made an important provision: there were no language restrictions and students could present in whichever language they felt most comfortable, including their local languages. To everyone's surprise, Rafiullah volunteered to represent his group and chose Pashto for his presentation. Unexpectedly, he demonstrated greater confidence and fluency, eloquently articulating the content of the group's work. His body language, gestures and overall demeanor reflected newfound confidence and engagement. Later, Rafiullah explained that his lack of fluency in both English and Urdu had previously hindered his classroom participation. Language had been a significant barrier to his active involvement.

This episode was a revelation for me – it highlighted how official language policies can inadvertently silence and exclude marginalized and socially disadvantaged students. A minor adjustment in the classroom's linguistic practices had empowered Rafiullah, giving him a stronger voice and sense of representation. It is important to note that in Pakistani universities, the use of languages other than English or Urdu is highly uncommon and few teachers would dare to challenge this norm. Theoretically, embracing less prestigious languages, such as Pashto, in classroom settings underscores the limitations of focusing exclusively on dominant languages like English and Urdu. Such an approach barely qualifies as translanguaging, as uncritical translanguaging can still reinforce dominant languages and sustain traditional language hierarchies. Therefore, scholars rightly emphasize the importance of critical translanguaging to promote genuinely more inclusive, equitable and responsive educational practices (Mendoza et al., 2024; Sah & Kubota, 2022).

In retrospect, when I reflect on the experiences and responses of the learners, not only did this form of culturally and contextually responsive pedagogy positively affect the classroom teaching and learning environment, but it also massively transformed students' linguistic orientations and ideological outlook. For instance, students began to develop attributes such as language as a resource orientation, valuation of the native/indigenous, acceptance of linguistic and ethnic identities and considering translanguaging as a natural practice of multilingual speakers. Thus, in implicit ways, the learners' whole linguistic repertoires found an enabling environment to grow and become optimally capitalized. To sum up, the dismantling of deeply entrenched sociolinguistic hierarchies and the imagined superiority of English led to creating meaningful ideological and implementational spaces for multiple languages and identities (Hornberger, 2003). As a result of such responsive pedagogy, the whole linguistic repertoire of all the students would grow and flourish rather than getting stifled or shrunk.

Author 2

At the beginning of my teaching career, I failed to see that most of the students in my classrooms were denied access to the proceedings of the class due to my strict adherence to the English-only policy. Later, reflecting upon those experiences, it occurred to me that those students had to face a two-fold challenge: one, it was hard for them to understand the delivered lectures; second, their lack of confidence in English proficiency prevented them from participating in the classroom discussions. Due to the English-only policy within the classrooms, they would be in the class but not part of the class. This exclusion was addressed when I gave them the liberty to switch between languages whenever they deemed necessary. This, coupled with my translanguaging practices during the class proceedings, encouraged more participation. Language was no longer a barrier and the English language was no longer looked upon as the end. Moreover, their responses to written exams turned more sophisticated, for I told them to use any language they felt comfortable with whenever they believed they would not be able to articulate arguments and answers adequately in English.

In general, within the span of one semester, all these strategies and discussions combined would demythologize the English language among my students. To have lived most of their lives in a context where the power and prestige of English are internalized in its superlative form, making it the most sought-after capital – a panacea to all their problems, making students look at their first languages as a cultural capital can be very challenging. However, by the end of every semester, besides facilitating learning processes, the reclaiming of spaces for languages other than English in the classroom through translanguaging and other strategies would also sensitize most of the students to see the historical and current role of global politics and the uneven distribution of wealth in the dominance of English around the world.

Author 3

As I started translanguaging in my classes, I could observe that the English-only policy in my context was not working. Translanguaging from English to Urdu and other languages and vice versa created an equitable space that helped me to connect with students and students with each other. I felt my classes were lively and meaningful. Not only were they lifeful and engaging, but most of the students also felt liberated. Thus, the majority of those who could not join in the debates and discussions due to their weak English proficiency felt it easy to join and be part of those events. They could easily ask questions and give PowerPoint presentations. Moreover, as I reflect on my decision of moving from the English-only policy to using English along with Urdu/other languages in my class, I see that I could be an effective teacher in the sense that I negotiated my teaching with my context. I also felt that I was successful in making clear all those concepts and ideas that my students hardly understood in English. This all resulted in a win-win situation both for me and my students. Although this was a win-win situation, there was always a fear if any top management official visited my classes and caught me lecturing in Urdu/Balochi, or any other language and English code-mixing mode or asked for students' feedback on my teaching. In addition, there was also a fear that those students whose English was adequate would take me as a weak teacher – one whose English is weak. These fears were compromised at the cost of the majority of the students who came from government schools and who understood, participated and felt included.

Conclusions and Implications

In this section, we discuss the significance of the findings and suggest implications for policies, practices and the community of practitioners. The discussion draws on recurrent themes from the preceding sections and the observable commonalities in the theoretical stances and pedagogical trajectories of all three narratives. The most common concern that the three narratives share is the influence of a hard-core, traditionalist TESOL/ELT orthodoxy and the pervasive Anglophonic linguistic norms that dominate curricula, assessment, day-to-day teaching practices, teachers' beliefs and ideologies about the profession of language teaching. Anglophonic norms refer to teachers' exclusive reliance on and supposed celebration of the orthodox English-only policy and practice. This has direct implications for the younger and fresh teachers of the country because the system, in such cases, instills in them the same Anglophonic tendencies that subsequently translate into their practices. As we can see, all three authors indicated a strong inclination towards monoglossic orthodoxy and conservative approaches in the early years of their teaching careers. They demonstrated exclusionary, essentialist and intolerant tendencies towards the local languages, translingual practices, or any form of flexibility around language use in the classroom contexts. Language purism appeared to be their only obsession. In this pursuit, the local languages and local multilingualism were rendered stigmatic, deficient and redundant in the teaching and learning processes. Instead, it aroused in them guilty feelings (Manan *et al.*, 2020, 2022). Based on the evident Anglophonic norms, we suggest for a paradigmatic shift and a radical departure from the current traditional paradigm to an alternative paradigm that dismantles the Anglophonic essentialist norms and narrow monolingual bias. The alternative paradigm that we envision essentially derives inspiration from the 'postmethod conditions' (Kumaravadivelu, 2006) and it seeks the 'decolonial option in English teaching' (Kumaravadivelu, 2016). According to this paradigm, policy, curriculum, teaching, assessment and all other relevant academic activities are deeply grounded in the particular local multilingual classroom contexts and decisions around all the above aspects are more sensitive to and synchronized with the local cultural, linguistic realities and learners' conditions. In his proposed 'postmethod conditions' and 'decolonial options', Kumaravadivelu (2006) aptly criticizes the traditions of importing language teaching and learning theories and methods, especially from the Native countries, while he emphasizes the understanding of the local conditions. He suggests that the fundamental principle of 'particularity' must guide English language teaching and learning, which means that any language teaching and curriculum development program,

> …must be sensitive to a particular group of teachers teaching a particular group of learners pursuing a particular set of goals within a particular institutional context embedded in a particular sociocultural milieu. (2006: 171)

Lin (2013) also observes that many postcolonial societies and developing countries such as Pakistan mostly draw on knowledge claims of the monolingual principles and often rely on the import of overseas experts (in most cases, the native speakers). Lin also contends that these societies often embrace imported teaching methodologies as the most advanced language education principles. Such outsourcing and knowledge import also signifies the hegemony (Gramsci, 1985) and symbolic domination (Bourdieu, 1991) of the Western applied linguistics and English language (May, 2014). Similarly, pedagogies in the alternative model are mainly founded on collaborative rather than on coercive relations of power (Cummins & Early, 2010), in which educators tend to collaborate rather than coerce linguistically disadvantaged students. In collaborative relations of power, students may be 'enabled' or 'empowered' to achieve more in their academic studies. This approach promotes and recognizes students' 'identities of competence'. Teaching and learning are aimed to amplify rather than silence students/learners' 'power of self-expression' (Cummins, 2009: 263). Students' power of self-expression in this context alludes to their own fund of knowledge and their native/Indigenous languages that normally benefit and enable them to express themselves powerfully and confidently. Thus, a teacher at the classroom level could potentially abstain from exercising coercive relations of power and, instead, create interpersonal spaces with students for collaboration so that the knowledge they generate becomes mutual, inclusive, negotiated and equitable (Manan, 2018). Collaborative teaching and learning environment also facilitates greater cognitive engagement and investment or affirmation of students' various identities (Cummins *et al.*, 2010).

The second most important theme emanating from the three narratives is the transformed theoretical and ideological position that visibly translates in their liberatory, equitable and inclusive pedagogical approaches, approaches that are free of linguistic biases. The transformation then engenders their agency and makes them realize the potential of their agentive response to the dominant Anglophonic norms. In practice, the theoretical reorientation and transformation manifest in the flexible stance towards language use and the allowance for the use of the native/indigenous languages, promoting greater inclusion, equity, cognitive engagement and identity affirmation. From the perspective of agency, the evidence reveals an important theoretical consideration that individual teachers can mostly exercise their agency and execute their 'pedagogy of choice' even if they encounter institutional constraints (Cummins, 2009; Cummins *et al.*, 2010; Manan *et al.*, 2022). As Cummins *et al.* (2010) aptly argue, teachers are 'never powerless, although they frequently work in conditions that are oppressive both for them and for their students' (2010: 156). This also signifies that teachers need to recognize and develop a theory that power is not always fixed in a few powerful hands, who may always be in absolute control of the classroom practices. Rather, power can be generated, shared and distributed. As evident in the narratives of the authors, Cummins *et al.* (2010) aptly theorize that,

> There are always options with respect to how educators orient their practice to students' language and culture, to the forms of parent and community participation they encourage and to the ways they implement pedagogy and assessment. (2010: 156)

This also implies that the classroom is not a fixed space; teachers can generate their own powers and the spaces of their choicest pedagogy if they want so. Thus, language policy may be understood as multilayered, dynamic, fluid and open for teachers' choices and teachers, after all, are the ultimate arbiters, implementors and negotiators of any language policy (Cummins *et al.*, 2010; Hornberger & Johnson, 2007; Johnson & Freeman, 2010; Manan & Hajar, 2022; Menken & García, 2010b). Inspired by our own experiences, we would also stress that through their reflective activism, teachers have the potential to act as change agents and help in creating ideological and implementational spaces for transformative pedagogy, critical multilingual language awareness and multilingual identities of learners (Hornberger, 2005; Manan, 2020; Manan *et al.*, 2019). Similarly, Cummins *et al.* (2010) are optimistic that teachers have the potential, individually and collectively, to work towards the creation of 'contexts of empowerment' and the generation of 'interpersonal spaces' where they can appropriate and negotiate the policy to promote students' identities of competence. Thus, teachers and students together can 'generate power that challenges structures of inequity in small but significant ways' (2010: 156).

Finally, we would conclude by emphasizing that the way forward for a linguistically and culturally responsive, egalitarian and inclusive educational environment is to seek alternative paradigms than the traditionalist and Eurocentric approaches that are imported from socioculturally alien contexts and environments. Santos (2016) aptly suggests that what is 'missing is an alternative thinking of alternatives' (2016: 4). We understand that the alternatives in this case rest in shifting the lenses of scholarship and intellectual thinking towards the 'epistemologies of the South' or that of 'Global South' (Makalela, 2018). 'Epistemologies of the South' or 'Southern' theory, as we use here, constitutes the various epistemologies of the South discussed and debated in the past couple of decades. The Australian sociologist Raewyn Connell (2007) viewed it as the case of epistemic violence, as he argued that the Northern theorization largely ignored the majority of people in the world and claiming their knowledge to be universal and applicable to the Global South and the North alike. Connell postulated that the 'idea of a universal science of human behavior and society has a certain grandeur and a certain usefulness' (Connell, 2007: viii). However, this 'supposed universality' (Santos, 2014) was motivated by the 'hubris' of the 'zero point' epistemology (Walter D Mignolo, 2009) is ultimately flawed, as it best draws on partial data and it develops in the context of inequality, power and problematic ethicality. Southern theory, on the other hand, is a response to the domination of the North and its claims to the universality of knowledge. Thus, it seeks to accord power to the Global South and attempts to redress the epistemic harm caused by the Global North. In this regard, Sultana (2022) aptly contends that 'Minimizing intellectual dependency on northern theories may help gain the intellectual sovereignty of the South' (2022: 1).

In view of the upsurge of scholarship produced recently on the Global South theory and epistemology and the call for relocating applied linguistics from the Global South standpoint, the emerging scholars and researchers from Pakistan-like contexts need to take stock of related debates and locate possibilities of how they could expand the range of applied linguistics scholarship. The shift should focus on much deeper and more critical probing of the broader theoretical debates, controversies and challenges around multilingualism and related concepts, which could be the need of time because, as Pennycook and Makoni (2019) contend, 'the southern epistemologies offer fresh perspectives, new understandings, and alternative ways of doing applied linguistics' (2019: 9). The idea of southern epistemologies or a southern view of applied linguistics is crucial as it potentially encourages applied linguists to engage in much more profound ways with concerns about some critical issues such as disenfranchisement, colonial histories, global inequalities or the exclusion of scholars and contexts from many parts of the world. Thus, local scholars from any part of the global South can capitalize on the possibilities and theoretical openings, which the Southern epistemologies open for reinvention, innovation and renewal in applied linguistics. This lens also allows the local/indigenous knowledges and languages to reclaim value and help them decolonize from the clutches of the North (Canagarajah, 2005; Manan & Tul-Kubra, 2022).

Other studies presented in this volume also offer profound insights into translingual practices, policies and pedagogies that foster celebratory spaces by drawing on local linguistic, semiotic and epistemic resources. These studies highlight how such practices can challenge normative structures of 'unequal languaging' (Sah & Li, 2022). For instance, Ara and Sultana (in this volume) argue convincingly that linguicism and nationalist language ideologies are often perpetuated through English-medium instruction in Bangladesh. They caution that if translanguaging is romanticized without critically engaging with its ideological complexities, it risks reproducing the very inequalities it seeks to dismantle. In the context of Nepal, Phyak and Ghimire (in this volume) conceptualize translanguaging as a form of 'decolonial pedagogy', noting that it not only creates flexible and inclusive interactional spaces for multilingual teachers and students but also enables them to assert their epistemic identities. Similarly, on an epistemological as well as operational front, Boruah (in this volume) outlines a forward-looking vision for translingual practices in English language teacher education. She proposes three key goals: (a) fostering integrative rather than assimilatory pedagogies; (b) positioning English within broader multilingual identity formation; and (c) promoting shared responsibility in supporting the healthy use of all languages.

Finally, in operational and policy terms, the paradigmatic shift we propose may be actualized by integrating critical courses into university curricula, such as critical pedagogy, critical applied linguistics and critical theory. These courses would foster critical awareness among both teachers and students. Furthermore, exposing prospective university teachers to successful case studies of linguistically responsive teaching across diverse multilingual contexts would deepen their understanding and dismantle myths and misconceptions they may hold about multilingualism and multilingual pedagogy. This approach could also be incorporated into teacher education programs for both pre-service and in-service teachers. Such initiatives would create opportunities for the implementation of critical multilingual awareness and practices, encouraging more flexible attitudes toward language use. Ultimately, this shift could contribute to transforming rigid linguistic stances, advancing the multilingual agenda in EMI, something that is critically important, particularly in multilingual contexts like Pakistan (Manan *et al.*, 2023).

References

Bouchard, J. and Glasgow, G.P. (eds) (2019) *Agency in Language Policy and Planning: Critical Inquiries*. Routledge.

Bourdieu, P. (1991) *Language and Symbolic Power*. Polity.

Canagarajah, S. (1999) *Resisting Linguistic Imperialism in English Teaching*. Oxford University Press.

Canagarajah, S. (2005) *Reclaiming the Local in Language Policy and Practice*. Lawrence Erlbaum.

Channa, L.A. (2014) English medium for the government primary schools of Sindh, Pakistan: An exploration of government primary school teachers' attitudes. Doctoral dissertation, University of Georgia, USA.

Channa, L.A. (2017) English in Pakistani public education: Past, present, and future. *Language Problems and Language Planning* 41 (1), 1–25. https://doi.org/10.1075/lplp.41.1.01cha

Connell, R. (2007) *Southern Theory: The Global Dynamics of Knowledge in Social Science*. Allen & Unwin.

Cummins, J. (2009) Pedagogies of choice: Challenging coercive relations of power in classrooms and communities. *International Journal of Bilingual Education and Bilingualism* 12 (3), 261–271. https://doi.org/10.1080/13670050903003751

Cummins, J. and Early, M. (2010) Introduction. In J. Cummins and M. Early (eds) *Identity Texts: The Collaborative Creation of Power in Multilingual Schools* (pp. 3–21). Institute of Education Press.

Cummins, J., Early, M., Leoni, L. and Stille, S. (2010) 'It really comes down to the teachers, I think': Pedagogies of choice in multilingual classrooms. In J. Cummins and M. Early (eds) *Identity Texts: The Collaborative Creation of Power in Multilingual Schools* (pp. 153–164). Institute of Education Press.

Dobinson, T., Dryden, S., Dovchin, S., Gong, Q. and Mercieca, P. (2024) Translanguaging and "English only" at universities. *TESOL Quarterly* 58 (1), 307–333. https://doi.org/10.1002/tesq.3232

Doiz, A., Lasagabaster, D. and Sierra, J.M. (eds) (2013) *English-Medium Instruction at Universities: Global Challenges*. Multilingual Matters.

Dovchin, S. (2021) Translanguaging, emotionality, and English as a second language immigrants: Mongolian background women in Australia. *TESOL Quarterly* 55 (3), 839–865. https://doi.org/10.1002/tesq.3015

Dryden, S. and Dovchin, S. (2022) Translingual English discrimination: Loss of academic sense of belonging, the hiring order of things, and students from the Global South. *Applied Linguistics Review* 15 (4), 1231–1252. https://doi.org/10.1515/applirev-2022-0065

Fang, F. and Xu, Y. (2022) Commonalities and conflation of global Englishes and translanguaging for equitable English language education. *Teaching English as a Second or Foreign Language (TESL-EJ)* 26 (3). https://doi.org/10.55593/ej.26103a9

Foucault, M. (1991) *The Foucault Effect: Studies in Governmentality with Two Lectures by and an Interview with Michael Foucault*. Harvester Wheatsheaf.

Friedrich, J. and Shanks, R. (2021) 'The prison of the body': School uniforms between discipline and governmentality. *Discourse: Studies in the Cultural Politics of Education*. https://doi.org/10.1080/01596306.2021.1931813

García, O. (2019) Decolonizing foreign, second, heritage, and first languages. In D. Macedo (ed.) *Decolonizing Foreign Language Education: The Misteaching of English and Other Colonial Languages* (pp. 152–168). Routledge.

García, O. and Li, W. (2013) *Translanguaging: Language, Bilingualism and Education*. Palgrave Macmillan.

Giddens, A. (1986) *The Constitution of Society: Outline of the Theory of Structuration*. University of California Press.

Gramsci, A. (1985) *Selections from Cultural Writings* (D. Forgacs and G. Nowell-Smith, eds, W. Boelhower, trans.) Harvard University Press.

Haidar, S. (2018) The role of English in developing countries: English is a passport to privilege and needed for survival in Pakistan. *English Today* 35 (3), 42–48. https://doi.org/10.1017/S0266078418000469

Haidar, S. (2021) Designed for failure: English instruction as a tool for the perpetuation of students' dependent and dominated status. *International Multilingual Research Journal*. https://doi.org/10.1080/19313152.2021.1928843

Hornberger, N.H. (2003) *Continua of Biliteracy: An Ecological Framework for Educational Policy, Research, and Practice in Multilingual Settings*. Multilingual Matters.

Hornberger, N.H. (2005) Opening and filling up implementational and ideological spaces in heritage language education. *The Modern Language Journal* 89 (4), 605–609.

Hornberger, N.H. and Johnson, D.C. (2007) Slicing the onion ethnographically: Layers and spaces in multilingual language education policy and practice. *TESOL Quarterly* 41 (3), 509–532. https://doi.org/10.1002/j.1545-7249.2007.tb00083.x

Hult, F.M. (2012) English as a transcultural language in Swedish policy and practice. *TESOL Quarterly* 46 (2), 230–257.

Irfan, H. (2019) *The Policy and Practice of English Medium of Instruction (EMI) in Pakistani Universities*. Cambridge Scholars Publishing.

Johnson, D.C. (2013) *Language Policy*. Palgrave Macmillan.

Johnson, D.C. and Freeman, R. (2010) Appropriating language policy on the local level: working the spaces for bilingual education. In K. Menken and O. García (eds) *Negotiating Language Policies in Schools: Educators as Policymaker* (pp. 27–45). Routledge.

Johnson, D.C. and Johnson, E.J. (2015) Power and agency in language policy appropriation. *Language Policy* 14 (3), 221–243. https://doi.org/10.1007/s10993-014-9333-z

Kumaravadivelu, B. (2006) *Understanding Language Teaching: From Method to Postmethod*. Lawrence erlbaum Associates, inc.

Kumaravadivelu, B. (2016) The decolonial option in English teaching: Can the subaltern act? *TESOL Quarterly* 50 (1), 66–85.

Lee, E. and Canagarajah, S. (2019) The connection between transcultural dispositions and translingual practices in academic writing. *Journal of Multicultural Discourses* 14 (1), 14–28.

Liddicoat, A.J. (2019) Constraints on agency in micro-language policy and planning in schools: A case study of curriculum change. In J. Bouchard and G.P. Glasgow (eds) *Agency in Language Policy and Planning: Critical Inquiries* (pp. 149–170). Routledge.

Liddicoat, A.J. and Taylor-Leech, K. (2020) Agency in language planning and policy. *Current Issues in Language Planning*, 1–18. https://doi.org/10.1080/14664208.2020.1791533

Lin, A.M.Y. (2013) Toward paradigmatic change in TESOL methodologies: Building plurilingual pedagogies from the ground up. *TESOL Quarterly* 47 (3), 521–545. https://doi.org/10.1002/tesq.113

Lipponen, L. and Kumpulainen, K. (2011) Acting as accountable authors: Creating interactional spaces for agency work in teacher education. *Teaching and Teacher Education* 27 (5), 812–819.

Mahboob, A. (2017) English medium instruction in higher education in Pakistan: Policies, perceptions, problems, and possibilities. In B. Fenton-Smith, P. Humphreys and I. Walkinshaw (eds) *English Medium Instruction in Higher Education in Asia-Pacific* (pp. 71–91). Springer.

Makalela, L. (2018) Introduction: Shifting lenses. In L. Makalela (ed.) *Shifting Lenses: Multilanguaging, Decolonisation and Education in the Global South* (pp. 1–8). Centre for Advanced Studies of African Society (CASAS).

Makoni, S., Kaiper-Marquez, A. and Mokwena, L. (2022) *The Routledge Handbook of Language and the Global South/s*. Taylor & Francis.

Maldonado-Torres, N. (2007) On the coloniality of being: Contributions to the development of a concept. *Cultural Studies* 21 (2–3), 240–270.

Manan, S.A. (2018) Silencing children's power of self-expression: An examination of coercive relations of power in English-medium schools in Pakistan. *L1-Educational Studies in Languages and Literature* 18, 1–25. https://doi.org/10.17239/L1ESLL-2018.18.01.14

Manan, S.A. (2019) Myth of English teaching and learning: A study of practices in the low-cost schools in Pakistan. *Asian Englishes* 21 (2), 172–189. https://doi.org/10.1080/13488678.2018.1503041

Manan, S.A. (2020) Teachers as agents of transformative pedagogy: Critical reflexivity, activism and multilingual spaces through a continua of biliteracy lens. *Multilingua* 39 (6), 721–747. https://doi.org/10.1515/multi-2019-0096

Manan, S.A. (2021) 'English is like a credit card': The workings of neoliberal governmentality in English learning in Pakistan. *Journal of Multilingual and Multicultural Development*. https://doi.org/10.1080/01434632.2021.1931251

Manan, S.A. and Hajar, A. (2022) "Disinvestment" in learners' multilingual identities: English learning, imagined identities, and neoliberal subjecthood in Pakistan. *Journal of Language, Identity & Education*. https://doi.org/10.1080/15348458.2022.2083623

Manan, S.A. and Tul-Kubra, K. (2022) Reclaiming the indigenous knowledge(s): English curriculum through 'Decoloniality' lens. *Journal of Multicultural Discourses* 17 (1), 78–100. https://doi.org/10.1080/17447143.2022.2085731

Manan, S.A., Dumanig, F.P. and David, M.K. (2015) The English-medium fever in Pakistan: Analyzing policy, perceptions and practices through additive bi/multilingual education lens. *International Journal of Bilingual Education and Bilingualism* 20 (6), 736–752. https://doi.org/10.1080/13670050.2015.1080659

Manan, S.A., David, M.K. and Channa, L.A. (2019) Opening ideological and implementational spaces for multilingual/plurilingual policies and practices in education: A snapshot of scholarly activism in Pakistan. *Current Issues in Language Planning* 20 (5), 521–543. https://doi.org/10.1080/14664208.2018.1543162

Manan, S.A., David, M.K., Channa, L.A. and Dumanig, F.P. (2020) The monolingual bias: A critique of idealization and essentialization in ELT in Pakistan. In N. Rudolph, A. Fuad Selvi and B. Yazan (eds) *The Complexity of Identity and Interaction in Language Education* (pp. 25–42). Multilingual Matters.

Manan, S.A., Channa, L.A., David, M.K. and Amin, M. (2021) Negotiating English-only gatekeepers: Teachers' agency through a public sphere lens. *Current Issues in Language Planning* 22 (3), 290–307. https://doi.org/10.1080/14664208.2020.1839219

Manan, S.A., Channa, L.A. and Haidar, S. (2022) Celebratory or guilty multilingualism? English medium instruction challenges, pedagogical choices, and teacher agency in Pakistan. *Teaching in Higher Education*. https://doi.org/10.1080/13562517.2022.2045932

Manan, S.A., Channa, L.A. and Haidar, S. (2023) Fostering the multilingual agenda in EMI: Researchers as reflective thinkers and stance shifters. In P.K. Sah and F. Fang (eds) *English-Medium Instruction Pedagogies in Multilingual Universities in Asia*. Routledge.

May, S. (2014) Disciplinary divides, knowledge construction, and the multilingual turn. In S. May (ed.) *The Multilingual Turn: Implications for SLA, TESOL, and Bilingual Education* (pp. 7–31). Routledge.

Mendoza, A., Hamman-Ortiz, L., Tian, Z., Rajendram, S., Tai, K.W.H., Ho, W.Y.J. and Sah, P.K. (2024) Sustaining critical approaches to translanguaging in education: A contextual framework. *TESOL Quarterly* 58 (2), 664–692. https://doi.org/10.1002/tesq.3240

Menken, K. and García, O. (2010a) Introduction. In K. Menken and O. García (eds) *Negotiating Language Policies in Schools: Educators as Policymaker* (pp. 1–10). Routledge.

Menken, K. and García, O. (2010b) Stirring the onion: Educators and the dynamics of language education policies (looking ahead). In K. Menken and O. García (eds) *Negotiating Language Policies in Schools: Educators as Policymaker* (pp. 249–261). Routledge.

Mignolo, W.D. (2009) Epistemic disobedience, independent thought and decolonial freedom. *Theory, Culture & Society* 26 (7–8), 159–181.

Mignolo, W.D. (2010) Coloniality at large: The Western hemisphere and the colonial horizon of modernity. In A.B. Pinn, C.F. Levander and M.O. Emerson (eds) *Teaching and Studying the Americas: Cultural Influences from Colonialism to the Present* (pp. 49–74). Palgrave Macmillan US.

Ngunjiri, F.W., Hernandez, K.-A.C. and Chang, H. (2010) Living autoethnography: Connecting life and research. *Journal of Research Practice* 6 (1), E1-E1.

Nguyen, H.T.M. and Bui, T. (2016) Teachers' agency and the enactment of educational reform in Vietnam. *Current Issues in Language Planning* 17 (1), 88–105. https://doi.org/10.1080/14664208.2016.1125664

Pacheco, M.B., Daniel, S.M., Pray, L.C. and Jiménez, R.T. (2019) Translingual practice, strategic participation, and meaning-making. *Journal of Literacy Research* 51 (1), 75–99.

Pennycook, A. (2001) *Critical Applied Linguistics : A Critical Introduction*. L. Erlbaum.

Pennycook, A. and Makoni, S. (2019) *Innovations and Challenges in Applied Linguistics from the Global South*. Routledge.

Phillipson, R. (1992) *Linguistic Imperialism*. Oxford University Press.

Priestley, M., Biesta, G. and Robinson, S. (2015) *Teacher Agency: What Is It and Why Does It Matter?* Routledge.

Rahman, T. (1996) *Language and Politics in Pakistan*. Oxford University Press.

Rahman, T. (2005) Passports to privilege: The English-medium schools in Pakistan. *Peace and Democracy in South Asia* 1 (1), 24–44.

Ricento, T.K. and Hornberger, N.H. (1996) Unpeeling the onion: Language planning and policy and the ELT professional. *TESOL Quarterly* 30 (3), 401–427. https://doi.org/10.2307/3587691

Sah, P.K. and Kubota, R. (2022) Towards critical translanguaging: A review of literature on English as a medium of instruction in South Asia's school education. *Asian Englishes* 24 (2), 132–146. https://doi.org/10.1080/13488678.2022.2056796

Sah, P.K. and Li, G. (2022) Translanguaging or unequal languaging? Unfolding the plurilingual discourse of English medium instruction policy in Nepal's public schools. *International Journal of Bilingual Education and Bilingualism* 25 (6), 2075–2094.

Santos, B. (2014) *Epistemologies of the South: Justice Against Epistemicide*. Routledge.

Santos, B. (2016) Epistemologies of the South and the future. *From the European South: A Transdisciplinary Journal of Postcolonial Humanities* 1, 17–29.

Shahjahan, R.A. and Edwards, K.T. (2021) Whiteness as futurity and globalization of higher education. *Higher Education* 1–18.

Skutnabb-Kangas, T. (2000) *Linguistic Genocide in Education or Worldwide Diversity And Human Rights?* L. Erlbaum Associates.

Sultana, S. (2022) Applied linguistics from the Global South: Way forward to linguistic equality and social justice. *Applied Linguistics Review*. https://doi.org/10.1515/applirev-2022-0071

Thiong'o, N.w. (1986) *Decolonising the Mind: The Politics of Language in African Literature*. Zimbabwe Publishing House

Tollefson, J.W. (2006) Critical theory in language policy. In T. Ricento (ed.) *An Introduction to Language Policy: Theory and Method* (pp. 42–59). Blackwell.

Tollefson, J.W. (2013) Language policy in a time of crisis and transformation. In J.W. Tollefson (ed.) *Language Policies in Education: Critical Issues* (2nd edn, pp. 11–34). Routledge.

Van Viegen, S. (2020) Translanguaging for and as learning with youth from refugee backgrounds. *Australian Journal of Applied Linguistics* 3 (1), 60–76. https://doi.org/10.29140/ajal.v3n1.300

Xu, Y. and Fang, F. (2024) Promoting educational equity: The implementation of translanguaging pedagogy in English language education. *International Journal of Language Studies* 18 (1), 53–80. https://doi.org/10.5281/zenodo.10468187

Afterword: Translanguaging for English or Social Justice?

Ajit Kumar Mohanty

Introduction

The volume *Translingual Practices in English Language Education in South Asia: Inclusivity and Equity* offers a compelling examination of translanguaging as a pedagogic practice in English Language Teaching (ELT) in South Asia. It examines the processes and consequences of leveraging students' multilingual repertoires in English Medium Instruction (EMI) classrooms in linguistically diverse South Asian societies. Several chapters underscore the social, affective, cognitive and pedagogic benefits of classroom translanguaging for English learners in South Asia. Classroom freedom to use a familiar national or indigenous language in teaching-learning of English does increase learners' comfort level, confidence and participation and gives them a sense of agency (Rafi, Ch. 5; Phyak & Ghimire, Ch. 6; Anbreen & Sah, Ch. 9; Manan, Khan & Channa, Ch. 11). Translingual communication using a language of proficiency along with English promotes learners' cultural identity, and is perceived as inclusive, democratic and liberating (Rafi, Ch. 5; Wijesekara, Ch. 8; Anbreen & Sah, Ch. 9; Manan, Khan & Channa, Ch. 11). Rafi (Chapter 5) documents how Bangladeshi students draw on their prior knowledge and skills in Bengali to make sense of English texts, effectively using translanguaging as a cognitive, metacognitive and metalinguistic resources to 'scaffold knowledge construction' (Wijesekara, Ch. 8).

Translanguaging in ELT is seen as a decolonial strategy which allows learners to reclaim their 'epistemic identity' or their 'discursively co-constructed positionality' recognizing their agency (Phyak & Ghimire, Ch. 6). Phyak and Ghimire suggest that Translanguaging pedagogy is not to be interpreted 'only as an approach to access knowledge in a dominant language'; it should be a 'transformative pedagogy that contributes to reclaiming epistemic identities' in multilingual contexts of teachers and students. Translanguaging, according to Phyak and Ghimire involves a holistic and integrated system of languages of multilingual learners. In the Sri Lankan context, Wijesekara (Ch. 8) suggests that recognition of the value of learners' language may decolonize/democratize English.

However, it must be pointed out that, while TL pedagogy in South Asian classrooms allows learning of English to be supported by the nationally dominant language (e.g. Nepali in Nepal, Bangla in Bangladesh), it also involves the denial of the less powerful languages of the Indigenous Tribal Minority and Minoritized (ITM) students. Mohamed (Ch. 7) expresses this concern in the context of the Maldives. Analyzing the linguistic landscape of classrooms, Mohamed shows that despite the overtly translingual space for Dhivehi, English and Arabic, there is a clear bias towards English and, often, teachers taught curricular content in English even if the policy directives were for prioritization of Dhivehi, the medium of instruction as well as the official language of Maldives. In their analysis of the translingual practices in the English Medium University level classrooms in Bangladesh, Ara and Sultana (Ch. 10) show a strong presence of Bangla along with English. However, as they pointed out, ITM languages do not have any presence in classroom translanguaging. Ara and Sultana suggest that the exclusive English-Bangla translanguaging and the absence of minority languages of the country show 'elite bilingualism' rather than translanguaging, as such. Although they do not elaborate on the assertion, Ara and Sultana draw a forceful conclusion that 'translanguaging, as a pedagogic resource, is still a romantic pursuit of international academia when the reinforcement of linguicism in the form of EMI and nationalistic reinforcement of Bangla is a bitter reality in Bangladesh'. The Editors of this volume, in their Introductory chapter, discuss this concern about the dominant presence of English and the national languages and the neglect of ITM languages in EMI or ELT classrooms in the South Asian nations. In Chapter 3, Boruah expresses her concern that translanguaging practices in the classroom driven by Eurocentric epistemologies in education may not acknowledge the rights of minority languages and their speakers. She suggests that translanguaging pedagogy needs to be seen as a tool for minority language maintenance, with an emphasis on using learners' existing funds of knowledge in teaching English. Mukhopadhyay (Ch. 4) emphasizes the need to focus on the home language of marginalized and low SES children in translanguaging practices in teaching reading and in reading assessment.

Thus, the insightful analyses of translanguaging practices in teaching English in South Asian classrooms raise some concerns which need to be addressed in taking off from the significant groundwork that this comprehensive volume documents. In this discussion, I seek to briefly touch upon some issues primarily related to translanguaging as a pedagogical practice in multilingual societies. I will reflect on how translanguaging pedagogy has been addressed in the context of hierarchical multilingualism in South Asian societies with reference to the positioning of ITM languages in particular from a social justice perspective. I will then examine the relationship between the spontaneously and naturally developed communicative repertoire of children in multilingual societies and the notion of translanguaging as a pedagogic tool, and end the discussion with the role of English as a 'target' language in South Asia.

The Blind Spot in Translanguaging Pedagogy and Social Justice

As the reported studies in this volume show, translanguaging practices in South Asian classrooms often reinforce existing sociolinguistic hierarchies by privileging dominant national language(s) over ITM languages. Mohanty (2010, 2019) shows that languages (and, hence, their speakers) all over the world are placed in a hierarchical power structure, typically with a 'double divide'. Usually, one of the many languages in each society, a colonial/*international* language like English or, in some cases, a national or official language, is the dominant language of power at the top of the hierarchy with the major national or regional languages in the second rung of the power hierarchy and the ITM languages at the bottom. There are two major power cleavages in the 'double divide' structure – one between the most dominant language and the major national/regional languages, and the other between the latter group of languages and ITM languages. The ITM languages are discriminated against and stigmatized, while the powerful languages are relatively more privileged depending on their position in the hierarchy. The twin processes of stigmatization and glorification are variously rationalized hegemonically benefiting the dominant language users while the ITM languages are disadvantaged and displaced from significant domains of society such as education, economy and democratic processes (Skutnabb-Kangas, 2000). This leads to a vicious circle of language disadvantage (Mohanty, 2019); the ITM languages are cumulatively weakened by long-term neglect and displacement from significant domains and the resultant weakness is used to justify their continued neglect in major social domains such as education. The risk of endangerment of the ITM languages is furthered by the fact that without educational use, these languages remain mostly spoken languages (McCarty, 2009). The translanguaging practices in South Asian classrooms often reflect and reinforce this hierarchy by placing English at the centre of educational discourse followed by national languages such as Hindi, Bangla and Nepali and keeping the ITM languages in a blind spot. Educational use is vital to the maintenance and development of languages and societal multilingualism. Unfortunately, the language-in-education policies perpetuate inequality and linguistic homogenization which favours the dominant language(s) with gross neglect of the languages in the lower rungs of the power hierarchy. Prioritization of dominant languages in translingual instruction can be viewed as an extension of the broader processes of social discrimination and violation of linguistic human rights (LHRs) ['fundamental rights protecting language-related acts and values' (Mancini & de Witte, 2008)] of ITM pupils. In their study of translanguaging practices in EMI classrooms in Nepal, Sah and Li

(2024) show that, apart from English, the nationally dominant language Nepali was used and students' home languages such as Bhojpuri were excluded. This practice, according to them,

> ...demonstrated a *selective nature of translanguaging*. Such a translanguaging practice reproduced hegemonic language ideologies (e.g. English-Nepali elite bilingualism) and it did not guarantee equity and equality due to excluding students' mother tongues (i.e., Bhojpuri) in content classes. In other words, this selective translanguaging driven by nationalist ideologies and the stigmatization of the mother tongue (i.e. Bhojpuri), resulted in the symbolic power of hegemonic languages (i.e. English and Nepali) in EMI classrooms and perpetuated language hierarchy that excluded local languages, thereby creating epistemic injustice for minoritized students. (2024: 8)

Padmini Boruah (Chapter 3) calls for a 'bottom-up constructivist' approach to translanguaging that genuinely includes minority languages, ensuring that translanguaging serves as a tool for both English learning and minority language preservation. Translingual pedagogy is often projected as a transformative approach that dispenses with the societal power relationship between languages and valorizes the identities of multilingual pupils, including those from the ITM groups. I will return to this purported relationship between translanguaging and multilingual identity in the next section. However, it needs to be reiterated here that, in its applications in EMI in South Asian classrooms as illustrated in different South Asian contexts, classroom translanguaging does not prioritize ITM languages in these multilingual societies.

Cenoz and Gorter (2017) point out that translanguaging can be a threat to minority languages under certain conditions. According to them:

> ...the situation of translanguaging in the case of English-Spanish bilinguals in the US is (also) different from that of speakers of regional minority languages. Translanguaging can be a tool for empowering language minority students in the US because it accepts the way bilinguals communicate. The direction is then 'from minority to the majority' because it legitimises the features that bilinguals have in their whole linguistic repertoire and takes them to spaces where English (and in some cases Spanish) is the main language. When referring to the regional minority languages, however, translanguaging goes in the opposite direction, 'from majority to the minority' and this is related to the differences in the status and demography of the languages involved. (2017: 7–8)

Cenoz and Gorter (2017) suggest some guiding principles for sustainable translanguaging for regional minority languages as in the case of the ITM languages in South Asia. These include free use of ITM languages in classroom translanguaging without any perceived threat to the majority of languages, developing the need to use ITM languages in translanguaging, developing metalinguistic and language awareness and linking spontaneous translanguaging to pedagogical activities. Thus, '(T)he celebration of translanguaging without taking into consideration the specific characteristics of the socio-linguistic context can hurt regional minority languages' (Cenoz & Gorter, 2017: 10).

Translanguaging Pedagogy, Multilingual Repertoire and Multilingualism as a First Language[1]

Translanguaging as a pedagogic process is claimed as classroom engagement with the total linguistic repertoire of the learners. As we have seen above, this claim is weakened by the absence of ITM languages in classroom translanguaging in the South Asian context even when minority language students are present. Further, as suggested by Cenoz and Gorter (2017), translanguaging in the case of Spanish English bilinguals is not the same thing as in the case of the classroom contexts in complex multilingual societies with regional minority language users. To appreciate the limitations of classroom translanguaging in ELT classrooms in South Asian societies we need to recognize that the translingual communications in these classrooms are not spontaneous; they are necessarily anchored in the goal of teaching English with teacher-initiated interpretive and managerial purposes and student-initiated interactive processes (Wang, 2019). As such, the pattern of language use in translingual communication in ELT classrooms is constrained by the long-term goal of learning English and the immediate purposes of classroom transactions. Thus, the limited classroom translanguaging in learning English as a 'target' language in multilingual societies is different from routine spontaneous exchanges reflecting multilingual speakers' communicative repertoire in natural settings (Mohanty, 2023a). To appreciate this difference, we need to understand the nature of the multilingual communicative repertoire of speakers in multilingual societies as it evolves through the processes of multilingual socialization.

Children's communicative repertoires in multilingual societies are progressively shaped through social interactions and participation in cultural practices in multilingual socialization. Our studies in India (see Mohanty, 2019, 2023a; Mohanty & Skutnabb-Kangas, 2022, for details) with 2- to 9-year olds from different regions/contexts show three broad periods of development (each further divided into two stages): (i) Period of language differentiation, (ii) Period of social awareness of languages, and (iii) Period of competent multilingual functioning (which most children in India attain by 9 years of age).

Through multilingual socialization, children progressively develop a communicative repertoire of integrated systems of interrelated and overlapping languages 'constituting a composite set of tools complementing each other and forming a synergistic network to make communicative acts more effective' (Mohanty, 2023a: 56). This integrated system can be seen as *'multilingualism as a first language'* (MFL) (Mohanty, 2023a; Mohanty & Skutnabb-Kangas, 2022). Our multilingual socialization studies show the development of MFL, which, involves:

(1) Competent engagement with societal multilingualism to communicate effectively and holistically.
(2) Learning multilingualism as the norm of communication rather than learning to use languages as separate systems.
(3) Learning to differentiate languages and developing an understanding of the interrelationship between languages, their functions and mutual complementarity.
(4) Developing an understanding of variations and diversity of languages in social contexts.
(5) Pragmatic knowledge of context-appropriate choice of languages.

Cognitive processes associated with learning to use MFL and to negotiate complex multilingual social contexts enrich children's sensitivity to languages and to linguistic and paralinguistic communicative cues, metalinguistic awareness and multilanguaging/translanguaging skills, all of which have noted neuro-psychological reflections (Mohanty, 2019, 2023a). Ethnolinguistic fieldwork in the Kumaun region of Uttarakhand (India) by Groff (2018) and sociolinguistic surveys of children and adults in rural and tribal areas in the Indian states of Madhya Pradesh and Rajasthan (Panda, 2018, 2019a, 2019b) show routine daily life use of multiple languages with porous boundaries and subjective awareness of languages, and the norms and community practices of multilingual communication. Panda (2018, 2019a, 2019b) also shows that children follow similar normative patterns of multilingual communication and display metalinguistic awareness of languages in the region, the nature of domain-specific language use as well as the hierarchical relationship between languages. Multilingual speakers' repertoire as an 'integrated system' (Canagarajah, 2011: 401) does not negate subjective awareness of languages and language identities.

Children's MFL reflects their multilingual repertoires. It is developed and co-constructed through collaborative processes of multilingual socialization. It seems that multilingual socialization needs to be viewed as a prototype for planning effective processes for classroom development of languages in multilingual societies.

Cummins (2021; Cummins & Early, 2011), has repeatedly pointed to the effectiveness of instructional practices that encourage students to use their full multilingual repertoire to engage with learning. In linguistically diverse classrooms in India, engaging students' multilingual repertoire as cognitive resources enables the use of their languages as powerful tools for cross-linguistic reflections and learning (Mohanty, 2019; Mohanty *et al.*, 2010). This, in my view, is the essence of additive language pedagogy that expands students' multilingual repertoire. MFL, as a construct, negates the 'solitude' orientation to language and language teaching. It presupposes a shared cognitive, linguistic and conceptual space which evolves to enable dynamic interaction between languages and multi-directional cross-linguistic transfer. From this perspective, language education in multilingual societies needs to involve instructional processes that acknowledge students' MFL and seek to expand their multilingual repertoire through a second layer of multilingual socialization in the classroom.

Classroom processes that value and use the multilingual repertoire of students have been variously characterized as translanguaging, multilanguaging pedagogy, plurilingual pedagogy, cross-linguistic pedagogy, multilingual instructional strategies and teaching through the multilingual lens with overlapping approaches. Of these, translanguaging pedagogy is the most used term. Cummins (2021) has used these terms 'interchangeably to refer to classroom instruction that acknowledges, engages and promotes the multilingual repertoire of students in linguistically diverse schools' (2021: xxxvii).

The term 'translanguaging', introduced by Cen Williams (1996, 2000; also, Baker, 2011) in the context of Welsh-English bilingual programs in the 1980s, was popularized by Ofelia García. In her early use (e.g. García, 2009), García viewed translanguaging as *'multiple discursive practices'* extending into 'hybrid language use' (2009: 45). However, with the growing popularity of translanguaging among language educators, García (García & Lin, 2017) introduced a distinction between 'weak' and 'strong' versions of the translanguaging theory. The strong version (which she now supports) denies the notion of 'language'; bi-/multilingual people 'do not speak languages but rather, use their repertoire of linguistic features selectively' whereas the weak position 'supports national and state language boundaries and yet calls for softening of these boundaries' (García & Lin, 2017: 126). Cummins (2021) has used the expressions *Unitary Translanguaging Theory* (UTT) and *Crosslinguistic Translanguaging Theory* (CTT) corresponding to the strong and weak versions, respectively, and has critiqued the UTT claims as lacking 'empirical basis' and as being 'logically flawed, and devoid of clear pedagogical directions for educators' (2021: 288). The proponents and allies of the UTT position view the notions of language, MT, or bi-/multilingualism as non-entities; for them, these terms do not reflect the way languages are used and understood. In my analyses (Mohanty, 2023a, 2023b), such denial ignores the mental state of language users and their self-construal (Singh, 2022) as users of a language or MT or as multilingual. As I have pointed out, 'Underneath the "squishiness" of languages, languaging, multilingualism, there are anchor beliefs of speakers/communities in their language(s); denial of this mental state or belief system in any theoretical discourse amounts to denial of social justice' (Mohanty, 2023b: 158). Further, we need to appreciate that 'At the grassroots level, languages and mother tongues are not linguistic categories; they are community (and individual) ascriptions' (2023a: 58). As Cummins (2021) shows, claiming the primacy of *languaging, multilanguaging* and *multilingual francas* while denying their root terms *language, multilanguage* and *multilingualism* does not lead to any practical insights.

Let me now return to the translanguaging pedagogical practices for multilingual classrooms. We know that classrooms in the Global South are multilingual and that, to make sense, teachers often engage in translingual communication (see Mukhopadhyay, Ch. 4) despite the imposed language solitude policy. Focus on MLE and translanguaging classroom practices in the recent academic and policy discourses calls for planned and systematic translanguaging pedagogy. A host of strategies, such as engaging students' multilingual repertoire, reinforcing linguistic identities, using 'identity texts', fostering conscious metalinguistic and crosslinguistic reflections, promoting multilingual literacy engagement, scaffolding comprehension and production of languages across the curriculum have been discussed/practised by language pedagogy professionals. The list of specific translanguaging (or similar) strategies used by practitioners worldwide is quite long and, often, overlapping. The diverse strategies for education in multilingual societies need to be critically evaluated from the Global South perspective. The work from the South Asian countries reported in this volume is a positive step in this direction.

Translanguaging for English as a 'Target Language'

Translanguaging pedagogy is perhaps most frequently discussed in the context of teaching English, that too for learners of English as a foreign language or as a second/third/other language. Considering that the routine transactions in all classrooms with linguistically diverse ITM students, mostly in the Global South, involve translingual communication, it is somewhat intriguing that attention in the research literature on language teaching is more focused on ELT. ITM children in most parts of the Global South are quite often subjected to schools where the medium of instruction in the Primary/Elementary grades is a dominant regional/national language and most of the teachers are from dominant language communities with no or limited knowledge of pupils' home language. It is quite common for these teachers to use code-mixed translingual communication involving the home language and the school language and, sometimes, other languages too. In India, it is not uncommon to find at least three to five languages used in elementary-grade classrooms. The spontaneous translingual communication in such classrooms has not received adequate attention in research. Tribal children in Odisha (India), for example, with Kui, Saora and, at least, 21 other tribal languages as mother tongues, are subjected to schooling in the dominant state language,[2] Odia.

Our studies on the classroom processes in tribal areas in Odisha (Mohanty *et al.* 2010) show that teachers frequently used pupils' tribal language along with Odia (and, less often, some Hindi and English[3] words) in their classroom transactions even if the official language of instruction (as well as the textbooks) was Odia. When, as we have reported, some teachers did not know the home language of children or could not explain a concept due to limited proficiency in the language, they asked another teacher/community adult or even another older pupil from the tribal language community to help by explaining the concept in the home language. These processes of spontaneous translanguaging in multilingual contexts are quite challenging and pedagogically significant. However, translanguaging in ELT programs in multilingual contexts in the Global South seems to have drawn much more attention from researchers than translanguaging in teaching other Indigenous languages.

This volume is about classroom practices in South Asia for teaching-learning of English. Unfortunately, the social construction of English as a 'language of development' (Mohanty, 2017) and its 'uncritical acceptance' in the Global South perpetuates its hegemony (Tsuda, 2013, cited in Phillipson & Skutnabb-Kangas, 2022). The eminent South Asian researchers in this volume have discussed English language education, which targets 'English'. English has been seen as a language of discrimination and inequality. Earlier, the perception of English as a valued commodity all over the world, particularly in the Global South, was associated with discrimination between those who knew English and those who did not; now, with the proliferation of low- and high-cost English-medium schools (which generally correspond to English language education with and without classroom translanguaging, respectively), the discrimination is between those with 'good' quality English and others with 'bad' quality (Mohanty, 2017, 2019). Linguistic imperialism (Phillipson, 1992, 2009) and the consequent linguicism (Skutnabb-Kangas, 1988, 2000) seem to grow unabated. The decolonizing project of translanguaging is supposed to change this perception of English as a 'target' or valued language. What then is the end-product of using translanguaging pedagogy in ELT? Is it another unnamed language to flatten the implicit hierarchy (García, 2023) which enriches the languaging repertoire of the students with 'translanguaged' English? Translanguaging is projected as a process which seeks to use and develop learners' communicative repertoire – '…the trans- in translanguaging connotes the transcendence of named languages, going *beyond* named languages as have been socially constructed' (Li & García, 2022: 314). Therefore, it is ironic that, in the literature on translanguaging pedagogy in EMI classes, English is often mentioned as the 'target' language. Despite the celebration of *World Englishes*, and now, translanguaged Englishes, British-American English continues to be seen as a 'target'. And, hence, even when classroom translanguaging *(albeit selective)* is accepted, there is a reluctance to accept the new form of (English) enriched repertoire in assessment processes in translingual education for English. The target of *British-American English* continues to be reflected in the tests of proficiency in English language teaching programs in the Global South. In setting the standards and norms of English proficiency in these programs, the influence of the standard/standardized gate-keeping tests, such as TOEFL and IELTS, still seems to loom large. The hegemony of English continues to deny social justice for the dominated ITM language communities all over the world. Assessment of proficiency in English is largely responsible for creating a hierarchy among the English-aspiring ITM communities in the Global South. The decolonizing project of the translanguaging pedagogy proposes to change this unjust hierarchy in how proficiency in English is assessed. 'Changing the assessment regime to better reflect bilingual *(and multilingual)* learners' translanguaging capacities is a top priority in decolonizing education in the 21st century' (Italics added) (Li & García, 2022: 322). Almost a quarter into the century, we are yet to see any appreciable signs of such a 'changing assessment regime'.

Conclusion

English language education in South Asia is not just about languages and the medium of classroom transactions. It is inextricably linked to the wider economic and political processes. Applications of translanguaging pedagogy, as we have seen in this volume, are selective and hierarchical and influenced by forces that go beyond the choice of teachers and students in ELT programs. They are reflections of the structural realities of double-divided multilingual societies, as I have discussed. Therefore, as Sah and Li (2022) argue, the movement towards equitable and effective translanguaging in English language teaching needs to effectively engage with the full range of multilingual repertoire of the learners, including those from the ITM communities and reassess and reform the nature of assessment itself in ELT programs. 'Uncritical adoption of translanguaging without considering the(se) local realities and systemic barriers can be harmful to minoritized students' academic success' (Sah & Li, 2022: 2092). Adoption of critical translanguaging for teaching English must accord primacy to the issues of equity and social justice in planning for inclusive classroom practices that respect the Linguistic Human Rights of multilingual learners particularly from ITM communities. While translanguaging has the potential to disrupt entrenched language hierarchies, its current application in South Asian ELT often reinforces the dominance of English and other powerful languages. Future efforts must prioritize the inclusion of ITM languages to ensure that translanguaging serves as a useful tool for both linguistic and social justice. It is also equally important to appreciate the nature of multilingualism and multilingual repertoire not just at the level of theoretical discourse, but in how translanguaging and other pedagogical processes are used in classrooms. A 'bottom-up' understanding of the multilingual reality from the subjective perspectives of the multilingual users and communities in the margins is necessary for socially just education in the Global South including education for English'. To advance the development of equitable English language education, future studies should aim to gain deeper insight and understanding into the role of mother-tongue and mother-tongue-based translanguaging, as well as identify more effective ways to sustain linguistic and epistemic equity' (Sultana & Fang, 2024: 8). This captures the agenda for translanguaging studies in South Asia.

Notes

(1) Part of the discussion in this section is taken from my inaugural talk in the International Conference on Language Education in Multilingual Contexts held in English and Foreign Language University, Hyderabad, India (26–27, July 2024); the discussion is also based on Mohanty (2023a, 2023b).
(2) There is a limited program of mother tongue-based multilingual education (MLE) for tribal children which offers education in their mother tongue in 1485 (out of over 25000) Primary Schools in Odisha (for details see Mohanty, 2023c)
(3) Many English words, such as ball, mobile, phone, TV, radio, chair, table, balloon, pencil, biscuit, phone etc., have become part of the common daily life vocabulary of Odia and other Indian languages (including tribal languages) in India due to prolonged contact with English. For the common language users, tribal language speakers for example, these borrowed words are accepted and used as a part of the vocabulary of the Indigenous languages and, therefore, young children and adults including those without formal education use these words as their native language without any awareness of their origin. There are, however, many other recently borrowed English expressions which are used in common code-mixed and translingual communications in India.

References

Baker, C. (2011) *Foundations of Bilingual Education and Bilingualism* (5th edn). Multilingual Matters.
Canagarajah, S. (2011) Codemeshing in academic writing: Identifying teachable strategies of translanguaging. *The Modern Language Journal* 95 (3), 401–417. https://doi.org/10.1111/j.1540-4781.2011.01207.x
Cenoz, J. and Gorter, D. (2017) Minority languages and sustainable translanguaging: Threat or opportunity? *Journal of Multilingual and Multicultural Development* 38 (10), 901–912. https://doi.org/10.1080/01434632.2017.1284855
Cummins, J. (2021) *Rethinking the Education of Multilingual Learners: A Critical Analysis of Theoretical Concepts*. Multilingual Matters.
Cummins, J. and Early, M. (eds) (2011) *Identity Texts: The Collaborative Creation of Power in Multilingual Schools*. Trentham Books.
García, O. (2009) *Bilingual Education in the 21st Century: A Global Perspective*. Basil Blackwell.
García, O. (2023) Translanguaged TESOL in transit. *NYS TESOL Journal* 10 (1), 5–18.
García, O. and Lin, A.M.Y. (2017) Translanguaging in bilingual education. In O. García and A.M.Y. Lin (eds) *Bilingual and Multilingual Education (Encyclopaedia of Language and Education, Vol. 5)* (pp. 117–130). Springer.

Groff, C. (2018) *The Ecology of Language in Multilingual India*. Palgrave Macmillan.

Li, W. and García, O. (2022) Not a first language but one repertoire: Translanguaging as a decolonizing project. *RECL Journal* 53 (2), 313–324.

Mancini, S. and de Witte, B. (2008) Language rights as cultural rights – a European perspective. In F. Francioni and M. Scheinin (eds) *Cultural Human Rights* (pp. 247–284). Martinus Nijhoff Publishers.

McCarty, T. (2009) Empowering Indigenous languages – What can be learned from Native American experiences? In A.K. Mohanty, M. Panda, R. Phillipson and T. Skutnabb-Kangas (eds) *Multilingual Education for Social Justice: Globalising the Local* (pp. 114–127). Orient Blackswan.

Mohanty, A.K. (2010) Language, inequality and marginalisation: Implications of the double divide in Indian multilingualism. *International Journal of the Sociology of Language* 205, 131–154.

Mohanty, A.K. (2017) Multilingualism, education, English and development: Whose development? In H. Coleman (eds) *Multilingualism and Development* (pp. 261–280). British Council.

Mohanty, A.K. (2019) *The Multilingual Reality: Living with Languages*. Multilingual Matters.

Mohanty, A.K. (2023a) Multilingual socialization and development of multilingualism as a first language: Implications for multilingual education. In B.E. Antia and S. Makoni (eds) *Southernizing Sociolinguistics* (pp. 47–66). Routledge.

Mohanty, A.K. (2023b) Multilingualism, mother tongue and MLE. *Language and Language Teaching* 12 (23), 155–167.

Mohanty, A.K. (2023c) Linguistic human rights in education in India: Odisha's partial success story. In T. Skutnabb-Kangas and R. Phillipson (eds) *The Handbook of Linguistic Human Rights* (pp. 561–575). Willey Blackwell. https://doi.org/10.1002/9781119753926

Mohanty, A.K. and Skutnabb-Kangas, T. (2022) Growing up in multilingual societies: Violation of linguistic human rights in education. In A. Stavans and U. Jessner (eds) *The Cambridge Handbook of Childhood Multilingualism* (pp. 578–601). Cambridge University Press.

Mohanty, A.K., Panda, M. and Pal, R. (2010) Language policy in education and classroom practices in India: Is the teacher a cog in the policy wheel? In K. Menken and O. García (eds) *Negotiating Language Policies in Schools: Educators as Policymakers* (pp. 211–231). Routledge.

Panda, M. (2018) *A Sociolinguistic Survey of Barwani District, Madhya Pradesh*. Room to Read & NMRC.

Panda, M. (2019a) *A Sociolinguistic Survey of Sirohi District, Rajasthan (Phase I)*. Room to Read.

Panda, M. (2019b) *A Sociolinguistic Survey of Sirohi District, Rajasthan (Phase II)*. Room to Read.

Phillipson, R. (1992) *Linguistic Imperialism*. Oxford University Press.

Phillipson, R. (2009) *Linguistic Imperialism Continued*. Routledge.

Phillipson, R. and Skutnabb-Kangas, T. (2022) Communicating in 'global' English: Promoting linguistic human rights or complicit with linguicism and linguistic imperialism. In Y. Miike and J. Yin (eds) *The Handbook of Global Interventions in Communication Theory* (pp. 425–439). Routledge.

Sah, P.K. and Li, G. (2022) Translanguaging or unequal languaging? Unfolding the plurilingual discourse of English medium instruction policy in Nepal's public schools. *International Journal of Bilingual Education and Bilingualism* 25, 2075–2094. https://doi.org/10.1080/13670050.2020.1849011

Sah, P.K. and Li, G. (2024) Toward linguistic justice and inclusion for multilingual learners: Implications of selective translanguaging in English-medium instruction classrooms. *Learning and Instruction* 92, 1–9. https://doi.org/10.1016/j.learninstruc.2024.101904

Singh, M. (2022) Language priming effect on self-description: Contextual variations. PhD dissertation, Jawaharlal Nehru University.
Skutnabb-Kangas, T. (1988) Multilingualism and the education of minority children. In T. Skutnabb-Kangas and J. Cummins (eds) *Minority Education: From Shame to Struggle* (pp. 9–44). Multilingual Matters.
Skutnabb-Kangas, T. (2000) *Linguistic Genocide in Education – Or Worldwide Diversity and Human Rights?* Lawrence Erlbaum Associates.
Sultana, S. and Fang, F. (2024) English as the medium of instruction and mother-tongue-based translanguaging: Challenges and prospects for tertiary education in Bangladesh and China. *International Journal of Educational Development* 104, 1–10. https://doi.org/10.1016
Tsuda, Y. (2013) Speaking against the hegemony of English: Problems, ideologies and solutions. In T.K. Nakayama and R.T. Halualani (eds) *The Handbook of Critical Intercultural Communication* (pp. 248–269). Wiley-Blackwell.
Wang, D. (2019) *Multilingualism and Translanguaging in Chinese Language Classrooms.* Palgrave MacMillan. https:// doi. org/10.1007/ 978-3-030-02529-8
Williams, C. (1996) Secondary education: Teaching in the bilingual situation. In C. Williams, G. Lewis and C. Baker (eds) *The Language Policy: Taking Stock* (pp. 39–78). CAI.
Williams, C. (2000) Welsch-medium and bilingual teaching in the further education sector. *International Journal of Bilingual Education and Bilingualism* 3 (2), 129–1.

Index

ABOE (Activity-Based Oral English) 150
academia 2, 5, 224
academic language 92
accents 54
action research 149, 154, 193
active translanguaging 207
additive bi/multilingualism 83, 143, 245–6
Adhikari, B.R. 168
Afghanistan 4–5, 12
agency 18, 118, 125, 149, 153, 171, 217, 223–7, 232–3
agentive learners 10–11, 93
Agnihotri, R. 52
Ahmad, A. 5
Akter, S. 189
Alamyar, M.N. 5
Al-Azami, S. 7
Alobaid, A. 45, 48, 49
Anderson, J. 49, 55, 64, 82, 94, 165
anglocentrism 3
Anglophonic norms 215–39 *see also* English-only policies
Anglo-vernacular schools 28
Annual State of Education (ASER) 2023 report - India 53
Ao 48
Arabic 27, 126, 127, 130–1, 132–3, 143
Ascenzi-Moreno, L. 169
Ashraf, H. 177
assessment
 –Bangladesh 83, 84, 201–3, 204
 –bi/multilingual assessment practices in higher education 168–9
 –bi/multilingual reading abilities 71–5
 –decolonization 19
 –dynamic translanguaging assessments 75

 –inclusive and adaptive framework 180
 –monolingual ideologies 168
 –Pakistan 165–6, 171, 226
 –reading comprehension 74–5, 86
 –research on translanguaging in 166–8
 –standardized tests 249
 –test instructions 181
 –translanguaging 74–5, 176–80, 201–4
asset-based approaches 50
assimilation 50, 83, 234, 245
Atmacharita (Phakhirmohan Senapati) 35–6
autobiographies 35–6
autoethnography 215–39

background knowledge 68, 71, 107, 115, 158
Backhaus, P. 128
Baker, C. 10, 26, 94
Bangla 6, 7, 12–13, 82–3, 87–93, 188, 194, 196–8, 201, 203, 207, 208, 241, 242
Bangladesh
 –colonialism 4
 –higher education 101, 187–214, 234, 241
 –indigenous languages 1, 6
 –number of languages 1–2
 –reading comprehension 81–98
 –translingual practices 12–13
Batra, P. 46
Bell, N.D. 8
Bengali 31–2, 36, 82 *see also* Bangla
Bhutan 4–5, 12
Bialystok, E. 61, 64, 72
bilingual education
 –India 40
 –Pakistan 170
 –Sri Lanka 148–64

Bill & Melinda Gates Foundation 83
bi/multilingualism, problematization of terms 190
Blackledge, A. 7, 26, 191
Block, D. 51
Blommaert, J. 8, 9, 127
body languages 9
Bonnin, J.E. 43, 44
books in classrooms 131
border thinking 101
Boruah, P. 46, 47, 63, 64
bottom-up constructivism 53, 217, 243, 250
Bourdieu, P. 8, 64, 100, 124, 148, 152, 154, 157, 161, 220, 231
Bourhis, R. 122
British colonialism 4, 5, 27, 30–5, 218
Brown, C.P. 32
Brown, K. 122
bureaucracy 28

Canagarajah, S. 3, 7, 9, 10, 11, 27, 124, 152, 171, 191, 196, 245
capitalism 102, 117 *see also* neoliberalism
caste 103
Cenoz, J. 11, 65, 122, 128, 142, 143, 168, 207, 243–4
Centers of Oriental Learning and Translation 28
Chakma 203
Chalhoub-Deville, M. 179
Charamba, E. 19
Chatterjee, P. 29
Child's Easy First Grammar 32–3
China 124
Chinese 85, 86, 94, 206
Cho, B.Y. 86
"choice" logic 43
Chu, C.S.S. 86
civil services 28
classical Indian languages 28
classroom displays and signage 127–8
classroom instructions 177
CLT (Communicative Language Teaching) 95, 215, 220
co-construction 93, 110, 114, 116, 118, 245
code meshing 27, 196–7, 204, 206, 207, 209, 227

code mixing 170, 190, 196, 227, 229, 247
code switching 46–7, 61–2, 64, 72, 190, 196, 227
Coffey, S. 11
cognate expressions 41, 67, 88, 90, 91–2
cognitive benefits of bilingualism 60–1, 63, 245
Coleman, H. 5, 124, 142
collective identity 11, 143, 157
colonialism
 –Bangladesh 82, 84
 –beauty standards 87, 88–9, 92–3
 –challenging the matrix of power 101, 118
 –coloniality of English 3, 4, 64, 117, 220
 –decolonization 11–12
 –dominance of English 124
 –English as global linguistic capital 64
 –epistemic access 102
 –India 29
 –linguistic habitus 152
 –linguistic hierarchies 142
 –mindset based on grammar teaching 43
 –multilingual identity construction 50–1
 –national identities 29
 –neutralization of 161
 –Pakistan 218
 –in SA 4
 –Whiteness as futurity 226
colonilingual ideologies 43, 45
communicative competence 10
comprehensible input and output 158
compulsory language study 2, 42, 172, 218
Connell, R. 233
consciousness raising 153, 154, 158, 159
constructivism 153, 193
content-based instruction (CBI) 227
contextual meanings of words 92, 196
Cooperative Groups 154
coping strategies, translanguaging as 12, 62, 66
corrective feedback 159
creativity in language learning 11

Creese, A. 7, 26, 191
critical multilingual language awareness 45, 117, 118
critical spaces 109
critical thinking 11, 12, 65, 68, 91–2
critical translanguaging 14, 228, 234
criticisms of translanguaging 193, 246
crosslinguistic mediation 49, 61
Crosslinguistic Translanguaging Theory (CTT) 65, 246
cultural capital 28, 228
cultural heritage 42
culturally responsive pedagogy 101, 123, 226, 227, 233
Cummins, J. 61, 65, 66, 143, 174, 217, 225, 228, 231, 232, 233, 245, 246, 247
Cushing, S.T. 74
Cushman, E. 11–12

dance 25
Daniel, S.M. 192, 209
Das, Acharya Harihara 33
Das, Pandit Gopabandhu 33
De Costa, P.I. 10, 11, 45, 46
decolonization
 –classroom pedagogy 19
 –decolonial pedagogy 10, 99–121
 –decolonial praxis 118
 –decoloniality theory 100, 102–3
 –early childhood education (ECE) 142
 –EMI (English as a medium of instruction) 227, 231
 –epistemic decolonization 18
 –higher education 210
 –second language acquisition 152
 –social justice 240, 248
 –teacher education 45–6
 –translanguaging as decolonial approach 188
 –translingual practices 11–12
deficit ideologies 43, 45–6, 54, 72, 101–2, 104, 117–18, 152, 220
defining bi/multilingual abilities 61–2
Dendrinos, B. 169
Dhivehi 6, 126, 127, 130–9, 140–1, 143, 241
dialect of the supervernacular 9
dialects 42, 208
dictionaries 28, 30–5, 91–2, 200

Dictogloss Activities 154, 159
diglossia 41–2
discourse abilities 73
diversity of knowledge 106–12, 113–14, 116
Dobinson, T. 221
domain-specific language policies 148, 162, 242
double divide 187, 209, 242
Dovchin, S. 2, 9, 12, 125, 143, 188, 190, 216
Dravidian languages 25
Durbar School 5
Dutch 9
Dutch colonialism 4
dynamic bilingualism 26
dynamic translanguaging assessments 75

early childhood classrooms 122–47
East India Company 4, 28, 30, 32
ecological affordances 7
ecological stance of language learning 153
elite bilingualism 13, 151, 189, 193, 203, 207, 241, 243
English
 –Bangladesh 208
 –"choice" logic 43
 –colonialism 3, 4, 64, 117, 220
 –desirable commodity 2, 83, 220, 225
 –dictionaries and textbooks of Indian languages 30–5
 –education in India 25–6, 29, 30
 –elitism 151, 160
 –hegemonic and neoliberal political roles 3, 14
 –hegemony of 50, 52, 151, 187, 220, 242, 248
 –India 1, 27–9, 37, 40–58
 –as linguistic capital 64
 –Maldives 126, 127, 128–9, 130–41, 143
 –monolingual biases in South Asia 4
 –neoliberalism 13
 –non-standard varieties 14
 –Pakistan 169–70, 173–6, 180–1, 218, 219–20
 –prestige 4, 6, 142, 151, 169–70, 189, 194, 209, 228

English (*continued*)
 –proficiency 53
 –reciprocity value of English 51
 –shift to 126
 –Standard English ideology 9
 –'target language' 75, 85, 95, 169, 192, 247–9
 –tuition and coaching in 2
English as a foreign language 2, 5, 30
English as a global language 124, 142
English as a lingua franca 5, 51, 194
English as a medium of instruction (EMI)
 –Afghanistan 5
 –Bangladesh 82, 83, 90, 94, 189, 194, 196, 207
 –coloniality of 117
 –growing demand for 2
 –India 40, 44, 62–4, 66–76
 –low socioeconomic status 63
 –Maldives 6, 124, 126
 –maths and science in India 47
 –mismatch between policy and practice 207
 –mother tongue-based MLE 62–4
 –neoliberalism 187
 –Nepal 5, 99–121, 103, 104, 112
 –non-colonial areas 5
 –Pakistan 165, 167, 170, 215–39
 –'policy dumping' 3
 –Sri Lanka 149, 150, 162
 –teacher attitudes to 45–6, 47, 116
 –translanguaging to support 64–5
English as a Second Language (ESL) 43, 50, 148–64, 230
English as an additional language (EAL) 7, 127
English as an international language 188, 242
English as 'neutral' language 151
English-only policies
 –assessment 166, 168, 177–80, 201
 –autoethnography 219–30
 –mismatch between policy and practice 207, 218
 –Pakistan 215–39
 –reading comprehension 82
 –Sri Lanka 148, 151, 157, 161
 –teachers' resistance 116
Environmental Studies 104, 128, 150
epistemic access 102

epistemic decolonization 18
epistemic diversity 106–12, 113, 114, 116, 233
epistemic identities 99–100, 117
epistemic spaces 106
epistemological racisms 43–4
ethnocentric identities 149, 207
ethnography 104, 127, 215–39
ethnolinguistic integration 155–9
Eurocentrism 43–4, 102, 233, 241

face-value 89–91
failure, sense of 90
Fakatsa writing 8
Fang, F. 188, 189, 208, 216, 250
Fielding, R. 51
Flores, N. 209
flouting of conventions 8
folk art forms 25
Forbes, K. 51
Foreign Language Classroom Speaking Anxiety 149, 152, 161
funds of knowledge 54, 227

Gagarina, N. 72–3
Gao, L. 193
García, O. 3, 7, 8, 26–7, 62, 65, 84, 85, 100, 115, 117, 118, 141, 142, 143, 152, 158, 166, 167, 168, 171, 178, 180, 188, 191, 192, 207, 209, 216, 217, 225, 246, 249
gender stereotypes 92
German 7–8
gesture 9, 199, 200
Ghimire, N.B. 104
Giddens, A. 217
Gillies, D. 19
Giri, R.A. 5, 124
globalization 83, 218, 226
Goldman Sachs Foundation 83
Gonzalez, N. 54
Gorski, P.C. 101
Gorter, D. 11, 65, 122, 128, 142, 143, 168, 207, 243–4
grammar, assessing multilingual 73
grammar books 28, 30–5
grammars, languages without written 43
Groff, C. 245
group interventions 71

group membership 157 *see also* collective identity
group work 156, 160
Gu, M. 206
'guilty multilingualism' 124, 142–3, 152, 215, 220

Halhed, N.B. 32
Hamid, O. 3, 208
Hebrew 8
heteroglossia 148–9, 152, 153, 154, 156–7, 160–1, 162
Heugh, K. 102
hierarchies, linguistic
  –assimilation 50
  –Bangladesh 189
  –colonialism 11, 29
  –flattening 248
  –India 29, 42
  –Indigenous languages 242–4
  –linguicism 3
  –linguistic landscapes (LL) 122, 125, 128, 142, 143
  –multilingualism as a first language 245
  –Pakistan 219–20
  –Sri Lanka 152, 153, 161
  –structural inequities 54
  –teacher education 45, 47, 50–2
  –uncritical translanguaging can perpetuate 13, 228
higher education
  –Bangladesh 83–4, 87, 89–90, 94, 189–210
  –India 28
  –internationalization 2, 4
  –Pakistan 165–86, 215–39
Hindi 13, 25, 67–8, 92, 126, 242
Hinduism 149
Hirsu, L. 82
home languages
  –assessment making use of 73, 74–5
  –classroom strategies to support 49
  –early childhood education (ECE) 123
  –epistemic access 102
  –feedback in 73
  –heteroglossia 148
  –India 42, 45, 47–8, 52–3, 60
  –Indigenous languages 203
  –for learning content 174, 190

  –legitimization of 10
  –metatalk 153
  –Nepal 103–4, 116–17
  –reading comprehension using multilingual pedagogy 67
  –revival of support for 125
  –teacher attitudes to 47–8, 206
  –teacher education 45
home-school connections 102, 125
Hornberger, N.H. 125, 142, 217, 228
Horwitz, E.K. 149, 152, 161
Hu, G. 124
human capital development 189
hybridization 7, 246

identity
  –bilingual identities 13
  –co-construction of identity 111, 115, 176
  –collective identity 11, 143, 157
  –cultural identity expression 174, 175–6
  –early childhood education (ECE) 123
  –epistemic identities 99–100, 115–17, 118, 240
  –ethnocentric identities 149, 156–7, 207
  –fluidity of 181
  –legitimization of 125
  –linguistic identities 29
  –Maldives 125–6
  –mother tongue 148
  –multilingual identity construction 50–1, 53, 119, 234, 243
  –national identities 175
  –negotiation of 11, 89, 189
  –regional nationalisms 29
  –teachers' 51, 99–100, 224
  –trans-identity 101
idiolects 152
illeism 138
illusion 152
images/pictures 105, 108, 111, 199
immersion education 124
inclusive language practices 10, 18, 27, 118, 125, 141, 156, 181, 182, 228
India
  –colonialism 4
  –education in modern Indian languages 25, 28–9

India (*continued*)
  —elite bilingualism 13
  —English as pathway out of exclusion 189
  —English language education (ELE) 40–58
  —multilingual practices 27–9, 101
  —multilingualism 245, 247–8
  —Odisha 25–39
  —official languages 1
  —reading development and assessment 59–80
  —teacher training 44–54, 59
Indigenous languages
  —Bangladesh 1–2, 187–8, 203, 207, 208
  —denial 241
  —home languages 203
  —as impediment to English learning 220
  —India 25, 28–9, 248
  —linguistic hierarchies 242–4
  —Nepal 5–6, 102
  —Pakistan 219–20
  —sustainable translanguaging 243–4
  —threatened by 'national' languages 6
  —translingual practices 13
individual learner differences 71
individualism 93 *see also* agency
inequality 64, 89, 94, 102, 123, 151, 189, 227–30, 248
inferential skills 67, 69, 73, 86
'inner lives' 153
Input, Interaction, Output 152–3, 154
integration versus assimilation 50, 234, 245
interactivity 111
international centres of ELT 94
international schools 150
international students 2
internationalization of higher education 218
interpretive translanguaging 206–7
Islam 149, 156
Izadi, D. 9

Jahan, A. 101
Japan 167
Jaspers, J. 13, 43, 193

Johnson, D.C. 216–17
Jones, R. 11, 82
Jorgensen, J.N. 190

'kaduwa' 148
Kano, N. 84, 100
Karki, J. 203
Kenner, C. 7, 8
Khan, A. 5
Kleyn, T. 85
knowledge activism 19
Kohn, K. 152
Korean 86
Kothari Commission 42
Kress, G.R. 128
Krishnaswamy, N. 28
Kubota, R. 12, 13, 14, 27, 43, 62, 63, 66, 101, 148, 151, 152, 161, 165, 188, 193
Kumaravadivelu, B. 216, 220, 231

LAC (Language-across-the-Curriculum) 44
Landry, R. 122
language ecologies 1–2
language loss 54, 63
language of instruction *see also* English as a medium of instruction (EMI); medium of instruction
  —indigenization of 209
  —negative consequences of not using home languages 68
  —teachers ignoring official policy 138, 143
language policy and planning (LPP) 18, 216–17
language revitalization 19
language shift 126
language-activist-scholars 18
Language-Related Episodes (LREs) 153, 154, 159, 161
Larsen-Freeman, D. 153
Lasker, S.N. 47
Lee, E. 11
Leiva, C. 192
Leung, C. 11
Lewis, G. 26
Li, G. 5, 13, 27, 64, 101, 124, 142, 200, 210, 249

Li Wei 3, 11, 26–7, 45, 62, 100, 107, 118, 152, 158, 166, 167, 171, 178, 180, 188, 248, 249
liberal translanguaging practices 101
Lightfoot, A. 27, 62, 64, 65, 66, 68, 165
Lin, A.M.Y. 65, 125, 141, 142, 148, 231
linguicism 3, 12, 14, 152, 234, 241, 248
linguistic agency 89 *see also* agency
linguistic capital 64, 124
linguistic habitus 152, 161
linguistic hierarchies *see* hierarchies, linguistic
linguistic ideologies 12, 13 *see also* deficit ideologies; monolingual ideologies; separate/named language ideologies; standard language ideology
linguistic imperialism 187, 209, 224, 248
linguistic justice 151, 161
linguistic landscapes (LL) 122–47
linguistic marketplaces 152
linguistic repertoires
 –assessment 180
 –decolonial pedagogy 118
 –diverse sets of knowledge visibility 106
 –equitable spaces 227–8
 –India 29
 –mother tongue-based MLE 63
 –multilingual literacy development 66
 –multilingualism as a first language 244–7
 –purposeful translanguaging 84–5
 –subtractive multilingualism 124
 –teacher attitudes to 46, 206
 –teacher education 44–5
 –translanguaging as metalanguage 158–9, 161
 –trans-movement in Applied Linguistics 190
 –transnational contact zones 191
 –unique meaning-making systems 158
linguistic rights 12, 14, 63, 72, 188, 201–3, 242, 249 *see also* right to speak
Link, H. 125, 142
Lippi-Green, R. 100
listening comprehension 73

literacy *see also* reading comprehension
 –early childhood education (ECE) 123
 –home languages 42
 –multilingual literacy development 66–76
 –purposeful translanguaging 85
 –Sri Lanka 149
lived experience 111
Lo Bianco, J. 161
local epistemologies 177
Logic of Practice 154
logocentrism 6, 187
longitudinal studies 19
low proficiency students 159, 160, 218, 220, 223
low socioeconomic status 60, 63, 66, 69, 150–1, 241

Macaulay's Minute 28, 83
Macmillan Education India 48, 49
MacSwan, J. 41
Mahapatra, Chakradhara 34–5
Makalela, L. 102, 216, 233
Makoni, S. 6, 8, 54, 216, 234
Malaysia 2, 224
Maldives 4–5, 6, 12, 101, 122–47, 241
Malinowski, D. 122
managerial translanguaging 206–7
Manan, S.A. 215, 217, 218, 220, 225, 228, 231, 232, 235
Manipravalam 25, 29
mapping languages 1
Marvi, Sanam 19
Maseko, K. 85, 94
mathematics 27, 47, 128, 204–6
May, S. 59
Mbirimi-Hungwe, V. 87
medium of instruction *see also* English as a medium of instruction (EMI); language of instruction
 –home languages in India 42
 –local languages in India 30
 –Pakistan 170, 218
 –Sri Lanka 149
 –Urdu 170
Meierkord, C. 5, 6, 45
Meighan, P.J. 43
memorization 178–9, 189

Mendoza, A. 125
Menken, K. 115, 119, 216, 217
Meredith, K. 51
metacognitive resources 94
metalinguistic awareness
  –assessment 73
  –decolonization 12
  –EMI classrooms 94
  –Indigenous languages in the classroom 207
  –Language-Related Episodes (LREs) 153
  –linguistic repertoires 8
  –metalinguistic skills 61
  –minority languages 244
  –multilingualism as a first language 245
  –reading comprehension 66, 86
  –translanguaging as metalanguage 158–9, 161
  –translanguaging stance 125
metatalk 153, 154, 159, 161
metrolingualism 190
Mevawalla, Z. 2
Mignolo, W. 11, 100, 101, 233
Miller, M.E. 192
Milligan, L.O. 2, 3, 189
minority languages *see also* Indigenous languages
  –Bangladesh 203
  –harm to 207, 243
  –identities of resignation 54
  –Indian education policy 43
  –linguistic human rights 63
  –maintenance 54
missionaries 28, 31
Mitul, S.M. 189
Mkhize, D.N. 85, 94
Moghul Tamsa 25, 29
Mohamed, N. 101, 126
Mohanty, A.K. 42, 60, 64, 66, 124, 167, 187, 209, 242, 244, 245, 246, 247–8
monoculture 43
monolingual ideologies
  –assessment 166, 168, 177–80, 201
  –Bangladesh 188, 208
  –forcing use of English 106–7
  –India 43, 45, 63
  –mismatch between policy and practice 218

  –Nepal 100–1
  –Pakistan 165, 167, 220
  –preschools in Maldives 131, 138, 142
  –in South Asia generally 4–6
  –Sri Lanka 148
  –teachers' resistance 104–17, 119
  –trans-turn in applied linguistics 192
  –written assessments 167, 171, 177
monolinguals as comparator for assessment 71–2
Morgan, A.M. 12, 13, 82, 86, 87, 94, 101, 188, 207
mother tongue-based linguistic performance 10
mother tongue-based MLE 62–4, 104, 148, 250
'mother-tongue' as concept 3
mother-tongue instruction 149 *see also* home languages
motivations to learn 68, 71, 160
Mukhopadhyay, L. 65, 66, 68, 69, 71, 73, 75
MultiLiLa 67–8
Multilingual Assessment in Narratives (MAIN) tool 72–3
multilingual awareness 115
multilingual education 29–30, 59–80, 104, 148, 250
multilingual epistemic subjects 106
multilingual identity construction 50–1, 53, 119, 234, 243
multilingual knowers 114
multilingual learners, learning advantages of 60–2
multilingual socialization 244, 245
multilingualism, societal 41–4
multilingualism as a first language 244–7
multimodality
  –Bangladesh 209
  –classroom displays and signage 128
  –literacy 142
  –multimodal pedagogies in ELE 46
  –polysemiotic practices 9
  –translingual pedagogy 11
multisensory practices 11

Nagaland 47–8
named languages *see* separate/named language ideologies

names (personal) 134, 225
National Education Policy (NEP) - India 40, 42–3, 50–1, 218
national identities 175
national languages 3–6, 13, 42, 170, 187, 209, 218, 242
nationalism 29, 33, 83, 89, 208
native speakerism 72, 157, 224
naturally-occurring translanguaging 94
neocolonialism 142
neoimperialism 151
neoliberalism
　–Bangladesh 13, 187
　–"choice" logic 43
　–and English 3, 6
　–India 40–1, 53, 54
　–Maldives 144
Nepal 4, 5–6, 13, 27, 99–121, 177, 193, 207, 234, 242–3
Nepali 5–6, 103–7, 109, 110, 113–16, 118, 242
Ngunjiri, F.W. 219
Nguyen, H.T.M. 3
Nihmathulla, M.C.B. 101
non-standard varieties 14
Norton, B. 116
note-taking, translanguaging in 174–5
number of languages 1

Odia 25, 30–1, 33–5, 36
Odia self-taught 34–5
Odisha 25–39, 247–8
Odugu, D.I. 117–18
official languages
　–Bangladesh 187
　–India 1
　–Maldives 6, 126
　–monolingual biases in South Asia 4
　–Pakistan 218
　–Sri Lanka 149
official recognition of translanguaging practices 86, 162, 167
onion metaphor 217
online reading strategies 86
oral comprehension 66
oral proficiency 69, 71, 72, 73
Orientalist-Anglicist controversy 28–9
Orientalists 28, 32
Ortega, L. 59

Otheguy, R. 152, 161, 169, 191
Otsuji, E. 9, 190

Pacheco, M.B. 11, 217
Padwad, A. 151
Pakistan 4, 19, 101, 165–86, 215–39
Palkhiwala, S. 2
Panda, M.P. 167, 245
paraphrasing 90–1, 93
particularity 231
Pashto 177, 222, 228
pedagogy of choice 232
Pennycook, A. 3, 6, 8, 9, 54, 187, 190, 216, 234
Perera, C. 153
performative arts 25, 29
'permission' to translanguage 90, 94
　see also official recognition of translanguaging practices
Persian 4, 27, 35–6
Phakhirmohan Senapati 35–6
photographs as research tool 127–8
Phyak, P. 18, 27, 43, 54, 63, 69, 101, 102, 103, 118, 174, 177, 187
pictures 105, 108, 111, 199
plurilingual environments 192
polylingualism 190
polysemiotic practices 9
Pomerantz, A. 8
Portuguese colonialism 4
postmethod conditions 216, 231
Poudel, P.P. 168
power
　–challenging the colonial matrix of power 101, 102, 118, 143
　–collaborative relations of 231–2
　–double divide 187, 209, 242
　–English as elite language 151, 170
　–to impose reception 161
　–and legitimacy 148
　–teachers' 232
pragmatic competencies 61, 73, 158
preschools 126–7
prestige 4, 6, 142, 151, 169–70, 189, 194, 209, 228
Priestly, M. 226
primary education
　–Bangladesh 82
　–English as a 'Target Language' 247
　–Maldives 126
　–Nepal 103

primary education (*continued*)
—Odisha 30
—Sri Lanka 150
principled eclecticism 192–3, 207
proficiency *see also* assessment
—defining bi/multilingual abilities 61
—higher education in Bangladesh 189
—language of instruction 63
—low proficiency students 159, 160, 218, 220, 223
—memorization 179
—proficiency-based discrimination 12–13
—right to speak 148
—showcasing using translanguaging 200
pronunciation 7–8
proverbs 92
public sphere paradigm 216
Punjabi 171
purposeful translanguaging 125, 167, 177

Quijano, A. 101, 102

racism 92, 101, 102
Rafi, A.S.M. 12, 13, 82, 83, 84, 85, 86, 87, 88, 90, 91, 94, 95, 101, 188, 207
Rahman, M.M. 2, 207, 218
Rajendram, S. 192
Rana, Jung Bahadur 5
reading comprehension 59–80, 81–98, 172
regional languages 11, 42, 170
regional nationalisms 29, 33
register 65
religious segregation 149
'remedial' English 90, 94
Ricento, T.K. 217
right to speak 116, 148, 161, 228
Roshid, M.M. 189
rote learning 179, 189
Rowe, D.W. 192
Rutgers, D. 51

Sah, P.K. 5, 6, 12, 13, 14, 27, 62, 63, 64, 66, 101, 124, 148, 151, 152, 161, 165, 187, 188, 189, 193, 200, 203, 210, 249

Saha, M. 101
salience 128, 129, 130, 136, 141, 143
Sánchez, M.T. 101, 115, 119
Sanskrit 25, 27
Santos, B. 225, 226, 233
Satyabadi school 33
Savage, R. 68, 69, 71
Saville, N. 168
scaffolding
—English language education in India 54
—home languages 63
—L1 as 45
—reading comprehension 66, 88–9
—translanguaging as 101, 155–9
—translanguaging spaces 107
Schissel, J.L. 168
schoolscapes 122–43
scripts 8–9, 104, 126
second language acquisition 50, 60, 81, 152–4
secondary education
—Bangladesh 82
—Odisha 30
self-esteem 63, 90, 124, 149, 159, 228
self-reflexivity 52, 54, 154
semiotic resources
—classroom displays and signage 127–8
—classroom pedagogy 10–11
—definitions of translanguaging 100
—heteroglossia 148
—Nepali translanguaging pedagogy 110
—reading comprehension 85, 91–2
—schoolscapes 142
—teacher education 45
—teaching and learning 9, 10, 11
—techniques of using 198–200
—translingual literacy 10
—trans-turn in applied linguistics 7
separate/named language ideologies 3, 7, 8, 10, 41, 44–5, 85, 89, 125, 246–8
sequential multilingualism 41
Shah, M. 177
Sharma, B.K. 54
Sharma, S. 102
Shohamy, E. 168, 180
Showstack, R.E. 209
signage 126, 128

simultaneous multilingualism 41, 61
Sindhi Language Authority (SLA) 19
Singapore 85
Singh, M.K.M. 2
Sinhala 149, 151, 152, 154, 155, 156, 158, 161
Skutnabb-Kangas, T. 63, 64, 124, 152, 242, 244, 245, 248
Social Constructivism Theory 154
social justice
 –asset-based approaches 50
 –Bangladesh 188, 189, 201–3
 –focus on 14, 240–52
 –healthy use of one's languages 52
 –linguistic landscapes (LL) 123
 –multilingual education 59
 –multilingual identity construction 51
 –potential backfiring of 43
 –reading comprehension 94
 –second language acquisition theory 153
social mobility 40, 124
societal multilingualism 48–9
socioconstructivism 70
sociocultural contexts 26, 48, 88, 150, 180–1, 233
sociolects 152
Song, K. 86
South Africa 85
South Asian Association for Regional Cooperation (SAARC) 83
Southern Epistemologies 216, 233–4
Spanish 8, 243
spatial repertoires 9
speech communities 50, 62–3, 148, 158
Spolsky, B. 148, 162
spontaneous translanguaging 7, 11–12, 26–7, 66–8, 125, 177, 192, 198, 201
Sri Lanka 4, 101, 148–64
St Priere, P. 36
Standard English 9
standard language ideology 9, 100–1, 118, 125, 208, 249
Steele, C. 168
STEM 47, 198, 207, 218
stigmatization 148, 151, 153, 160, 221, 228, 231, 242

strong translanguaging theory 125, 246
subtractive multilingualism 124
Sultana, S. 1, 6, 9, 13, 14, 84, 90, 187, 188, 189, 190, 208, 233, 250
superdiversity 92
supervernacular 9
sustainable translanguaging 192, 243–4
Sutton, A. 30–1
Swain, M. 153, 158
syntactic awareness 73

Taiwan 86
Takaki, N.H. 19
Taliban 5
Tamang 103, 104, 106, 112, 113–14, 118
Tamil 25, 149, 151, 152, 154, 155, 158, 161
teachers
 –agency 18, 102, 223–7, 232–3
 –attitudes to translanguaging 85–6, 91, 94, 102, 104–15, 162, 191, 206
 –availability in rural areas 151
 –critical multilingual language awareness 117, 118
 –'guilty multilingualism' 124, 142–3, 152, 215
 –interactions with linguistic landscapes 136–9
 –micro-level translanguaging policies 167
 –multilingual agency 65, 69
 –perceptions of multilingual teaching 46–8
 –resisting oppressive EMI policies 99, 104–12, 226
 –taboo translanguaging 220
 –teacher education 44–54, 143, 144, 181, 208–9
 –teacher enjoyment 91
 –teacher-focused education 91
 –teacher-interventionist action research 154
 –translingual competence 12
technocratic processes 216–17
Telegu 32, 67–8
'Tell me now' activity 90, 92
TESOL *see* English as a Second Language (ESL)

test instructions 181
textbooks 28, 30–5, 109
thematic analysis 89, 173
Three Language Formula (TFL) 42–3
Tian, Z. 52, 166
time and space, embeddedness in 9–10
tourism 6
Tran, T.T. 128
transcultural experiences 11, 12
transformative acts 101
transglossia 188
translanguaging
 –as assessment tool 74–5
 –as classroom technique 64–5
 –as decolonial pedagogy 101
 –definitions 3, 11, 26, 62
 –as formal pedagogy in India 36–7, 66–76
 –as metalanguage 158–9, 161
 –pedagogical stance in English teacher education 45–6
 –planned pedagogy 27
translanguaging pedagogies 10–11, 13, 65, 68–75, 81–98, 166, 188
translanguaging spaces 27, 107, 109
translanguaging stance 115–16, 119
translations
 –assessing reading comprehension 72
 –assessment 169
 –Atmacharita (Phakhirmohan Senapati) 35–6
 –classroom pedagogy 105–6
 –as classroom technique 12
 –code meshing 199
 –simultaneous multilingualism 61
translators 28
translingual competence 10, 12
translingual literacy 10
translingual negotiation 171
trans-turn in applied linguistics 6–12, 190–3
Treffers-Daller, J. 61, 65, 72, 73
Tsimpli, I.M. 45, 54, 67–8
Turner, M. 125, 141, 142
Tywoniw, R. 74

Unamuno, V. 43, 44
unbiased learning environment 192
unconscious use of translanguaging 165, 177
Unitary Translanguaging Theory (UTT) 246
universities *see* higher education
University of Dhaka 83
unplanned translanguaging 68 *see also* spontaneous translanguaging
Urdu 25, 169–70, 171, 173–6, 180–1, 218, 219–20, 222, 223, 226, 228, 229
USA 93, 243

Vaish, V. 85, 94
Vaisman, C. 8
Van Leewen, T. 128
Van Viegen, S. 216
varieties 161
Vertovec, S. 92
virtual spaces 8
vocabulary knowledge 67, 69–70, 72–4, 85, 91–2, 106, 127
Vulli, D. 189
Vygotsky, L. 154

Walling, S. 47–8
Walsh, C. 100, 102–3, 118
Wang, D. 206
weak translanguaging theory 125, 141–2, 246
Wei, Li 3, 11, 26–7, 45, 62, 100, 107, 118, 152, 158, 166, 167, 171, 178, 180, 188, 248, 249
Western epistemologies 3, 43, 52, 92, 101, 102, 231
Whiteness as futurity 226
Wijesekera, H. 150, 151, 152, 153, 155, 162
Wiley, T. 143
Williams, C. 26, 100, 191, 246
Wolf, M.K. 168–9
word-meaning correlates (L1-L2) 67
world Englishes 9, 248

Xu, Y. 216

Yaakthung 103, 104, 106, 107, 108, 109, 110, 111, 112, 116, 118
Yilmaz, T. 101

For Product Safety Concerns and Information please contact our EU Authorised Representative:

Easy Access System Europe

Mustamäe tee 50

10621 Tallinn

Estonia

gpsr.requests@easproject.com

www.ingramcontent.com/pod-product-compliance
Lightning Source LLC
Chambersburg PA
CBHW070023010526
44117CB00011B/1685